The
HARROWSMITH
CountryLife
R E A D E R

The HARROWSMITH CountryLife READER

The Best of North America's Award-Winning Journal of Country Living

———————— ◆ ————————

Introduction by James M. Lawrence

CAMDEN
◆HOUSE◆

PUBLISHING

Camden House Publishing, Inc.
Charlotte, Vermont 05445
A division of Telemedia Communications (USA) Inc.

ISBN 0-944475-09-4
Library of Congress Catalogue Card Number: 90-083426

Designed by Susan McClellan, Leslie Fry, and Eugenie S. Delaney

Trade distribution by
Firefly Books Ltd.
250 Sparks Avenue
Willowdale, Ontario
Canada M2H 2S4

Printed and bound in Canada by
D.W. Friesen & Sons
Altona, Manitoba

A number of people were involved with the articles included here (taken from both the U.S. and Canadian editions of the magazine), and with the production of this book. Special thanks goes to: James M. Lawrence, Thomas H. Rawls, Michael Webster, Barry Estabrook, Sandra Taylor, Craig Canine, Wayne Grady, Jake Chapline, Jennifer Bennett, Rux Martin, JoAnne Cats-Baril, Paul H. Dunphy, Tim Snyder, Frank Edwards, Merilyn Mohr, Pamela Cross, Alice Z. Lawrence, Susan Dickinson, Howard White, Sharon Smith, Susan Mc-Clellan, Ulrike Bender, Pamela Wimbush, Suzanne Seibel, Anne Rutherford, Jody Morgan, Eugenie S. Delaney, Pamela Orr, Suzanne Fay, Marcy Gibson, Janice McLean, Charlotte DuChene, Tracy C. Read, David Archibald, Denise Fisher, Lisa Rathke, Wendy Ruopp, Régan Eberhart, Judith Knopp Brown, Jill Walker, Euan Bear, Wistar Rawls, Patricia R. Motch, Patricia Denard-Hinch, Eileen Whitney, Catherine De Lury, Lois Casselman, Ellen Brooks Mortfield, Laura Elston, Sharon Alanna Schneider, Sheryl Fletcher, and Chris Landry.

About the Authors

Lamont Bassett lives part-time on the tiny island of Nevis in the British West Indies and part-time on a ranch in northern British Columbia. In addition to working as a rodeo clown during summers, he is a freelance writer, and recently finished a novel, based on his childhood experiences of growing up on a ranch in Wyoming. (ARK DE TRIOMPHE)

Jennifer Bennett is a senior contributing editor for *Harrowsmith*. She is author of *The Harrowsmith Northern Gardener* (Camden House, 1982) and co-author of *The Harrowsmith Annual Garden* (Camden House, 1990). She lives in Verona, Ontario. (A MOMENT IN THE SUN)

Rick Boling is a frequent contributor to *Harrowsmith Country Life* and *Equinox* magazines. He lives in Tallahassee, Florida, where he publishes a billiard magazine entitled *Snap*. (Breeding for Self-Defense – INSECT WARS)

Sandra Buckingham lives in Point Grey, Vancouver. She is fluent in French and German and has a Ph.D. in zoology. Author of *Stenciling* (Camden House, 1989), she plans to write her next book on renewable resource management. (BORDER LINES)

Max Burns lives in the North Bay area of Ontario. He is the northern correspondent for *Cottage Life* magazine and an associate editor for *Cycle Canada*. (SECRETS OF THE HEARTH)

Craig Canine, former senior editor of *Harrowsmith Country Life*, runs a corn and soybean farm in Norwalk, Iowa. In addition to farming, he is a freelance writer and contributes frequently to *Harrowsmith Country Life* magazine. (PADDLING INTO THE MAINSTREAM; SOLAR DELIVERY; BUILDING BY THE BOOK)

JoAnne Cats-Baril, former *Harrowsmith Country Life* food editor, is author of *The Harrow-*smith Cookbook Volume 3 (Camden House, 1987) and co-author of *Simmering Suppers* (Camden House, 1988). She lives in Charlotte, Vermont. (MEMORABLE MUFFINS; SUMMERTIME SOUPS; GARDEN PIZZA, SAUSAGE SAVVY)

Jake Chapline is managing editor of *Harrowsmith Country Life*. He lives in Charlotte, Vermont. (THE HEN-PECKED HOMESTEADER)

Andrea Chesman lives in New Haven, Vermont, and is a food writer for *Vermont Life* magazine. She is author of *Summer in a Jar: Making Pickles, Jams & More* (Williamson Publishing Co., 1985), *The Great American Dessert Book* (Crossing Press, 1990), and *Sundried Tomatoes!* (Crossing Press, 1990). (SMALL-BATCH CANNING)

Jack Cook lives in the small town of Walden in the wilds of the Northeast Kingdom of Vermont. He frequently writes for *Harrowsmith Country Life, Country Journal, Organic Gardening,* and *Horticulture.* Currently, he is writing a book about work horses, which will be published by the Stephen Greene Press. (THE LIVING GARDEN)

Formerly food editor of *Harrowsmith,* **Pamela Cross** is now attending law school at Queen's University in Kingston, Ontario. In addition, she is writing a cooking/kitchen almanac which will be published by Camden House in 1991. (A TWIST OF TRADITION)

Karan Davis Cutler is senior editor of *Harrowsmith Country Life* and garden columnist for *The Rutland Herald* and *The Barre Times Argus.* She lives in Essex, Vermont. (Lettuce Man – SUMMERTIME LETTUCE)

Cheryl Dorschner is advertising director for *Country Journal* magazine. She lives in North Williston, Vermont, where she grows 54 varieties of vegetables in a 40' x 50' garden. Other interests include singing shape-note music (four-part folk harmony). (ELEMENTARY, MY DEAR CHANDLER)

Jane Dwinell and Sky, her husband, now live in the "big house" they had planned to build, and are making a living selling eggs, vegetables, and maple syrup. Jane continues to write, and is working on a book about child birth philosophy. She is expecting a second child. (AVOIDING THE RAT RACE)

Adrian Forsyth spends half his time at his home in eastern Ontario and the other half in Indonesia, where he is directing a conservation program. He writes an ecology column entitled "Natural Liaisons" for *Equinox* magazine and is a frequent contributor to *Harrowsmith*. His books include *Portraits of the Rainforest* (Camden House, 1990), *Mammals of the American North* (Camden House, 1985), *The Nature of Birds* (Camden House, 1989), and *The Architecture of Animals* (Camden House, 1989). (FLOWERS THAT BLOOM IN THE NIGHT)

Dr. Michael W. Fox is director of the Center of Respect of Life and Environment in Washington, D.C., an affiliate of the Humane Society of the U.S., of which he is vice president. This article appears in part in his latest book, *Inhumane Society: The American Way of Animal Exploitation* (St. Martin's Press, 1990). (THE NATURAL DOG)

Linda Gilkeson, an entomologist, is director of biological pest control research at Applied Bionomics. She lives on Vancouver Island and writes frequently for Rodale Press. (INSECT WARS)

Sophia Hauserman still lives in Patricksburg, Indiana, where she grows and sells lettuce, spinach, flowers, and eggs. She is attending nursing school and plans to eventually work for a community health program. (AVOIDING THE RAT RACE)

Marshall Helmberger and Jodi Summit write, edit, and publish a weekly newspaper called *The Timberjay*. Marshall works part-time as a naturalist and Jodi's knitting business fills her spare time. Together they lead weekly birdwatching and nature tours in the summer and gather rice in the fall. (AVOIDING THE RAT RACE)

Eva Hoepfner lives in Oakville, Ontario, near Toronto, where she writes on gardening topics and tends to her vegetable and flower gardens. She is currently working on a book about gardening with native plants. (WILDFLOWER MEADOWS)

Des Kennedy lives on Denman Island, British Columbia, in the Georgia Strait. He writes on rural lifestyles, gardening, and environmental issues, particularly forestry in British Columbia. (LIFE IN THE CLEARINGS; WOODLOT WIZARDRY)

Robert Kourik is author of *Maintaining Your Edible Landscape* (Metamorphic Press, 1986) and *Gray Water Use of the Landscape* (Metamorphic Press, 1988). A resident of Occidental, California, he writes for a number of gardening publications and is a contributing editor for *Garbage* magazine. (GROUND RULES FOR PLANTING TREES)

Allen Lacy lives in southern New Jersey, where he is professor of philosophy at Stockton State University and a garden columnist for *The New York Times*. His most recent book, *Garden in Autumn*, published by the Atlantic Monthly Press, will be available in October 1990. (STEADFAST PERENNIALS)

Patrick Lima lives on the Bruce Peninsula in Ontario where he tends to Larkwhistle, his large, 15-year-old organic garden of perennials, fruit trees, vegetables, and herbs. He frequently writes for *Harrowsmith* and *Harrowsmith Country Life* and is author of *The Harrowsmith Perennial Garden* (Camden House, 1987) and *The Harrowsmith Illustrated Book of Herbs* (Camden House, 1986). (SUMMERTIME LETTUCE; STALWART HERBS)

Charles Long lives in Ontario. When he's not writing, he builds stone structures. He is a frequent contributor to *Harrowsmith* and author of *Life After the City* (Camden House, 1989), *How to Survive Without a Salary* (Summerhill Press, 1988), *The Stonebuilder's Primer* (Camden House, 1981), and *The Backyard Stonebuilder* (Summerhill Press, 1985). (LIFE IN THE CLEARINGS; GETTING THE HANG OF IT)

Senior editor of *Eating Well* magazine and food editor for *Harrowsmith Country Life*, **Rux Martin** is co-author of *Simmering Suppers* (Camden House, 1988) and contributing editor of *The Harrowsmith Cookbook Volume 3* (Camden House, 1987). She lives in Underhill, Vermont. (SAUSAGE SAVVY; RISING AGAIN; BUBBLE, BUBBLE, NO TOIL OR TROUBLE; CULTURED COOKING; A TWIST OF TRADITION)

Michael McRae lives in Ashland, Oregon, where he is gentrifying a 19th-century farmhouse. He is a contributing editor for *Outside* magazine and has written frequently for *Harrowsmith, Harrowsmith Country Life,* and *Equinox* magazines. (PADDLING INTO THE MAINSTREAM)

Catherine Mills, a freelance garden writer, still lives both a rural and urban life, dividing her time between San Francisco and her country home in northern California. The number of wild pigs on her land has grown since she wrote this article, and she now has drip irrigation and tiles on her kitchen floor. (AVOIDING THE RAT RACE)

Merilyn Mohr is shelter editor of *Harrowsmith* and author of *Sunwings* (Camden House, 1985), *A Chronicle of Our House* (Camden House, 1988), *The Art of Soapmaking* (Camden House, 1979), *Canoecraft* (Camden House, 1983), and *Home Playgrounds* (Camden House, 1987). She lives in Kingston, Ontario. (SUNWINGS)

Helen Molitor died in 1989. A professor of English at the University of Calgary and later at the University of Manitoba, she was a specialist in 18th century English and published a number of academic articles. She lived in Winnipeg, Manitoba. (THE GREAT CODE)

John C. Pullen lives in Old Saybrook, Connecticut. Formerly an advertising copy writer, he has retired and now oil paints, gardens, and plays golf. (DEVIL ROOT)

Leigh Seddon lives in Montpelier, Vermont, where he runs Solar Works Inc., a renewable-energy contracting and engineering company. He is a frequent contributor to *Harrowsmith Country Life* and author of *Low Cost Green Lumber Construction* (Garden Way Publishing, 1981) and *Practical Pole Building Construction* (Williamson Publishing, 1985). (SITTING PRETTY)

"We now have hot water," says **Linda Tatelbaum**, who still lives off the land in Burkettville, Maine. An assistant professor at Colby College, she recently finished writing *Under the Milk Weed*, a book of essays, and a novel. (AVOIDING THE RAT RACE)

Michael Webster is editor of *Harrowsmith* and author of *Home Farm* (Camden House, 1989). He and his family live on a 75-acre homestead in eastern Ontario, where he raises chickens and pigs, gardens, and sings in a choir. (LIFE IN THE CLEARINGS; CARVED IN STONE; ANIMAL PHARMACY; CREATURE COMFORTS) 🌸

Contents

Introductions

"Chickens?" our new acquaintance asked. "Why ever would you?"

Indeed, even after years of keeping a small flock of birds, the rationale for a desk-bound publisher to raise chickens is not always apparent or readily explained. Urban friends mostly consider it quirky madness, and we have to admit to recent moments of self-doubt.

Having made do with rickety old sheds and, for the past five seasons, a dark, old horse stall in the corner of the barn, we moved up this spring to a full-blown, renovated henhouse, complete with south-facing windows, fenced runs, a supposedly predator-proof floor and all the amenities.

It has proved to be the worst year ever.

Seemingly alerted by our efforts, all manner of predaceous chicken lovers have converged on the new coop. A weasel somehow maneuvered its way up and in from below to decimate a batch of Buff Orpington chicks; raccoons scaled the walls, slipped through the windows and attacked the Cornish Rock Giant broilers, and just to add interest, a hawk has from time to time plundered us from above, taking a Barred Plymouth Rock hen that our 6-year-old daughter brought home from a school incubator-hatching. We are left with a greatly diminished flock and a renewed respect for the wild forces that separate us from our urban and suburban friends.

Raising a year's supply of chicken each spring may be a perversity that typifies everything in this book. HARROWSMITH was born in the wake of the great oil crisis of the early '70s, and over the years, many of us have retained the spirit of self-sufficiency spawned in those days. We continue to be serious about food gardening, we have wood stoves and compost heaps and beds of herbs and perennials. We still believe that homegrown chicken is better.

Fortunately, we are not alone. More than 500,000 people regularly read HARROW-SMITH in Canada, and HARROWSMITH COUNTRY LIFE has more than a million U.S. readers. It is an audience quite unlike any other: approximately 95 percent have gardens, almost half have wood heat as a primary or secondary source of heat, and more than a third have built their own homes. Curiously, among this group of neofarmers, 80 percent have university educations and the majority hold down professional or managerial jobs.

For years, these readers defied explanation to many media observers and advertisers. We had to be either barefoot hippies or plain-dirt farmers. What is finally emerging is an awareness that people are still interested in moving out of the city and taking up country skills. If our full-time farming neighbors at times find our poultry-raising prowess laughable, at least we share a basic rural ethic that society as a whole considers archaic. As the chapters in this book amply illustrate, our readers and contributors have more than an armchair interest in preserving rural values: a deep respect for the land, a love of nature and an uncommon interest in knowing where our food comes from.

This book is a collection of what we think are some of our most lasting articles from the past five years. It is both a celebration of country life and a warning that things are not always as simple or as easy as others might present them.

Country Life

Country Life

"Practically, the old have no very important advice to give the young, their own experience has been so partial, and their lives have been such miserable failures . . . . I have lived some thirty years on this planet, and I have yet to hear the first syllable of valuable . . . advice from my seniors."

WALDEN, Henry David Thoreau

Oh, to be so young again and to know so much. But twenty or more years ago, a young man or a young woman had reason to dismiss society's elders, who had given their sons and daughters a nation divided over war, race, the sanctity of the environment and the integrity of the President. Casting back, memory can only dimly recapture the turmoil and disaffection of the time—their singular intensity.

"One generation abandons the enterprises of another, like stranded vessels," Thoreau wrote in *Walden,* a book that served both to explain and justify a radical remaking of lives.

"I went to the woods because I wished to live deliberately, to front only the essential facts of life, and see if I could not learn what it had to teach, and not, when I came to die, discover that I had not lived," Thoreau said, in explaining why he decided to move to the shores of Walden Pond and live in a house a mere 10 feet wide by 15 long. Hundreds of thousands chose to follow his example, and the back-to-the-land movement was reborn.

"Simplify, simplify," Thoreau counseled, and the homesteaders did. Conspicuous frugality became a badge of honor.

Ultimately, moving to the country offered a lesson in humility, if nothing else. The fact is, Thoreau lasted only two years in the cabin by Walden Pond.

And his spiritual heirs, more than a century later—what has become of them? As the profiles that follow suggest, there is no simple answer. Some have endured in ways that put to shame the master's brief fling at self-sufficiency, and some might feel uncomfortable if called to face Thoreau's gaze. Most, of course, now occupy some middle ground between faith and blasphemy.

— The Editors

Avoiding the Rat Race

FIVE HOMESTEADERS IN SEARCH OF CONTENTMENT

Sophia Hauserman

The first winter in the country, I slept on the couch in the living room to keep the fire going. It was one of the hard winters. The high point came early in December when our hens started to lay. Benj, then a fourth-grader, was responsible for the flock. One morning, he came in from his before-school chores elated. He showed me our first egg: smooth, small, pale brown – a milestone.

Back in the '70s, the main thing I'd noticed about the back-to-the-land movement was that it was a lousy deal for women. Washing clothes on rocks by the river is not my idea of a good time. The great upheavals of that era – civil rights, environmental concern, protest against the Vietnam War, and the women's movement – sprang from a common root and began in the cities. The last, especially, flourishes in the city. So when the end came to my marriage, I stayed in town with women and children and graduate school. Benj's dad moved to the woods and built a yurt.

Some time later, on a fall day, I stood with Minnie, my Polish neighbor, in the silver-maple leaves by the fence, watching Benj play. She was telling me about the old days, not so long ago, when in the fall there would be a pile of coal in the cellar and shelves of canning jars filled and waiting. Food and fuel. I fastened onto the picture. To me, they spelled safety. My life at the time held nothing but in-security – an incomprehensible jumble of working, going to class, raising a child alone, grieving over my mother's recent death. Food and fuel. Not wages, not supermarkets, not gas furnaces. They weren't safe enough. I needed food and fuel where I could touch them, under my eye, under my hand. Under my control. I figured food and fuel would be easier to get in the country, so after a while, we left the city.

The Nearings had cautioned: do not go homesteading alone. But by the time Benj and I had worked ourselves, in a series of fits and starts, from western Massachusetts to south-central Indiana, I had no choice. If I didn't go alone, I stayed in the city. So I shrugged and leapt in.

At least I was careful enough to define "country" appropriately. Looking at one old house sitting in solitary splendor on a bend in the state highway, I knew instantly to let it be. If we bought it, pretty soon every yahoo who traveled that road would realize a single woman lived there alone. No sense asking for trouble. It was town for us, a small town. We found our place in a village of 200. The house has running water, electricity, two and a half acres and neighbors. Fifty yards away are the woods.

About that first winter I remember most clearly the deep paths I tramped in the snow. They were clean and white, and I walked them most of the day, it seemed – bringing in armload after armload of wood, taking feed and hot water to the chickens, gathering the eggs.

Also clear in memory is the day the pipes froze. I spent several hours bent over in the dark crawl space, wrapping rags around the hot-water pipe, soaking them with kettles of boiling water Benj brought down from the kitchen and handed gingerly in through a window in the cellar. Our victory was exhilarating. That summer, just in case, I bought a hair dryer at a tag sale.

By the end of the second winter, we were well on our way to acquiring a partner. The only other organic gardener in the township and a native, Jim had noticed my Garden Way cart and knew it for the mate to his own. Moreover, he'd seen me chasing Benj around the yard. "Probably I was trying to catch him for chores," I explained. "No," he said firmly, "you were playing."

A beekeeper and skilled gardener, Jim had been growing his own food for years. "For business or pleasure?" I asked brightly, early in the game. "Why, to *eat*," he answered.

Despite that prophetic exchange, indicating clearly a basic and profound difference in outlook, we took up together. Our first joint project was the cow, a venture I was just embarking on when Jim came into the family. I liked butter and the pretty brown eyes of Jerseys.

On my own, I'd have been minus a cow fast. My comprehension of the vastness of the undertaking was imperfect.

To make butter, first you repair the barn. Then build fence, buy hay, get a cow, learn to milk, skim the milk, get out the blender – and you're all set. That first taste of butter taught me a lesson: homesteading is hard work. Like pounding clothes on rocks, I'd rather not.

I now understand why, in my county, there are no women homesteading alone, and few women living alone out here under any cir-cumstances. As an end in itself, homesteading is too hard. It's not worth the effort. Car care, babysitting, food and fuel are easier to arrange in the city. The wages necessary to arranging them are easier to find. Besides, it's too lonely out here for most women. All the people I know who live alone in the country are men.

Jim gardens and takes care of the cow and cuts firewood and makes maple syrup and keeps bees because that's his notion of a

Left, Sophia Hauserman moved to the country, where she met her multitalented husband, Jim Doyle. "We've made a version of country living that suits us."

proper way to live. I weave rag rugs and write and two days a week run the local Senior Nutrition Project – known colloquially as the Eats for Old Folks. To my surprise, I've found I'd rather sweep a floor or make cheese than hoe corn when it's 100 degrees or milk when it's minus 10. But I value the fact that I've done both – and can do it again, if need be.

Not long ago, I asked Jim if he were disappointed that I hadn't turned out to be the Perfect Pioneer Woman. "Well," he answered carefully, "I knew when I married you that you didn't have a high tolerance for physical discomfort." I let it go at that, content with the affirmation that I hadn't put one over on him – and pleased by the delicacy of his answer.

Over the years, we've made a version of country living that suits us, but sometimes I look around and wonder, "Where is everyone?" In my county, the back-to-the-landers flourished in the late '70s. There was a substantial network of people who'd come from the city and kept goats and made sorghum and gathered for potlucks and midwinter sledding parties.

By the time Benj and I arrived in 1980, the group was beginning to disintegrate from the effects of divorce, hard work and money problems. The animals were the first to go, starting with the goats and their need for twice-a-day milking. Then there'd be a job in town and hours spent commuting instead of working on the place. Or one of the market gardeners, faced with the loss of a crop, would abandon the organic faith and turn to chemicals.

Now in our county of 15,000 people, I know one other family I call true homesteaders – meaning they spend most of their time providing directly for their own needs. Two other families at least support themselves by their land, one as a nursery and landscaping service, the other as an herb farm. Some of the others are still here, but they are not homesteaders – they just live in the country.

And what's wrong with that? I'm fully aware that as a homesteader, I hang on my husband's coattails. The title belongs to him. Left to myself, I would still keep a garden, but a tiny one; keep chickens, but no cow; keep the wood stove, but buy firewood. I'd live in the country, but I wouldn't be a homesteader.

For me, it was never a religion, so I escaped the pain of losing my faith. I'm here because I like it here. I get my clean food, I walk in the woods – and I notice with delight something that Ozark beekeeper Sue Hubbell remarked on. "I wonder," she wrote in *A Country Year,* "if I am becoming feral. Wild things and wild places pull me more strongly than they did a

few years ago." It seems to me, too, that, growing older, I grow wilder, more nearly feral. A new direction to explore.

At the same time, my son in school, my native husband and my job with the old folks bind me to the community. When I go around to the homemakers' extension clubs to talk about the Senior Nutrition Project, I introduce myself in concrete terms: "I'm the woman who bought Walter White's house seven years ago and married the oldest Doyle boy."

Even so, I won't ever belong here totally. There are too many memories of other places and people that crowd my head, demanding part of my allegiance. Besides, I have always treasured the curious freedom of the foreigner: license to be a little strange, a little fierce.

Well, I've got the control over food and fuel that I craved. Never mind that it turns out that my husband is the prime mover. I've learned to function as part of a unit, filling out parts of his life while he does the same for me.

More than that, more than the safety of securing control over the basic needs, in the country I've found a setting for my life that suits me. Not just a physical setting, though sometimes at dusk, when I look down the yard, the last sunlight giving a rosy-tan glow to trees I never planted and a few that I did, my throat tightens with love.

This setting also means a community – something I never considered when I moved here – where relationships can be prickly, tricky and, at times, infuriating. The climate is new to me. One day, my strong-willed mother-in-law, who lives next door, gathers signatures around town to complain about the roads. A few days later, the county truck comes out and fills the potholes.

At the same time, this is a community that fired the librarian because she didn't keep the library the way it was in 1913. How to adjust to such a climate, let alone contribute to it? A hard problem, one that will prove a lifelong study, I expect.

At least, while learning to look severely at systems of thought, I now look less severely at the people bound up in those systems. Maybe because we were younger then, we thought it possible to find a simple life. Now I figure that life is not simple anywhere, city or country. Those of us who went back to the land because we wanted to be in touch with earth are still here, if we still want to be. We've made adjustments with partners, incomes and expectations. The rest have moved on, properly so. Times change. Those who left took with them skills they didn't have before and maybe some of the self-respect that comes

RICHARD W. BROWN

from being capable. The best thing we did, those who left and those who stayed, was to open up possibilities—for ourselves and for the souls and imaginations of those who didn't come along physically.

What an adventure we had. Once I was telling my son how it was in the '60s, to help him understand that his experience in the '80s in a rural Indiana high school is not the sum total of experience possible. He said sadly, "It must have been neat to live then." And I told him what Wordsworth said about his youth during the French Revolution:

Bliss was it in that dawn to be alive,
But to be young was very heaven!

—*Sophia Hauserman*

Jane Dwinell

Fifteen years ago, my dream was to homestead. It has now become a reality. I am a seventh-generation Vermonter, come from a long line of farmers and hardy early settlers. I have wonderful memories from my childhood of the peacefulness of sitting on my grandmother's hillside under an apple tree, always wanting the quietness, the joy and delight of being in the country close to earth and sky.

Ten years ago, I thought I had begun my dream. Settled in a small Vermont town in a rented farmhouse with incredible old flower gardens engulfed by weeds, I had made the

It took Jane Dwinell 15 years to realize her homesteading dream. Today, she shares the reality with her husband, Sky Yardley, and daughter, Dana.

move from the city ready to become self-sufficient. Armed with a wood stove, pressure canner, dozens of canning jars and my gardening tools, I set about reclaiming the gardens and developing some of my own. I canned 300 jars of food that summer, staying awake into the night snapping beans and cutting corn off cobs. I was in heaven.

Two complications took over my life, however. My partner, who supposedly shared my dream, became depressed. Life became a nightmare as days stretched into weeks when he would barely emerge from bed to eat one meal a day or to put wood in the stove when I was gone. I lived in fear that I would return home only to find it gone – he having lived out his suicidal wish to torch the house and die within. We were surviving, but only by my sheer will and determination to provide warmth and food. It was a winter I'll never forget.

During that time, I attended nursing school, a 50-mile commute one way, five days a week. When I arrived in the country, I had little money, no skills and a worthless degree in history. I searched for a profession that would enable me to work part-time yet bring in enough money for land, taxes, supplies and other needs. I chose nursing and was enjoying school tremendously.

After two years, I graduated, left my partner and the old farmhouse and moved to Seattle, Washington. My stay in Vermont taught me several things, most importantly never to attempt to homestead without a willing partner, enough money to get started, and a marketable skill to help the cash flow. In Seattle, I was determined to save lots of money and find that partner I was looking for.

A year later, I returned to Vermont with a pleasantly large savings account, some wonderful memories of the West Coast and a determination to get back to the country. I got a full-time job in Vermont's first in-hospital birthing center, renovated an old barn on my grandmother's farm and settled in, once again planning to make my dream come true. This time, I had money and skills, but no partner. The strong feminist in me said, "To hell with it. I can do it myself."

Running a chain saw scared me, my pipes froze every week that first winter, and I was still eating the food I had canned in "the year of 300 jars." My first garden was a disaster – between the burdock, the chickens and the raccoons, I harvested almost nothing. But I loved my job and told myself that things would get easier in time.

That year, I was asked to teach classes on wood stove cooking, food preservation and quilting at the Good Life Get Together, a homesteaders' festival in upstate New York. I returned excited and inspired. I blamed my homesteading failures on not having spent enough time on my little place. I figured out just how much money I needed to pay the bills and was prepared to tell my head nurse that I wanted to work part-time. I could then spend the time I needed and wanted at home.

Karma and circumstances being what they are, I was approached by her first, was told she was leaving, and that *I* had been appointed head nurse. Although I was excited to take the position, I found myself working more than 40 hours per week. My homesteading dream disappeared again. I was so busy at the hospital that I installed a gas furnace and started buying my produce at the farmers' market. For the next few summers, my only brush with homesteading was the class I taught at the Good Life Get Together, my vacation every year.

Working full-time did not allow for true self-sufficiency, living off the land, homesteading, whatever you may call it. There was no time to run wood fires, let alone cut wood. I began to pay other people to do jobs for me – repair work, carpentry, snow removal. Every garden I attempted went by or turned to weeds. I gave up.

In due time, I said.

I need a partner, I said.

I need more money, I said.

After I'd been at the hospital for several years, working more than full-time began to wear on me. I had turned 30; I was banging my head against hospital politics; I wanted out. I wanted to homestead. But I was still lacking a partner, and several years alone had shown me I could not do it without one. I decided to fulfill another long-held fantasy – owning a restaurant.

I quit my job, made a deal with the bank, invested my life savings and, with a friend, converted a run-down greasy spoon into an upscale vegetarian café. My plan was to run it for five years, sell it and have enough money to retire to the country for good. I would spend the five years working hard, investigating homesteading possibilities elsewhere, looking for a partner or perhaps a group situation. I was sick of careers and conspicuous consumption. I was getting closer to my dream.

Well, it was not to be as I had planned it. No one had warned me that most restaurants fail, and partnerships are hard to make work. We ended the partnership – and the friendship – and to keep the café afloat, I sold everything I owned except my house and my car. Still determined to save face and maybe make a little money, I decided to stick with the café a little longer, even though 60-hour weeks and no money were beginning to wear thin.

And then I fell in love – out of nowhere and when I least expected it. And behold, my lover held the same dream that I did – only he had been living closer to it for many years. An early and continuing member of a northern Vermont commune, he had the skills of self-sufficiency. Food production, maple sugaring, dairy farming, logging, woodworking, make-do living had been his for 13 years. He only lacked a partner to share his dream of building a house, having a family and homesteading on their own land.

We began to build a small cabin on the communal land. I sold my house and business and moved into the 10-by-15 cabin in the middle of the sugarbush. I was so happy. I marveled at my ability to build, run a big chain saw and like it, split wood, live without running water, plumbing or electricity. We loved our location, walking a mile in from the road to be deep in the maple woods. But because we wanted children, we began to plan for our "big house," with running water and plumbing, in a more suitable location.

It all seems like a fairy tale sometimes. We are now living on our own land (no banks involved), 45 acres of young sugarwoods, mature softwoods and open pasture. Our first project here on Full Moon Farm was to get married. We then built a barn, insulated a 16-by-20 hunting camp that was on the property, developed a spring for running water (only cold, mind you, but it runs out of the faucet), acquired a generator for power (so we would not have to hook into the nuclear-powered "system") and had a baby.

I sit here in the peacefulness of winter, looking out the window from the top loft. The blue jays and the red squirrel share the bird feeder; a downy woodpecker is at the suet. I see my husband, Sky, and our draft horse, Lil, arrive with another log to add to the growing pile in the yard. A portable sawmill will come in the spring to saw those logs into lumber for the "big house" that we plan to build this year. As I look off the loft in the other direction, I see our daughter, Dana, asleep in her crib and the cats cuddled together on the bed. I am content. I am here. My dream has come true.

The homesteading dream, to me, means simple living, making do with what you have and doing for yourself as much as possible. Providing our own power, heat, food, lumber and skills is deeply satisfying to me. I feel safe; I feel secure; I feel proud.

As for cash flow, we make do. My husband is training to be a mediator. My nursing degree comes in handy as I suspected; part-time and on-call work is always available. We have a small home business making fresh salsa, which is sold in health-food stores and co-ops around the state. When the house is done, we will build a sugarhouse and start maple sugaring again. In the meantime, we are still selling the syrup we made at our last home. Barter also works well around here.

New challenges will come. Still, my husband and I often say to each other, "You know, I really love our life." I wouldn't change it for anything.

—*Jane Dwinell*

Marshall Helmberger

At the age of 11, I bet my skeptical older cousin $20 that, someday, I would live in a log cabin. Well, someday came three years ago, and I have yet to collect my due. Nonetheless, I feel more than compensated for the decision.

It was the spring of 1984 when my wife, Jodi, and I left Minneapolis, pickup loaded with our implements of construction, subsistence and edification, bound for our 20-acre chunk of the Minnesota Northwoods. We were fresh from the university scene and with ideals to spare – hoping to find satisfaction among the tall pines and balsam fir.

By our own hands and with the occasional help of friends, family and our ever-reliable chain saw, we built a house – and a way of life. The house is one room, with a loft and a passive-solar design that works well in the summer and fall, but is largely ineffectual against the northern winter. We heat with wood. For electricity, we recently installed a couple of solar-electric panels, and we have a well that we pump by hand. But we still have no phone.

Our livelihood, to date, has been based primarily on reforestation. We plant trees, on a contract basis, for the state of Minnesota and the federal government. So far, we estimate that we've planted 350,000 trees, mostly red pine, and our goal is one million. It's a tough yet satisfying way to earn a living, and with only a six-week season, it leaves us free the rest of the year.

My writing, mostly political journalism and how-to, helps to supplement our income. Jodi keeps busy with her fledgling knitting business, selling custom sweaters and hats. In the fall, we gather wild rice from lakes in nearby Superior National Forest and Boundary Waters Wilderness. We hand-parch our rice in the traditional Ojibwa manner, which en-

New blood: recent back-to-the-landers Marshall Helmberger and Jodi Summit.

hances the taste considerably. We sell most of it and still have more than enough for our own use. With no mortgage and almost no utility costs (bottled gas runs our lights, stove and refrigerator for about $20 a month), we do quite nicely on a yearly income of $7,000.

Our agricultural efforts have been small-scale so far—this area is not a gardener's paradise. Our land sits firmly on the Canadian Shield, where the latest glacier has made soil a rare commodity. Through the use of raised beds, however, and imported soil (mostly peat), we have managed some success. And the climate is extreme: Tower, the nearest town, has an average frost-free period of 41 days, and two summers ago we had only 14. Still, we've had fun pushing our luck. Last year, I shoveled the snow off a couple of beds on April 1 and covered them with plastic to help thaw the soil. Following a week of sunny weather, I planted starts on April 10 and, using cloches and lots of blankets, saw them through temperatures in the single digits. By May 25, a full two weeks before the accepted planting date around here, we had full-grown Romaine lettuce and all the chard we could eat.

Beekeeping, long an interest of mine, has proven quite difficult because of almost daily visits by bears. We speculate that the house sits on an ancient ursus burial ground, which accounts for the bears' virtually constant presence during the summer.

The isolation of rural life was a bit rough on us the first couple of years. We sometimes don't realize what social creatures we are until we find ourselves in such a situation. We knew there were kindred sorts in the area, but finding them was hard.

Thanks to the Minnesota National Guard, however, we've greatly expanded our social horizons. Last summer, the Guard proposed building a 200,000-acre military training facility in Superior National Forest, not far from our house. We got involved in successfully opposing the facility and, through our activism, met lots of folks with philosophies similar to ours. We became good friends with many of them and, with the defeat of the Guard, we have begun working on other environmental and economic issues. Political activism, which isn't new to us, has changed our lives to the point where any evening spent quietly at home is now the exception. We're still looking for a happy equilibrium.

Above all, Jodi and I are pragmatists, rather than romantics. Our living here was not so much an attempt to "get back to nature" as it was simply to pursue and promote a sane and sustainable way of life. A deep respect and appreciation for the Earth and natural systems is an inevitable outgrowth of our basic philosophy, a philosophy of permanence. And for us, I feel, there is an order that is beginning to emerge. For along with the many new friends, this year has also brought us a growing sense of community with and commitment to the area. Like the thousands of pine seedlings we have planted here, I think we too are growing permanent roots.

— *Marshall Helmberger*

Catherine Mills

When Thoreau left the woods after two years of confronting "only the essential facts of life," the world he returned to hadn't changed in his absence. A large degree of self-reliance was expected, even in the cities. The service industries were not paramount. "Consumerism" was not yet a word. If Thoreau were making his decision today, I think he'd have stayed at the pond.

I can understand the urge many homesteaders have to return to civilization. Living on the land is simple (or can be), but it is not easy. Living in the city is, in its way, easy, but it is never simple. I prefer the difficulties of rural life over what I experience as the oppressive complexity of the city, and I consider it a privilege that I am able to indulge that preference most of the time.

I moved to the isolated beauty of northern California's Coast Range in 1982 when I was in my late 30s and felt I knew clearly what I wanted. I had lived in four countries, in small towns and a city of 2 million, on a farm and in a trailer. Unlike many who took up rural life in their 20s, I had had a lot of experience — both in practical skills and in everyday situations. I may not spend the rest of my life here, but then, I well may.

I live at the end of nine miles of dirt road on a half-section of oak woodland, which I own with four friends. Once a massive sheep ranch, the land was subdivided in the '70s into parcels of 160 acres and up. I have three full-time neighbors within walking distance, but the other nearby parcels are owned by city men who come now and then on weekends to hunt. One doesn't just pop over to the neighbors here. Each is a mile or more away and 500 to 1,000 feet up or down. We are good acquaintances and can rely on each other in a pinch, but we haven't become close friends. My closest friends are in the San Francisco Bay Area, three hours away. When the weather is fine, I have a lot of weekend guests.

I am alone here most of the time. Until last year, when my friend Tom was not away working or traveling, he called this home as well. He used to live down the hill, and we met when he volunteered to help build my house, saying he was forgetting how to use power tools and could use the practice. At that time, the place he lived in had no power, although now it has a solar-electric setup far, far more elaborate than mine. He has since moved back there. We visit often, and I can still count on him to help with heavy chores.

I'm the only co-owner who lives on the land.

The others visit with varying frequency and talk wistfully of retiring here – but not until their children are grown. It's a long commute from here to the nearest town, and the education it offers is worse than mediocre. Having no children makes it easier for me to live as I do. If orthodontists or college tuition loomed in the future, I would not feel secure living in splendid isolation on a marginal income.

It's hard to make a living here, near impossible to make a good living. Rural northern California has an almost Third World economy, exporting raw materials, agricultural products and illegal drugs and importing finished goods. The service industries are mostly tourist-related, labor largely seasonal, hourly wages low. I came to the land with savings from several years of farming, and now earn money by doing carpentry, substitute teaching, freelance writing and odd jobs. And occasionally, working in the city. Yes, I could grow dope, and the income from a single successful year could support me well into the future. But the consequences of a single bust could also be devastating. Since CAMP (the federal/state Campaign Against Marijuana Planting) began its raids, the summer skies are full of helicopters and spotter planes. For me, growing raises a number of moral as well as legal questions and is not an option.

I have no illusions about making my living from the land or being self-sufficient. I also know that this land hasn't the water or the soil for commercial farming. I realized before moving here that my demands on the land would have to be kept modest. There is a large vegetable garden, a small orchard – and a raging overabundance of wild pigs, which we are trying to eliminate. The land does provide, but we don't ask too much of it.

The land is paid for, the house nearly so, and while I can live on little, I'm 43 and don't want to exist hand-to-mouth forever. Ideally, I would devise a way to live here full-time and not have to commute, but after five years here, I have recently begun to spend two weeks a month in the Bay Area. I have fairly steady work doing freelance writing and research and find that I *can* stay sane living in the country only half-time. I don't want it to be a permanent arrangement, however.

Perhaps because I read a great deal and can populate my environment in my imagination, I am more content than most when by myself. Some chores, like gardening, lend themselves well to working alone. Others, like carpentry projects, do not. I'm not paranoid about it, but I am always aware that, if hurt, I might not be found for several days. I take reasonable precautions: I don't go onto the roof when there's no one else around. It's like living with the rattlesnakes around here; if you have foresight, the chances of getting bitten are almost nonexistent. If you want to eliminate the "almost" as well, then this isn't the place for you.

This place is not wilderness, but it is both wild and remote. Yet I feel far more confident of my ability to cope with this environment than with urban threats. If I am bitten by a snake or fall off the roof, it is likely to happen because I let my attention wander and grew careless. The things I fear in the city are quite out of my control. Leaving a friend's house in San Francisco, I am cautioned to be careful – a woman was raped a block away. I wonder how it is possible to be "careful" of such random violence.

In the city, agencies and authorities assume responsibilities that I, in the country, retain for myself. If my lights go out, I check the charge on my battery or turn on the generator. If the roads are flooded, I must find the clogged culvert or ditch. I prefer this to calling the power company or the city engineers.

I have a high tolerance for what most people would consider adversity and a low tolerance for what many take in stride: crowds, noise, locks, curtains, cement, bottled water, shopping. I can cope with these but they fuel a discontent, a dis-ease, which soon triggers an urgent need to escape. I like knowing where the Big Dipper is and what phase the moon is in. They provide a kind of orientation and a rhythm I am attuned to. In the country, I can easily forget what day of the week it is. In the city (San Francisco, which is temperate), I sometimes can't remember what season it is, but I always know when it's Saturday.

Just as the days of the week mask time, the city's skin distorts my sense of space. Even San Francisco seems flat (or flattened), because the surface has been planed relatively smooth. Here, it is not so much the steep hills that let me know I am walking on the Earth, as it is the micro-geography of each trail. There are always changes – new flowers, fallen branches, mudslides, pig ruts, a flush of mushrooms. These remind me that there are forces other than "man" always on my path.

Life in the city can seem easy because, for a price, there are services and products to meet every need. But I can't buy peace to soothe me or an environment to remind me that I, too, am an animal, and I need to rest more than I need to buy something. When I am on the land, although I have little, I find I want nothing.

I don't mean to imply that I am some sort of ascetic living in a backwoods treehouse. The house is small, but as the insurance agent said when he looked at the photo, "It's a normal house!" Given my location, he'd expected a "hippie shack." I'm an outlaw as far as the county is concerned. The house is built to code, but without permits. That's not uncommon here. The hill people are isolated and individualistic, and they are not fond of bureaucracy.

I have provided myself with some conveniences that back-to-the-landers might once have considered luxuries: solar electricity, for example, and a classy fiberglass composting toilet, a modest sound system, a generator and full complement of power tools.

There is still a long list in my wish book: finish the house, increase water storage, fence as many acres as possible against the pigs and deer so the trees can grow back, build a pond, get drip irrigation, plant trees. I consider it a measure of my privilege that that list concentrates on preserving and restoring my environment rather than insulating me from it.

From a distance, northern California's hills may seem wild and empty, but they are not "natural." They've been overgrazed since the Spaniards came, logged out, burned and eroded. The Grizzly State has no grizzly bears, and government trappers take more and more coyotes every day. I've seen only a single mountain lion in five years. Some species of oak haven't regenerated in 80 years; many wildflowers are endangered; the spotted owl can't find its habitat. However lightly I tread, I know I can't live here without further altering the landscape and local ecology. Neither

"I am more content than most when by myself," writes Catherine Mills, who finds her isolated life simple, but not easy.

I nor the dogs, cats, house or garden is native to this place, but we can try to naturalize gracefully and make our decisions and choices with more than just our own species in mind. People who have left the land and sought success in the city say they're getting "back into the mainstream." But that's only the mainstream if the river you are in flows exclusively with people. It is important to me to live where I don't have to get away from it all, but am surrounded by it all—midstream in a more all-inclusive river.

—*Catherine Mills*

Linda Tatelbaum and Kal Winer were the "last pure homesteaders around," but they've given up eking out a living to engage—selectively—the broader world.

Linda Tatelbaum

It's 1974 and I am a professor at a college in New Hampshire. The college goes bankrupt. Watergate bursts open. The Arab oil crisis hits home. With my good friend the dean of students, I decide to drop out, do physical labor, earn my keep on this planet. I work for barter, trading my labor on a farm for cordwood, cow's milk, maple syrup, old canning jars. I think I will never need money again or "good clothes" or anything made of plastic, or light bulbs, extension cords, ice-cube trays, books that aren't "how-to" manuals. Good-bye to all that.

We eat from wooden bowls, drink from stoneware mugs, use chopsticks. Nothing metal or plastic or china will ever touch our lips again. No alarm clocks, radios or newspapers, except to start the cookstove. We eat beans and rice, vegetables, yogurt, whole-wheat bread. The seasons will rule us. We are one with the woods.

1975: I marry my woods-companion. I chop wood and carry water. He operates a lathe from 9 to 5 at a factory in town and comes home gray.

1977: We buy land in Maine and build our own house, plant a garden. We use only hand tools.

1979: I am pregnant. The nurse says I must drink milk, eat liver and fish once a week. I have no refrigerator and don't want to break my vows of simplicity, but not doing what she says fills me with doubt. Two weeks before delivery, I go into a discount store and stand, bewildered, in front of rows of consumer products – Kleenex, baby wipes, ointments. I feel I've re-entered a world I once knew and rejected. I spend $20 on things not made by hand. The baby comes, hospital-delivered. I change his cloth diapers by flashlight at night; I lug a bushel basket of diapers to the Laundromat every week; I haul water while baby sleeps; I grind grain for his pabulum and cook it on a wood stove. I am exhausted. I want my mother or canned soup or baseboard heat. Or do I? At least I wish I could switch on a light when baby cries at 2 a.m., rather than fumble with kerosene lamps while my milk leaks down my chest and baby howls. I wish I didn't have to go down cellar every time he wants apple juice. I wish I had a drain, so I didn't have to lug water in *and* out. I wish my mother could come and I didn't have to write her a manual for how to boil water for a cup of tea in my kitchen. I'm so tired.

1981: I go back to work as a professor, part-time. I get up in the dark and eat breakfast by kerosene light. Dressed up in my new clothes, I haul water, trying not to perspire or spill water on my stockings. Our dirt road is the last in town to get plowed, so I leave extra early in snow, and then mud, to make the hour commute for an 8 a.m. class. I read student papers by Aladdin lamplight at night. At the college, I feel like a creature from another planet, until I find out my colleague in his three-piece suit in the next office lives in a log cabin and has to ski out to his car in the dark each morning. I begin to see how funny it all is.

1983: We build an addition with a bedroom for our son, a study for me. We install photovoltaics for lights and a water pump. We put in a drain. We get a 12-inch black-and-white TV. Our friends are shocked. They are homesteaders, too, who have long since put in power, washing machines, freezers, taken jobs in town, and they regret to see *us* change. We are the last "pure" homesteaders around. They want us to die for their sins. But we want to live and not just subsist. I begin to write again, seriously, in the time gained not hauling water or cutting wood by hand.

Present: I still garden. I still eat homegrown food. I still cook on a wood stove. But I do buy bananas and an occasional fresh broccoli in winter. I still make my own yogurt and bread, but I don't grind my own flour with a hand-mill anymore. I still eat from my same wooden bowl, but once in a while I do like drinking wine from a stemmed glass or setting the table with my grandmother's china. I still live on the same rutted narrow dirt road, but now I drive a recent-model four-wheel-drive Toyota, no longer an old Volkswagen. I still walk in the woods for entertainment, but I do like TV and going out to dinner. I still like to watch my son growing up close to nature, but I do cook him hot dogs and let him buy gum sometimes.

I don't *want* to make my own Grape-Nuts or grow my own mustard seed. I've stopped reading magazines that extol the "simple life." Call it enough to eat from the garden year-round. Call it enough to be minimally responsible for the world's pollution. There's work to do "out there," human-to-human work, and if I'm home hauling water uphill from my spring and eking out a living from the soil, how can the world be served? After all, even wood smoke from my two stoves is an air pollutant, and my solar electric panels are made from silicone, copper, plastic, rubber. I'll never be pure unless I live in a cave and wear animal skins. But then I'd have to kill animals, wouldn't I?

I believe in compromise. I believe in finding my own way. Conforming to anything makes a warped life. Keeping up with the Nearings is just another form of rat race. A self-created life is the only one worth living. And watch out: as soon as we've saved enough money, we're getting hot water. 🔥

—Linda Tatelbaum

Life in the Clearings

IS THE BACK-TO-THE-LAND MOVEMENT DEAD?

Elizabeth & Charles Long

I still get an uncontrollable urge to roll down a grassy hill, especially on a summer day, with the grass mown smooth and the earth smelling warm. There is a simple wholeness to it, a clarity of cause and effect. The best part is the beginning, at the top, feeling the rolling first in the dreaming of it: rolling straight and fast, faster still, gathering force as I fall.

In reality, I still lie on the brink occasionally, surrendering all dignity to the simple joy of letting go. Then I flop over crookedly two or three times and trace a little arc that leaves me beached and deflated, feet pointing back up the hill.

And if you're asking what that has to do with going back to the land, then you've never stood on your own new acres, with your arms around someone you love, imagining how it will be . . . in the dreaming of it: the trees you'll plant, how the shade will lie, the pond over there, animals grazing in organic fields and apples sweet on the tree.

We did that one day, bringing a picnic out from the city, carrying the baby and showing the land to our friend Marcel. We sprawled on the hill, basking in the sun and the wine and the new meadow smells. We solemnly agreed that life was meant to be lived that way.

The baby is 15 now, the hill is overgrown with sumac, and I bumped into Marcel the other day. I didn't recognize him at first. His mass of curls had given way to a shiny bald pate. He looked worried. He asked about the farm and talked about the pressures of budget fights and person-years.

"You know," he said, "what I'd really like to do is get a little piece of land someplace, plant a garden and say, 'To hell with all this,'" waving at the plush seats, the necktied people, the life-sized television tennis players and the dark mirror behind the bar.

Now this is a man fully capable of surrendering all dignity to the simple joy of letting go. This is a man who once had a little inflatable wading pool – before he had children – just so he could come home from work on a hot afternoon, grab a beer and the garden hose and sit in the inflatable pool with Barney, his big Doberman.

To be fair, however, I should give the whole accounting. You know all about the sunsets and the hummingbirds, about drinking great draughts of sap in spring, moonlight skiing, open fires and the taste of food taken ripe from the vine. The reality of that is even sweeter than the dreaming of it, but there *are* worms in the apple, as well as prickly ash, poison ivy and the sheer perversity of nature. Some of us were beaten by the unexpected drudgery, others by the different aspirations of growing children, by the economics of self-sufficiency or by the Byzantine diplomacy of surviving in rural society. Even those of us who stayed the course had our ideals dented just a little bit by all those things. It wasn't quite the way we had dreamed it when we took off for life on the land. All in all, it had a lot less to do with agriculture, which we thought would be the essence of it, than we had imagined.

There were visions of life as self-employed peasants. For a year before we left the city, we collected scraps from the vegetarian restaurant on the corner. That, plus scroungings from the riding stable, built us the biggest urban compost heap outside of the House of Commons. And so, on moving day, we sold the furniture and loaded the compost onto the truck. What the heck, we reasoned, it's the soil that matters; we can eat off an old door or something until there's time to make furniture. The compost served us well. So did the door – we still have a keyhole in the dining table. There never was time; time would always be the fat man on our teeter-totter.

There would be gardens and goats, pigs, rabbits, poultry and pets, a Noah's Ark of our efforts at husbandry. Most of it ended up on the table. Some of it even paid for the feed. And every animal had a lesson for us.

JIM MERRITHEW INSET: KIRKINTILLOCH HERALD

There was Isadora the self-milking goat, for example, who made a mockery of our grand designs on self-sufficiency. We tried splints and collars to keep her from reaching her own udder. We tried milking her early, feeding her more, even telling her she'd go blind if she kept it up. But Isadora stubbornly continued to short-circuit the dairy plan . . . in one end and out the other.

The hard lesson in farm economics came with the first pig slaughter. The procedure, according to *Harrowsmith*, Number 14, was clear: a clean kill, scrape off the hair, hang it and gut it. We started early. By dusk, we had it hung. The head wasn't quite off the floor, and the hair wasn't entirely gone, but it would have to do in the fading light. Liz held the lantern and read out instructions from our trusty back-to-the-land magazine while I groped elbow-deep inside the carcass, feeling for glands that I would not have recognized in a supermarket, even with overhead lights and labels. By midnight, the slithery gap felt more or less like meat. The floor was awash with the overflow. As the lantern began to flicker, we split the carcass to speed the cooling, and the two halves flopped off the hanging arrange-

ment and onto our heads. In total darkness, ankle-deep in blood and urine, struggling to keep the precious pork off the floor, we considered the fruits of an exhausting 18-hour day . . . and tomorrow we would start on the next pig; the fat man chuckled from the other end of the teeter-totter.

The next day, we called the local butcher and learned that he would gladly do the job for $7 per pig. He had vats and machines and electric lights. So much for self-sufficiency.

If life on the land, at least in the way we have come to live it, now has less to do with subsistence farming than we had imagined, then what is here apart from the garden and the hummingbirds? What is here that we hadn't expected?

The simplest answer is that this is a place where life can still be lived on a human scale. I'm sure it still happens in other places, perhaps even in some urban places; it may be a state of mind as much as a place. Perhaps it is merely one means of mental survival when the gap between public crisis and

Elizabeth and Charles Long before their escape from the city, inset, *and with their children, Ewan and Kirsten.*

private impotence has grown so wide. It is a way of life in which an individual can still fix most of the things that go wrong and dismiss the rest as unimportant.

Consider our neighborhood housing crisis, for instance. With Alden's third child on the way, his little bungalow was becoming cramped. He bought a pile of lumber and put out the word. One fine Saturday at dawn, neighbors began to arrive, more than 20 in all. By 8 in the morning, the old roof was off and the house was open to the sky. By noon, there was a floor where the ceiling had been, second-story walls and rafters for the new roof. By sundown, there were still seven of us on the roof, nailing down the last of the shingles. Then we retired to the lawn, sprawling in a circle on the grass, passing around a green unlabeled bottle of wild-grape wine in the dusk, admiring both our work and our aches. There were casualties: some of us had sunburns; Alden's budget took a beating on the beer; and RJ fell through the ceiling into the living room below. But the housing crisis was over for a time, without a penny of public money, without a word of partisan debate.

Nobody keeps accounts on such occasions, or so I thought. But some time later, the fat man found us with an empty woodshed and winter coming on. I merely mentioned the fact, and the next fine Saturday at dawn, the neighbors began to arrive. Alden was there with Carl and Lisa and some other friends we barely knew. By the afternoon, there were five full cords of wood in the shed and our energy crisis was solved for another year.

The system, as it is practiced at this level, is much more human and far more workable than most people could ever envisage. Sports is another instance. I used to go to the big-league parks and pay to watch the pros play. Here, I play catcher for the County Fair Maulers. Last year, in the league play-offs, we faced a powerful team from the candy factory. We Maulers only mustered seven men, so we put the two teams together, chose up sides and played anyway. Nobody kept score. I hit my only home run of the season in a game that didn't count and had more fun than was provided in a lifetime of World Series watching.

Liz and I still smile at those breathless news accounts of some city crippled by a few hours without electricity. We remember the Christmas when the power went off for days. Liz took the dinner out of the oven and put it on the wood stove. We lit candles and pumped water by hand. We sang carols and did puzzles. We skated on the beaver pond and hardly noticed when the power came on again. Like our neighbors, we have never considered producing our own electricity or doing without on ideological grounds. But a blackout doesn't really spoil our day.

This kind of self-sufficiency enjoys the means and doesn't worry unduly about the ends. We may never slaughter a pig again, but if we have to, we can; and we'll keep on growing tomatoes in our own inefficient way, even if California can strip-mine them cheaper. Owner-builders understand that. So do parents who turn off the television and play with the children. So do those County Fair Maulers who play for the joy of it and not for the score.

We haven't rolled straight to the bottom of the hill without hitting a cowflop or two on the way. A dozen years of coddling the organic orchard have yet to produce one worm-free apple. But I've learned enough about grow-it-yourself to let the worm have his. It doesn't spoil my day anymore.

—*Charles Long*

Noel Taylor & Merrick Anderson

It was not an auspicious beginning. In the spring of 1970, 12 hippies, resplendent in beards and beads and amplitudes of hair, disembarked from the small ferry and clomped up the wharf onto Lasqueti Island, in the middle of British Columbia's Georgia Strait. They had, in their minds, escaped from a collapsing civilization by going out into the wilderness to live off the land. Before they had departed from Vancouver, debate had erupted as to whether they should dine in the purity of hand-carved chopsticks and boards or compromise themselves by bringing along plates and cutlery. They had almost nothing in the way of tools, skills or cash—but they had jointly bought a quarter section with an old log house on Lasqueti Island, and had arrived "back to the land."

Within days, a cocker spaniel attached to the party had run a sheep to death. An early pruning expedition into the neglected orchard saw a pear tree hacked down for deadwood because it lacked leaves in January. Word rippled along the coast that there was a groovy commune on Lasqueti, everyone welcome. The islanders, 57 of them, were not amused.

"We looked like freaked-out weirdos," says Merrick Anderson, "but we were just a bunch of kids living together, trying to make a go of it." Merrick, a genial 6-footer, now 36, is no longer as hirsute as in those early days. His partner Noel Taylor, who was 17 when they arrived on that first spring day, smiles now as she prepares a homegrown supper on the

wood cookstove. We are sitting in their comfortably cluttered little kitchen, with 2-year-old Tom burbling and chattering at the table. Smart money might have bet against those 12 kids making a go of it in the wilds of Lasqueti Island, but today, all but one of the original commune members hold their joint shares in the property, and most still live here.

Once part of a ragtag radical threat to the status quo, Noel and Merrick are now blue-chip members of the establishment. She is the island's elected director of the board of the regional district and can be seen periodically flying off to meetings in a chartered floatplane. Merrick is the island fire chief and, as chairman of the Advisory Planning Commission, helps formulate zoning and subdivision bylaws. Yet despite the changes, these two—and the 300-strong community generally, most of whom arrived in the 1970s—remain remarkably faithful to that youthful vision of

getting themselves back to the garden and not getting caught up in some devil's bargain.

"Our original plan," Noel says, "was to divide the land, not to live as a commune forever." After a year and a half jammed together in the old log house, with often as many as 25 people for dinner—"The women were stuck in the kitchen, constantly cooking and doing dishes. It was drudgery!"—Noel and Merrick fled to their one-sixth of the property where, in a little natural clearing ringed with white-stemmed alder trees, they set about building a temporary shelter. For footings, they stuck cedar posts in the ground. With nothing but a hatchet and a Swede saw for the slow cutting of fir framing poles, they tore down an old house to salvage nails and boards and hand-split innumerable shakes from cedar blocks off the beach. Heated with a smoke-belching wood stove, lit with kerosene lamps, poorly angled to the sun, swathed in tar paper and plastic, the little two-story house cost a grand total of $45. And with a living room added on one side, a bedroom for little Tom and a pantry now bulging with canned goods, juices and homemade wines on the other, that original structure is still home.

Merrick Anderson and Noel Taylor arrived on Lasqueti Island in 1970, inset, *and are still there, now with son Tom.*

The airtight cookstove heats the house, and its water jacket gives ample hot water. The shower, a minimalist contraption hanging off the back of the house, delights city visitors with the charm of starlit soapings. The outhouse is defiantly Woodstockian—a leaflike shake roof held up by poles at the base of a large cedar tree, the throne itself magnificently open to the world. Behind the house sits a lovely stone-and-cedar sauna. Farther back rises the most ambitious building of the lot—a 24-by-40-foot, two-story edifice containing a toolshop, a meeting area, a massage room where Noel maintains an acupressure practice and holds workshops and a rehearsal space for Merrick's rock band, The Lasqueti All-Stars.

The 25-acre clearing has grown over the years—and is still growing—to include a small hayfield, an orchard of over 50 fruit and nut trees, pasture and barn for a small flock of sheep, several catchment ponds (fresh water can be a problem on the island), flower, vegetable and berry gardens and a chicken run. The greenhouse, fashioned from a strong, light aluminum alloy that was once part of a Boeing 747 fuselage, can be moved around the garden. Ornamental trees and shrubs ring the lawns. The entire compound is fenced to keep out deer and wild sheep, and Noel and Merrick park their ancient Dodge pickup far from the house and walk in.

When the homestead was built, it became clear to the residents that the island would only remain a sanctuary through the assertion of political will. Thus began—with Noel and Merrick in the thick of it—Lasqueti's version of the politics of paradise. First, the regional district decided to impose building codes and small-lot subdivisions on the island. "We decided," Noel says, "that would be a disaster." Islanders defeated the building code, created a community plan and density bylaw to prevent small-lot subdivisions and elected a conservationist candidate to the regional board. When an upstart municipal affairs minister named Bill Vander Zalm tried to abolish the Islands Trust—an NDP attempt to protect the Gulf Islands from overdevelopment—Lasqueti led the charge to Victoria. In the teeth of fierce opposition, the legislation was withdrawn, and Vander Zalm quit the government.

These preliminary tussles were mere skirmishes compared with Lasqueti's main event—a two-year knock-'em-down, drag-'em-out brawl with a real heavyweight: B.C. Hydro. The utility was determined to use the island as a stepping-stone for a high-voltage transmission line feeding power from the mainland to Vancouver Island. "We put our whole lives into fighting that line," Noel says.

"It was going to come right through the backside of our property. It was going to destroy our whole life-style. It would be the end: we'd have had to move. And basically, the whole island felt that way." The islanders raised funds, researched exhaustively, wrote newsletters, performed plays and concerts, held meetings and news conferences. Eventually, Hydro dusted itself off and withdrew, like a bear retreating from a hornet's nest.

With Hydro's transmission towers out of their lives, Noel and Merrick decided to erect their own steel tower—this one to capture wind for power. They already had a small 12-volt wind charger mounted atop a tall fir tree, but Noel wanted more. Newspaper advertisements eventually turned up just what they needed—a Jacobs 32-volt wind generator, circa 1940. That was the easy part. Designing, carting in, cutting, sandblasting, erecting and anchoring a 90-foot steel tower on top of bedrock and then winching up the 500-pound generator—that was another matter. Now the two of them roar with laughter at the madness of the undertaking, but at the time, it meant hundreds of hours of heavy, heartbreaking, dirty and dangerous work. Sustained by their dream of alternative energy and by the need to prove it could be done after the Hydro fight, they saw it through. "The windmill gave us power and light," says Noel. "It was such a major achievement, any project after that was nothing."

Now things are a little less frantic. "We have always had some major project on the go," Noel says. "Now, we're basically down to maintenance; there isn't that great sense of urgency to get things done." They are in no particular hurry to start working on the new house they plan to build. Merrick, who has taken a pounding over the years in the frenzy of homesteading—he lost an eye to a flying Rotovator tine in the worst of several accidents—is learning to relax: "As we get older, we learn a few lessons. You learn how to live a bit better." There is time now for windsurfing around Lasqueti's coves and islets—although Noel still has a hard time visiting the shore without dragging home some gravel or seaweed.

Living better keeps them satisfied with their life on Lasqueti. "In an urban situation," Merrick says, "we'd be paupers. But here, we're wealthy because we own what we've got and don't have payments going out every month." They earn a modest income from Noel's massage business, her regional board honorarium and Merrick's seasonal work with his small Kubota tractor. "We have the self-sufficiency thing down pretty well," Merrick says. "We grow most of our food, and the barter system is alive and well here."

With dinner over and the blackberry wine flowing freely, we watch home movies of the homestead, filmed by Merrick's father. "I grew up seeing my dad miserable," Merrick says, "running the rat race, always too many bills to pay, lots of pressure and constant complaints about what a hellish life it was. My ambition was to have a place of my own where I could just do my own thing, and that's what we've got here. We're about as free as you can be in this society."

— Des Kennedy

Susanne & Frans Anema

Nobody promised them that the road to paradise would be paved. Frans and Susanne Anema knew that better than most, having come to the decision to go back to the land by routes that would have wiped the dew from any eye: from a Japanese camp in occupied Indonesia, through the chaos of postwar Europe, to the United States and Canada; coming of age in the 1960s, going to Paris in the 1970s and finally arriving at the common belief that life should be simpler and better than it is.

Frans, a tall, thin Dutchman, was an economist at the Paris headquarters of the Organization for Economic Cooperation and Development in 1974. He was also a painter, a musician and a potter. Susanne, a dark-eyed Hungarian with a degree in economics, studied mime and movement, painted and performed. They immersed themselves in a city in which life itself may be an art. But it wasn't paradise.

"I found my job becoming ridiculous," says Frans. "The absurdities of pushing paper, all the negative aspects of the city—"

"The smell of Gitanes in our hair," Susanne interrupts.

"—made it clear that that life was not for us."

So they saved and planned and finally bought a homestead in Quebec's Gatineau Hills, 18 miles northeast of Ottawa. The road to it at the time inched through an industrial detritus of pulp mills, potholes and an honest-to-goodness topless bowling alley. Frans, with a Paris gloss on his orderly Dutch soul, seethed inside until the car turned away from the broken pavement and onto the little dirt road, staggered up the rocky hills, sloshed through the ruts and finally petered out completely in the narrow valley that would be their home.

They stopped the car at the final turning and tumbled out for the long view—across the creek and up the valley to the farm. It was a rundown wreck.

"It was paradise," Frans remembers.

Susanne laughs affectionately. "Those were not your first words. Your first words were: 'Yep, we're moving to British Columbia.'"

But they stayed. They plunged into the rigors of self-sufficient homesteading with a vigor that only comes when philosophy and necessity are joined. For a while, they made

Susanne and daughter Aranka Anema, inset. With the addition of son Yosha, the family now lives in Ottawa.

Jim Merrithew Inset: Frans Anema

paradise happen. But the seeds of what would change the dream had already been planted: Susanne was pregnant.

Sitting today in their comfortable Ottawa home, where the sun floods in through the big Pella bay window, it is hard to credit the early ordeals of life on the pine-cloistered farm. "Susanne had a difficult pregnancy," Frans recalls. "She had to lie on her back on the floor, and I could see the snow through the cracks in the wall behind her. I had to get the house ready."

"And that was the beginning of a pattern," Susanne sighs. "Frans and the neighbors and the hired workmen put in the plumbing and fixed up the house while I occupied myself with motherhood and serving coffee."

Aranka, born in October of that first hard year, had always been part of the dream. "She was the symbol of our starting this whole project together," says Susanne. "But I hadn't realized that a child would have such an effect. For me, the dream of the farm was being outdoors, working side-by-side with Frans. Instead, I found myself in the kitchen. It began with the physical weakness of the pregnancy, and it continued. Who else could nurse Aranka? I hadn't expected the division of labor. That was part of our naïveté."

"Once we went back to pioneering, to more self-sufficiency," says Frans, "we no longer had the technology that had liberated women from the kitchen. We were almost forced to go back to the old roles. Susanne could have helped in the bush, but it would have been less efficient than dividing our labor."

"And I thought we had left the idea of efficiency behind in Paris," she bristles.

"The question is," says Frans, "were we too romantic?"

The economics of self-sufficiency were admittedly tinged with romance. From the heady springboard of Paris, it had seemed possible to retire from salaried labor, to maintain Susanne's involvement in theatre and to pay for it all with bees and goats. But the labors of living off the land were more than the Anemas had bargained for. Frans went back to part-time consulting. Susanne turned to writing and tried to make art and mime pay.

"But that didn't change the dream," Susanne adds quickly. "We loved that place. And we always had choices; we never felt trapped, financially or otherwise."

"We would have been happy to stay there forever," Frans agrees. "But then I had it easier . . . I got away from time to time for the consulting jobs."

Susanne stayed behind. And every time Frans was away, some crisis arose. One winter, he was gone for four months. Susanne was left to cope with Aranka, the new baby Yosha, 30 goats, chickens, a wood stove and the hard road out. There was an accident with the car. The well went dry. "The neighbors were wonderful," Susanne recalls, "but there's a limit to how much you can ask them to do."

In a single memorable season, late frost wiped out the garden. They replanted, and a hailstorm destroyed it again. A wandering horse ate what was left. Then a tornado leveled the hardwood bush and ripped the roof off the barn. Whitey, one of the goats, drowned in the well, and a drought finished the final attempt to replant the garden.

Incredibly, none of those hardships diminished the goal. In fact, the mix of art and the raw force of nature added to the romance. "The most sublime moment of my life," says Frans, "was playing Bach on the piano while a blizzard raged at the window a few feet away." They converted the little barn into a studio, in which Susanne rehearsed with the mime troupe that had followed them from Paris. The artistes in their tights danced in the wood-heated barn to the bemusement of the local farmers.

Four years into the dream, the wear and tear began to show. "Frans was away again," Susanne recalls. "We had pigs then, as well as the goats. The children were sick. There were tensions in the mime troupe. I realized we were exhausted, overextended. I wanted a change of pace." When Frans was offered a year's work in Nepal, Susanne and the children went along.

"It was a year of revelation," she says. "Before Katmandu, we had never seen the children playing in a group. We had never been able to compare them with their peers or to offer them lessons. We had never realized that the children didn't respond to the isolation of the farm in the way we did."

When they returned home in 1982, the old dream was still alive, but there were two new, independent voices to be heard. It was the time in the life of a family for piano lessons, hockey, swimming and the cultural outlets that they could find in the city. The long drives between paradise and the city proved too much for the parents and not enough for Yosha and Aranka. The homesteading days were numbered.

Family Anema moved to Ottawa in 1984, to an old, three-story house on a quiet street. It was the original farmhouse in the neighborhood, says Frans, waving at imaginary fields beyond the walls, fields that have been peopled for so long that the houses have big trees in the yards. There are touches of country in this city house—plants in the windows, a new wood stove in the family room—reminders that some dreams are reluctant to die.

They have even kept the Gatineau farm, renting out the house but using the piney hills for weekend skiing. And they both use the studio for quiet afternoons of painting. "Our sweat and blood are invested there," says Frans. "Everywhere we look, we see traces of our work. It's something we love."

And the city place? Can any family keep its heart in two places? "Moving back to the city was one of the best decisions we ever made," says Frans, "but without the children, we would never have moved."

"Moving to the country was one of the best decisions we ever made," counters Susanne. "When the children are grown, we'll go back."

They nod together, somehow managing to achieve common understanding from the apparent contradiction. Emotional roots do have more than one dimension. And keeping a country heart happy in the city is, I suppose, as simple as transplanting a Paris mime troupe to the Gatineau Hills or rediscovering the joys of civilization in Katmandu.

For now, Susanne clearly enjoys Ottawa. "I was amazed at how easy life can be, how many things can be done in a day in the city."

Frans is finding the adjustment more difficult. He still misses the trees and his evening chats with the goats. Somehow, even the sky is different, hemmed into narrow spaces within the geometry of urban rooftops.

They'll go back to the land again. The details might be different, but the dream that drew Frans to a communal farm in Ontario, to the windscoured North Sea isle of Texel and then to the Gatineau Hills, will strike again. "I want to build a house from scratch, perhaps of stone, or fix up an old ruin in the south of France. Building is essential to man." But he insists that next time it will not be the same. It will be more comfortable, less work.

"Our values haven't changed," Frans insists today. "But we have become more realistic, taking greater advantage of the civilization around us."

Life is comfortable for the Anemas now. They have taken the children to Europe for Christmas and gone to Bali in the spring. That seems a giant leap from the summer they pulled poor Whitey out of the well and watched the wind blow the barn roof away. But life, old friends, is a matter of circles, not of lines. You'll be back. This time, may your road be paved.

— *Charles Long*

Cathleen & Brewster Kneen

He had degrees in economics and theology, she had one in English literature. They were living in Toronto, working, active politically, embroiled in neighborhood projects and rapidly burning themselves out. "We were working hard and not seeing any results," says Brewster Kneen. "I felt it was time to stop dealing with the theoretical side of food production. I wanted to be involved at the production level."

Both Brewster and his Newfoundland-raised wife Cathleen liked the Maritime hill country, so in 1971, they loaded the car and, with their two children, headed for Nova Scotia. Knowing they could not afford shoreline property, they had decided to look for what Brewster calls "a relatively central location—much to the consternation of those who said, 'How can you move somewhere without knowing where?' " In Nova Scotia, they inquired at gas stations until they found a suitable place near Salt Springs, midway between New Glasgow and Truro. Near the Trans-Canada Highway, the 200 acres of eroded glacial soil was hardly prime farmland, but it contained pockets of good soil, and they felt it could be productively managed for livestock.

"We didn't intend to farm right away," says Brewster, "but we got the place cheap, and it came with a tractor, a line of machinery in reasonable working order, 12 cows with their calves and a bull. We had no experience, so we had to learn what we were doing quickly."

"It's not something I would recommend," Cathleen adds. "I'm grateful to all those sheep who let us learn on them." Sheep replaced the cows early in the Kneens' rural experience.

"I don't know why we switched to sheep," Brewster says, frowning.

"Romance," Cathleen deadpans. "They're such nice animals."

"I guess it was a financial choice," he concludes. "Sheep had a better return." Also, good land in the area was spotty—they eventually rented four other farms to accumulate 200 acres of workland—and sheep were easier than cows to walk from one pasture to another. "Mind you," Brewster says, "we walked some cows home too. I remember returning one along the Trans-Canada. That was before we got electric fencing." He pauses. "You liked the sheep better anyway, didn't you, Cathleen?"

"No. I really missed the cows."

The Kneens' political natures and organizational skills found an outlet in 1973, when they coordinated the first of eight annual Sheep Fairs. Centered around an auction sale

Cathleen and Brewster Kneen, with their children Jamie and Rebecca, inset, spent 15 years on a Nova Scotia sheep farm before moving to a duplex in Toronto's east end.

of breeding stock, the fairs drew farm families and city folk alike with craft sales, dog trials, shearing contests and electric-fence demonstrations. "It developed a freezer trade for us and gave us confidence in the sheep industry as a family-based operation," Brewster recalls.

After an unsuccessful attempt to start a coöperative abattoir – "I got recruited on the wrong side, with the free marketers" – he changed direction. Middlemen, he says, made more profit on a market lamb overnight than the farmer who raised it earned for a year's work. "I decided the only way for us to survive was to return the drovers' profits to farmers." He organized a shipment of lambs to the New Brunswick Lamb Marketing Cooperative in 1976 and started to concentrate his efforts on the marketing of agricultural products. Three years later, he began selling Nova Scotia-raised lamb to the Sobeys chain of grocery stores, and in 1981, he organized the Northumberland Lamb Marketing Cooperative, a successful venture that kept fresh lamb on supermarket shelves year-round. At that time, Brewster was a director of the Nova Scotia Federation of Agriculture and owned a 400-ewe flock, one of the largest east of Montreal.

His new ideas, campaigns for a change in the marketing system and activism in the National Farmers Union earned him the respect of many area farmers – and the enmity of many others. "We were profoundly threatening to some of the locals," he says.

Cathleen, in addition to shouldering her share of farm responsibilities, became deeply involved in the women's movement, eventually serving on the board of a women's center that offered counseling on birthing, family planning, matrimonial law, parenting, welfare, job skills and violence against women. "The farm and the women's movement were my educational background," she says, and she obviously found the work invigorating and fulfilling. After a decade on the farm, the couple were active and making progress, but there were problems. The first was the cancellation of a radio farm report that she taped regularly for a local CBC affiliate. It started her thinking about the future.

Brewster, too, was becoming increasingly frustrated, both with what he calls "the lack of imagination" of the federal and provincial departments of agriculture and with the reluctance of local farmers to improve their lot. "We met some very, very good people," he says, "but they were the exception. Most people were interested in not being disturbed, even if they knew the price would be high."

"I recognized it as the same attitude as that of battered women who go back to their husbands," Cathleen adds. "A structurally induced failure of imagination, a profound fatalism."

"One of the frustrations was the extent to which the mainstream will lock you out," says Brewster, who admittedly is somewhat bitter.

Their growing interest in long-term agricultural policy sharpened concerns about global economic and agricultural issues: the politics of world hunger, genetic erosion, the increasing control of food production by corporations. They founded the Nutrition Policy Institute and began publishing *The Ram's Horn*, a food-issues newsletter. "We wanted to move in larger circles," says Brewster, "but it was difficult to find like-minded people."

The final blow came in 1984, when both children left for university. "We had no more free labor, and we realized we couldn't do it ourselves." Red-meat prices were down, and the Kneens found their net income shrinking at a time when they wanted to do more traveling. "We could have got by if we had stayed home," Brewster says, "but we needed more cash income for our off-farm activities. We were forced into making choices." In 1986, after 15 years on the farm, they chose to move back to Toronto. It was a heart-wrenching decision that seemed to some of their rural friends like a betrayal of principles and loyalties. They now live on a dead-end street in Toronto's east end ("the cheapest housing in town") in a narrow, brick duplex with a paved-over backyard.

"I was aware not long after arriving here that it was like coming home," Brewster says with obvious satisfaction. "I've picked up where I left off before we went away."

They were pleased to learn that much of their earlier work in Toronto had been continued by others. "I was surprised by how many people were glad to see us," says Brewster, remembering the resistance they had encountered in the Maritimes. "Knowing what we were, they welcomed us. It was stimulating and encouraging and energizing."

"Yes, but you felt the same way about the farm," injects Cathleen, just to keep the record straight. "You said it was an immense relief to get away from the city. You said, 'I feel as if I'm coming home.'" She is not as enthusiastic about the move as Brewster is. "Physically, I don't like living in the city—the air and water and stuff. Brewster and I are partners, but I have a secondary role here—not like on the farm. I'm not sure what my calling is in the city." Currently, she is an administrator and fund-raiser for the Latin American Working Group, an organization they helped found 20 years ago. She enjoys the job, but in their pre-1971 Toronto days, she cared for two pre-schoolers, helped establish a parent co-operative daycare and struggled to become one of CBC Radio's first female announcers. Now, with the children gone and daycare centers as common as female broadcasters, she is at a bit of a loss. "In Nova Scotia, the women's movement was growing," she says. "I felt that people were sorry to see me go."

She doesn't regret moving, but she misses the self-sufficiency, the sense of community and the feeling of general competence she felt on the farm. "In the country, we had to do everything, and because of the isolation, it was an act of will for people to pull together. There isn't the same wholeness to life here." Of the future, she says, "I can see getting old and going back to the country and gardening."

Brewster, already writing, lecturing and traveling to the occasional speaking engagement, has received a one-year grant as an "independent scholar" to study technology and agriculture. A book on the food system "needs to be coughed up now." He is doing what he enjoys, and from this standpoint, he remembers the decision to leave the farm: "I asked myself, 'Would I want to grow old here?' The answer was an emphatic, 'No.'"

Cathleen smiles. "We're going to have an interesting discussion in about 20 years." ❧

—Michael Webster

Paddling into the Mainstream

Where Have All the Homesteaders Gone?

Anne & Jack Lazor

Jack Lazor is performing a yogurt test. Dressed in farmer's dungarees, a plaid flannel shirt and a striped stocking hat, he reaches into the dairy case of a health food store on his delivery route. A sticker on one of the cooler's sliding glass doors says, "Have you rinsed your tofu today?" He removes a quart of Butterworks Farm yogurt, which he and his wife, Anne, made only yesterday. He opens the container's lid, revealing a smooth white surface with the consistency of well-set custard. "Ah! It hasn't broken down a bit," he says. "That's what we work so hard to do: make the firmest, sweetest yogurt you can get."

The Lazors do indeed work hard, rising at 5 on most mornings and at 3:30 on Thursday, delivery day. But the routine has not dampened their enthusiasm for rural life. They still live on the same land, perched on a windy plateau near Vermont's northern border, that they bought as self-styled "hippie homesteaders" in 1976. In spirit and appearance, they are still anchored firmly in the same brand of 1960s-inspired idealism that brought them to the country in the first place. They have parlayed that idealism into a successful small-scale dairying and yogurt-making operation. Yet they sometimes wonder if their business has led them to compromise their original vision of agrarian independence. "Once you paddle into the mainstream a little bit," Jack says, "it's easy to get carried away by the current—and it's hard to paddle back."

Neither of the Lazors grew up around farming. Anne comes from an old Boston family. She attended Concord Academy near Boston (Jack calls her an "ex-preppie"), then earned a degree in anthropology at the University of Wisconsin. Jack grew up in suburban Connecticut and graduated from Tufts University. In college, both Anne and Jack became fascinated with nineteenth-century American agriculture—an interest that led them independently to Old Sturbridge Village, a re-created nineteenth-century farm in Massachusetts. They met there in the summer of 1974, when Anne had a job as a milkmaid and Jack was a historical researcher.

Within a few years, they were homesteading together in Vermont. With a small inheritance from Anne's grandfather, they bought 60 acres of woodlot and old, over-cropped hay pasture. Their main goal was to "heal the land" by adding rock phosphate, limestone and other natural amendments to the soil while they lived off what they could produce on it. They dreamed of setting up a diversified farmstead with chickens, a pig or two, a few milk cows, and maybe some draft horses for logging. They planned to rejuvenate the old sugarhouse among the maples in their woodlot, to plant a small orchard and a big vegetable garden.

Jack's fondest ambition is to grow and harvest grain crops, a practice that is rare on the dairy farms of New England, though common on dairy farms in Quebec and Ontario. He collects old farm equipment and has acquired a cultivator, a combine, a grain cleaner, a grain binder, a threshing machine, three 1954 tractors and an assortment of other machines, working and nonworking. He also has bought a small grain mill, which he set up in the "garage," an enclosed shed attached to the house that he and Anne began building with their own hands in 1978.

"Here we are with all these dreams," Anne says one evening as she milks the cows. "But the reality is that you've got to make a living."

The Lazors got into the yogurt business almost by accident. The family cows were producing more milk than Anne, Jack and their daughter, Christine, could drink, so they started making yogurt, butter and soft cheese in their kitchen. Jack peddled their surplus dairy products to a few neighbors and nearby food cooperatives. Butterworks Farm has been expanding ever since. Two cows became four, and four became six – too many to milk by hand in the garage, so they built a big post-and-beam barn in 1982, installing a 1950s vintage surge-bucket milker powered by an ancient motorized pump. The milking barn is currently set up for 12 cows, Jerseys with names like Gooseberry, Tinkerbelle, Rosebud and Sundance.

Somewhere along the way, the Lazors gave up making butter and cheese, concentrating on whole yogurt, maple-flavored yogurt, lowfat yogurt and its inevitable by-product, cream. "We'd be selling plain old milk just like everybody else if we could get a decent price for it," Jack says. "But there's no living in selling raw materials to the processors – they're the ones who make all the money, not the poor grunts who actually produce the stuff. So we do the processing ourselves." He figures it costs them about a dollar to produce a gallon of milk. The local milk cooperative would give them around $1.25 a gallon; instead, they make it into yogurt and clear about $4 a gallon (excluding the cost of containers). Any profits left over after deducting overhead and living expenses are plowed back into the land in the form of fertilizer.

To keep down distribution costs, Jack delivers the yogurt himself to a network of health-food stores, restaurants and food co-ops spread all over Vermont, plus a few in New Hampshire. In one recent week, he delivered 153 pints of cream and 1,050 quarts of yogurt. Business may be too good: demand for Butterworks Farm yogurt nearly exceeds the Lazors' capacity to produce it in their meticulous fashion. "The barn chores alone take six hours a day," he says. "Processing yogurt takes another five hours. We're so busy keeping up with the yogurt thing that we don't have time to do the farming we always wanted to do."

Now they face a dilemma. "Sometimes I think we should get bigger and increase our economy of scale," Jack says. "The alternative is to chuck everything and start living closer to our means. We could spend all our time just surviving, and it would be fun."

Having paddled this far into the mainstream, however, Jack would just as soon

paddle in a little farther. He has visions of converting the barn to a 20-cow operation, complete with more up-to-date milking equipment (1960s technology, perhaps) and an automatic gutter cleaner. What is his ultimate dream? "Probably to be a big farmer," he confesses. "I *love* sitting on my tractor, planting and harvesting grain. I could be happy just going round and round in the fields all day."

Whether they decide to scale up or down, the Lazors are likely to do things the slow, old-fashioned way. "There must be some reason why I look backward for inspiration instead of forward," Jack says. "Maybe it's because

Ann and Jack Lazor with daughter Christine. In 1977, inset, they harvested their first wheat crop.

RICHARD W. BROWN INSET: JIM REHRMAN

Peepers, an orphaned starling, perches on Vic's glasses in 1982, inset. Today, Sussman lives and writes in Washington, D.C.

when you do as much as you can for yourself, it's easier to understand your society and where you stand in it. Life wouldn't be very satisfying if you weren't in *some* kind of control."

— *Craig Canine*

Vic Sussman

Vic Sussman is a man given to epiphanies—sudden rushes of insight that have, more than once, changed the course of his life. One such moment came on a squeaky-cold winter's night in 1982 when he was out walking the family's two dogs. He was on a snow-packed road near the homestead in

northeastern Vermont where he, his wife, Betsy, and their two children had been living for a year. During that year, and in the previous 11 years while the Sussmans were homesteaders in Maryland, Vic and Betsy had mastered the finer points of goat keeping, gardening, wood splitting, canning and other assorted country skills. Vic had even achieved a modest celebrity among some '60s refugees for his books and articles on vegetarianism and organic gardening.

But on that subzero night of revelation in Vermont, under a sky so clear and dark he could see Andromeda, Sussman suddenly had the feeling he was in the wrong place. "I looked up at the stars and began wondering, 'What have I proved living out here?' " he recalls. "I

"I've always wanted to perform for a big audience. Now I write for two million people who read the *Post*, and I'm the happiest I've ever been in my life."

His exile from the city got its impetus when he was a graduate student in communications at American University in Washington, D.C., working part-time for NBC news. He read Adelle Davis's book *Let's Eat Right to Keep Fit* in a single evening in 1964. "I came away thinking I had to change my life," he says. "Suddenly, I wanted to live simply, to grow my own food and be outdoors." His first step was to abandon his habitual diet, which consisted largely of junk food, and "put some thought into what I ate." He planted his first garden in a weed patch at a friend's house. His urban garden, he says, was a disaster – he went to the beach for a week and returned to find that it had reverted to weeds – but the dream of self-sufficient living had taken root.

He was soon married to Betsy, who had grown up in a small New Jersey town about 20 miles from New York. A yearning for a life in the country was the glue that knit them together, but neither of them knew the first thing about surviving outside the city limits. In 1969, they bought their two-acre "suburban homestead" in Potomac, Maryland, to serve as a halfway house between the city and the country, a place where they could learn the skills that would equip them to live on a larger, more rural piece of land someday. Vic chronicled their early years as homesteaders in his book *Never Kiss a Goat on the Lips* (now out of print). The other book he wrote in their Maryland homestead, *The Vegetarian Alternative*, has sold 90,000 copies and been translated into three languages.

The Sussmans spent 11 years in training before they moved to the homestead of their dreams: 23 acres of highland plateau in Vermont's isolated Northeast Kingdom. Betsy was ecstatic, but (at least in retrospect) Vic had moments of doubt. Shortly after they moved, a friend came to visit from New York. "She saw how hard we were working just to keep warm, dry and fed," Vic recalls. "She said, 'Is this how you're going to live when you get old?' That made me think."

Today, Sussman can make light of his constant fight against the elements. "Summer was the worst," he recalls. "The people in our town called it the blackfly capital of the world. One of our neighbors used to say, 'Blackflies don't bother me. Whenever I feel weak from loss of blood, I just lie down.'"

Moments of humor aside, the unrelenting work of homesteading weighed heavily upon him. "I lived in Vermont for five years," he

had learned to do all I had set out to do in the country. Big deal. This was the high point of my day: waiting for the dogs to pee. I said out loud, 'I'm meant for more than this.'"

Sussman was born in the city, raised in the city, and now, after 15 years as a back-to-the-lander, he has come back to the city. He suspects that he was never cut out for country living in the first place, and sees his 15 years of rural life as a self-imposed exile, a departure from his youthful dreams of becoming a comedian and an entertainer. At age 46, he has picked up those ambitions where he left them in his 20s. He writes a weekly column for *The Washington Post* called "Personal Tech," a sometimes whimsical account of the relationship between people and technology.

says, "and I realize now that I was angry most of the time. There was always this oppressive sense of being behind – behind in the garden, behind with getting in the wood supply. And for what? Weeding carrots just wasn't enough for me. I thrive on contact with people, but you don't meet that many people in the woods. And the natives weren't exactly scintillating company: they were all busy stringing barbed wire around their satellite dishes so the cows wouldn't knock them over."

About a year and a half ago, things fell apart. Sussman was exhausted with the hard work and isolation of country life. His marriage suddenly went on the rocks, and he found himself driving southward with all his worldly possessions – a stereo, a computer, an 18-foot kayak and some clothes – in the back of his station wagon. He gravitated back to Washington where, unexpectedly, he landed a steady writing assignment for the *Post*. His daughter, Rachel, stayed with her mother in Vermont. Their son, Noah, who had had enough of the country, accompanied Vic. ("The only outdoor stuff I like," Noah says, "is skiing and sunbathing.") The two of them live in a rented split-level house in Bethesda, Maryland, within a half-hour's commute of downtown D.C.

Sitting on the couch in his living room, Sussman looks like a man in his element. He cranks up the volume of his stereo system, basking in the sound with a look of satisfaction that he may once have felt among his broccoli plants. He is stylishly dressed in pressed khakis and a crew-neck sweater. "When I got back to the city, I didn't own a tie," he says. "I bought an entry-level wardrobe at Sears. Somewhere in there I started reading *GQ* and caring about clothes. Then I began grooming my beard with an electric beard trimmer and getting my hair cut – what hair I have left."

He pauses to take a sip of beer from a tall, fluted glass. "When I lived in the country," he says, "I used to preach about living the simple life, with *Walden* as my text. I took *Walden* at face value – I read it as an exhortation to 'live deliberately' in the woods. What I sometimes forgot was that Henry Thoreau's cabin was only a mile from his mother's house and that he often went home for dinner.

"I think I'm living the simple life right now, in the city. I wake up in the morning and the furnace is running, the pipes aren't freezing. That's simplicity. I love it."

He pauses, takes another sip of beer. "In a way," he adds, "I'm still gardening – but now I'm cultivating myself instead of the earth."

– Craig Canine

David & Micki Colfax

When David and Micki Colfax settled in rural Boonville, California, 14 years ago, they were a family on the lam. "We were not motivated by the same concerns that motivated others who moved here," David says. "We came up here as a beleaguered family, as political refugees."

In the heat of the anti-war movement, David was one of academia's most strident activists. Founder of the Union of Radical Sociologists, he ran afoul of the draft laws in 1968. The FBI began investigating him. The right-wing Minutemen threatened to murder his young son. By 1972, driven out of two universities and blacklisted as a troublemaker, he accepted a position to teach in Uganda. With Idi Amin in power, he prudently decided to stop short in North Africa. Finally, holed up in Morocco, with a wife and three sons and a dwindling bank balance, David Colfax needed a port in the storm. Boonville was it.

The town was then a hippie Mecca – "Haight-Ashbury North," David calls it. Only two hours from San Francisco, it lies at the head of the vineyard-and-orchard-studded Anderson Valley in Mendocino County. But the family was less interested in communing with nature than in putting a roof over their heads. With a grubstake of $25,000, they made a down payment on 47 acres of hilly, logged-over, brush-ridden land and put out the word: "We made it very clear that no one had better come around unannounced," David says.

For the first winter, the family lived in a trailer and did little else besides clear the land. Huge bonfires of deadfall and brush blazed day and night. The next spring, a group of hippies celebrating the vernal equinox on a distant ridge saw the fires and assumed the Colfaxes were kindred spirits. When the celebrants arrived, dressed as Indians and chanting, David decided to have a good time of it – but the political rhetoric flowed as fast as the jug wine. "We had a bemused contempt for the people who had dropped out of the politics of the era," he said. "Everybody who came around got stuck in a political dialogue whether they wanted to or not."

The Colfaxes made a snug, comfortable house by trial and error and dug a septic system by hand, a job that still makes David wince. But their major preoccupation was to build an economy that would sustain them. Over the years, they have variously considered contracting, real estate sales, raising rabbits, a printing business, a bookstore-coffeehouse, a cheese factory. He taught

briefly at a college in Thunder Bay, Ontario, was a field representative for the National Center for Appropriate Technology, wrote freelance magazine articles.

In the end, though, their mainstay has been raising dairy goats, for which the region is nationally renowned, and registered Suffolk sheep. They have a large garden, raise poultry, tap the local barter economy, rent out a guest cottage, edit a newsletter called *Goat Notes.* "Generally, we're regarded as working all the time and not terribly mellow," David says. "That's been our image from the start."

The other preoccupation, of course, has been their sons. (Two are their offspring: Grant and Drew; two are adopted: Reed, who is racially mixed, and Garth, an Inuit.) In spite of the difficulties of making Shining Moon Ranch work, the couple has insisted on educating their boys at home. David's denunciation of the local schools is blistering, but the reason is mainly pragmatic. "It is simply more efficient to teach them at home," he says. "Two hours a day, six days a week, equals what they would get in school. That means

they have five hours to work on other projects."

That logic has turned out to be unarguably sound. Grant and Drew are on full-tuition scholarships at Harvard. Grant, a senior studying pre-med, is a candidate for Fulbright and Luce scholarships. Drew, who installed the photovoltaic system at the ranch and built his own telescope, is a freshman studying mathematics and chemistry. The two younger boys, still at home, are self-assured beyond their years. "All of my kids, except Garth [who is 11], could build a house from the ground up," David boasts. "That's quite a thing for a boy."

David takes a certain fatherly pride in that knowledge but is quick to point out the larger lesson: "You're less likely to make compromises to keep the house when you can build your own," he tells Garth while cutting

David Colfax with wife, Micki, and sons Grant, Drew, and Reed, inset. **Today, with Garth and Reed.**

studs for an addition to their house. The years have not mellowed David, and his outlook on country living — at least in Boonville — continues to be one of bemused contempt. A year ago, he ran in a school board election, because of what he sees as the board's "outrageous corruption," and he won. His opponent, the incumbent, calls herself Morning Star Little Feather Who Sits Under a Shaft of Light.

David delights in telling that story, but he has little tolerance for what he calls "reentry hippies." "Our orientation is towards the economics and aesthetics of living in the country," he says, "but when it comes to the social dimension of country living, we've seen people become even more right-wing, more acquiescent, more gray-flannel than anyone in the '50s, when we came out of school and sneered at it [David is 50; Micki, 49]. The first naked woman I saw in Mendocino County is now the superintendent of schools in one of the districts. She went through the whole Mother Earth trip and finally said, 'To hell with it, I want to make $60,000 a year too.'

"The bureaucracies all over the county are full of ex-hippies, all of them scared shitless when they didn't have any money. One woman lives in splendor and says, 'I've been there, honey. I was a hippie once.' This justifies the most reactionary, acquisitive behavior."

The reentry syndrome is no surprise, David says. "It confirms what we thought when we first came up here, that there wasn't much substance behind this scene." The demise of Boonville's food co-op and child-care collective only fueled the Colfaxes' cynicism about the local counterculture's commitment to self-sufficiency. "A lot of people have simply not had the motivation to work as hard as we do," he says without sounding smug. "We work hard all the time, and we're constantly shifting gears." A few years ago, for example, an "abortion storm" devastated their goat business. "We were looking at $600 embryos all over the ground," he says. In four days, they lost about $4,000-worth of kids.

Why have they survived such calamities when others have given up? "We're not up here as romantic back-to-the-landers," David explains. "We're about as successful as anyone who's tried it. On the one hand, we are saying, 'Yeah, you can do it.' But on the other we're saying, 'You're out of your head to try.'"

— *Michael McRae*

Shelter

Building by the Book

USING *A PATTERN LANGUAGE* TO DESIGN A HOUSE WITH HEART

BY CRAIG CANINE WITH PHOTOGRAPHY BY GEORGINA E. FRANKEL

It is not the Golden Gate or the George Washington, but it is a bridge nonetheless, and Bruce Johanson must cross it each day on his way to and from work. Made of wood and suspended just high enough above the ground to be a tempting handhold for chin-ups, the footbridge connects the Johansons' house with the upper story of their garage, which serves as Bruce's office. The small upper room, walled with knotty pine and furnished with an old couch, a small desk and miscellaneous chairs, looks more like a music studio than the office of a building contractor. Bruce demonstrates a set of chimes that sits on a shelf near his desk, taps a few metallic notes on a steel drum and plucks the strings of a dulcimer. Then he nearly jogs past a music stand and two dumbbells, stops near the door and picks up the edge of a rug, revealing a trapdoor that leads to the garage below. "This is in case I have to make a quick getaway," he says with a grin. Surveying the room with obvious delight, he says, "This is my little fort, my cabin in the woods."

Now we are in the house, touring the bedroom of Bruce and Sharmaine Johanson's 5-year-old son, Arne. One wall is covered with a mural inspired by *Star Wars* — rockets dueling in outer space. In the middle of the wall, a small, silver-painted door has a sign on it. "No admittance without security code," it says. Bruce apparently knows the code: he ducks down low and darts through the door into a cubbyhole beneath a set of stairs. "And here," he says, gesturing expansively with his arms, "is Arne's office."

A few minutes later, we are upstairs in a cheerful room festooned with artwork by Arne and his 8-year-old sister, Vanessa. The room is lined with shelves filled with books, blocks and other toys. A well-worn ladder mounted on one wall leads upward to a play-loft, where a small table is apparently set for

tea. In this room, the "children's realm," Arne and Vanessa content themselves by the hour while their mother, Sharmaine, works nearby in the kitchen or in the adjacent "music realm" or in her own small office. "In this house," Bruce says, "we either have several offices or a lot of playrooms, depending on how you look at it."

However you look at it, this is not an ordinary three-bedroom, split-entry house. Bruce and Sharmaine have lived in their share of those: during their first seven years of marriage, they occupied seven different houses, unremarkable dwellings built by past owners who evidently lacked the Johansons' passion for individuality. Five years ago, when Bruce and Sharmaine started to think about building a house, they vowed that it would be different — an embodiment, in some way, of their own personalities. "People spend more money on their houses than on anything else," Sharmaine says. "Yet they're encouraged to accept this boring uniformity of houses that fit the norm. They're made to feel that a boring, normal house is what they want — and worse than that, they're made to feel that that's what they *are.* I think that's a crime. We wanted a house that would reflect who we are, as individuals."

By their seventh move, the Johansons had become fairly articulate about things they did *not* like in a house, but they found it much more difficult to identify and describe the things they *did* like and want, things that might make their new house comfortable, soothing and uniquely their own. Furthermore, they had a limited budget to work with. They were determined to build their house for less than $70,000.

First they had to find a place to build it. They wanted a piece of land in open country or near

Tired of living in "boring houses that fit the norm," Bruce and Sharmaine Johanson wanted to design a place that would reflect their own personalities. They built their house, left, for about $75,000.

a small town within easy reach of Minnesota's Twin Cities. One day, Bruce found a small lot two blocks from the north shore of White Bear Lake, which is about 10 miles from downtown St. Paul. The land was priced well below the area's going rate, since one-third of the parcel was swamp. Convinced that he had found a great deal, he told Sharmaine about it – but not before he had made an offer, which was accepted.

When Sharmaine saw the swamp, she could only envision drowning children and hordes of mosquitoes the size of hummingbirds. Bruce's enthusiasm for the land's southern exposure and proximity to a community beach on White Bear Lake was not enough to dispel her misgivings, though she set them aside in order to face the next challenge: deciding what to build.

They read many books, ranging from architectural texts to a dog-eared library volume called *Build Your Own Home for $50.* Nearly everything they read was either too theoretical or too mundane and practical, leaving their imaginations stranded somewhere in the middle, uninspired. Then, during a vacation, Bruce picked up a book called *A Pattern Language,* at the recommendation of his brother. A few moments after opening it, he was convinced he had found the single most valuable tool ever invented for designing a house. The discovery struck him with the intensity of a religious conversion – an experience that not only guided the construction of his family's house, but also changed the course of his life.

A Pattern Language, published in 1977, might best be described as an anatomy of comfortable places. Its authors – Christopher Alexander and five architectural colleagues at the Center for Environmental Structure in Berkeley, California – spent eight years trying to describe exactly what makes a building or a community seem "alive," "comfortable" or "timeless." The group traveled around the world studying buildings and towns made by preindustrial, traditional societies. Whenever they found a place that struck them as especially humane and attractive, they asked themselves, "What makes this place special?"

Certain patterns began to show up again and again. The architects gave names to these recurring features. They found that the most appealing towns, for example, often shared such characteristics as "identifiable neighborhoods," "access to water," "street cafés," "corner groceries" and "food stands." In their favorite buildings, they identified such recurring pat-

The house's main living areas are located on the second floor in order to take advantage of views overlooking a swamp. The sunroom, right, doubles as an informal dining room, where the Johansons often enjoy summer suppers. In winter, solar gain from the sunroom helps heat the house.

terns as "wings of light," "arcades," "light on two sides of every room," "six-foot balconies," "alcoves" and "windows overlooking life." They also identified specific details of construction and ornamentation that contribute to what they call "buildings which live," including "columns at the corners," "perimeter beams," "low sills," "radiant heat," "solid doors with glass," "soft tile and brick," "climbing plants" and "paving with cracks between the stones." *A Pattern Language* is a collection of 253 of these patterns, numbered and arranged in order from the largest and most general (such as 2, THE DISTRIBUTION OF TOWNS and 4, AGRICULTURAL VALLEYS) to the most specific and intimate (251, DIFFERENT CHAIRS and 253, THINGS FROM YOUR LIFE).

Each pattern consists of a statement describing a common problem of design, followed by a discussion of the problem and a recommendation, based on the authors' research, about how to solve it. For example, LIGHT ON TWO SIDES OF EVERY ROOM (159) begins with the statement, "When they have a choice, people will always gravitate to those rooms which have light on two sides, and leave the rooms which are lit only from one side unused and empty." After several paragraphs in which the authors describe how they arrived at this conclusion, they end the pattern with a prescription: "Locate each room so that it has outdoor space outside it on at least two sides, and then place windows in these outdoor walls so that natural light falls into every room from more than one direction."

Patterns with higher numbers address more specific issues. For example, CHILD CAVES (203) — the blueprint for Arne Johanson's "office" — begins by stating, simply, that "children love to be in tiny, cavelike places." Some rough sketches of children playing under stairs, beneath a tablecloth and below a kitchen counter are followed by a recommendation: "Wherever children play — around the house, in the neighborhood, in schools — make small 'caves' for them. Tuck these away in natural leftover spaces: under stairs, under kitchen counters. Keep the ceiling heights low — 2 feet 6 inches to 4 feet — and the entrance tiny."

None of the other design books the Johansons had read said anything like these things. Yet these and many other passages in *A Pattern Language* seemed intuitively true to Bruce and Sharmaine, describing things they felt they had always known but couldn't articulate. Like children learning to speak, they discovered in the book a new vocabulary with which they could expand

A Pattern Language *describes 253 features that help make human environments "alive" and comfortable. The nook off the kitchen,* above, *was inspired by the pattern "Alcoves," which says that larger rooms should have intimate places for people to sit and chat.*

upon their vague desire for friendliness, warmth and character. "It validated the feelings we had about building a house that would reflect us," Sharmaine says. "Suddenly, here was this book that told us that some of our fantasies weren't crazy, but legitimate."

Perhaps even more important, the book confirmed their strong belief that good design is not necessarily expensive. "It taught me that there are many things that don't cost anything that will make a house better," Bruce says. "First, it emphasizes designing for the site and taking the play of natural light into consideration when laying out the rooms. Second, it suggests ways of placing rooms to make the most of limited space. And third, it encourages people to establish priorities—to decide what things are really important in their lives and design the house around those things. Is a formal dining room important to you? Then have one. Do you like to dance? Then instead of having a 'rec room'—what a crummy word—maybe have a room with a little stage

and dance floor in it. The book unleashes people's creativity, and I don't know of anyone who doesn't like to be creative."

At the top of their own list of priorities was a warm and commodious kitchen—a place where the whole family would naturally tend to gravitate. Pattern number 139, FARMHOUSE KITCHEN, spoke eloquently to those needs (see excerpt, page 54). Several other patterns provided more specific details for the kitchen. For example, pattern 179, ALCOVES, says that large rooms are cold and uninviting unless they have small places around the edges where people can gather in groups of two or three to "sit, chat or play." Accordingly, the Johansons' kitchen has a small nook on one side that contains a trestle table and four chairs. It is a sunny place, especially in the morning, with windows on three sides. A stained-glass pastoral scene mounted in the east-facing window obscures a view of the house next door.

The kitchen occupies the southeast corner of the house, with a long U-shaped counter

The "music realm," center, embodies the patterns "Common Areas at the Heart" and "Window Place." The Johansons' children, Arne and Vanessa, content themselves for hours in the "Children's Realm," above, a few steps from the kitchen.

around the perimeter and large casement windows on the south and east sides. This arrangement grew out of pattern 199, SUNNY CORNER, which says, "Place the main part of the kitchen counter on the south and southeast side of the kitchen, with big windows around it, so that sun can flood in and fill the kitchen with yellow light both morning and afternoon."

Reluctant to endow the kitchen entirely with OPEN SHELVING (200), the Johansons combined some open shelves with enclosed cabinets. They also observed the spirit, if not the letter, of pattern 184, COOKING LAYOUT, which addresses the problem of striking a balance between a kitchen work area that is too compact and one that is too spread out. It counsels: "Place the stove, sink, food storage and counter in such a way that:

1. No two of the four are more than 10 feet apart.

2. The total length of counter – excluding sink, stove and refrigerator – is at least 12 feet.

3. No one section of the counter is less than 4 feet long."

The Johansons' U-shaped counter helps to satisfy these rules of thumb. One leg of the U also serves as a WORKSPACE ENCLOSURE (183) to help define the cook's domain and as a HALF-OPEN WALL (193) to create a sense of separation, though not a complete barrier, between the kitchen and the adjacent "music realm" – an informal living area, defined by its own cathedral ceiling, where Bruce and Sharmaine sometimes gather with friends to play guitar, flute and other musical instruments.

The kitchen, like the rest of the house, is a patchwork of overlapping and interweaving patterns. Picking them out is a game, like spotting all the hidden monkeys in a picture from a child's puzzle book. Sharmaine puts it another way. "One pattern leads to another," she says. "It's like a magical mystery tour."

After Bruce discovered *A Pattern Language,* he and Sharmaine lived with the book for nearly a year before they proceeded any further. They steeped themselves in it, memorizing so many patterns that, eventually, they could quote one that seemed appropriate for any situation, like missionaries reciting scripture by heart. "We carried the book around with us everywhere we went," Sharmaine recalls. "We called it our bible."

They assumed it must be every architect's bible, too, though they quickly learned otherwise. They had decided to seek out a professional designer who could help them make the best use of space in applying the *Pattern Language* approach. Most of the architects they

Bruce Johanson, above, pictured with his daughter, Vanessa, on the bridge leading to his office, acted as general contractor during construction. The experience changed his life: after several years of selling musical instruments, he is now a professional builder specializing in "pattern language" construction. His ultimate ambition is to design an entire town.

ly," he says. "But others are intimidated. They think, 'Uh-oh, what kind of weird religious tract is this outfit into? Do we have to master this philosophy before we can design our house?'"

Sarah Susanka is less reluctant than her partner to proselytize. "Put *A Pattern Language* into the hands of most of our clients," she says, "and they're immediately absorbed. It reinforces what they know instinctively—a love of alcoves, for example—and it says, 'That's right.' They find that tremendously exciting. We see ourselves as facilitators to help people put those ideas into practice in aesthetically pleasing ways. People need an assistant, not a person who comes in and says, 'Look, I'm an architect, a godlike figure who will now tell you what your house should be like.' Instead, we help people get on the right track. We try to help make their houses dense with patterns, to achieve what Alexander calls the 'poetry' of the pattern language."

Mulfinger and Susanka were just the collaborators the Johansons were looking for. Bruce and Sharmaine typed up a two-page list of their favorite patterns, along with some other priorities, and took it to their first meeting with the architects. Because clients and architects shared a common vocabulary of design, there was little wasted time and, from the outset, a reduced likelihood that expensive misunderstandings might occur. A good rapport quickly developed, which, not insignificantly, endures to this day.

Mulfinger and Susanka visited the building site several times. At first, it seemed unprepossessing—a sloping woodlot with a swamp covering the back 40 feet. A town ordinance requiring that the house be placed at least 35 feet from the front of the lot left only about 30 feet in the middle to build on. But Mulfinger also saw possibilities. He sensed that the view toward the swamp from 15 feet above the ground was promising, so he shinnied up a tree to check it out. "It was a rewarding climb," Mulfinger says. "There *was* a nice view. Since we didn't have room to build outward, I decided that the house should go up," he says, pointing skyward with his thumb.

The floor plan that began to suggest itself was roughly square in shape. At first, the Johansons found this distressing, since *A Pattern Language* says that the most efficient and satisfying houses are long and thin (109, LONG THIN HOUSE). But the book also suggests that some patterns—those the authors felt might be improved upon, which are marked with an asterisk—should be treated with "a certain amount of disrespect."

Taking the authors at their word, Mulfinger

talked to had never heard of the book; others were not interested in working with the Johansons for other reasons. "I was literally laughed out of one architect's office after saying we wanted to build a custom house for $50,000 to $70,000," Bruce recalls. "They laughed because I had the audacity even to consider having an architect on a budget like that. But I was thinking, why not?" In frustration, he tried to call Christopher Alexander at the Center for Environmental Structure.

He reached Sara Ishikawa, one of the co-authors of *A Pattern Language*. Coincidentally, she had recently been to the Twin Cities area to attend a conference conducted by Dale Mulfinger and Sarah Susanka, two Minneapolis architects who admire Christopher Alexander's approach to design and use it in their professional practice. Ishikawa gave Johanson their names.

Bruce and Sharmaine Johanson were the first prospective clients who had ever approached Mulfinger and Susanka with their own previous knowledge of *A Pattern Language*. Mulfinger has found that few nonarchitects have ever heard of it, and he does not make a habit of recommending the 1,171-page, $50 doorstopper to clients. "I've found that some people take to it very quick-

suggested an alternative to the long, thin house: the tall, square house. He pointed out that in Minnesota and other places with cold climates, cube-shaped houses are more common than long, thin ones, since the cube encloses more interior space with proportionately less surface area exposed to the outdoors. "We were really set on the long, thin house thing for a long time," Sharmaine says. "But eventually we realized it was much more energy-efficient, and made more sense on our lot, to build a square house."

Mulfinger and Susanka drew up three preliminary plans and met with the Johansons for an all-day design workshop. By the end of the session, the group had produced a design that all four of them liked, largely because each person had contributed to it and felt that it was, in some way, his or her own.

The floor plan they came up with has a 27-by-28-foot "footprint," with jut-outs for a bay window, a sunroom porch, and two alcoves (one in the kitchen and another in the children's room). The main living area, including the kitchen, music room and sunroom, is on the second floor, affording views of the wooded swamp. Three bedrooms and a full bath are on the first floor (actually a finished walk-out basement). The third floor is now used as a TV and exercise room. It is plumbed for a second full bathroom, where fixtures will be installed someday when the children are older and the Johansons are ready to convert the space into a separate COUPLE'S REALM (pattern 136).

The house seems larger than its actual 1,800 square feet. This is due mainly to the inclusion of alcoves and the organization of space according to the patterns STRUCTURE FOLLOWS SOCIAL SPACES ("on no account allow engineering to dictate the building's form"; rather, "place the load-bearing elements . . . according to the social spaces of the building"), SHORT PASSAGES ("keep passages short") and INTIMACY GRADIENT ("lay out the spaces of a building so that they create a sequence which begins with the entrance and the most public parts of the building, then leads into the slightly more private areas, and finally to the most private domains").

Thanks to good planning, even Sharmaine agrees that the swamp now seems like an asset rather than a liability. On warm days, family members enjoy lounging on a small deck outside the kitchen windows—the perfect vantage point for watching frogs, ducks and other wildlife moving among the reeds and cattails. The wet lowland has proven to be a benign adventure playground for the children, and furnishes some good ice skating in winter.

If good design is the art of making every square foot count, *A Pattern Language* helped the Johansons achieve that goal on a modest budget. Final costs amounted to about $75,000 (not including land)—somewhat more than they hoped to spend, though less than the $95,000 to $100,000 that Dale Mulfinger estimates the house might easily have cost if its owners had been less involved in planning and construction.

Bruce acted as general contractor for the project, which took place during one of the worst winters in Minnesota history. Since he was on the building site every day, he was able to ad-lib with the plans during construction, implementing patterns in ways that no one had anticipated at the design stage. "Some of the best features of this house weren't planned," he says, "like my bridge, the play-loft in the kids' room and the oak beams in the kitchen and music room." The exposed oak beams, which give the main living areas an added dimension of rusticity and warmth, were an unexpected find in a small Amish community in southern Minnesota. Bruce salvaged some of the other materials in the house, including several oak French doors (one of them leads into the sunroom) and some maple boards, which became the flooring in the sunroom and Bruce's office. Though these materials have a charm that could not be

Nestled into its small wooded lot, the Johansons' house is just what Sharmaine wanted: "a house to daydream in."

Farmhouse Kitchen

A PATTERN LANGUAGE SAMPLER

You have laid out, or already have, some kind of common area at the center of the building. In many cases, especially in houses, the heart of this common area is a kitchen or an eating area since shared food has more capacity than almost anything to be the basis for communal feelings – COMMON AREA AT THE HEART (129), COMMUNAL EATING (147). This pattern defines an ancient kind of kitchen where the cooking and the eating and the living are all in a single place.

The isolated kitchen, separate from the family and considered as an efficient but unpleasant factory for food is a hangover from the days of servants; and from the more recent days when women willingly took over the servants' role.

In traditional societies, where there were no servants and the members of a family took care of their own food, the isolated kitchen was virtually unknown. Even when cooking was entirely in the hands of women, as it often was, the work of cooking was still thought of as a primal, communal function; and the "hearth," the place where food was made and eaten, was the heart of family life.

As soon as servants took over the function of cooking, in the palaces and manor houses of the rich, the kitchens naturally got separated from the dining halls. Then, in the middle-class housing of the nineteenth century, where the use of servants became rather widespread, the pattern of the isolated kitchen also spread, and became an accepted part of any house. But when the servants disappeared, the kitchen was still left separate, because it was thought "genteel" and "nice" to eat in dining rooms away from any sight or smell of food. The isolated kitchen was still associated with those houses of the rich, where dining rooms like this were taken for granted.

But this separation, in a family, has put the woman in a very difficult position. Indeed, it may not be too much to say that it has helped to generate those circumstances which have made the woman's position in mid-twentieth-century society unworkable and unacceptable. Very simply, the woman who accepted responsibility for making food agreed to isolate herself in the "kitchen"– and subtly then agreed to become a servant.

Modern American houses, with the so-called open plan, have gone some way toward resolving this conflict. They very often have a kitchen that is half-separated from the family room: not isolated, and not entirely in the family room. This does create a circumstance where the people who are cooking are in touch with the rest of the family, while they are working. And it does not have the obvious stigma and unpleasantness of separated sculleries and kitchens.

But it does not go far enough. If we look beneath the surface, there is in this kind of plan still the hidden supposition that cooking is a chore and that eating is a pleasure. So long as this mentality rules over the arrangement of the house, the conflict which existed in the isolated kitchen is still present. The difficulties which surround the situation will only disappear, finally, when all the members of the family are able to accept, fully, the fact that taking care of themselves by *cooking* is as much a part of life as taking care of themselves by *eating*. This will only happen when the communal hearth is once more gathered round the big kitchen table, as it is in primitive communities, where the taking care of necessary functions is an everyday part of life, and has not been lost to people's consciousness through the misleading function of the servant.

We are convinced that the solution lies in the pattern of the old farmhouse kitchen. In the farmhouse kitchen, kitchen work and family activity were completely integrated in one big room. The family activity centered around a big table in the middle: here they ate, talked, played cards, and did work of all kinds including some of the food preparation. The kitchen work was done communally both on the table, and on counters round the walls. And there might have been a comfortable old chair in the corner where someone could sleep through the activities.

plenty of room

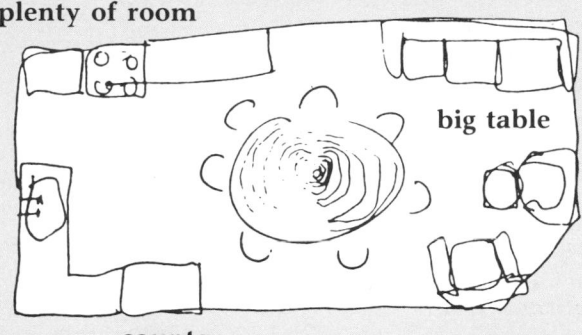

big table

counter

Therefore:

Make the kitchen bigger than usual, big enough to include the "family room" space, and place it near the center of the commons, not so far back in the house as an ordinary kitchen. Make it large enough to hold a good big table and chairs, some soft and some hard, with counters and stove and sink around the edge of the room; and make it a bright and comfortable room.

Give the kitchen LIGHT ON TWO SIDES (159). When you place the kitchen counters later, make them really long and generous and toward the south to get the light – COOKING LAYOUT (184), SUNNY COUNTER (199); leave room for an alcove or two around the kitchen – ALCOVES (179); make the table in the middle big, and hang a nice big warm single light right in the middle to draw the family around it – EATING ATMOSPHERE (182); surround the walls, when you detail them, with plenty of open shelves for pots, mugs, bottles, and jars of jam – OPEN SHELVES (200), WAIST-HIGH SHELF (201). Put in a comfortable chair somewhere – SEQUENCE OF SITTING SPACES (142). And for the room shape and construction, start with THE SHAPE OF INDOOR SPACE (191).

◆

Excerpted from A Pattern Language, © *1977 by Christopher Alexander. Used by permission of Oxford University Press, Inc.*

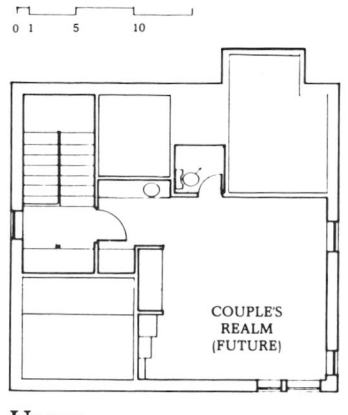

UPPER LEVEL

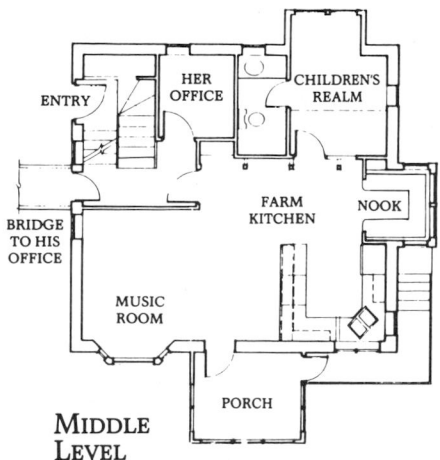

MIDDLE LEVEL

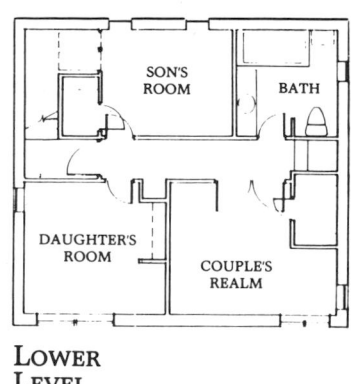

LOWER LEVEL

duplicated with newer components, they required many extra hours of labor to remove from their original settings, clean, store, reinstall and refinish. A new French door, prehung, costs about $150, which now seems to Bruce like a pretty good deal.

He also has second thoughts about the double-wall construction method used in the house's exterior walls. The idea of thick walls appealed to the Johansons, not only because they wanted to build an energy-efficient house, but also because of patterns 211, THICKENING THE OUTER WALLS and 223, DEEP REVEALS ("reveal" is the authors' word for the framing around windows, including the sill). The exterior walls are about a foot thick. An outer frame, made of 2x4s on 16-inch centers, supports the structure. Three-and-a-half inches inside this, a second 2x4 frame augments the inner wall cavity to a total thickness of 10½ inches – room enough for three layers of fiberglass batt insulation. The composite R-value of the sandwich is about 37, three times greater than the insulating value of a standard 2x4 exterior wall.

The double walls do indeed conserve energy, even though some of the windows and doors were built on site and, by Bruce's own admission, "aren't exactly the tightest." Solar gain from an ample array of south-facing windows supplies some of the house's heat. The rest comes from baseboard electric units, chosen mainly because of their low initial cost. So far, the Johansons have spent less than $400 each year for heat in a climate where $1,000 seasonal heating bills are not uncommon. Even so, Bruce is not sure the energy savings justify the high cost of double-wall construction. If he were to build the house again, he would frame the exterior walls with 2x6s, fill the cavity with fiberglass batts, apply rigid foam insulation outside the sheathing and, on the interior side, nail up a layer of 2x2 strapping over the vapor barrier to make a space

beneath the gypsum board for electrical wiring. The R-value of this wall would be about 20 percent less than that of the double 2x4 wall, but it would require 20 percent less framing lumber and considerably less labor to build.

Bruce has had plenty of opportunities to put such lessons to work. As a result of his pattern language "conversion," he is now a building contractor – a big change from selling musical instruments, which he did for several years before contracting his family's house in 1983-84. Since then, he has built new houses for three customers and remodeled another house, all with the help of Dale Mulfinger, Sarah Susanka and *A Pattern Language*. Several more projects are now in the works. The construction business, Bruce says, "gives me a little platform I can use to push this philosophy of mine." Using ideas from the "Towns" section of the book, he also made some disciples in his neighborhood by organizing support for, and planning the layout of, a small local playground. Someday, he would like to build an entire town based on *A Pattern Language*. The book's influence in his community, he says, "started with our little house and has just radiated outwards," much like the waves from a pebble thrown into White Bear Lake. ❧

The floor plan is based on a 27-by-28-foot rectangle. Various bays and alcoves add to the house's living space, visual interest, and "warmth."

SOURCES

The Center for Environmental Structure
2701 Shasta Road
Berkeley, California 94708
(415) 841-6166

A Pattern Language, by Christopher Alexander and others, is available for $49.95 through bookstores or from the publisher: **Oxford University Press**
2001 Evans Road
Cary, North Carolina 27513
(800) 451-7556

Sunwings

SOLAR ADDITIONS FOR NORTHERN HOMES

BY MERILYN MOHR

On a frigid February day, Carol and Arthur Keil of Littleton, Colorado, lounge on their deck, basking in the hot afternoon sun. The panoramic landscape before them lies buried in deep snow and ice, but here they are surrounded by luxuriant green foliage and baskets of flowering geraniums. Like hundreds of snowbound country dwellers from Portland, Maine, to Portland, Oregon, the Keils have found a way to bring the tropics north for less than the price of plane tickets. While their neighbors mutter about the weather or fly south to escape the cold, the Keils simply step into their sunwing to enjoy the warmth and greenery of summer.

A Classic

A "sunwing" is an updated version of the classic British conservatory, an addition designed to capture and hold the sun's radiation. Properly designed, a sunwing can be a greenhouse for growing food and flowers in the dead months, a collector for supplementing the heating needs of the house, or a solarium for warm sunny midwinter living. A sunwing can extend from any kind of house – Victorian mansion or clapboard cottage – and can be as large or small as fancy and finances allow. A carefully planned sunwing need cost no more than a conventional home addition and it can be virtually energy self-sufficient, exacting no payment for opening an otherwise ordinary house to the unique pleasures of the sun.

"As I built this room, I had an image floating around in my head," recalls sunwing owner Rory Dowler of Ontario, Canada. "I saw myself sitting in the sun on a Christmas morning surrounded by vegetation, eating a toasted tomato sandwich – the tomato and lettuce freshly picked."

That vision has materialized. While numbing winds howl outside, the Dowler family eats fresh leaf lettuce, radishes and salad tomatoes. By early spring, their sunwing is a profusion of seedlings for transplanting to their vegetable garden and flower beds. In summer, they enjoy the cool night breezes out of range of marauding mosquitoes.

Since putting a sunwing on their house, Donna and Larry Steele of Princeton, New Jersey, enjoy limes off their indoor tree in the middle of winter, and the Keils take a soothing dip in their hot tub, while outside the sun reflects off the heavy mountain snowdrifts.

Sunwing owners typically credit their additions with giving them a whole new outlook on winter. They bring a shaft of sunlight into northern homes when it is needed most, especially where the local climate is characterized as "nine months of winter and three months of poor sledding." In such areas, the land wakes up slowly in the spring, enjoys a short frantic burst of growth in summer, then has a prolonged fade-out in the fall before the full dormancy of winter sets in.

A sunwing effectively shortens the winter by incorporating principles of passive solar design and energy-efficient construction. The addition is oriented toward the south, its glazing positioned to collect as much of the winter sun's heat and light as possible. The building materials are chosen to absorb that warmth and keep it inside and are put together using construction techniques that combat heat loss and allow for solar gain. None of this adds significantly to total cost: it is just as easy to build on the south side of a house as on the north, and the windows are the same price whether they are concentrated in the south wall or distributed on three sides. The concrete that absorbs the heat is already part of the structure, as is the air/vapor barrier that

Left: **The key to planning a successful solar addition is in understanding what different types of sunwings can and cannot do.**

seals the warmth inside the room. What makes the difference is how these elements are arranged in the design and how they are detailed during construction.

Many of the hard-learned lessons of the solar home industry are being brought to bear on sunwing design. There is more to this than simply throwing up walls of south-facing glazing and sitting back to soak up the benevolent rays. Many passive solar sunrooms became living nightmares – plants seared by day, heat sucked out of the house by night – inviting spaces for neither man nor magnolia. The key to planning a successful solar addition is in understanding what different types of sunwings can and cannot do.

T-Shirts at 10 Below

In most parts of the country, a sunwing can be self-sufficient or use little backup heat. As a bonus, it may slightly lower home heating costs by acting as a "buffer," reducing heat loss through the wall to which it is attached. Most homeowners report that although the sunwing needs an occasional heat infusion to keep it above freezing in the depths of winter, by February it can collect enough heat from the sun to help warm the main house.

Concern with home heating costs is a fairly recent phenomenon. People have spent millions to stuff their attics and walls with insulation, but in their single-minded attempts to improve thermal efficiency, many have ignored other approaches to home comfort. Remember the tale about the north wind and the sun vying to make the young man take off his coat? As the north wind blew, the youth only gathered the folds of his cloak more tightly around him, but when the sun gently shone, the youth willingly doffed his wrap. Likewise, though bundling a house in insulation offers some protection against the blasts of winter, a great measure of comfort can be gained by opening the house to the sun.

"The best thing," says Kathy Boyle of Aplaus, New York, who recently added a sunwing to her Victorian home, "is that you can have a cup of coffee and sit in the sun, wearing shorts and a T-shirt, when it's 10 below zero outside."

For many homeowners, that psychological benefit of a warm, sunny space outweighs the potential energy savings of a sunwing. The broad expanse of glazing in a sunwing offers a wider vista and a direct connection with the fundamental rhythms of nature. The sunwing itself becomes a massive sundial that marks the passing of the hours and the seasons as the sun's rays slant across the floor.

Tuning a house to its environment is not an avant-garde idea. In fact, it is only recently in human history that people have ignored such natural forces as sun and wind and have situated their houses to accommodate sewer lines and zoning bureaucracies. One of the first references to passive solar principles is a lecture by Socrates, in which he advises students to "build the south side loftier to get the winter sun." On a more mundane level, Canada's early farmers built their barns banked on the north and open to the south, with hay stored in the "attic" acting as insulation for the animal pens below. The farmhouses that squatted nearby often included a sun room – an unheated area that was closed off in winter but reopened in early spring – as an intermediary indoor-outdoor room.

Sunwing design is rooted in such sensitivity to specific needs. There is no single "correct" passive solar addition that can be slapped onto the side of any house. There are, however, basic principles of solar gain and heat loss that, once understood, can be adapted to suit a particular climate, property and house. The sunwing that results will not only be efficient, it will look like an integral part of the original structure, blending unobtrusively into a heritage home or improving the character of more modern buildings.

Most homeowners have several goals in mind when they design their sunwings. Like the Keils, they want a pleasant living space for sunny winter days and room to grow a wide variety of plants – decorative plants, seedlings in spring and the makings for fresh salads in winter. Furthermore, they want an energy-efficient addition that will not cost a fortune to heat.

To avoid the disasters of the early solar additions, it is necessary to decide what you want out of a sunwing and then to realize that certain design compromises may have to be made to achieve it.

A sunwing can be many things – a heat collector, a greenhouse or a solarium where people bask in the sun. As with any building, the design of a sunwing is determined by its proposed use. Every structure is a climate-control unit, with roof, walls and floor combining to create a unique interior space that can be insulated from the conditions around it and then heated or cooled to become anything from a deep-freeze to a sauna. The artificial climate inside the enclosed space is created partly by the design of the structure and partly by the heating and cooling systems that are added to it. Exactly what form that inside climate takes depends on how the space will be used: while it may be obvious that cacti and watercress need vastly different environments, the same

holds true for people.

Each of the three main sunwing functions requires different and sometimes conflicting design features. A single sunwing *can* collect heat, grow plants and house the hot tub, but not without compromise: a true greenhouse will not be an efficient heat collector, and a solar furnace is certainly no place to serve afternoon tea. If heat is the goal, the sunwing's use as a greenhouse or living room will be restricted; if growing plants is the primary objective, sacrifices will have to be made in heating efficiency and livability; and if the space is designed as a sun room for people, growing conditions and heat collection will have to be adapted to human needs.

Therefore, the first and most crucial step in planning a sunwing takes place before a single piece of sod is moved – even before pencil meets drafting paper: The homeowner must ponder his or her priorities.

Function dramatically affects the design of the sunwing. A sunwing devoted solely to **heat collection** is tall and narrow, with only enough floor space to create the correct angle for the collector. The glazing, oriented unerringly toward solar south, is perpendicular to the sun's rays when they are at their midwinter low so that the collector can gather maximum heat when it is needed most. Such a sunwing will likely be two stories high to increase the collector area and to encourage warm air to rise so it can be immediately distributed to the house. Because a collector-sunwing is designed to heat the main house and not itself, it includes no heat-loss controls, thermal storage or backup heating system. Consequently, the temperatures in the sunwing itself swing wildly from the outside winter low to a sunny-day high of up to 150 degrees F. There may be a few hours in-between when the space is habitable, but the conditions are too inconsistent for plants and too unpredictable for most people.

A sunwing intended as a **greenhouse** is designed to provide adequate light and heat for the kinds of plants the homeowner wants to grow. Its south glazing, chosen for solar transmission rather than visual clarity, is sloped or continued overhead to provide maximum, even light. The addition is narrow, generally 8 to 10 feet deep, so that the winter sun can penetrate to the back wall, and it includes east and west wall glazing, allowing plants to be bathed in light from early morning to late afternoon. Although a high proportion of glazing is necessary for active growth, in a cold climate too much glass will create

The "breakfast room" has reduced heating costs by 40 percent. Water tubes store heat, which can be vented to upstairs bedrooms.

COURTESY PRINCETON ENERGY GROUP

The laminated arches of James Ahlstedt's spacious, customized, kit-built sunwing in Ossining, New York, create a handsome area for sunny relaxation; plus there's room for 12-foot trees.

temperature swings that most plants cannot tolerate. To moderate the extremes, a greenhouse includes backup heat and movable insulation to counter nighttime heat loss, storage mass to absorb daytime solar gain, shade to protect the plants from intense summer sun and ventilation to flush out excess heat and provide a fresh supply of carbon dioxide. The humidity inside a greenhouse is higher than is comfortable for humans and creates more dampness than conventional building materials can tolerate. For this utilitarian design, finishes are chosen not for aesthetics but for their ability to reflect light, for easy maintenance and for resistance to rot.

A **solarium** is much less stringent in its design demands than either a greenhouse or heat collector. Instead of trying to maximize light or heat, a solarium-sunwing concentrates on collecting and retaining comfortable levels of solar heat. Instead of a sloped south wall, a solarium has vertical glazing that collects as much solar heat energy as a slope, but loses less heat and is easier and cheaper to install. East-west and overhead glazings are eliminated in the interest of energy efficiency, and orientation can be modified to accommodate human rather than plant preferences.

As a primary function, there is no doubt that the solarium offers the most design freedom. Indeed, cold-climate designers generally agree that a sunwing designed exclusively for heat collection does not make economic sense for northern latitudes: a room-sized "solar furnace" is a large investment with only limited potential return, since a sunwing cannot hope to fulfill a house's heating needs. Likewise, a true greenhouse demands an investment of time and money that few homeowners anticipate. In many northern states, the intensity and duration of light is so low around the winter solstice that grow lights are necessary to stimulate active plant growth. Because plants are dependent on their environment, a greenhouse must be automatically regulated with thermostatically controlled fans, vents and heaters to maintain growing conditions. Though the cost of operating a greenhouse depends on local climate, the crops grown and the type of backup used, it can be expensive: when a family in central Minnesota grew tomatoes in their sunspace, it cost as much to keep the addition at growing temperature as it did to heat the rest of their low-energy house.

However, heat collection is a reasonable

secondary function for a solarium-sunwing. The vertical glazing promotes good solar gain, and the two-story profile typical of a heat collector meshes well with human needs: the lower floor level remains a comfortable temperature, while hot air pools near the ceiling where it can be manually or mechanically vented into the main house. In midwinter, the sunwing will likely need backup heat to keep temperatures above freezing, but on an annual basis, depending on the design and use of the space, solar gain and energy consumption will usually even out.

"It's not necessarily economically advantageous to create solariums simply for reduced heat loss," warns Dale Mulfinger, an architect in Minneapolis, Minnesota. Sometimes, however, a sunwing will produce a slight drop in overall energy consumption because the addition converts an exterior house wall to an interior wall. In other words, if a sunwing has a positive effect on home heating costs, it will probably stem more from its buffering effect than from solar gain. Even if the sunwing is unheated, its temperatures will not be as extreme as those outdoors, so there will be less heat loss through the wall blanketed by new construction. If the common wall between the house and the addition is large and uninsulated, with ill-fitting single-glazed windows, the sunwing's effect on fuel bills can be significant.

A solarium really comes into its own, however, when plants are included in the plan. This, in fact, is what many people have in mind when they decide to build a "solar greenhouse"—a pleasant place to sit and somewhere to start seedlings and grow houseplants. According to Brian Marshall of Sun Shelters, a Canadian firm specializing in energy-efficient sunwing design and construction, "many clients *think* they want a greenhouse, but we've found that most people just want a table in the corner to start seedlings, maybe a hanging fern or two and a place to sit and enjoy the warm, bright winter sun."

The Ideal Solution

Instead of designing a climate-controlled space for particular plants, species are selected that are flexible in their light and heat needs. There are many varieties that thrive on the relatively Spartan conditions of an unheated sunwing: jasmine needs a drop to as low as 35 degrees F to bloom profusely the next season; hydrangea, oleander and geraniums likewise enjoy the semi-dormancy induced by low temperatures; and winter-blooming plants like azaleas and cyclamens can adapt to tem-

ILLUSTRATIONS BY JOHN BIANCHI

AUTOMATIC ROOF VENTS

GLAZING ON ALL SIDES

HIGH TRANSMISSIVITY GLAZING

ACTIVE VENTILATION

BACKUP HEAT

HIGH THERMAL MASS

SOLID ROOF TO REDUCE HEAT LOSS

OPERABLE PANES FOR VENTILATION

VERTICAL GLAZING TO PREVENT OVERHEATING

BACKUP HEATING SYSTEM TO MAINTAIN COMFORT LEVEL

Whether it is intended as a greenhouse-sunwing, top, or as solarium-sunwing, bottom, the solar addition must be defined before it can be designed.

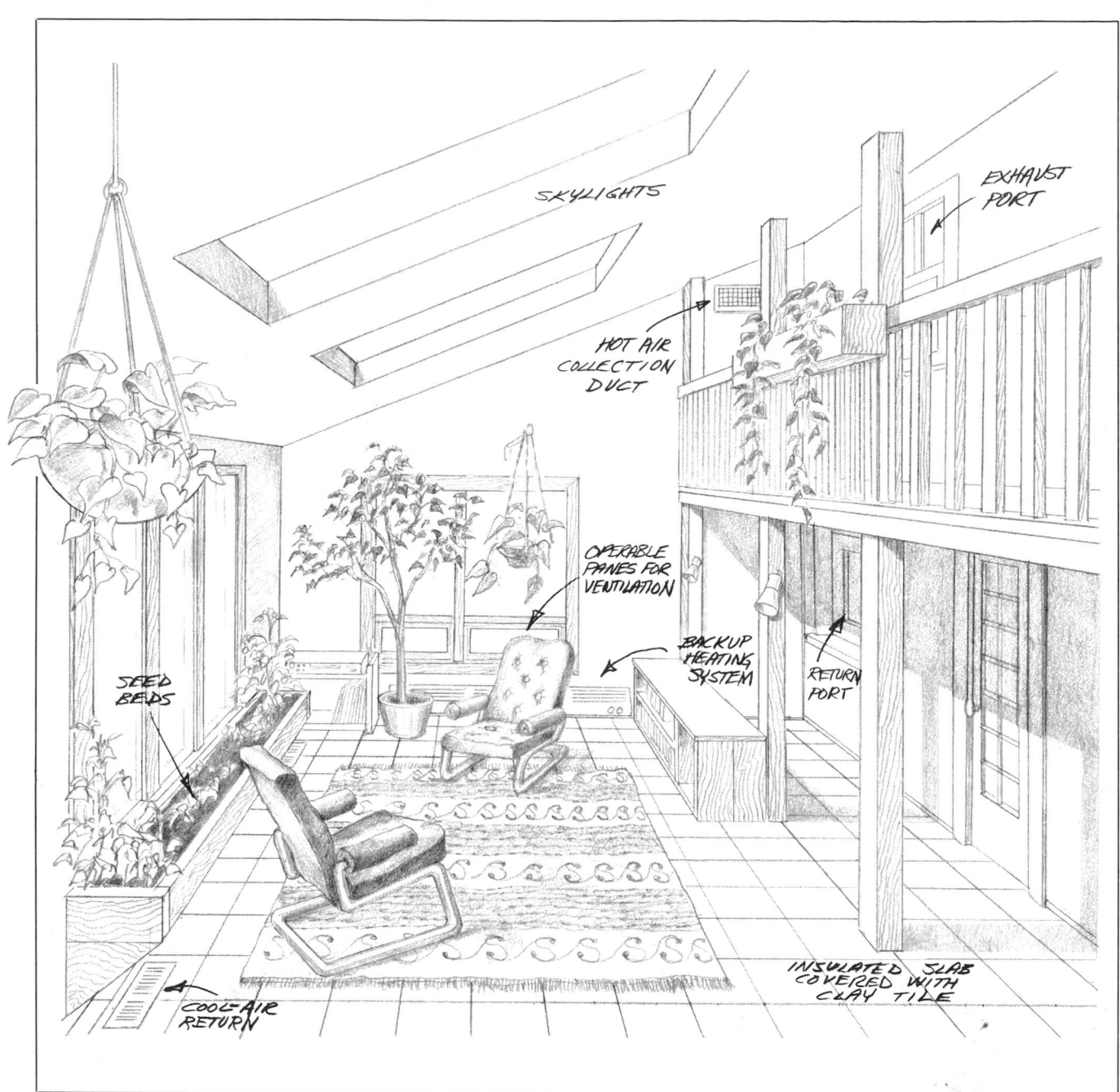

SKYLIGHTS

EXHAUST PORT

HOT AIR COLLECTION DUCT

OPERABLE PANES FOR VENTILATION

SEED BEDS

BACKUP HEATING SYSTEM

RETURN PORT

INSULATED SLAB COVERED WITH CLAY TILE

COOL-AIR RETURN

With good planning, a hybrid sunwing can collect enough solar heat to be energy efficient and will be light enough to grow spring seedlings and houseplants without compromising its primary function as a bright, inviting living space.

peratures close to freezing.

We've got to learn to give more appreciation to those plants that are willing to stick with us through the rigors of a northern winter – cool, low-light plants such as salad greens and herbs. Indeed, many vegetables can survive the relatively cool, low-light conditions of a sunwing. In an unheated sunwing, you can routinely expect winter harvests of salad greens, celery, leeks and herbs. And cold-resistant vegetables transplanted from the garden in late autumn can provide the family with fresh vegetables during the coldest part of the winter when light levels and temperatures are too low for young seedlings.

There is no question that a well-thought-out master plan can produce an effective compromise – one with vertical glazing and good orientation for maximum heat collection, a little overhead glazing for good light penetration, narrow built-in beds for plants, with lots of room left over for the Ping-Pong table. It will not grow plants as well as a nursery greenhouse or produce the maximum heat of a passive solar collector, but it will be light enough for healthy plants, collect enough heat to be self-sufficient and create an incomparable living space.

"My mother didn't enjoy flowers before I built the sunwing," James Ahlstedt of Ossining, New York, says. "She thought they were too difficult. Now she has 12-foot-high trees, in addition to a comfortable sitting area."

Thermal Break

Single-purpose greenhouses and heat collectors are recognized as functional appendages to a house, but there is a strong temptation to integrate this "hybrid" sunwing fully into the living area of the house. With no barriers between old and new construction, heat could flow freely from sunwing to house when the sun is shining and from house to sunwing at night and on cloudy days. In a cold country, however, it is expensive to maintain consistent human comfort levels in a highly glazed structure. Even constructed to energy-efficient standards, an **integrated sunwing** – an addition that is not connected to the main part of the house by an insulated wall – will likely increase total heating bills as it drains house heat out through its large windows.

An integrated sunwing can, however, be transformed into a **buffered sunwing**, an addition outside the thermal envelope of the house. The wall between the addition and the house is fully insulated, and the sunwing becomes a transitional indoor-outdoor space, more than a porch, less than a living room. The homeowner can use the solar heat when it is available, but can close off the space so that heat from the house is not drained when the temperature drops. The sunwing itself can swing with the weather or can contain heating and ventilation systems to counteract the heat loss/gain cycle. Aligning sunwing windows with house windows allows people to see out of and sun to shine into the main part of the house. At the same time, the sunwing creates a thermal break between the house and outdoors. Because the temperature differential across the buffered wall is thus narrowed, there is less heat lost from the house.

This buffered sunspace is flexible and always usable – as a game room, as a mudroom after cross-country skiing, as a greenhouse for starting seedlings, as a summer sleeping porch.

Being outside the thermal envelope need not limit the sunwing's use. Two or three thousand dollars can create a 200-square-foot sunwing that brings daily pleasure. It becomes a breakfast room, a station for bird-watching, a sanctuary for plants and, at the appropriate season, a place to force bulbs and start tubers and seeds.

That kind of satisfying sunwing stems from sound planning. The homeowners should start by taking an honest look at the house to

The slate floor of Kathy Boyle's two-story sunwing absorbs heat from the sun's rays, so "even in winter you can go barefoot."

Finding Solar South

When Yukon homeowner Wayne Wilkinson decided to add a sunwing to his house in Whitehorse, he found that Grey Mountain to the east blocked the winter sun until late morning, a neighboring house shaded the site in the afternoon, and instead of facing south, his house tilted sharply to the southeast. At that latitude, the winter sun barely rises above the horizon, and when it does, its rays have to filter through a haze of wood smoke that persistently hangs over the valley. Nevertheless, Wilkinson overcame these seemingly insurmountable obstacles and built a sunwing that feeds his family year-round, saves $425 on his annual heating bill and is "a warm, sunny retreat from the grasp of winter."

As Wilkinson proved, a sunwing can be added successfully to any house as long as its design takes into account the idiosyncrasies of the local climate, the site and the house. The amount of solar heat and light energy the sunwing collects depends entirely on how many hours of sunshine the region receives, the sunblocks that shade the property and the orientation of the sunwing itself.

Here in the northern hemisphere, windows have to face south to catch the sun. Yet the sun is constantly on the move, or so it seems. As the Earth spins, the sun tracks across the sky from east to west on a daily cycle, and from low on the horizon to high overhead and back down again on a yearly cycle. It rises and sets at its most northerly points on the summer solstice (on or around June 21), and on that day, the sun is as high overhead as it gets. By the winter solstice (around December 21), the sun rises and sets at its most southerly points on the horizon and is at its lowest zenith. The spring and fall equinoxes, around March 21 and September 21, mark the midpoints of this annual cycle.

In order to catch all the available solar radiation, a window would have to pivot with the sun, a feasible solution for active collectors but not for sunwing glazing. The next best thing is to face the glazing toward the midpoint in the sun's arc across the sky. That midpoint occurs at solar noon, exactly halfway between sunrise and sunset. The sun's position in the sky at solar noon is called solar, or true, south. A window oriented precisely toward solar south collects the most light and heat energy available to a fixed surface.

How close sunwing windows can come to this ideal depends to a large extent on the relationship between the house and the sun. Unfortunately, because solar orientation was not a priority when most of our houses were built, few homes will be perfectly oriented for a sunwing. To figure out where the house lies in relation to solar south, establish which wall faces most nearly south (look for windows that admit direct winter sun). The exact orientation of that wall can easily be determined by using a compass.

If there are no windows or doors in the south wall, the homeowner will have to go outside to locate solar south. In an unshaded area of the yard, about 10 feet out from the south side of the house, drive a 6-foot stake into the ground, checking with a level that it is vertical. (In spring and summer, the shadow may be too short to give an accurate reading, in which case a plumb bob suspended from a tree

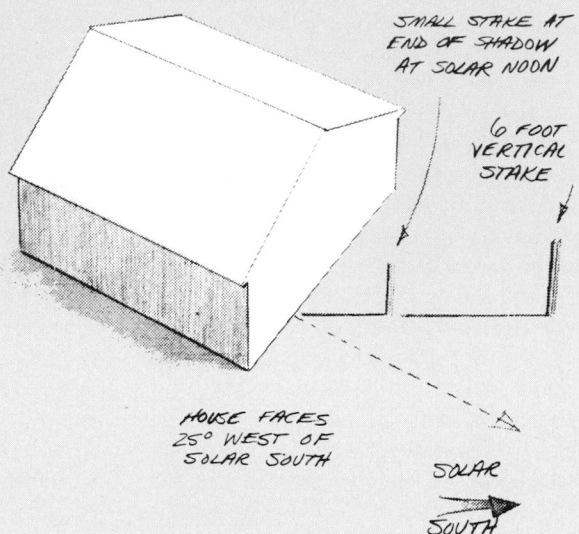

or clothesline may produce enough cast shadow.) At exactly solar noon, the cast shadow indicates the solar north-south axis. Use stakes to mark the beginning and end of the shadow, then extend the line to the wall of the house. The angle between this north-south line and a line perpendicular to the wall indicates how much the house deviates from solar south.

Fortunately, orientation is not a solar-south-or-nothing proposition. The house, and thus the sunwing, can face within 30 degrees of solar south and still garner 90 percent of the potential solar energy. Most designers recommend orienting passive solar structures within this 30-degree limit, though some consider even as much as 45 degrees off south acceptable. At that angle, a quarter of the available solar energy is sacrificed, so it is not recommended for far northern latitudes or where heat gain is a priority.

Although a certain measure of play is possible without abandoning solar principles, the amount of deviation from south will affect the time of year the sunwing gets the most sun. The east and west walls of a house receive two to three times more solar energy in summer than they do in winter. Thus the farther east or west a sunwing faces, the more winter solar gain is reduced and summer solar gain is increased.

Whether a sunwing faces east or west of south also affects the time of day that it receives the most sunshine. A western orientation exposes the sunwing to less morning sun, which is much-needed by healthy plants: in the low-light winter months, they need direct sunlight as early in the day as possible to renew photosynthesis. Therefore, greenhouse-sunwings that face more than 15 degrees west of solar south should include east wall glazing to provide enough light for active growth. However, for people who are late risers or who want a bright sunny space after a hard day's work, the afternoon sunshine of a west-facing sunwing may be welcome.

—*M.M.*

ILLUSTRATION BY JOHN BIANCHI

determine if its structure and condition merit the expense of adding a sunwing. Is a passive solar addition really the top priority, or would the family's resources be better spent on overdue maintenance or upgrading insulation? A sunwing will not do much to improve the comfort of a house that is underinsulated or leaking air like a sieve.

Once the decision is made to go ahead with a passive solar addition, priorities must be set. Make a list of everything the sunwing will be used for, then number the functions from most to least important. "When you start to talk with people who want sunwings, you often find that they want a lot of contradictory things," says Kyle Van Dyke, a New Jersey architect who has designed a number of sunwings. Setting priorities may sound easy, but it will likely take some soul-searching to come to grips with the fundamental purpose of the space. Once the primary function has been established, each of the secondary functions can probably be incorporated into the design with varying degrees of success. Beside each one, jot down the design features required for the activity. For instance, if the sunwing will contain planting beds, the homeowner may want an outside entrance or a special potting area. Finally, establish a rough dollar figure the family is willing to invest in a sunwing.

This initial stage can take days, weeks, months or even years, with the sunwing evolving as family interests change. In the meantime, keep a file of magazine clippings of promising design features. Perhaps you can convince a friend to build one first while you help out.

Another good way to understand the implications of your final decisions, aside from reading, is to visit as many sunwings as possible. Talk to people who live with passive solar additions to discover what works and what doesn't in a particular locale. As humorist James Thurber once said, "Always look before you leap. The conclusion you jump to could be your own." ❧

———————————— ◆ ————————————

Excerpted from Sunwings: The Harrowsmith Guide to Solar Addition Architecture *by Merilyn Mohr. Camden House Publishing, Ltd., 1985.*

Ark de Triomphe

STRANDED HIGH IN THE MOUNTAINS, AN OLD BARN BECOMES A NEW HOME

BY LAMONT BASSETT WITH PHOTOGRAPHY BY GARY FIEGEHEN

My first impression of the building was of a great log ark landlocked in the middle of a hayfield, its hull turned a deep coffee umber from years of brilliant summers and blazing winters. For half a century, the structure had been a barn, but its character conveyed a grander purpose than that of a mere manure mill; the logs were too big for a barn, the dovetail joints too fine, the seams between the logs too precise. "Someone should renovate it," I mused in passing; now, 20,000 worker-hours and 10 years later, the restoration has been for us like a sled ride on black ice: though seldom in control, we have been committed to seeing the trip through to its end.

Located near Smithers, in northwestern British Columbia, the property sits on a bench overlooking the serpentine Bulkley River, with Hudson Bay Mountain looming across the western horizon. The southern sky is defined by the rugged Telkwa Range, while the gnarly Kitseguecla peaks dominate the north. Thick fingers of deep boreal forests ascend the mountains between clean avalanche chutes reaching down to the valley floor. The seasons here are abrupt and vibrant, and the long arc of the sun changes the mountains with each sunrise.

The first people to travel the land were Gitksan and Carrier Indians, but the original Crown title was awarded to czarist Russia as a gesture of goodwill during the Canada/Siberian telegraph-line attempt. When the overland communications venture went bust, title reverted to the Crown and was finally issued to Henry Gunderson, a tie hack who homesteaded here in the early 1920s. During the winter, Gunderson cut trees to clear the land, squared the pine for railroad ties and saved the spruce for buildings. Using only a team of horses, a water level and a broad axe,

he built the 30-by-40-foot barn, 18 rounds high, with such precision that the second-floor purlins deviated only 1¼ inches when checked with a surveyor's transit 50 years later.

The standard of excellence set by Gunderson was the catalyst for the barn's renovation. Quentin Robbins, an artist of considerable talent, saw the potential in the building and bought the property in the early 1970s. Rot had started in the bottom round of logs, so he had to jack up the entire structure, cut out the bad wood and pour a ring foundation beneath. Water lines were brought into the building from a gravity well, a root cellar was dug, and the septic system was laid. But the project cut heavily into Robbins' painting time, and after laboring for four years, he decided to sell.

When my wife, Keith, and I arrived in the valley and heard the Gunderson farm was for sale, we had not thought of settling here. Though the barn captivated us, it was an unseasonably rainy summer, dulling the landscape and obliterating the mountains. "There's a peak wrapped around a glacier there," Robbins would say, pointing to the cloud cover, "another one there and a beautiful river

Ten years and 20,000 worker-hours have turned this 50-year-old log barn, *near left,* into a beautiful, energy-efficient home, *far left.*

there in the canyon." Taking Robbins at his word, we purchased the place, and that afternoon, the clouds parted to expose our ark surrounded by a sea of mountains.

We had to return to New Orleans to pack our belongings, so the first fall, we fixed up a granary to stay in when we returned. We felt certain we would only live one summer in the small outbuilding before moving into the barn (of course, we also calculated the cost of renovation to be around $10,000, one-eighth the final figure). In New Orleans, providence set up another encounter, this time with the project's chief carpenter, Andy Webster. The meeting took place on a street curb, with the full gale of Mardi Gras only inches away. "What do you do?" I asked. He shrugged nonchalantly, "Most everything." Knowing nothing about basic building skills, I invited him to British Columbia to teach us in exchange for wage and board. He considered the offer for a few seconds, and we shook hands on a relationship that would change both our lives.

Closing the Barn Doors

To understand the renovation, one must know the crew. In its course, roughly two dozen people helped with the project, with skills as basic as cutting saddle notches with a chain saw and as exact as glass cutting. (Each left a signature of his or her trade on the barn.) We were escapees from the 1960s, a crew of extremes from hirsute vegetarians to bushed big-game guides. But we shared a common pilgrimage to that vague Mecca, "back-to-ism": back to the land, to self-sufficiency, to self-expression through one's work. And Webster, a devout discile in the renaissance of craft, infected the rest of the crew. That year, there were Mike Seltzer, a student who carried Immanuel Kant in one pocket and Ken Kesey in the other; Gaston Porterie, a bayou expatriate; Lovely LaRae; and Keith, pregnant with our first child. For my part, I was along for the learning, reasoning that when the nest you are building is yours, you are much more attentive to the lessons.

The first summer, we began where Robbins had stopped. Though he had bulldozed tons of old hay, manure and stall stanchions, the interior walls had to be scrubbed and rescrubbed with steel brushes, then scoured with soap and ammonia to cut the smell. We also leveled the fireplace pad started by Robbins, using broken tractor parts, bedsteads and springs for reinforcing, and thought ourselves quite clever for saving money on re-bar and simultaneously cleaning junk from the yard. We even laughed about the poor archaeologist

Though the renovations continue, Bassett feels "we've learned about ourselves through our labors on this barn," right.

Many furnishings in this renovated barn are also second-hand: the stained glass window was salvaged from a church in New Orleans and is back lit by a terrarium in the kids' bedroom.

lem considered. Then Keith simply took a hydraulic jack and a board and lifted the log over the sill. It was a pivotal lesson in self-reliance and pragmatic problem solving, an attitude we would continue to rely upon during the renovation.

Once the purlins were in place and the third floor laid on them, the roof was straightforward. Tongue-and-groove decking was nailed directly onto the original rafters. A lattice of 2-by-8-inch lumber set on edge was made on the decking to hold sheets of Styrofoam insulation, giving the roof R40 value. We further framed in four dormers, two on each side, located according to weight-bearing supports and visual symmetry: we did not foresee that one winter, after a heavy snowfall, the wedge effect between the dormers would keep the snow from sliding, creating an ice bridge that would have to be broken free by hand.

By the end of the first summer, the ground-level flooring was laid and the gable ends framed in. But our dream of a closed dwelling in a single summer had been grossly naïve, as evidenced by the squadron of barn swallows still zooming in and out of gaping holes at each end. The crew disbanded with the first snowfall, and Keith and I turned our attention to the necessities of surviving the winter in the granary. Still, we did save our firstborn, Nicole, from the stigma of actually having been "born in a barn."

For the next couple of summers, we filled holes in the log walls with windows, doors and fireplaces. Robbins had planned for a walk-in fireplace on the pad we had previously leveled, but we were warned that an opening of that size would suck all the internal heat out of the house. Instead, we opted for a small fireplace and, beside it, an alcove for a central heating stove. Also, a second-floor fireplace was built immediately above the one on ground level. To stop the vacuum effect, we fitted each fireplace with a metal heatilator shell, reinforced with ¼-inch metal plate to curtail burning out, a tight flue damper and glass doors.

Masons Ed DeWitt and Eric Anderson joined the project and constructed a chimney system of three adjacent flues, 35 feet high. Anticipating chimney fires, we built the chimneys to accommodate creosote combustion by laying two courses of building blocks around the flue liners and offsetting each block so no single joint went to the outside.

With the rough fireplaces sealing the south end, we turned our attention to the doors and windows. The front door is the original barn door laminated onto tongue-and-groove oak and hung on hinges salvaged from a 150-year-

who would have to excavate it with torch and jackhammer to discover the secrets of our culture. Ironically, the pad would instead become a nightmare to haunt me.

The first major challenge was the roof. Concerned that the weight of a new roof would roll the top sill logs from their seats, we decided to cross tie them with several log purlins. Because we wanted to save the rafters and keep the original shakes on the roof, we had to thread the logs through two holes cut into the shakes, one on each side of the building. With a backhoe bucket pushing on one end of the log and a winch cable pulling from a truck on the opposite side of the barn, it was a bit like spanning a gorge by pulling a bridge across the chasm. My concern was how to support the weight of each log as it extended over the interior of the building.

Our plan was for the crew to hang from ropes on pulleys attached to the rafters, thereby counter-weighting the advancing log. Unfortunately, we did not fill our pockets with enough rocks; when the end of the log reached the far side, it hit the sill 2 inches below the top. Hastily, ropes were tied off and the prob-

old Pennsylvania barn. We had brought with us a couple dozen beveled hand-stained glass windows, collected from backgrounds as diverse as the French Quarter in New Orleans and a Mexican backyard glass factory in Oaxaca. The problem with leaded glass in the north is that it leaks air like a sieve. Pennywise and dollar-foolish, I decided to make my own thermal panes to protect the leaded glass. Luckily, winter caught the project in midstream, and the following year, it was finished with commercial twin-seal units on the exterior of the leaded glass.

The first heating system was a potbelly stove, the kind that made cracker barrels and knee slappers famous. However, when the temperature dropped below zero and vapor trails feathered along the logs, there were dead-air spaces in the corners capable of freezing moose meat in minutes, and our fascination for the potbelly dwindled. Certain that the problem was the size of the stove, we put in a space heater twice its size. This only served to burn three times as much wood (15 cords), and we still wore mittens to supper. Passive heat, solar, radiators—we considered a number of alternatives, but each was abandoned in the face of one hard reality, you cannot achieve a complete vapor barrier in an old log building. The inevitable solution was to pressurize the building internally, thus stopping the inward flow of cold air.

Trial and Error

Because the building did not have a basement, a furnace room was built onto the back of the fireplace complex and ducting was laid under the floor. Having the firebox out of the house has its advantages. No longer was there a long trail of wood chips through the living room, and the building stopped smelling like a salmon smokehouse. Of greater importance, our wood consumption dropped to around eight cords. The only hitch was bringing the ducting through the pad—the same pad that three years before, we had laid with bedsteads and archaeological jokes. I thought the project would take three days with a jackhammer and a cutting torch. Nine days later, a hole to accommodate the ducting was finally punched through the pad. Lesson: plan your heating system first.

Though a log building will never be completely airtight, the technique and materials used to chink between the logs can make a considerable difference. We replaced the original exterior burlap and moss chinking with fiberglass covered with strips of triangular pine strapping. But crafting the wood

to the log contours was time-consuming and not very effective. Consequently, we began experimenting with mortar mixes, and after an alchemist's regime of trial and error, we settled upon a mixture of lime, white cement and silica sand (1:2:8). The cracks were first stuffed with fiberglass, then strips of expanded masonry screen, a couple of inches wide, were stapled to the logs. Once the mix was troweled through it, the screen provided lateral strength to withstand seasonal expansion and contraction. The other attraction of the white mortar is the bright visual relief it gives to the dark logs.

Living away from the project had helped to solidify our ideas for floor plans. For example, after three years in the small granary with two young children (by then, our second daughter, Samara, had been born), we realized that the parent-child relationship often is served best from a distance. Therefore, the children's bedrooms are on one floor and ours is on the next. Also, we saw that the layout of the ground floor should correspond to our day-to-day activities and thus should include the kitchen, living room, laundry, sauna, et cetera. Pur-

The first-floor bathroom tiles are delft antiques from the 19th century.

Floor tiles in the kitchen, top right, are thick and cool in the summer—but also in the winter. The salvaged marble-and-quartz fireplace, bottom right, is the focus of the living room.

suing the radial-arm saw, we moved into the barn by occupying each room as soon as the saw moved out.

The kitchen, the nucleus of rural life, is one of the few rooms where utility had precedence over decor . . . probably because Keith did the planning. Working with Webster, she started the design around a triangular relationship between the stove, sink and refrigerator. The main food-processing area in the center of the room is a movable butcher block, fitted with metal flour and sugar bins, utensil drawers and mixing-bowl storage. Close at hand is a floor-to-ceiling food pantry. Aware that much of one's time is spent around the sink, we located it in front of the best view in the kitchen.

The only thing worse for broth than too many cooks is too many non-cooks. Consequently, the main non-cook gathering points in the kitchen—the dinner table and the wood stove—were set apart from the work area. We reasoned that as many hours would be spent doing homework on the table as eating there and as much time passed visiting around the wood stove as cooking on it. The wood stove, by the way, is an Eatonia Climax, which came to us from two birder friends living up the road. Though in excellent condition (even the water jacket is tight), it was occasionally given to smoking: when we found a mummified duck wedged between the oven and the water jacket and removed it, however, the problem immediately cleared.

"Construction should be decorated, not decoration constructed," according to a Victorian maxim. Blissfully ignorant of it, we designed entire rooms around furniture, fixtures and pieces of art. For example, the decor of the first-floor bath was defined around a collection of hand-painted Dutch delft tiles we had discovered years before in a dusty antique shop, and the living room was developed around a 14-foot cherrywood armoire. Initially, we had planned heat-efficient, low-ceilinged rooms and closed stairwells. To accommodate the armoire, this idea was scrapped, and we created a two-story room by cutting out a section of an overhead purlin. The rest of the purlin was supported with a wall, against which the armoire sits, dividing living and dining rooms. In turn, this modification resulted in the mezzanine. From the mezzanine evolved the library and the location of the children's ward.

Many fixtures around which we incorporated the house were salvaged. Four cypress doors and the library fireplace mantle came from an antebellum home in New Orleans, and the doors on the built-in china cabinet in

the dining room were once windows on a turn-of-the-century Vancouver house. Friends also traded treasures they had collected. One of the more intriguing finds was the wood for the mezzanine railings. We had considered numerous woods, but when none fit our ideas, we fabricated a chicken-wire screen to keep the kids from plunging over the edge and resigned ourselves to waiting for the right material. A couple of years later, a Cat driver discovered an old ore crib buried in years of the tailings from an abandoned gold mine. Taking his pocketknife to it, he found the wood was yellow cedar, an increasingly rare commodity even in the northwest. After careful excavation around the crib, it was disassembled, planed down and finally made by Dave Gillespie into spindles and rails.

Finishing Touches

The extra effort and pride the crew took in their work became apparent as the finishing touches of the project evolved. Even fundamental tasks like lighting were handled with imagination. Allen Pickard's lighting around the library is a case in point. Besides the yellow cedar railing and the cypress mantle around the fireplace, teak inlay was set into red cedar frames on the bookcases and karpawood parquet laid on the library floor. Consequently, the room was dungeon-dark despite three floor-to-ceiling windows. The brown tones were offset with green marble around the mantle and lots of plants, but the atmosphere of the room was still too somber. Realizing that light, preferably from above the bookcases, was essential, we first considered track lighting but felt it would create a mood much different from the one we wanted. We also thought about recessed picture lights, but the cost was prohibitive. Noting the muddle, Pickard decided to handmake the light fixtures from scratch. Wiring was strung through the valance, and Pickard added the spark and instant ambience on his first try.

Like a totem, the barn was becoming a chronicle of the events and stories the carvers had shared with us. Following a trip Murray LaBrash and I took to the highlands of the Spatsizi Wilderness Park in northern British Columbia, he made two leaded windows with alpine flowers in the centers for Marley's (our third daughter) and Samara's bedrooms. And the mural in Nicole's room of Raggedy Ann and Andy skiing grew out of the opulent imaginations of artist Carl Chaplin and our children while they were snowbound one winter. The girls told Chaplin the story, he drew in the figures, and then with Job-like forbearance, he

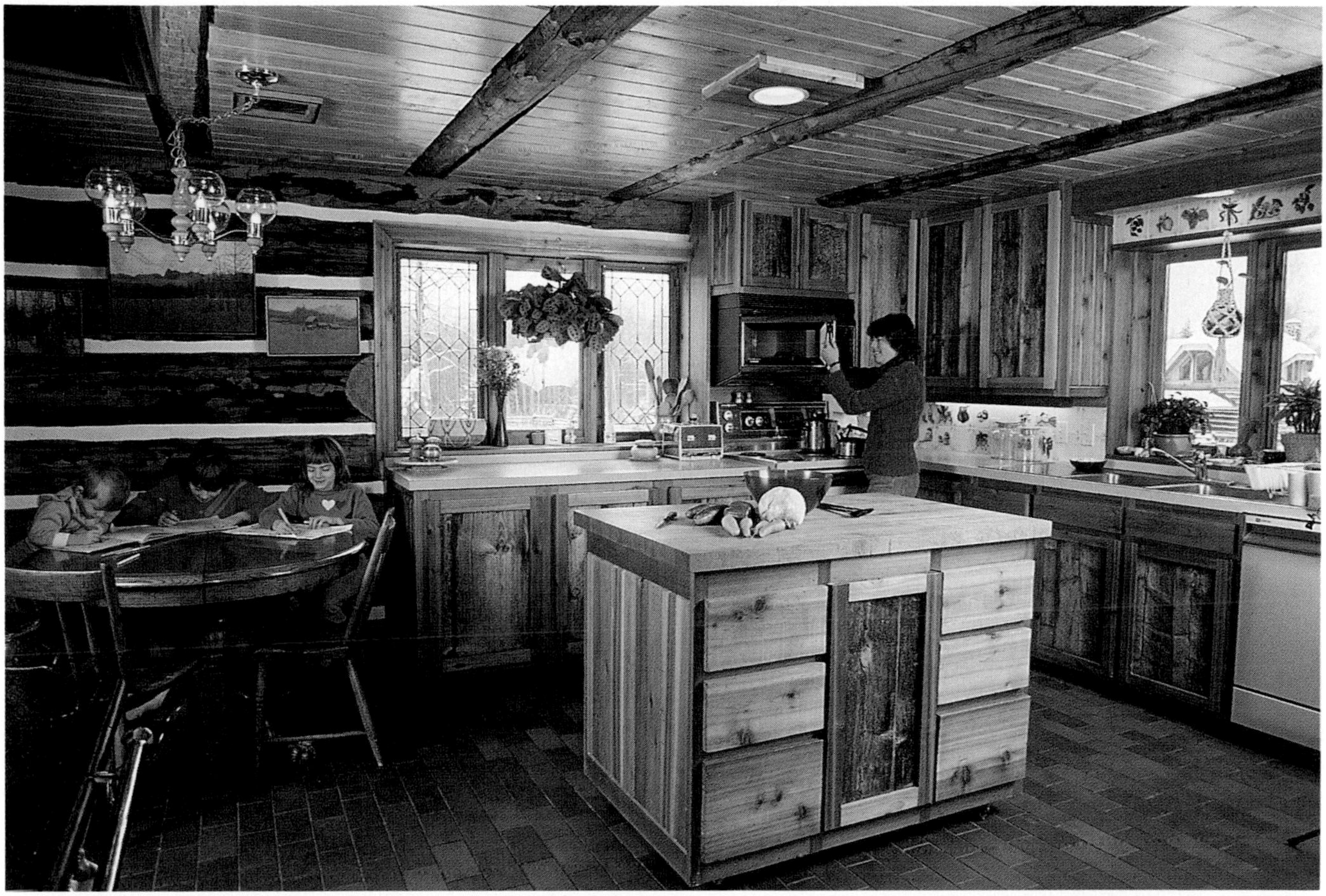

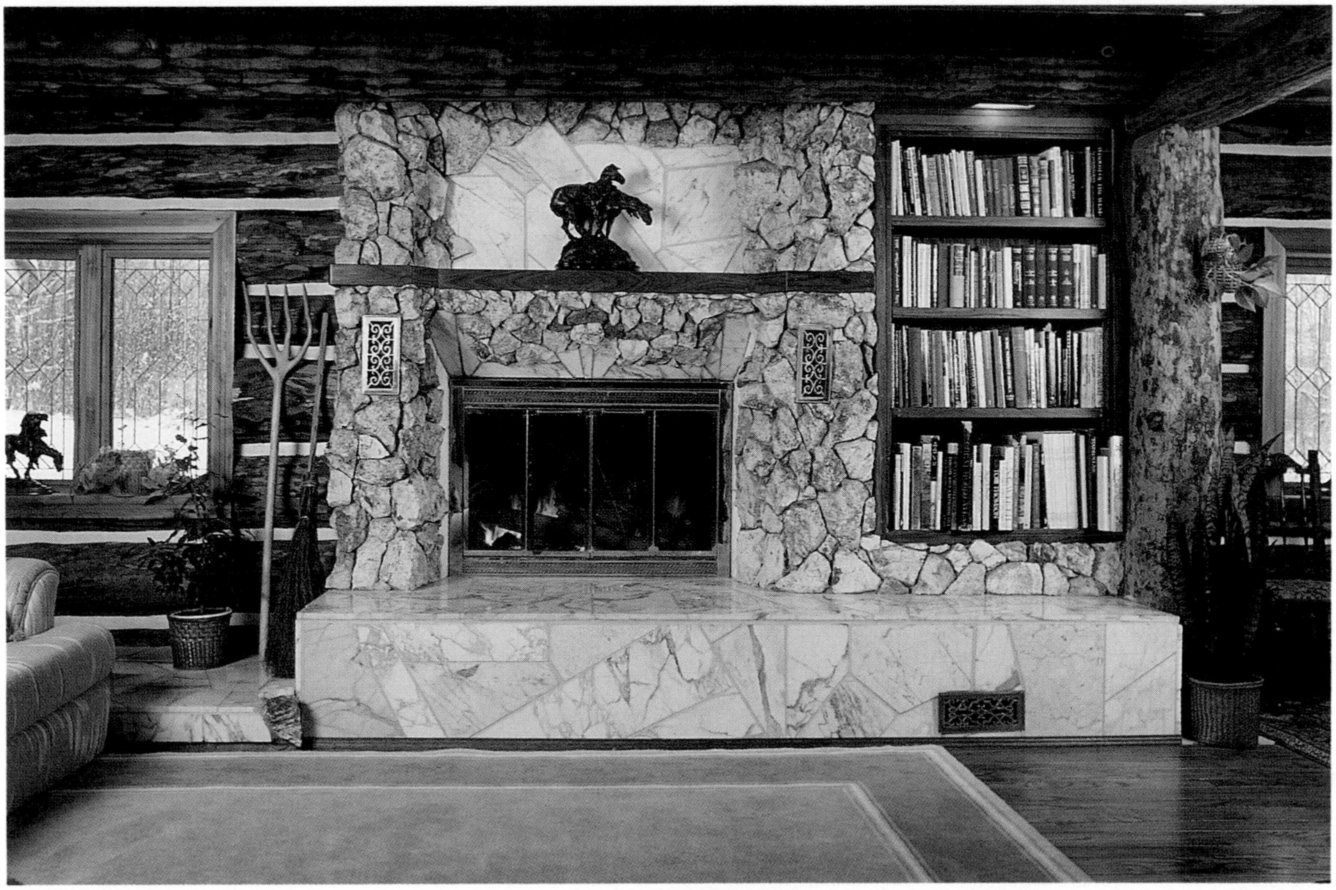

stepped back to let the children do the painting. The project was also becoming a family record as relatives showed up to help. The two-story cedar ceiling above the living room was fitted and finished by our niece, Carter Mannion. Even my mother was conscripted to make a stained glass window for the third-floor bath.

As the last pieces of the renovation puzzle fell into place, I could no longer put off doing the stonework on the living room fireplace. But the task terrified me. The fireplace would be the central focus of the first floor and would therefore set the mood for much of the house. To complicate matters, I wanted to try mixing the mediums of marble and stone (white quartz latticed with galena and pyrite) to accent a mantle sculpture, *Storm Driven*, by James Earl Fraser. What I saw in the statue was the rough, sinewy form of a wild horse detailed with emotive elegance. But faced with barbed wire and grey block, my goal seemed rather remote.

There was one encouraging aspect about working in marble and malleable quartz: both can be cut and shaped into patterns – unlike the red rust-colored rock used to face the exterior of the chimneys, which shattered like an iron skillet when struck with a chisel. Using off-cuts of polished marble, which cost a fraction of full slabs, a mosaic hearth was made by cutting the marble with a masonry blade in a skill saw, making shallow cuts and several passes and atomizing the rock with water to keep it from heating and chipping. To enhance the individual rocks in the fireplace, their joints were recessed.

Marble was inset behind the statue, using its grey streaks to accentuate the sweep of the sculpture. The fireplace doors were also framed with marble, thus drawing the eye to the fire chamber and reflecting light out across the galena and pyrite crystals. After experimenting with a number of woods, Lyle Lepky made the bookcase adjoining the fireplace and mantle around it out of moradillo wood because of its deep burgundy brown. Finally, Pickard did his magic with recessed lights in an adjacent log purlin.

It had been exactly 10 years from the day I had first seen Gunderson's barn to the day of completion of the fireplace and the laying of the final hardwood flooring. But not all that time was spent renovating. Considerable energy was expended building up the farm, clearing land, replacing fences, cutting hay. Also, with the barn in the service of humans, the livestock, robins and barn swallows needed shelter. So with Glen Buchanan and Stephen Fearing, we built the post-and-beam "barn barn." In addition, the logs from a derelict building on a neighboring ranch were numbered, disassembled and reassembled into a two-story shop adjacent to the main house. And finally, a chicken coop, which some warned was beyond saving, was stripped, set on a new foundation and eventually converted into a guest house.

Now that we are ensconced in the log ark with the storms of necessity at bay, I tend to forget that the rewards of the renovation have been as great in the going as in the goal. We have learned about far more than measurements and materials. For just as we learned about Gunderson through his work, we have learned about ourselves through our labors on his barn. It has also been a binding process, forming the crew into a large extended family: Andy Webster met and married Jane, the project's chief chinker; Gaston Porterie married Lovely LaRae; and Quentin Robbins is the godfather to one of our children.

And the process still is not finished. There are window seats to go in the dormers, a pipe in the root cellar has to be reset, and while I am there, I should counterbalance that heavy trapdoor. But sitting before the fireplace in the living room, where cows and porcupines once held sway, I sometimes wonder if even our efforts will be the last. Perhaps fate has destined another unsuspecting soul to look at Gunderson's barn, now Bassetts' home, and conjure yet grander dreams for it. 🌱

The yellow cedar for the mezzanine railings came from an ore crib found in an abandoned gold mine.

Solar Delivery

Neither Snow nor Dark of Night Can Chill This Owner-Built, Double-Envelope House

By Craig Canine with Photography by Richard W. Brown

Bambi Jones and Tracy Moscovitz lead double lives. They get up each morning at 5:30, don overalls, T-shirts and muddy boots, and start the day as vegetable farmers.

By 6 a.m., two helpers have arrived out at the barn. Tracy climbs onto a John Deere tractor with a front-end loader, its bucket brimful of wire baskets poised to receive the morning's harvest. Bambi and the helpers pile into a red pickup and follow Tracy as he drives the tractor out to the gardens. He straddles a vegetable bed with the tractor's wheels, moving forward at a creep while the three others toss lettuce, leeks and honeydew melons into the wire baskets. The baskets are soon full, and the group moves back to the barn to wash, sort and box the produce.

At 8 a.m., Tracy disappears into the house. He emerges 20 minutes later, his mud-spattered overalls exchanged for clean khaki trousers, a dress shirt and a sweater.

Along with his clothes, he has changed names: now he is David Moscovitz, one of three Public Utilities Commissioners in the state of Maine. David, his given name and professional moniker, is a lawyer and one of the nation's leading authorities on least-cost energy planning and conservation strategies for electric utility companies. Tracy, a nickname he picked up in college, is what his friends and agricultural acquaintances call him. On his way to the PUC offices in Augusta, David the commissioner will make a few appearances as Tracy the farmer as he drops off boxes of vegetables at some of mid-coastal Maine's finest restaurants.

After Tracy leaves for work, Bambi works around the farm for a few more hours until she, too, steps into the house and transforms herself from vegetable farmer to urban professional. She works long afternoons as an attorney for a small law firm in Damariscotta, a town on the Maine coast. She specializes in the legal aspects of real estate, land conservation and affordable housing. Bambi, too, is an adopted name. Her real first name is Barbara, though she hasn't been called that since she was a young child, when her father nicknamed her Bambi.

At the intersection of Jones and Moscovitz's double identities is the house they designed and built for themselves on the 115 acres they call Hidden Valley Farm. The house serves their needs well as a home base for their market-gardening operation, and it also reflects

concerns from their professional lives—especially their interests in affordable housing and energy efficiency. In 1982, their 2,400-square-foot house cost them about $60,000 to build (not including land), and it requires less than a cord of wood to heat each year. "It's a great house," Moscovitz says with justifiable pride. "We're very happy with it.

"Before we built it, we cut six or seven cords of wood a year to heat our old farmhouse. Now we cut a year's worth of firewood in an afternoon. Heating this house with wood isn't a hassle in any way."

Their home's low fuel requirement is only one measure of efficiency at Hidden Valley Farm. The daily routines of cooking, cleaning up, caring for the gardens and attending to livestock (feeder hogs and beef cattle) are all made simpler by various time- and labor-saving measures they have adopted over the years. The harvest procedure, with produce baskets carried by the tractor's bucket instead of by each human picker, is one small example. Another is the carefully planned layout of the barn, which enables Moscovitz to feed 22 pigs in less than two minutes a day.

Several modest expedients like these, scattered throughout the house, barn and greenhouse, add up to a large cumulative savings of time and effort, and make it possible for the hard-working couple to enjoy their dual occupations. "Tracy has an engineering background," Jones says. "He likes to be inventive and is always figuring out better ways to do things. I'm perfectly happy to sit in the garden all day and weed. He finds ways for me to do it faster."

Moscovitz pursues efficiency as though playing a game of chess, as much for the pleasure and challenge as for the practical benefits. "Efficiency isn't a religion or a belief structure for me," he says. "It just makes sense and saves a lot of money besides."

Bambi Jones and Tracy Moscovitz moved from Chicago to Maine in 1977 and bought a 120-acre farm near the village of Alna a year later. "It was your basic back-to-the-land impulse," Jones says. "I had started gardening in college in the Midwest and even had a small garden plot in downtown Chicago. We were looking for a place with some land and found this old farm with an abandoned farmhouse. We went to the FmHA (Farmers Home Administration) for a mortgage. They said, 'No,

This Maine hybrid combines features of a double-envelope design with those of earth-sheltered house construction.

A central hearth runs upward through the center of the house, absorbing heat radiated from the sun and giving it off when the sun sets.

we only make loans to farmers, and you really aren't farmers.' So we got short-term financing from the farm's previous owners and planted some vegetables – enough to persuade the FmHA that we were qualified. They were convinced, and we've been farming ever since.

"After we bought the place," she continues, "several people advised us to tear down the old farmhouse. It hadn't been occupied for eight years and had no plumbing or electricity. But the family who sold us the farm had lived in that house for generations. Some members of the family still lived in the area, so we decided not to tear the house down, out of respect for them. It took us a year to fix it up – longer than it took us to build our new house from scratch."

Neither of them had much previous experience in building or renovating houses. They learned as they went. "Tearing down and building back up an old house," Jones says, "you learn a lot by observing others' mistakes and fixing them."

They knew all along that they would eventually build a new house somewhere on the farm, but had no idea at first what kind of house it would be or exactly where they would build it. After a few years of living on the property, they chose a site on the north edge of a south-sloping hay meadow. Then they started pondering a design for their new house.

"The old farm setup showed us everything we didn't want in a new place," Moscovitz says. "We decided pretty quickly that we didn't want to have to lug water around for animals, carry hay to and from the barn or cut and burn seven cords of wood a winter." With a view toward selling the old farmhouse, they fixed it up

better than new, and also built a new garage nearby. At the same time, they began collecting ideas for a new place that would be simple and relatively inexpensive, yet elegant. "It was a casual but steady planning process that took place over three years," he says. "During that time, we took an adult-education course in drafting and house design. The teacher was a local architect whose work we liked. As we came up with questions during the designing, we could ask him. There was minimal formal instruction. We mainly used the time as a disciplined time for drawing."

They also visited several houses that appealed to them. In particular, they sought out examples of a type of house called the "double envelope," a solar design touted in the late 1970s as the ultimate in energy efficiency. A cross-sectional view of a double-envelope house reveals not one but two houses, one built inside the other. The outer shell encloses a greenhouse, or sunspace, on the house's south side. In the roof and the north side of the house, the double envelope's inner and outer shells are separated by at least 6 inches of air space. A plenum, or crawl space, below the inner shell completes a continuous gap between the two thermal envelopes, through which air can circulate in a loop.

The double-envelope house works this way: on a sunny day, air in the greenhouse warms, causing it to rise and enter the air channel in the roof. The warm air displaces cooler air, which falls downward through the void in the north wall and collects in the basement crawl space. Then, propelled by convection, the air moves south again and re-enters the greenhouse, where it warms up, rises and makes another circuit around the convective loop. The continuous bath of warm or lukewarm air circulating around the walls of the inner shell helps heat the living space.

In theory, the air circulating around the convective loop also gives up some of its warmth to the earth beneath the crawl space. This thermal energy is stored there until nightfall, when the convective loop reverses itself. As the temperature of the greenhouse drops below that of the crawl space, the relatively warm air in the crawl space rises up the north wall, moves south along the roof channel, then falls into the greenhouse, keeping it warmer than it would otherwise be at night.

There is no denying that houses built according to the double-envelope formula are highly energy-efficient – but not necessarily because the system works exactly as predicted. Skeptics have pointed out that any house with two insulated shells (forming a thermal barrier more than a foot thick) and an attached, south-facing greenhouse would perform extremely efficiently. The convective loop and earth-coupled crawl space, they suggest, may not be justified. Some energy experts would contend that the more straightforward technique of superinsulation could achieve similarly impressive results more cost-effectively than the double-envelope approach.

Jones and Moscovitz had a different qualm about the double-envelope houses they visited. "The thing that discouraged us about them was the buffer zone between indoors and outdoors," Jones says. "With the double walls, you were always separated from the outdoors by an intermediate space. Another problem was that we liked the idea of a greenhouse on the south side, but we'd had enough experience with horticultural greenhouses to know they generate huge amounts of humidity and pests. So an attached greenhouse didn't seem like a good idea."

The design they slowly developed combined some features of the double-envelope scheme with features from earth-sheltered house construction. Though the double envelope in its pure form is rarely built anymore, their variation incorporates the best features of the design while eliminating its disadvantages. Built into a small hillside, their house's north wall is almost entirely earth-bermed, while its south side is fully exposed to the sun. The earth's constant temperature, combined with tight, well-insulated walls, ensure that the temperature in the house never drops below about 50 degrees F. The difference between ambient earth temperature (which, a few feet below the surface, only varies by several degrees year-round) and a comfortable indoor temperature of 65 to 70 degrees (a difference of 15 to 20 degrees) is taken care of largely by solar heat, which enters through extensive glazing on the south side of the house.

The south walls on each of two levels are 40 feet long, and both consist almost entirely of double-glazed windows. Some of the windows can be opened for summer ventilation; the rest are fixed. The fixed windows are inexpensive patio-door replacement units, but Moscovitz worries that the silicone seal holding these units in place may someday leak. He plans to replace them with the latest in window technology: sealed, double-glazed units filled with argon gas and coated, on one surface, with a low-emissivity film. These replacement windows will have twice the insulating value of the existing units.

But a simple earth-bermed house with lots of south-facing windows would have major problems, which Moscovitz and Jones anticipated.

They realized that if there were no way to circulate the solar-heated air, the south side of the house would tend to overheat, even in winter, while the north side would remain uncomfortably cold and dark.

To avoid hot and cold spots, they adapted the convective loop idea from double-envelope theory. But they "opened up" the envelope by removing the separation between inner and outer shells on the south side and part of the roof. This eliminated the intermediate zone between indoors and outdoors on the south; it also did away with the enclosed greenhouse

Bambi Jones and Tracy Moscovitz.

and its attendant problems. Instead of warming the interior space indirectly by means of an attached greenhouse, the sun warms the living space of Jones and Moscovitz's house directly through the south-facing windows.

This modification aside, the house works much like a true double envelope (see diagram). "We decided to incorporate the partial envelope and convective loop because we wanted the house to be comfortable no matter where you were," Moscovitz says. "We wanted to have the feeling of central heat but without central heat. The loop accomplishes that pretty well."

They have discovered one drawback: a few years ago, they tested for, and found, traces of radon, a naturally occurring radioactive gas.

*Top, **the convective loop in a true double envelope with attached greenhouse. In the Moskovitz-Jones modification,** bottom, **the sun warms the living area directly.***

The carcinogenic gas seeps into the house from the earth beneath the crawl space. To eliminate the radon, they installed an air-to-air heat exchanger within the convective loop. When the level of relative humidity in the house reaches 40 percent, the heat exchanger turns on automatically, exhausting stale, humid air and bringing in a fresh supply.

On exceptionally cold days or during a cloudy spell, one of them lights a fire in a wood stove that nestles in an alcove of their massive brick hearth. The hearth, measuring about 6 feet wide by 2½ feet thick, rises upward through the middle of the house. It acts as thermal mass, absorbing some of the heat radiated by both the stove and the sun, and later slowly giving off the captured heat after the fire has gone out or the sun has gone down.

The wood stove is installed on the lower of the house's two levels, where the master bedroom and bathroom are located. "We designed the house upside down, with the kitchen, living room and dining area upstairs and the main bedroom downstairs," Moscovitz explains. "We like the space where we live during the day to be a little warmer than the space where we sleep. With this kind of construction, where the lower level is largely buried in earth and the main entryway is on the upper level, the upside-down floor plan works out pretty well.

"And, unlike most people's conception of an earth-bermed house," he adds, "it's bright and airy inside." Two large roof windows, as well as several windows on the east and west sides of the upper level, reduce glare from the south glazing and admit natural light into the far northern reaches of the house. An open well containing a spiral staircase allows some of the daylight to penetrate to the lower level.

Artificial lighting is also plentiful, though the cost of the lighting is a fraction of what it might be. Nearly every fixture is equipped with an adaptor for a super-efficient fluorescent light bulb. These bulbs, made by companies like Panasonic, Phillips and Mitsubishi, put out about the same amount of warm, pleasant light as a normal 60-watt incandescent bulb, but they consume a quarter as much electricity and last 10 times longer.

The house at Hidden Valley Farm is a quarter-mile from the road, but Jones and Moscovitz never considered generating their own electricity with a photovoltaic (solar-electric) setup. They hooked up to the grid just before the local utility company started charging customers for bringing power lines to off-road house sites. "We're efficient," Moscovitz says, "but we do use electricity. It's hard to have a welder and a VCR without it."

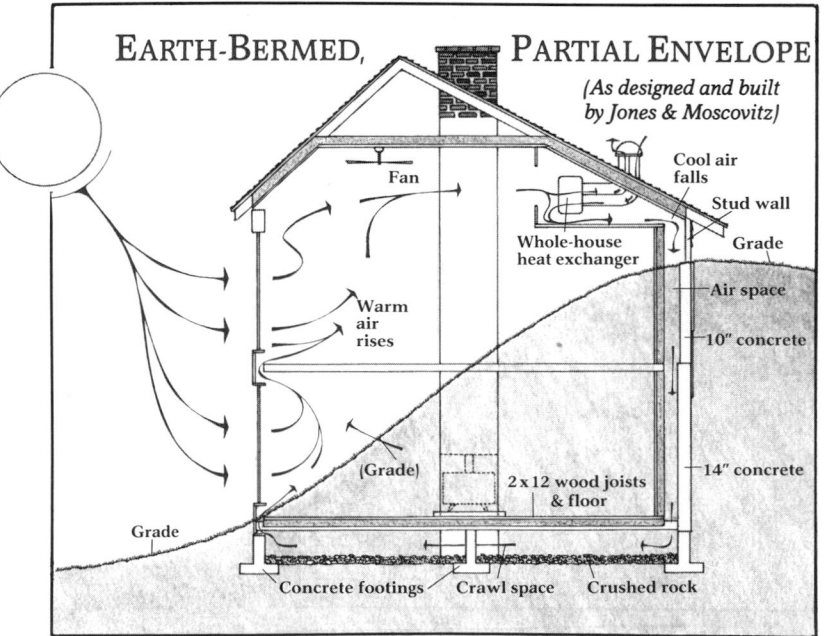

TRUE DOUBLE ENVELOPE

Sunny Day
(Loop reverses at night)

Outer shell

Attached greenhouse

Air channel

Inner shell

Concrete

Grade

Gravel   Crawl space

EARTH-BERMED,   PARTIAL ENVELOPE

(As designed and built by Jones & Moscovitz)

Fan

Cool air falls

Stud wall

Whole-house heat exchanger

Grade

Air space

Warm air rises

10" concrete

(Grade)

14" concrete

2 x 12 wood joists & floor

Grade

Concrete footings   Crawl space   Crushed rock

Though frugal and hard-working, Jones and Moscovitz are anything but ascetics. They put extra care and money into many details that make their house a more pleasant place to live. A carpenter friend did the kitchen cabinetry, bathroom cabinetry and upstairs trim using oak and maple cut from the 100-acre woodlot at Hidden Valley Farm. Countertops in the kitchen and two bathrooms are 4 inches higher than the usual 36 inches, making them noticeably more comfortable to use for people who are even slightly taller than average.

The 2-inch-thick oak floorboards on both levels were also cut from native timber, then taken to a nearby mill to be tongued-and-grooved. More native wood is visible in the maple wainscoting that surrounds the living and dining areas. The wainscoting is built out from the walls about 4 inches. It conceals electrical wiring. "That way," Moscovitz says, "we didn't have to penetrate the vapor barrier for wiring and outlets."

Jones and Moscovitz made the built-in, closet-sized cabinets in their bedroom themselves, also from wood cut off their own property. They finished the inside of the large shower in the master bathroom with cedar clapboards—a water-resistant surface that is both easier to install and less expensive than good ceramic tile, yet just as attractive.

One material they did not economize on was concrete. Their house contains 80 cubic yards of it—three times as much as most conventional houses use. But this house is, in effect, about half basement, buried below grade. Its owners didn't want to worry about cracks or leaks in the foundation. "We're real believers in foundations," Moscovitz says. "If the foundation isn't right, nothing else can be right. There's a lot of frost in this part of the world, and frost heaves can easily ruin a poorly made foundation. We want our buildings to last more or less forever. So we used a lot of concrete, with steel in all the right places."

The earth-bermed north foundation wall is 14 feet tall, while the east and west walls of the foundation step down in height, following the contour of the gentle hillside into which the house is built. The steel-reinforced foundation walls are 14 inches thick at the bottom and 10 inches thick at the top. Building the forms and pouring the concrete for these walls was one job Jones and Moscovitz contracted out. They had already built a foundation to similar specifications for their new barn. "We knew we could build the house foundation, too," Jones says, "but our time was better spent supervising a professional crew than doing it ourselves."

Once the foundation walls were poured and the forms stripped, Jones and Moscovitz ap-

Moskovitz and Jones built their greenhouse with a truss system adapted from their barn plans.

plied sheets of bentonite waterproofing to the outside of the concrete. "The waterproofing comes in 4-by-4-foot sheets that look like corrugated cardboard with a fine powder [bentonite, a natural clay] in the flutes of the corrugations," Moscovitz says. "When the powder gets wet, it turns to a gelatinous mass that can expand to 25 times its original volume. The wetter it gets, the more it expands and tries to fill any holes or cracks that might develop in the concrete. With black tar [the usual substance used to waterproof foundations], if the wall cracks, you've got a crack in your waterproofing. The bentonite sheets were about three times more expensive than black tar, but it's worthwhile insurance. We've never had any trace of moisture in the lower floor of the house."

Besides being well-waterproofed, the foundation is also well-insulated. "There are 4 inches of rigid foam insulation around the top 4 feet of the foundation," he says. "The next 2 feet have 2 inches of foam, and the next 2 feet have 1 inch. There's no insulation below that, since below 8 feet in the ground never gets colder than 50 degrees. Because of all that contact with the earth, the whole house is trying to be 50 degrees, year-round."

The house measures 40 feet by 30 feet on both of two levels, yielding more square-

The house was built "upside down" with the kitchen, dining area, and main living area upstairs. These rooms stay warmer, while bedrooms on the earth-bermed first floor remain cool.

moved into the house the following January. Roughly a quarter of the house (two large rooms downstairs) remains unfinished, and serves as storage space.

They brought the same degree of forethought to the design and construction of their barn and greenhouse. The barn is compact, yet serves several functions at once: hay storage, livestock shelter, equipment shed, toolshop and vegetable-washing station. One end of the barn is banked with earth, permitting a truck or tractor to drive into the upper level, where hay is unloaded and stored. There's a hole in the floor of the haymow directly above a manger in the livestock pen on the lower level. Feeding the animals is a simple matter of kicking a bale or two through the hole. A trickling hose keeps the watering trough full.

The greenhouse was last year's construction project. For it, Jones and Moscovitz scaled down the same truss pattern that they had previously used on the gambrel-roofed barn, built from plans they had obtained from the Maine extension service. The south side of the greenhouse is clad with Phylon, sheets of a translucent fiberglass material that is guaranteed to last for 20 years. To insulate the north side, they used foam-board with a foil facing. Sunlight reflects off the silver backing, making the greenhouse brighter in the daytime.

From late winter through August, Jones starts about 1,500 lettuce seedlings a week in the greenhouse, including some 30 varieties. She plants the seedlings in flats resting on large tables. Under the tables, 600 "sono buoys" stand upright, holding water that absorbs and stores solar heat. The sono buoys are plastic cylinders, about 6 inches in diameter, that the Navy and Coast Guard use for radar-detection purposes, then discard. Each one contains 7 gallons of water. "On a typical day," Moscovitz says, "they'll take in about 1.5 million BTUs, the equivalent of 10 gallons of fuel oil. That mass, plus the concrete floor and the insulation, make the greenhouse much more economical to heat. It takes about one-fourth the fuel to heat this greenhouse than it would take to heat a conventional greenhouse of similar size."

The cost of building such an energy-efficient structure is higher than that of buying and erecting a prefabricated greenhouse kit, in spite of the savings Jones and Moscovitz realized by building it themselves and by finding bargains on materials like the sono buoys. But the operating costs are so low that they figure they'll recover their extra capital investment in a few seasons, then reap a profit from the additional savings. It's the same principle that Moscovitz has spent his years as a Public Utilities Commissioner drumming into the heads of utility-

footage than the two of them have found ways to use – or time to finish. "We could have built a smaller house," Moscovitz says, "but given the design, it's hard to add onto. So we decided to build as big a house as we thought we might need, then finish the rooms as we needed them." By the time they built the house, Jones and Moscovitz were seasoned owner-builders. Their construction résumés already included the renovated farmhouse and its garage, as well as a barn by the site of the new house. This experience helped the house project proceed smoothly and quickly: they stripped the concrete forms off the foundation in July and

company executives—that a megawatt saved is better than a megawatt burned.

And it's the same principle he and Jones applied to building their house. They spent a little more time and money up front on efficiency features, but the investment has already paid off. In general, Moscovitz estimates that the premium for energy-efficient house construction is around 5 percent of the house's total cost. For them, that additional investment went for things like high-quality windows, extra insulation, excavation and concrete work for the earth-bermed foundation, plus miscellaneous items like caulking and materials for a vapor barrier.

"For an additional 5 percent over what we would have paid for conventional construction," Moscovitz says, "we have a house that's warm in winter, cool in summer, healthful, bright and cheery, and requires very little maintenance. I'd say that's a pretty good deal."

Moscovitz is taking time out from the office to eat lunch at Slates, a popular restaurant among Augusta's business-lunch crowd. During the meal, his two identities as David the commissioner and Tracy the farmer mingle inextricably—as when several executives from Maine Central Power, the state's largest utility company, walk past the table while he is in the middle of a conversation about vegetable farming. He greets the utility executives, then resumes the farm talk, pointing out that the bustling restaurant is Hidden Valley Farm's biggest single customer. "This place goes through about 20 cases of lettuce, 100 pounds of tomatoes and 5 pounds of basil a week," he says. When a large salad arrives, he proudly points out the ingredients he and Jones grew: the tomatoes, cucumbers, lettuce, red cabbage and red peppers—virtually the whole meal, except for the tuna.

Far from seeming incongruous, his professional and agrarian roles complement each other neatly: it is David the efficiency expert who makes it possible for Tracy the farmer to accomplish as much as he does in a day. He admits that holding down the equivalent of two full-time jobs imposes strains at times. But he and Jones have clearly found a formula they thrive on, and neither of them foresees curtailing one career in favor of the other. "I like both lives," Moscovitz says, "and would just as soon not give up either one." ❧

The barn is compact, yet serves as hay storage, livestock shelter, and toolshed.

Carved in Stone

REHABILITATING A 150-YEAR-OLD STONE HOUSE

BY MICHAEL WEBSTER WITH PHOTOGRAPHY BY JIM MERRITHEW

Entering the town of Merrickville, Ontario, is somewhat like boring into the trunk of an ancient, gnarled oak tree. After peeling off the outer bark of angelstone-and-aluminum-siding bungalows, one encounters the community's growth rings, irregularly concentric circles of history that reveal the life of the town. Although the outer rings indicate a 50-year period of drought with very little growth, a ring of pleasant 2-story and 1½-story clapboard-sided homes encloses a circle of imposing brick houses – not the square farmhouses typical of much of this area but imaginative buildings cluttered with such Victorian gewgawery as spires, turrets, arches, bay windows and gingerbread trim. Inside this circle is a band of 150-year-old limestone buildings in excellent condition, and inside that – nearly 200 years old and established when Merrickville was but a sapling in a wild meadow – are stone ruins, as picturesque and intriguing as any medieval castle.

At the heart of the town, and the rootstock from which it sprang, is a rapids on the Rideau River, now skirted by lock number 21 of the Rideau Canal. In 1793, when William Merrick, an entrepreneurial 33-year-old Loyalist, arrived from New England at what was then called Great Falls, he immediately saw the

Exposed stone and wood, far right, add texture to the rich colors in Devlin's 1½ century-old limestone house, right.

potential of the site and established an industrial complex that eventually included foundries, sawmills, a gristmill, a woollen mill, an ax-handle factory and more, each drawing some or all of its power from the fall and flow of the river. Today, though some of these buildings are in ruins, others remain in industrial use.

The commercial section of the town that sprang up in response to Merrick's initiative lies across the canal, and it is still the downtown core, now renovated with new sidewalks, clean façades and fresh paint as part of a newfound municipal sense of heritage, due in part, no doubt, to a desire to divert summer tourist dollars from the well-traveled canal. At the edge of the downtown strip, on a corner of the main street that separates a pub from the town's residential section, is an unimposing 1½-story stone house that serves as home and studio for artist Joyce Devlin. According to Nigel Hutchins, a local preservation consultant who specializes in pre-1900 architecture, "Joyce's house is probably one of the earliest houses in Merrickville."

Actually, says Hutchins, the T-shaped house was built in two stages: the first part, a simple workman's cottage, between 1825 and 1835, and the second around 1860 to 1880. When Devlin bought the house in 1981, the original portion provided a scant 900 square feet of living space, and the newer part was a disused motorcycle shop. Devlin has since renovated both sections of the house, living in the old part and turning the other into a studio with a sleeping loft for guests. Also, she has appended a 42-foot-long shed-roof wood addition clad in board-and-batten siding that spans the full length of the back of the building and provides space for kitchen and dining facilities as well as a room which was intended for flowers and a "privacy corner" but which in practice is used for storage. The decor throughout

Though it suits the 2-foot-thick walls and antique furniture, the Rumford fireplace smokes so badly, it is all but unusable.

is a unique combination of whimsy and practicality that offers a hospitable face to visitors without compromising Devlin's privacy. "I would class Joyce's house as a rehabilitation, rather than a historical renovation," says Hutchins. "It's well-designed – the aesthetics are great – and it's a functioning building that works as a studio as well as a home. I enjoy being in it."

The house was not Devlin's first choice. A sawyer's daughter from the Okanagan Valley, with a strong chin and lightly flecked brown eyes that exactly match her hair, she has been drawn to the eastern Ontario area since 1965 – "I think we gravitate to places that are a metaphor for ourselves," she says. "I am haunted by the landscape here" – and was living in Ottawa when circumstances forced her to look for a new house. "I wanted the country, but I couldn't find anything I could afford that suited me," she recalls. "I'd been to Merrickville 15 years ago, and this was not one of the houses that attracted me at all; but I drove here to visit a friend, and he said, 'Come and look at this little house on the corner.' I said, 'No way, I don't want to live in that little house.'

Well, we came in, and it was *so* little, but I looked around and crawled through the little door and finally said, 'Okay, cut this off, take that out, put an addition on – okay, I'll have it.' Because," she says with the confidential air of someone who still cannot believe her own good fortune, "I got it for $26,000 plus a mortgage of $8,000 at 8 percent. I came to Merrickville because I could afford it." Now in her 50s, Devlin is a respected painter, perhaps best known for her portraits – which hang in the Senate of Canada and in numerous public and private collections – and she has always earned a living from her art, even when still in art school, although she has never been wealthy. Financial considerations are, consequently, as important for her as they are for most Canadians.

Still, the purchase price was only a beginning – Devlin estimates she has spent another $25,000 to $30,000 in renovations. She started with the motorcycle shop, an 18-by-30-foot rectangle in which the second floor was unused and the first floor was divided into three small, dingy rooms. Although it was relatively easy to tear out the downstairs partitions

with the help of her youngest son and locally hired workmen, the floor was caked with years of grease. "We scraped and scraped and *scraped*," she recalls with an expressive flourish of hands. Lye soap finally lifted enough grease to allow the 6-inch boards to take a coat of paint, but before the space could become a studio, Devlin needed more light and more room for her large canvases than the low-ceilinged ground floor offered. Her solution was to tear out half the ceiling and raise the second-floor ceiling, then install skylights in the roof. What remains of the second floor, accessible only from the upstairs hallway in the other part of the house, is given over to a sleeping loft for guests. The old plaster was not salvageable, so Devlin tore it out, then reinsulated – "not the maximum amount, but adequate" – and, with fond memories of helping her father bring in firewood, installed a wood stove. The final phase of the studio rehabilitation was the enlarging of a low doorway – almost a crawl-through – to the rest of the house, and in the process of tearing out the old stonework, workers found, and used again, a stone arch that must have spanned a door or win-

dow. Devlin moved into the house in August 1981 and had the studio ready for an open house the following summer.

The older part of the house had been partially renovated when Devlin moved in, and indeed, the previous occupants had uncovered a stone fireplace on the east wall when they moved the staircase to the other side of the room. Devlin took out some nonbearing partitions and "stripped everything right down to the stone." And again, she found a forgotten doorway – the original front door. Since there was a "business entrance" in the studio already opening to the street, Devlin, who prefers the privacy of the back door, decided not to re-open this one; instead, she made it into a window that, on the inside, matches two other windows on the same wall. On the outside, it is framed in to ground level, thus giving the appearance of a doorway and retaining some of the authenticity of the original design. "That off-center door is a very Georgian feature," Hutchins notes.

After 150 years of use, the floorboards, all of them a foot or more in width, are worn, and some have more than the normal amount of

The house faces a busy main street, but Devlin enjoys the peaceful privacy of her addition: "It makes the whole house."

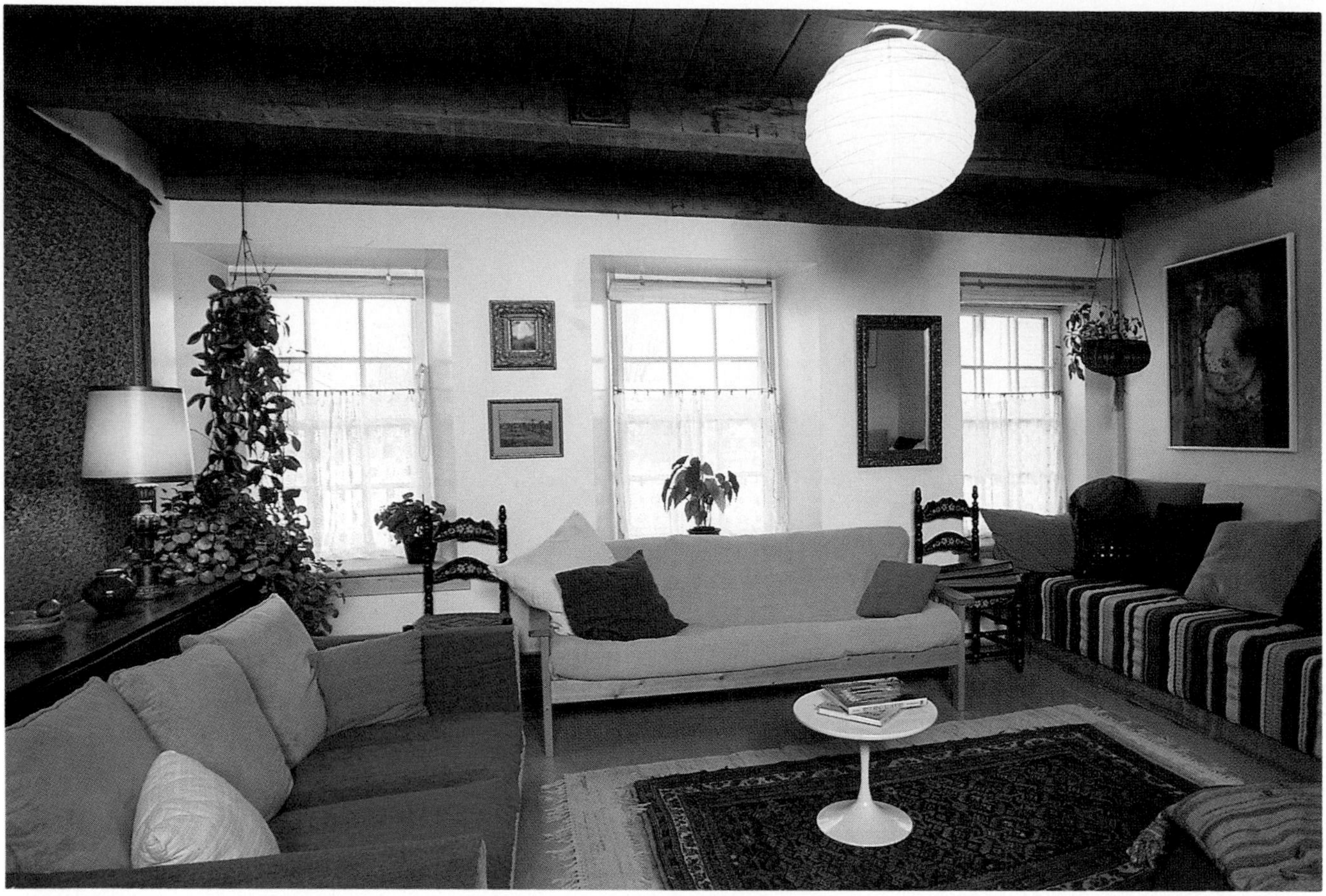

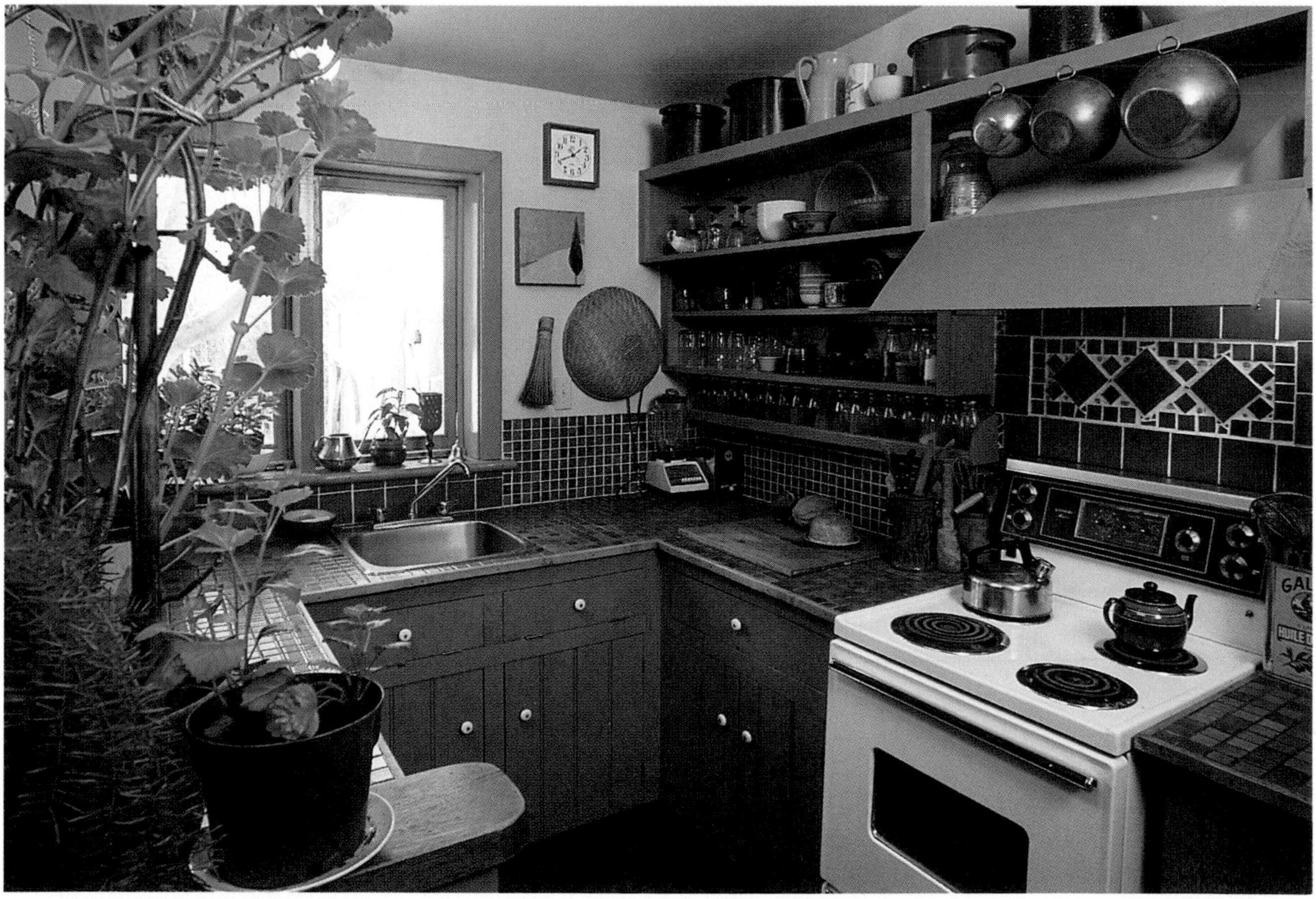

spring. Those by the old back door, now an interior door from the addition, are hollowed from years of first steps inside, except for knots which, like granite ridges in a soapstone plain, have better resisted the wear and stand defiantly above the surrounding contours. Devlin, once again opting for authenticity, added yet another coat of paint to the many that already covered the floor. Previous owners had stripped the ceiling and coated the exposed white ash beams with Varathane, giving them a mottled appearance Devlin dislikes. "It makes them look like hard rock candy," she says in disgust.

The fireplace, so recently unearthed, is an anomaly. Though it has the high, shallow firebox of the Rumford design, "it's the only fireplace in Merrickville with no smoke shelf and no damper," says Devlin. "Well, I wouldn't say it's the only one that doesn't have a smoke shelf," counters Hutchins, "but it's a peculiar style." He adds that the fireplace helps date the house to pre-1830, when a tax was levied on fireplaces, and cast-iron stoves became the norm. As would be expected of a fireplace with no smoke shelf, this one does not work very well and tends to smoke a lot. Devlin guesses that is why it was covered over in the first place, and she keeps the throat blocked with fiberglass insulation batts and a strip of polyethylene. Still, the exposed stonework is an attractive feature of the living room, though no more striking there than in the upstairs bathroom, where the chimney face serves as a backdrop for the vanity and mirror.

The rest of the second floor consists of a medium-sized master bedroom, a crooked hallway and lots of built-in storage space, all tied together with a rich broadloom, installed to control air movement and "to stop things from falling through the cracks in the floorboards." Although she has raised the ceilings in the bedrooms, replacing the rafter bracing with exposed 2-by-8 rough-cut cross ties, the bathroom and hallway ceilings are low, and the doorway to the loft is well under 6 feet. Such features, as well as the 2-foot-thick walls, the worn floorboards and the exposed stone, betray the age of the building: skylights and fresh plaster notwithstanding, there is no mistaking the house for a reproduction.

Beyond the normal wear and tear of 150 years of use, though, there is no sign of weakness or deterioration in the building, and the inherent strength and solidity of the stone structure is a tribute to the traditional styling and skill of the masons who built it. According to Hutchins, those masons came from the United Kingdom at a time when stonebuilding was in its heyday and were heavily influenced

Cushioned in comfort, the living room, far left, and a master bedroom, left, are lit by Georgian windows.

by the traditions they had left behind. "The Scots and some of the Irish were just A-1 stonemasons," he says, and the Georgian houses they built around Merrickville are as fine an example of neoclassical architecture as exists anywhere in English Canada. Though some of the buildings in the area are made of quarried limestone painstakingly cut and dressed, many, including the Devlin house, were built with uncut stone of lesser quality in a style known as rubblestone.

In this technique, a double row of rough stones is laid up either coursed or uncoursed—that is, either in discernible rows, like bricks, or randomly. In a typical 2-foot-thick wall, the inner and outer stones are 8 to 10 inches thick, and the resulting 4-to-8-inch gap between them is filled with smaller stones. "Rubblestone is a fantastic way of building," says Hutchins. "It's held together by nothing except gravity and a little bit of bonding, but it is very strong because it's like interlocked fingers." Theoretically, 24-inch-long stones that span the width of the wall give

A "one-woman kitchen," far left, is the focus of the addition. A high triangular window, left, vents excess heat.

added strength, but though Hutchins recommends one such stone every four feet in every fourth course, he admits that most of the houses from that period have none at all. "It's hard to say, after 100 or 200 years, that it doesn't work," he says with a grin, "but we sometimes pour the cavity full of cement for extra strength."

As well as going up quickly, rubblestone walls require relatively little expertise to erect – Hutchins says that while he would hire a mason to build a cut-stone house, he would likely attempt rubblestone on his own. He cites three reasons for the preponderance of rubblestone in Merrickville's architecture: the availability of material (several limestone quarries lie close by), the availability of the necessary skills, and tradition. Historically, rubblestone can be traced through Britain to medieval Europe, the Roman and Greek Empires and beyond, until its origin becomes lost in the ancient Middle East. "You could photograph parts of buildings in Turkey," says Hutchins with the enthusiasm of a true aficionado, "and the brick part looks like something you'd find in Toronto, while the stone part" – he pauses, visibly flipping through some mental file cards – "perhaps western Ontario."

But as widely used as it was, rubblestone was not held in particularly high regard by its early-19th-century practitioners. Viewed as a lesser technique, rubblestone was usually covered with parging or stucco that was sometimes tooled to look like cut stone. In typical fashion, the older part of Devlin's house is parged, while the studio – 40 or 50 years newer, when standards had changed somewhat – reveals its coursed rubblestone. There are other differences of style and structure between the two halves of the house related to the onset of the Victorian era, and though they are not marked enough to spoil its appearance, they help an expert like Nigel Hutchins pin down the respective dates of construction. The off-center front door, parged walls, 8/12 roof pitch and solid, rectangular design of the early building all identify the Georgian, neoclassical style, while the Gothic influence is visible in such details of the new part as its 12/12 roof pitch. "Socially, George was right off the wall, a liberal man," Hutchins observes, "and it's interesting that the Georgians were very into proportions, with low roofs and large windows to allow a lot of light into the house – very open. But as you go through the 19th century, the roof pitch grew steeper" – he demonstrates with his hands and flashes a grin – "as people became more uptight. Everything became taller – windows were high and narrow – and darker, even the woodwork."

Hutchins, a former set designer who became interested in old buildings while tracking down some log cabins for a film, does consulting, design work and general contracting on 19th-century stone, log and timber-frame houses. "It's mostly hands-on work," he says, a claim verified by his robust build and thick, stoneworker's hands. Though professing a fondness for Victorian architecture, he is obviously infatuated with the Georgian style. "It's the purity of it, the simplicity," he says. "There's a proportion – a cleanness of statement – to everything. It's the difference between a simple brass door pull and an ornate Victorian porcelain doorknob. Most people will go for the porcelain, but there's something quite magnificent in the simplicity of the brass. I'm intoxicated with that 1820s 1½-story Georgian style. I get shivers from one house, the proportions are so perfect."

Rather than remodel the house like Devlin did, Hutchins says he would have treated it with more historical accuracy, but he admits, "I tend to get locked into that. She needed that light, and I think it's very successful." Though passionately concerned about salvaging our architectural heritage, Hutchins wants to see the old buildings used as homes, or even offices and stores, instead of being turned into museums. "I don't mean save everything just because it's old, but if it's really exceptional, I think it should be saved," he says. "We have to get away from this heritage thing. Heritage is a word like 'love' was in the 1960s – it doesn't mean anything. It's all heritage, the whole lot: the house you built yesterday is heritage. It has got to become part of our lives, not some special thing we set aside."

After two years in the house, Devlin had completed most of the renovations but was feeling cramped. With half the house given over to studio and guest room, she was reduced to the equivalent of a one-bedroom apartment in which the kitchen kept spilling into the living room. "I needed a back entrance, so I looked at putting a porch out to there, then out to there," she says, indicating an airlock entry and a modest sun porch. "Then I thought, 'Well, if it was out to there, do you suppose I could have a kitchen?'" She drew up some sketches and approached then 76-year-old Edwin Pitcher, a local carpenter and handyman with a reputation for authentic, old-fashioned joinery, particularly his recreated windows. "I had heard he was too busy to do any work," Devlin recalls, "but I asked him to do some windows for me, and he ended up doing the addition."

With exposed beams, the stone common wall, textured plaster and lots of woodwork,

The worn sill of the old back door, right, is one of many clues to the age of the house.

the addition has a rustic, almost rough, appearance that is sympathetic to the well-worn disposition of the house itself. In practical terms, it houses what Devlin calls "a one-woman kitchen," a two-piece bathroom, closets and an all-purpose sun room used by turns for sketching, needlework, flower potting and storage. Devlin, who had always felt exposed to the main street, only the width of the sidewalk from her front windows, is delighted: "The kitchen makes the house. It's a world apart from the rest of the village, and it makes you able to get away from things." Since the house takes the full width of the west end of her 50-by-200-foot lot, the addition faces east, and while it is pleasant to sip coffee in the morning sun, solar energy does little to take the heating strain off the wood stove in the studio. But although the addition is not well-warmed by the winter sun, neither is it overheated in summer. Four factory-made skylights give extra light year-round but leaked with irritating regularity until Pitcher covered them with sheets of Plexiglas.

The board-and-batten exterior, painted a historically accurate blue, blends seamlessly into fences that extend partway down each side of the lot: on one side, joining with a woodshed to block the view of the neighboring pub's parking lot, and on the other, offering some privacy from the busy sidestreet without depriving passersby of a view of the extensive flower gardens in the backyard. "It was a junkyard out back when I came here," says Devlin. Though an inexperienced gardener, she made massive plantings and cultured some attractive yellow-blooming wildflowers—that turned out to be goldenrod. "I thought if I made it very beautiful, I would be accepted here," she says, and the strategy has worked. "People say, 'You don't know how wonderful it is to have this lovely garden here,' and I think, 'Oh, yes I do.' " More experienced now, she avoids unidentified wildflowers, and the whole backyard is alive with tulips, lilies, phlox, daisies, cosmos and more, planted between cedar hedges in beds and in raised boxes filled with soil from the addition's excavation. This summer, Devlin's yard will be added to a garden tour sponsored by the county horticultural society.

Devlin designed the addition herself, and though hardly authentic, it suits the house well and carries the approval of Hutchins, who feels that the shed roof and board-and-batten siding are in sympathy with the style and period of the original house. As well, Pitcher has added a measure of his own creativity to the carpentry throughout the house. Unwilling to work from the scant plans Devlin provided, he made alterations as he went,

most of which met with Devlin's approval. When Pitcher made two paneled exterior doors for the addition, he added Victorian glass inserts around the window and raised, diamond-shaped panels, knowing Devlin likes the shape. "I love the doors," says Devlin, with an obvious fondness for Pitcher and his work, "but they're both different. You can't get him to do them the same." She would plainly prefer to have matching doors, but – and this is typical of her attitude about the whole house – she is able to accept them the way they turned out. "In a way," she continues, "it's lovely, because it works, and that's the charm of it." Indeed, it is charming, and one of the most appealing aspects of the house is its uniqueness and individuality, much of it due to Pitcher's abilities and independent approach. Born only two miles from the house, he has worked on old houses for a good part of his adult life and still, at age 78, has as much work as he cares to accept. He carries his knowledge of historical carpentry lightly. "I just grew up with it," he says with a shrug, but Hutchins declares, "I can't compete with him. Someone should document the stuff he's done."

Although Pitcher did the construction and added what Hutchins calls "a nice folk influence," it is Devlin's expressive personality that makes the house come alive. An imaginative decorator who has done color consultations for many years, she has created a home that is an expression of herself to an extent that few other houses equal. Even the exterior of the house – neither tall nor slender, but with an innate strength of character – mirrors its owner. Inside, each corner has a different ambience, one to suit every facet of a complex personality. The studio, for instance, is a large and functional workroom, but it can quickly be made into an appealingly modern gallery by rolling up the paint-stained carpet, drawing curtains in front of the shelf clutter of brushes and cans, then hanging paintings and turning on the spotlights. The cooking area of the kitchen is private, an area that belongs indisputably to Devlin, and like her paintings, it is filled with light, color and texture: large windows, rich brown tiles, antique bottles, hanging baskets and pots, open cupboards and a limestone wall for the touching. In contrast, the kitchen table, though less personal, is an inviting social area where visitors are treated to a colorful display of dried flowers hanging in carefully arranged abandon next to the living room door like some floral welcome sign.

In the living room, one corner is finished in smooth drywall, and the angles around the window are clean and sharp; the opposite corner is finished in intentionally rough plaster with soft, rounded corners. Rusty old square nails left protruding from the rock-candy ceiling beams contrast with the gleam of antique furniture. One side of the staircase is bare, exposed stone, with tiny chips of un-slaked limestone visible in the mortar; on the other side, Devlin has fitted a Turkish *mandar*, a sort of combination bench and couch that is accented with cushions and tapestries. She has visited the Middle East, and its influence is clearly manifested in her choice of colors ("I love the rich blue and the soft Arab pinks"), the medieval Islamic wall hangings and the recurring geometric patterns. Given the Mediterranean beginnings of the stonework, none of this seems misplaced. As Devlin herself notes, "There are all sorts of nooks and crannies in the house that you can hide in," but they are held together with a constancy of color, texture and comfort. "It's really hard to achieve that kind of effect," says Hutchins with something approaching awe. "I mean, some of these placcs look great in a magazine, but can you live in them?"

But though the house is warm in winter, cool in summer and eminently livable, it is not perfect. "This is not the sort of house I would have if I were very rich, not the decor or anything," says Devlin. If nothing else, she says, she would like to "plunk it down in the middle of a field somewhere." And even with the addition, it is not as big as she would like. But given the limits of the house and of her finances, she is satisfied. "It's adequate, and it has come together for very little money." It is largely because of her expressive decorating that it has. "With a few things in a rustic setting," she says, "you can make it work." ❧

The Garden

Wildflower Meadows

TRIALS AND TRIUMPHS WITH THE NEWEST TREND IN GROUND COVERS

BY EVA HOEPFNER

Seed catalogues beckon you with glossy photographs of massed wildflowers: brilliant combinations of red, blue, yellow, orange and purple, like samples of old-fashioned cotton prints. At the garden center, shelves are stocked with cans, canvas bags, plastic sacks, even greeting cards of wildflower seeds, the containers so appealing that their contents hardly matter. Articles in popular magazines hint at low maintenance, no fertilizer or water costs, ecological health, the attraction of wildlife. One's head spins with visions of a gardener's paradise: gorgeous flowers waving among wispy grasses; birds, bees and butterflies darting through azure skies to nectar-laden blossoms, while the lucky gardener sits back with a long, cool drink, contentedly at one with a healthy, wonderful world. Can wildflower meadows be the answer to a gardener's dreams?

Well, the photographs don't lie, and the rumors are based on fact, but the truth is that a single meadow is unlikely to satisfy all your desires. A prairie meadow planted to native species requires little maintenance, for example, but only after years of thorough weeding. And native grasses and flowers may be in harmony with nature, but they never achieve a gaudy display. The commercial wildflower-seed mixtures, on the other hand, will provide a colorful explosion of flowers – enough to stop traffic on an eight-lane freeway – but some of the most photogenic examples have been planted on soil treated repeatedly with herbicides. The American Horticultural Society admits to spraying pesticides on its test plots every three or four years to destroy weeds, and then replanting from scratch. Furthermore, the colorful splash of mainly exotic flowers usually lasts less than two years. So however appealing a wildflower meadow appears on first acquaintance, the concept is

relatively untested as part of a well-tended landscape; and given the diverse climatic and soil conditions across the land, no single collection of wildflowers will suit all locales.

Of course, one must first define what one means by a wildflower meadow. Gardens and fields have been left to return to a natural state for as long as humankind has disturbed the soil, but the effect has more frequently suggested neglect than artfulness. Then again, a wildflower to one person may be a noxious invader to another, and a wildflower to your seed company may be grass to you.

Gardeners have long squabbled over what wildflowers are. Purists insist that they are native plants that grew before the arrival of the Europeans. Others include naturalized plants in the classification – those introduced from other parts of the world and that reproduce freely in their nonnative habitat. Opinion these days favors the definition that includes both native and naturalized plants. Weeds, incidentally, are just wildflowers that grow where they're not wanted. Noxious weeds are plants that the authorities have determined threaten human health or agricultural practices. Some common attractive weeds are Queen Anne's lace (*Daucus carota*), chicory (*Cichorium intybus*) and even ox-eye daisy (*Chrysanthemum leucanthemum*).

The definition of "meadow" is also blurry. Some define it as a grassland occurring in areas of high rainfall, in contrast to a "prairie," which occurs in areas of low rainfall; others say a meadow is a grassy spot found in a forested region. For our purposes, a meadow is a mixture of grasses and flowers growing in a sunny, open area.

As for appearance, one person's cherub is another's gnome. A meadow might inspire nostalgia or conservational righteousness, but it can equally incite your tidy neighbor to

organize a vigilante mower brigade. Many lawsuits attest to differences in perspectives. None other than Rodale Press, publisher of *Organic Gardening* magazine, was hauled to court in Emmaus, Pennsylvania, when parts of the once-manicured lawn around its headquarters were left to grow undisturbed. Stephen Kenney, an ecologist in Kenmore, New York, was convicted of contravening the local lawn ordinance and fined $50 for each day his meadow remained unmowed. Meanwhile, his neighbors, who cut down Kenney's meadow when he was out, were absolved of wrongdoing. Kenney ended up moving to less hostile territory. It might be noted, however,

that in the great majority of lawsuits, meadow advocates are winning their cases. In Wisconsin, wildlife biologist Donald Hagar defended his unmown meadow by proving it was not a fire hazard, health hazard or rat haven. And in Milwaukee, Lorrie Otto successfully sued the city for damages when it mowed her meadow without her permission.

The problems of naturalizing wildflowers are illustrated by the case of a developer near Toronto who agreed to turn parts of a new housing development into wildflower meadows. The object was to reduce maintenance and to make the buildings blend in with the natural parkland that weaves throughout the

Hardy Alpine meadows in the Wyoming Rockies include flowers like mountain buttercups, phlox, and forget-me-nots.

development. The town was enthusiastic, as were a good many local residents. A wildflower-and-grass seed mixture was planted, but the exotic grasses in the mix greatly outnumbered the flowers such as clover and yellow trefoil. The result was not what many residents expected.

The following year, a different wildflower mix was seeded into the existing meadow. The new mix contained mainly exotic annuals, with some perennials thrown in. The first year, most people were pleased with the results: a profusion of familiar garden flowers such as Shasta daisies, baby's breath, phlox and bachelor's buttons mixed with naturalized plants such as toadflax and yarrow. Only a few critics were heard to grumble, "You call these wildflowers?" The second season, ragweed, burdock, thistles and poison ivy made a strong show, and complaints were heard all the way to the Parks Board. Few annuals had reseeded, and the ornamental perennials that had taken root were in a life-and-death struggle with the unwelcome invaders. Some residents decided to take matters into their own hands, and their mowers roared into action. The fate of the project is still uncertain, but the landscape contractor who planted the meadows swears he will never plant another.

This example is not meant to discourage

Chicory, often considered a common weed, makes a striking accent in the garden.

wildflower enthusiasts, but to point out that often too much is expected, too soon, with too little research and labor. Before you attempt to sow a wildflower meadow, know exactly what effect you want, exactly what the seed company is selling you, and how the meadow might be greeted by your neighbors and your weed inspector. Walk ever so slowly – don't run – for a can, or whatever, of seed. If you are uninformed, you might not get what you bargained for.

Ecological Parade

For successful meadow gardening, it is important to understand natural processes. Most natural meadows are temporary stages in the ecological parade of succession. A bare field, left to its own devices, is soon invaded by grasses and forbs (nonwoody, broad-leaved plants such as dandelions and plantain). This is the meadow stage. Soon shrubs and other woody seedlings will enter, and over the next 50 to 150 years, the field will reach its climax stage, the forest. If you want a meadow to remain a meadow, you must intervene by weeding out woody seedlings or by regularly mowing or burning it.

Sometimes, depending upon climate, soil, moisture and on other factors, like available seed and the presence of fire or grazing animals, the meadow stage becomes the climax. In North America, these natural grasslands are found on the prairies (*prairie* is French for "meadow"). The indigenous plants form a community, a stable collection of diverse species that have evolved over the ages to adapt to the particular conditions of the area. They depend on each other for survival, tall plants sheltering short ones from sun and wind, ground-hugging plants protecting the soil from erosion, and all manner of organic litter enriching the soil. The community is a complex interaction of plants, insects and soil organisms, and it plays host to abundant wildlife. A meadow that comes closest to simulating the natural plant community of your region will require the least maintenance.

If you are looking for carefree summer days and you don't care much how your meadow looks, the simplest choice is to let the lawn grow. Be forewarned that, for a long time, this kind of meadow will look like an abandoned field, which some folks might call unkempt. It will yield a good crop of weeds: dandelions, quack grass, burdock, thistles and teasel are common invaders. But depending on how close you are to wildflower seed sources, you might also be pleasantly surprised.

Alice Hayek of Cobourg, Ontario, reduced

her lawn mowing to a winding path, and received her share of weeds. But since the property lies in a rural area, it took only two years for the lawn to transform itself into a small meadow of black-eyed Susans, sunflowers, goldenrod, milkweed, asters, pink fleabane, butter-and-eggs, wild strawberries and violets. Gardeners who are not as fortunate can introduce mature wildflower plants, but the plants will face fierce competition from the naturalized forbs and grasses. An annual mowing to about 6 inches with a string trimmer (or sickle-bar mower for large areas) will keep woody species in check.

But many of us don't plant a meadow to avoid work; for some it is a matter of principle. Planting a meadow of only native species can satisfy conservationists as well as those in search of a low-maintenance landscape. The only problem is that it takes a lot of time and effort to keep the weeds at bay until the native plant community is secure. Larry Lamb, an ecology technician at the University of Water-

loo, Ontario, labored for four years to establish pathways, prepare seedbeds, introduce plants and seeds, propagate rare species and weed his backyard prairie garden. Setting a fire each spring has helped reduce weeds, and now that the native plants have knit into a tight little community, overseeing the burn is about all the work that remains.

Lamb's low-maintenance miniature prairie looks nothing like an abandoned field. In winter, russet grasses and seed heads lace the snow; during the rest of the year, wave after wave of more than 200 species mark the passing seasons: "During the growing season," Lamb says, "an average of two species start blooming every day." Short flowers such as purple pasqueflowers, bird's-foot violets and shooting stars emerge in spring, followed by taller golden alexanders, purple bergamot and fiery butterfly weed. By midsummer, turk's-cap lily and blazing star edge up, to be topped by giant prairie dock and sunflowers. Goldfinches, meadowlarks, hummingbirds and

Coreopsis lanceolata *grows in most soils and competes well with grasses.*

*Deep in a garden of California poppies (*Eschscholzia californica*) and Western wallflowers (*Erysimum asperum*).*

butterflies flit through grasses that range from knee-high to 10 feet tall.

Lamb lives on the outer edges of what was formerly natural prairie. "However," he says, "you can grow prairie plants where there never was prairie. And if prairie plants are unsuited to the area, just plant those species native to the region – check your field guides – and fight the woody stuff. Natural grassland occurs anywhere you go."

Native Meadows

Prairie gardeners agree that one cannot recreate the feel of a sweeping prairie on less than an acre. You can, however, plant any sunny, well-drained spot with native plants. In fact, it is advisable to start small – with a former perennial border, for example, or a corner of the lawn – and increase the meadow once you find out what grows well. Meadows look especially pleasant set off by a solid background such as a wall, a fence or shrubbery. For visual interest, take advantage of land contours, perhaps creating a slope and adding a few shrubs, rocks or a bench. Paths add shape, invite closer scrutiny of wildflowers and promote weeding.

Make sure the area gets at least five hours of sun a day; less than that will result in spindly growth and little bloom. The soil should be neutral or slightly alkaline. It must be well drained and not too rich if you want blossoms instead of leaves and grasses. Add organic matter to heavy soils. If you are replacing a lawn, remove and compost the sod (sod cutters are a great help). Don't plow it under unless you plan to smother the area with

plastic or thick layers of newspaper for at least a year. In fall or spring, till the area to a depth of 4 or more inches. Try to remove all vestiges of lawn grasses, for each little rhizome that stays in the soil can generate a large grassy patch that will be extremely difficult to remove once the area is seeded to wildflowers.

Weeds are the prime enemies of meadows. Before you seed, cover the prepared area with black plastic for at least three months to induce weed germination and subsequent smothering. If you are a patient gardener, fallow the soil for a growing season: rake shallowly, water to encourage weeds, then cultivate; repeat several times to encourage as many weeds as possible to germinate. Before seeding, rake, just barely scratching the soil so as not to bring other weed seeds to the surface.

Plants can be introduced by seed or as mature specimens. The cheapest way is to use all seed, but you will have to wait at least a couple of years for the perennials to start blooming. Mature plants will give structure to the meadow and achieve earlier bloom, but they are expensive. Never dig native plants from the wild. Some species are protected by law. Even if the plant is not endangered, you could be taking it from a part of its range where it is scarce. Combine a few plants with seeds for results that are both inexpensive and fast. Illinois ecologist Robert Betz, who has restored more than 300 acres of prairie, believes that aggressive native plants – goldenrod, asters and sunflowers – should be introduced first to overcome foreign weeds. This creates a more amenable prairie environment for the delicate plants, which can coexist with aggressive natives but not with foreign weeds such as dandelions and burdock.

The first year, a native meadow can be discouraging. No matter how diligent you've been, some weeds will defy your efforts. And while the weeds are flourishing, your seeded species will stubbornly resist fleshing out. This is because prairie plants first develop strong root systems, as much as 20 feet deep, to protect against a harsh climate. Nature also staggers some seed germination over a period of years. Don't give up. The second year should see a lot of grasses and some flowers in bloom. If you continue to weed (know your weeds!), you will be amply rewarded by the fourth year.

In nature, prairie grasses undergo occasional burning, a process that kills alien plants, warms the soil, adds nutrients in the form of ash, and removes thatch that could eventually choke smaller plants. Larry Lamb is fortunate to live in an area where he can burn his meadow, which he has planted in areas di-

vided from one another by 4-inch-deep gravel paths that act as firebreaks. In most situations, however, burning one's yard is dangerous and illegal. If you can't burn, mow to 6 inches every spring with a string trimmer, scythe or sickle bar, then compost the clippings.

Exotic Meadows

Conservation is well and good, but the prevalence of exotic wildflower seeds in stores and catalogues shows there are other reasons for wanting a meadow. I spent my childhood in rural Germany, and nothing turns me to homesick jelly faster than a reproduction of Monet's poppy fields.

There is nothing wrong with indulging yourself in a passion for foreign flowers, but be aware, nostalgic gardeners, that a meadow from a commercial mix will rarely resemble one from your childhood. One popular seed mixture contains lots of corn poppies and cornflowers—the mainstays of my favorite meadow—but along with these is a crowd of unrelated species: yellow coreopsis, evening primroses and black-eyed Susans, orange Siberian wallflowers, purple loosestrife, pink Mediterranean dame's-rocket, red North African flax and more. Missing are the wispy grasses that formed the background of my childhood meadow. The gaudy display from the seed packet is a far cry from what I remember as a harmonious blaze of golden stalks and scarlet blossoms.

No seed mixture, of course, can satisfy everyone. Many people want spectacular color —all the time and quickly. Hence, most commercial mixes strive for a maximum variety of hues throughout the season and include lots of annuals that will bloom the first year. The inclusion of flowers that tolerate various growing conditions is supposed to ensure that at least something will grow everywhere. Not all species are expected to flourish, and few will over any length of time. While some dwindle, others may take over, and this can create unforeseen problems.

The trouble with introducing alien species into a region is that you never know how they will react. They can succumb to the climate, can naturalize in a quiet, reserved manner, or they can take over the land. Many of our common weeds—dandelions, Queen Anne's lace and chicory, for example—were introduced from Europe or Asia. Purple loosestrife (*Lythrum salicaria*), imported from Europe as an ornamental, is becoming a serious pest in various regions, yet it is still included in many wildflower seed mixes. We should also heed the warnings from foreign gardeners. Those

scarlet corn poppies, for example, are said to be the bane of every European farmer. What if they love their new environment in the prairie wheat fields too?

Even if an introduced alien doesn't ravage the countryside, it might crowd out other desirable species within your own meadow. Often, this means replanting your meadow from scratch, and having gone to all that trouble once, you might be reluctant to repeat the process.

Before buying seed, make sure the mixture lists the species by name. Check in a reliable reference book for potential troublemakers. These include lawn grasses, which are sometimes used as filler but will quickly choke out many flowers. (Prairie grasses, on the other hand, "are not really sod forming—there are openings for forbs to take hold," says Larry Lamb, who recommends the use of orna-

Larry Lamb's backyard prairie in Ontario includes paths to make viewing and weeding easier.

mental native grasses in a prairie meadow in a proportion of 50:50 to 80:50 with forbs.) For hardiness and longevity, select a mix with a mainstay of locally hardy perennials, and remember that the strength of a meadow lies in diversity: the more species you try, the better your chance of success. Start with a small area, a flower bed, for example, and study the effect before seeding large areas.

Directions for planting a commercial mix are like those for planting a native meadow. The secret is starting with a clean seedbed. Unless you want to spray the area two or three times with a nonselective herbicide such as Roundup, which kills all green plants on contact, you will have to cultivate repeatedly or apply black plastic for a year. Once the meadow is established, mow it in late summer or winter to help disperse seeds and open the area to light. (Do not burn after early spring, or you will kill most of the plants.) Reseed patchy places every couple of years – every year for continuous bloom – and keep weeding. Some people start from scratch every three or four years.

Commercial seed mixtures can be a good introduction to meadow gardening. They can supply many species you might not have considered; they let you become familiar with the attendant pleasures and problems. But don't be afraid to experiment. Lighten up a flower mix with noninvasive grasses; temper an all-native mixture with well-mannered, naturalized flowers. Add a profusion of spring bulbs for early bloom. If you are cramped for space, forget the seeds and create the essence of a meadow with a tidy little patch of perennial flowers and clumped grasses, each plant as carefully placed as in a perennial border.

There is one more thing. In *The Wild Gardener*, published in 1894, William Robinson asked, "Who would not rather see the saving grass with countless flowers, than a close surface without a blossom." Well, your neighbors. Tell them of your plans, show them that you work hard (at least initially) and keep your edges trim; share your delights and disappointments. Who knows, you might win them over to this new gardening adventure. ❧

SOURCES

Nurseries

Aimers Wildflower Seeds & Bulbs
Cotswolds, The Green Lane, R.R. 1
King City, Ontario L0G 1K0
Wildflower seeds and mixtures. Free catalogue.

Clyde Robin Seed Co.
P.O. Box 2366
Castro Valley, California 94546
Many wildflower mixes. Catalogue free.

Daystar
Route 2, Box 250
Litchfield, Maine 04350
Sells live plants. Catalogue $1.

Lafayette Home Nursery
R.R. Box 1A
Lafayette, Illinois 61449
Native prairie grass and wildflower seed mixes. Send large self-addressed, stamped envelope for catalogue.

Niche Gardens
1111 Dawson Rd.
Chapel Hill, North Carolina 27516
Wildflower plants. Catalogue $3.

Orchid Gardens
2232-139th Avenue, NW
Andover, Minnesota 55304
Information on many native plants, including orchids, club-mosses, violets, ferns and some woody plants, in their "Wildflower Culture Catalog," 50 cents.

Prairie Nursery
P.O. Box 306
Westfield, Wisconsin 53964
Prairie wildflower seeds and plants. Catalogue $2.

Siskiyou Rare Plant Nursery
2825 Cummings Road
Medford, Oregon 97501
Rock garden and woodland plants of the Northwest. Catalogue $2.

Thompson & Morgan
P.O. Box 1308
Farraday & Gramme Avenues
Jackson, New Jersey 08527
Seeds and live plants. Catalogue free.

Valley Creek
P.O. Box 475, Circle Drive
McArthur, Ohio 45651
Twelve wildflower mixes. Catalogue free.

Vermont Wildflower Farm
Route 7
Charlotte, Vermont 05445
Wildflower seeds and mixtures. Catalogue free.

We-Du Nurseries
Route 5, Box 724
Marion, North Carolina 28752
Southeastern native plants. Catalogue $1.

Wildginger Woodlands
P.O. Box 1091
Webster, New York 14580
Seeds and plants. Catalogue $1, refundable with first order.

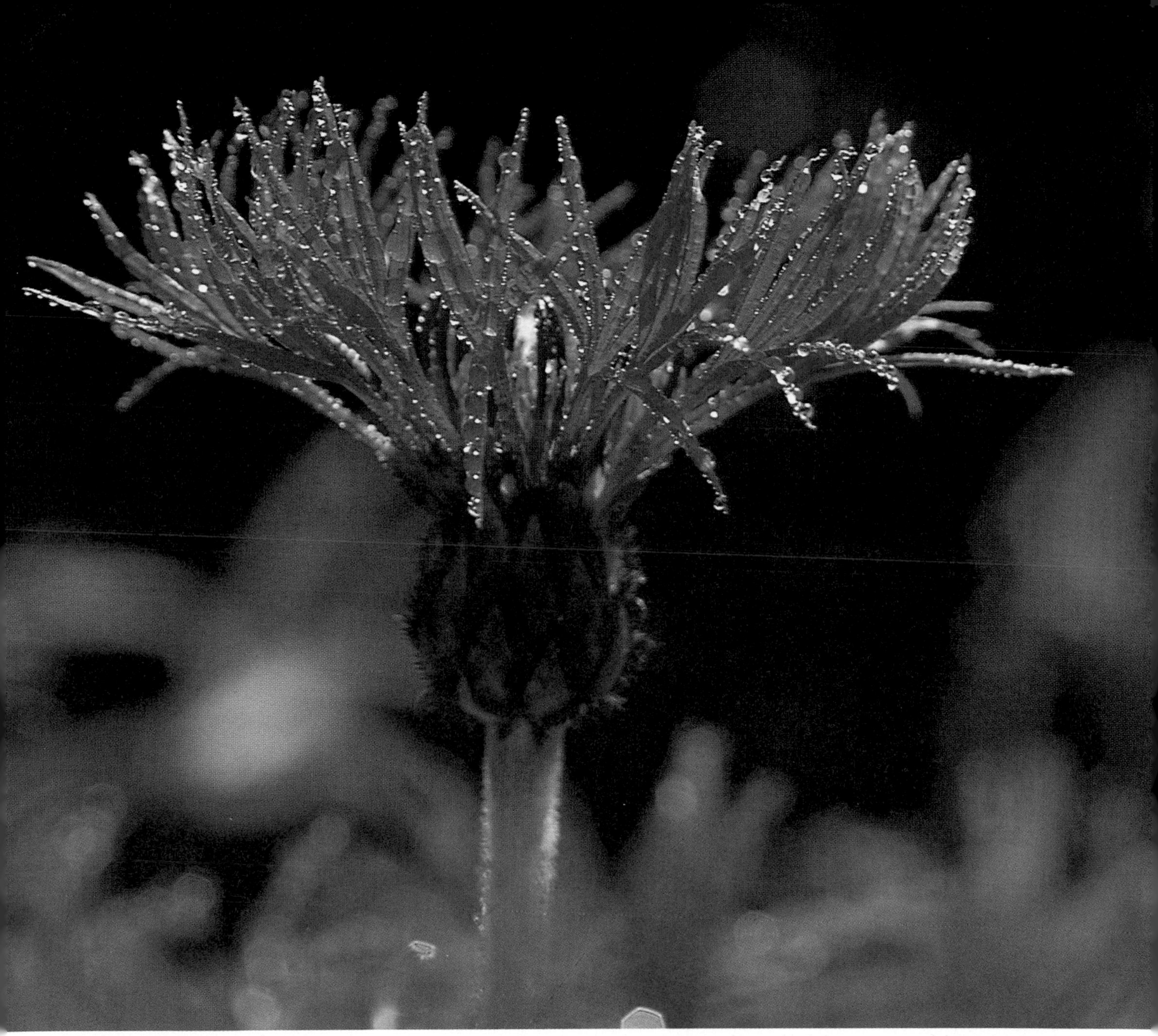

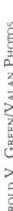

Wild Seed
P.O. Box 27751
Tempe, Arizona 85282
Southwestern desert and mountain wildflower seeds and mixes. Catalogue free.

Woodlanders, Inc.
1128 Colleton Avenue
Aiken, South Carolina 29801
Herbaceous and woody plants. Catalogue $1.50.

Books

A Garden of Wildflowers: 101 Native Species and How to Grow Them by Henry W. Art. (Storey Communications, 1986.)
Wildflowers from all over North America.

Wildflowers: Time-Life Gardener's Guide. (Time-Life Books, 1989.)
Guide to North American wildflowers.

Gardening with Native Plants of the Pacific Northwest by A.R. Kruckeberg. (U. Washington Press, 1982.)
Trees, perennials of the Pacific Northwest.

Growing and Propagating Wild Flowers by H.R. Phillips. (U. North Carolina Press, 1985.)
Eastern native plants.

Growing California Native Plants by M.G. Schmidt. (U. California Press, Berkeley, 1980.)
California wildflowers, woody perennials.

Growing Wildflowers by Maria Sperka. (Scribner's, 1973.)
Northeastern wildflowers.

Cornflowers* (Centaurea dealbata) *are a mainstay of wildflower mixes.

Harold V. Green/Valan Photos

The Great Code

THE FOLKLORE AND SCIENCE OF USING PLANTS AS TIMEPIECES

BY HELEN MOLITOR

Shortly after my husband and I moved to the Pacific Northwest, we asked our 80-year-old neighbor about garden schedules in the new climate. Her reply was succinct. "I never pay much attention to all that stuff about frost-free days and such," she said. "I just stick my earliest scallions in as soon as the violets bloom, and work from there."

We were disappointed for a moment. But then we realized that any seasoned gardener could "work from there." First, the earliest onion sets; then, a week or 10 days later, more onion sets, some peas and spinach, lettuce and kohlrabi; in another 10 days, early carrots and the first cabbage transplants, and the garden is under way in the new climate. All that is needed is a reliable reference point – in this case, the violets – from which to hang the rest of the garden schedule.

Our neighbor was, in fact, using the newest form of folklore to have attained scientific respectability. Gardeners may call it common sense; the scientific name is phenology, "the science of appearances," derived from the Greek *phainein,* to appear or to show. But phenology is more than the mere recording of appearances; it explains the relationships of various observations. It recognizes that every year when the violets bloom, a whole series of forces is involved – soil and air temperatures, hours of warmth and sunlight, inches of rain and percentages of humidity. Only when conditions are just right do those petals open. And when conditions are right for violets, they are right for other plants too, often domestic plants whose caretakers worry about planting schedules. For instance, the same combination of events that brings out the violets also constitutes near-perfect conditions for young onion sets.

In other words, certain plants, insects and animals may in themselves be complex, high-ly sensitive weather instruments that monitor the activities of many natural causes as well as any meteorological laboratory and can, therefore, be used to schedule other plantings. In Virgil's *Georgics,* written in the first century B.C., the Roman poet warns neophyte grape growers not to plant their young vines until the heat-loving white cranes have returned – a sign that spring is here to stay.

For most of us, plants are more readily observable phenomena than white cranes. Most phenological research has focused upon either plant-to-plant or plant-to-insect relationships, and the advantages of vegetative indicators become clear when one realizes that, for the cost of a notebook and some careful observation, even an inexperienced gardener can put this newest science to work. In Vermont, for instance, researchers have found that cool-weather crops, including lettuce, radishes and peas, can be planted when lilacs are at the first-leaf stage, while tender plants, such as beans and cucumbers, can generally be planted when the lilacs are in full bloom. Leonard Perry of the University of Vermont warns, however, that such a system is not infallible; the lilacs can be blasted by a late frost as easily as can the tomatoes. As always, keep blankets and newspapers handy in case of a frost warning.

Thanks in part to phenology, John Ritchie is one of the most successful corn growers in Calgary, Alberta. Long before the development of today's fast-growing northern strains, he was planting his seeds as soon as his lilac leaves were an inch and a half long. Both corn and lilac grew in a small area of southern exposure where the light hit his white garage and bounced across the garden patch to a low, white fence. The lilac indicated to him how warm and moist the soil was in that particular area, so Ritchie usually managed a jump of

Crocuses and other indicator plants can be used to determine the proper time to sow garden crops and to control pests, left.

three or four weeks on the rest of us in the neighborhood. We had corn every year, even if our crop failed, because he always shared his success.

Ritchie had learned this early-planting technique from a friend who came from southern Ontario, where the problem was not cool summers but corn borers. Recently, Robert McClanahan, an entomologist at Agriculture Canada's research station in Harrow, Ontario, recommended precisely this strategy. Planting a short-season corn "as early as possible" will reduce borer damage from 95 percent of the crop to just 15 percent. McClanahan measured the soil temperature day after day, planting his corn as soon as the temperature two inches below the surface had been in the 40s for several days.

Like Ritchie, I would rather use a lilac. If no lilac is available, one can always try Winnipegger Jim Keller's timing method: "Plant corn when oak leaves are as big as squirrels' ears"—an adage familiar to Minnesotans 50 years ago. Indeed, Samuel de Champlain was told in 1605 that the best time to plant corn seed in Cape Cod was when the leaf of a white oak was approximately the size of a red squirrel's footprint.

Indicator plants, like honeysuckle, have distinct growth phases that reveal subtle, underlying climatic conditions.

For orchardists and berry growers, phenology has already provided important information for dealing with insects. Until recently, growers of 'McIntosh' apples found the answer to one of their basic questions incredibly elusive: when should the hives of pollinating bees arrive in the orchard? Obviously, at full bloom or close to it, but the dates of full bloom vary greatly from one year

to the next. For example, in Vermont, where the original phenological experiments were conducted, those dates range from as early as May 10 to as late as June 3. To make the problem even greater, the intervals between first leaf and full bloom also vary, so the grower cannot use an early indicator to predict the later full bloom.

Now, however, scientists have discovered that the 'Red Rothomagensis' lilac reaches full bloom two days before 'McIntosh' apples, and the lilac's first leaves appear a predictable number of days before its full bloom. Thus 'McIntosh' growers, recording the dates of lilac first leaf and full bloom for several years, can use the average number of days between those events to predict the crucial apple-blossom date well ahead of time. As one of the growers said, "If you don't get the bees in spring, you don't get the apples in autumn. This lilac calculation gives us a better handle on pollination than we've ever had before."

Barton Hall-Beyer, co-author of *Ecological Fruit Production in the North* and an orchard owner in Quebec, also points out that the first adult codling moths emerge when the apple petals begin to fall. So if an orchardist is willing to spray at all, that is the best time to apply ryania, a biological pesticide. In many parts of the North, there is only one codling moth hatch.

Similarly, raspberry fruit worms feed on the young leaves and flower buds while they lay their eggs. Raspberry growers planning to use rotenone should apply it when the flower buds first appear and, with a bad infestation, again just before the buds open, to be most effective with the fewest applications of pesticides.

Such simple relationships between plants and pests exist everywhere in nature and need only be noted to be useful to gardeners. We can then intercede at the correct time, even though we have no control over the environmental factors, such as climate and weather, that cause particular events to occur.

In fact, it is partly because weather and climate are beyond our control that the scientific community's acceptance of phenology is increasing. The thesis is widely held that in the next 20 years, the weather will become more unpredictable and extreme; conventional agricultural methods may not suffice.

According to Professor P.A. Dubé of Laval University, the Canadian Committee on Agrometeorology has been trying for years "to develop strategies for food production under climatic stress conditions." Dubé and others

have been active in NE-95, a joint Canadian-American research venture, the largest phenological project yet undertaken, with more than 1,000 observers collecting phenological data at stations in 25 states and 6 provinces.

In Canada and the northeastern United States, indicator plants at the observation sites are mostly cloned—therefore genetically identical—hybrid lilacs, cultivars of the "Chinese lilac" (*Syringa chinensis* 'Saugeana'). This lilac, despite its name, seems to have been developed in Rouen, France; hence its other common name, the 'Red Rothomagensis' lilac (Rotomagus was the Roman name for Rouen).

Backing up the lilac are similarly cloned plantings of two kinds of honeysuckle, *Lonicera tatarica* 'Arnold Red' and *L. korolkowii* 'Zabelii.' Western centers use the common lilac, *Syringa vulgaris*, and southern areas, like North Carolina, have developed their own indicators, including dogwood, redbud, red maple and tulip poplar, because their winters are not cold enough to give lilacs and honeysuckles the dormant period they require.

One NE-95 project, in New York, focused on finding indicator plants that would help growers control cabbage maggots. According to L.H. Pederson and C.T. Eckenrode of the New York experimental station in Geneva, scientists have long known that cabbage maggots are able to hatch four times a year at six-week intervals. These hatches can be predicted with great accuracy using "heat-unit accumulations," that is, keeping track of how many degrees above zero have accumulated since a set date. But few farms can afford the necessary laboratory equipment and resident biologist to keep the records.

Since four flights of cabbage-maggot flies are spread over several months, the indicators had to cover a long span of time. One way to achieve temporal coverage is to choose a shrub like the lilac, that has several distinct, easily defined stages of development. The other way, particularly useful when the time span involves months and not just weeks, is to choose a variety of plants, each having at least one distinct identifiable stage—the method selected by the Geneva group.

The first indicator, the common yellow rocket (*Barbarea vulgaris*), serves also as a major food source for the flies that produce the maggots; it is no accident that full bloom occurs simultaneously with the peak of first flight.

There is clearly a shared set of environmental conditions favorable to both insect and plant. If the phenological grower wants to

know when to protect his cole crop from maggots, he watches for the first blooms, not the full-bloom stage, and then takes his protective measures—diatomaceous earth or tar-paper squares around the roots of cabbages and their relatives are the common organic methods of control. These measures prevent the flight from laying eggs that would otherwise hatch 2 to 10 days later and, once hatched, begin eating their way through the roots of the young, vulnerable plants.

The second hatch, in early July, is predicted by the blooming of the common daylily (*Hemerocallis fulva*). For gardeners unfortunate enough to have third and fourth flights, usually in mid-August and late September, the effects can be avoided by early plantings and early harvests of the vulnerable plants. But for fall crops and Brussels sprouts, the recommended indicators are full bloom of the otherwise baneful Canada thistle (*Cirsium arvense*) and the pale lavender New England aster (*Aster novae-angliae*). Where the thistle is absent, early goldenrod (*Solidago juncea*) in full bloom is the best indicator.

The aster presents another phenological complication and its solution. This indicator has an extended bloom period. Its full bloom continues for more than a week, and the maggot hatch may come either early or late in the stage. Thus, for nonorganic farmers who require a precise, two-day period in which to spray their insecticides effectively, the aster may not be precise enough. But for organic gardeners, whose methods are preventive rather than punitive, the aster's first blooms will give plenty of warning to protect plantings from this last and usually lightest infestation.

Common yellow rocket serves as a major food source for cabbage-maggot flies. It is no accident that full bloom occurs at the same time as the flies' first flight.

The easiest way for most gardeners to get started with phenology is to identify the plants that will help to determine when to try early plantings of various vegetables. Some of the scientific findings are helpful, for they suggest the range of plants that make the best indicators. The plants must be hardy in the area, and they must have recognizable stages, which observers can readily record.

Local wild plants, always present, can serve as useful indicators for early plantings. Growers in the northern plains could consider crocuses and such wild shrubs as wolf willow, native potentilla, saskatoons, wild plums and crab apples. In some areas, elderberries and thimbleberries bloom early enough in May to serve as indicators. Among the other plants sometimes suggested are milfoil, milkweed, chickweed, ox-eye daisy, spearmint and speedwell.

Alternate indicator plants are perennial bulbs, used in one of several ways. For example, there is the clump method, whereby a single type of perennial obtained from the same source is deliberately planted in identically sized clumps in locations suspected of being distinct microclimates. The reason for such plantings is that it is much easier to keep track of 8 out of 10 or 16 out of 20 tulips in a clump rather than 1 or 2. When clumps of bulbs are used, each planting should be the same size so that the observer can record first bloom, 25 percent bloom, 50 percent, 95 percent – and thus reach an easily observable and comparable set of data. Given several identical clumps, it is easy to differentiate between warm, cool and cold sites.

Of course, observations are relevant only if microclimate is taken into consideration. I planted a number of daffodil clumps, each containing two dozen bulbs, in several parts of our property and found the differences among them extraordinary, far surpassing my expectations. The earliest clump, in an open meadow along a tiny spring rill, had a dozen flowers almost an entire month before the first bloom opened on the shadiest clump. If I were going to time pea plantings by daffodil bloomings, I would have to know which daffodils to observe.

A second method for using perennial bulbs is the multispecies calendar. Here, a small bed or several beds containing a variety of indicators is used. Such beds already exist in many gardens. The very early bloomers are crocuses, snowdrops and hyacinths, whose blooming times overlap with the slightly later daffodils, grape hyacinths and early tulips such as *Tulipa kaufmanniana* and *T. fosterana*. The midseason tulips, including 'Double Early' and 'Mendel,'

are still blooming when the late tulips, the 'Darwins,' 'Parrots,' 'Rembrandts' and 'Cottages,' begin. Thus the assortment of bulbs provides a living calendar as decorative as and more functional than the "living sundials" of Renaissance gardens, in which at least one plant was in flower at any time during the day. And the useful season can be extended into summer by the addition of a selection of later-blooming lilies, for example.

The most popular indicators among scientists are domestic shrubs. Various sorts of lilacs and honeysuckles are found across the continent. Dubé of Laval, L.P. Perry and M.T. Vittum of the University of Vermont and the New York experimental station in Geneva, respectively, have listed instructions for the choice of a planting site for lilacs and honeysuckles. They recommend that the gardener choose a level, unshaded place away from footpaths, sidewalks and roads but close enough that the plant can be comfortably observed each day. The spot should not be subject to excessive amounts of snow from drifting or piling or to unusual weather conditions such as high winds or heavy frosts. Soil should be typical for the area. Leave at least 15 feet between plants.

The advantages of such plants as lilac and honeysuckle are obvious. They are cold-hardy, resistant to heat and drought and have few insect or disease problems of their own. Their bloom is spectacular and can clearly be observed to occur in several stages. Phenologists have identified five such "phenostages":
• *First leaf,* when the widest part of the first leaf has grown beyond the sheath or scale of the bud from which it emerges.
• *Full leaf,* when at least 95 percent of the active buds have leaves.
• *First bloom,* the definition of which depends on the type of flower. For lilacs, first bloom is the date when at least half the clusters have at least one flower open. For honeysuckle, the stage occurs when 5 percent of the flowers are open.
• *Full bloom,* when 95 percent of the flowers have opened but before many have wilted – in other words, observers should aim for the first day when 95 percent are open.
• *End of bloom,* when 95 percent of the flowers have withered.

Such recognizable stages are essential for productive observations, since there may be anywhere from one to six or more weeks between first and final flowers; hence the need to define what stage your indicator plants have reached when other natural events occur. Either a series of stages like those of lilac and honeysuckle need to be identified, or one such

stage should be chosen as the central point of your observations.

One of the most helpful record-keeping tools is a gardener's diary with room to record several observations each day or week: indicator-plant stages, vegetable plantings and insect arrivals, depredations and disappearances.

When I began experimenting with violets as my earliest indicators, I first toured my own garden and its vicinity, locating not only my violets but a number of other early wild plants, ranging from miner's lettuce to thimbleberries. I also made a list of shrubs and perennials on the inside cover of my diary – blueberry bushes, asparagus, elderberries, rhododendrons, Oregon grapes, domestic rhubarb and strawberries, and young apple, pear and cherry trees – that were potential indicators for events later in the season. For fall, I used chrysanthemums, the only plants I found useful for the late season.

If, as is commonly predicted, our weather is about to become even more volatile and pesticides are found to be even more dangerous, the advantages of phenology will be apparent. Phenological codes may become the only con-

stants in a changing world, and gardeners who have not learned them may be far more outdated than the merely computer-illiterate. In the near future, intelligent and prudent growers, large-scale and small, may find themselves planting and spraying at such magical times as the first of lilac or half past violets. 🌿

Lilac has five distinct indicator stages, the most impressive being full bloom.

SOURCES

Sequence of Bloom of Perennials, Biennials and Bulbs Including Height and Color Range
Publication IB 196, $1.60, from:
DISTRIBUTION CENTER
7 Research Park
Cornell University
Ithaca, New York 14850

Plant Phenology in Eastern and Central North America (B677) free from:
UNIVERSITY OF VERMONT
EXTENSION SERVICE
Agricultural Experiment Station
Publications Office
Morrill Hall
Burlington, Vermont 05405-0106

The Living Garden

A HEALTHY SOIL IS A WELL-FED SOIL – A MENU OF ORGANIC AMENDMENTS

BY JACK COOK

You may have an organic vegetable garden, but you cannot have a natural garden. Gardening, by its very nature, is unnatural. In nature, plants do not grow in rows, and seldom does a single species dominate a patch of ground to such a degree that all others are excluded. Rarely does a plant suddenly appear in a location where its species has never grown before. And in nature, when plants die, most of the nutrients they have taken out of the soil are returned.

With gardening, however, we make extraordinary demands on the soil. When the crop is harvested, the nutrients it has taken up are removed also. If we don't replenish the soil, it will, like a vein of gold being mined with dynamite and pickaxes, become depleted.

Unlike a gold mine, however, a garden can be replenished, nutrients can be put back. Through the alchemy of decomposition, organic waste becomes a precious material: humus. It is the basis of any soil in good tilth, rich with its own life and bursting with horticultural promise.

To maintain a productive garden, one need only follow the fundamental tenet of organic fertilization: feed the soil, not the plant. Every cubic inch of soil contains billions of organisms: bacteria, fungi, algae, actinomycetes, nematodes, mites, ants, millipedes, earthworms, slugs, to name a few. Their health and the soil's are indistinguishable. The ideal food for them and the soil is organic matter: materials that were once alive, like crop residues, hay, leaves, manure, wood chips, straw, grass clippings, eggshells and household garbage. As soil organisms break down organic matter, nitrogen – a major crop nutrient – is released, and the organic matter is transformed into humus. Humus is brown gold. A dark, porous, gummy substance, it contains acids that make other nutrients available to plants. Grace Ger-

shuny, a market gardener and author of *The Soul of Soil*, has written, "Soil health and humus are indivisible."

But most gardeners know about adding decayed organic matter – compost. What else does the soil need? A balance of minerals, which provide essential nutrients for all plants. Which minerals and in what proportions depends on the condition of the soil.

To find out what the soil's needs are, have it tested. At a minimum, a test done at modest cost by your state cooperative extension service will tell you whether your dirt has a deficiency in the availability of any or all of the major plant nutrients: nitrogen, potassium, phosphorus, magnesium, calcium and sulfur. Nitrogen is usually contained in a gas. The others are mineral nutrients. The test will also tell you the soil's pH, whether it is acid (below 7 on the pH scale), or alkaline (above 7). Most vegetables prefer a slightly acidic soil, in the range of pH 6.5 to 6.8.

To get soil for a test, dig a soil sample every 100 square feet in your garden at a depth of 6 to 12 inches. Mix the samples together in a plastic bucket, and send a small portion to the lab in the container it has supplied.

Nitrogen

Let's suppose that the test results show that your soil is deficient in nutrients, a mined plot in need of rebuilding. Prominent among the deficiencies will surely be nitrogen. A soil containing enough organic matter will, given appropriate moisture and temperature, produce nitrogenous gases continuously as soil organisms digest that organic matter. Warm, moist conditions promote nitrogen production; cool, dry conditions inhibit it. Whatever the conditions, the more organic matter and soil organisms there are, the more nitrogen is released

Plants don't care if nutrients come from synthetic or organic sources, but soil organisms do. Over time, synthetic fertilizers can hurt soil life.

and available to plants.

There are a number of organic compounds that will combat a nitrogen deficiency, the foremost of which is manure. Whether it comes from cows, horses, sheep, pigs or poultry, manure is magnificent soil food. It fosters the production of nitrogen and also contains a host of other essential nutrients. Moreover, it improves the texture of soil.

There is, however, one crucial caution to be exercised with the application of manure to the garden. If planting is soon to follow the application of the manure, it should be at least six months old, preferably twelve. Raw manure, especially from poultry, releases soluble nitrates into the soil. Leafy green vegetables will respond quickly and vigorously to an infusion of nitrogen, but they are prone to concentrate nitrates, which are toxic to humans, in their tissues.

Indeed, Louis Pulver, manager of Vermont Northern Growers, a small cooperative of organic farmers, and a vegetable grower himself, says flatly: "Manure can be the scourge of farmers. Most organic growers think they must use it. We tell our members not to unless it's at least a year old and, preferably, composted. What's in manure varies widely, depending on what the animals had been eating and, most important, what medications they'd been given. But the worst thing is, it usually carries zillions of well-fertilized weed seeds. Composting helps because the heat it generates kills a lot of the seeds."

A conservative rate of application would be 500 pounds of aged cow or horse manure for 1,000 square feet of garden, or about 150 pounds of poultry, sheep or goat manure (less of these because they are higher in nitrogen).

If you don't have access to manure or choose not to use it, nitrogen can be added directly. Chilean nitrate, once the most popular source of agricultural nitrogen, is derived from bird guano and contains about 16 percent nitrogen. Beware though, because Chilean nitrate is sodium nitrate and sodium tends to desiccate the soil and destroy soil life. (Many programs that certify organic growers disallow Chilean nitrate for that reason.)

Other useful sources of nitrogen include blood meal (8 to 13 percent nitrogen), alfalfa seed meal (3 percent) and cottonseed meal (6 percent). Some growers frown on the last because of the possibility of pesticide residues; more pesticide is used on cotton than on any other plant under cultivation in the U.S. today.

Fish emulsion (4 to 5 percent nitrogen, along with dozens of other nutrients) can be sprayed onto leafy vegetables, which take up the nutrients through the leaves. This source of nitrogen allows a gardener to combat a nitrogen deficiency in the short term, but its use runs contrary to the feed-the-soil dictum.

Finally, there is compost, the very heart of organic fruit and vegetable production. While everyone who makes compost knows what materials can go into the pile, it is also worth stressing that adding rock powders, such as rock phosphate and greensand, is a sterling idea. The rapid breakdown of organic matter that takes place in a well-built compost heap makes the minerals more readily available to plants than they are when minerals are simply broadcast onto the garden plot and tilled in.

There are, however, a few materials that should be excluded from the compost pile: lime, for one. It causes the release of ammonia, thus reducing the nitrogen content of the compost. For the same reason, wood ashes should not be added to working compost. Do not add synthetic fertilizers, which deter the growth of the microbe populations that break down the organic materials, and don't add meat scraps, which attract rodents.

Ken Burris

Langbeinite

Alfalfa Meal

Blood Meal

Sulfur

Phosphorus

The soil test, in addition to reporting on nitrogen, will describe levels of phosphorus, potassium, magnesium, calcium and sulfur. Besides being consumed by plants, these major mineral nutrients can be lost through leaching and volatilization (being driven off as a gas). They can also be locked up in compounds that make them unavailable to plants. These losses, collectively, are known as demineralization. In time, it can destroy a soil's fertility. Demineralization is combatted by a high level of organic matter in the soil and active soil life. Even so, any form of agriculture, no matter how meticulously carried out, will always result in some demineralization, which means that any form of agriculture requires the restoration of minerals in the soil. For organic gardeners, that generally means rock powders.

Phosphorus is crucial for early root development. Widely accepted organic sources of phosphorus are ground rock phosphate and colloidal phosphate. Both are mined in open pits, one in Florida, the other in Tennessee. Rock phosphate, which is ground into fine meal, contains about 30 percent phosphoric acid and 30 percent calcium. Colloidal phosphate, a fine clay, is about 22 percent phosphoric acid, 19 percent calcium.

Those total phosphorus percentages can be misleading, however. Both forms release phosphorus slowly, 2 or 3 percent a year. Also, unlike other minerals, phosphorus lacks mobility; it does not travel in the soil. That means, to benefit plants, it must be present in an available form, and it must be in the root zone. The breakdown of organic matter in the soil helps to make phosphorus available.

Because phosphorus from rock powders is released slowly, it needs to be added only every few years. If a soil test shows a moderate deficiency in phosphorus and a soil pH of 6.5 or higher, adding 35 to 50 pounds of rock or colloidal phosphate to a 1,000-square-foot garden should provide enough of that nutrient for the next four or five years.

For the most part, there is little to distinguish between rock and colloidal phosphate. The rate of phosphorus release is so low and similar that the choice might well be based on price and availability. Because its particle size is finer, the colloidal form does release the mineral at a slightly higher rate. The rock form is somewhat more effective on acid soils, making it the amendment of choice if soil pH is 6.2 or less. (If a soil is strongly acid, it will lock up phosphorus in compounds that make it almost completely unavailable to plants. Because both rock phosphate and colloidal phosphate contain calcium, the addition of either will raise the pH.)

Potassium

While potassium is abundant in most soils — usually 20,000 pounds or more to the acre — less than 1 percent is in a form plants can use. A deficiency of the mineral results in weak stems, stunted growth and susceptibility to disease. Common sources of potassium include greensand and langbeinite.

Greensand, an iron potassium silicate, comes mostly from just beyond the shoreline of New Jersey, where it developed in the interior of ancient shells. It contains 6 to 7 percent potassium, plus iron, magnesium, lime, phosphorus and some 30 trace minerals.

Langbeinite, a mineral mined in the Southwest, is sold under the trade names of Sul-Po-Mag and K-Mag. It contains 22 percent potassium oxide, 22 percent sulfur and 18 percent magnesium oxide. Thus, it is also a rich

Greensand

Cottonseed Meal

Soft Rock Phosphate

Organic grower Louis Pulver says that, despite being a good source of nitrogen, "manure can be the scourge of farmers."

source of sulfur and magnesium.

Manure also contains potassium, ranging from 10 percent for horse and cattle manure to 24 percent for sheep. The potassium content of ordinary grass hay ranges from 5 to 11 percent, and legume hay from 10 to 15 percent.

Adding potassium to your soil is not an altogether straightforward matter, demonstrating the danger of the proposition that if a little fertilizer is a good thing, a lot must be better. For example, a potassium deficiency can be induced if the soil has an excess of magnesium. So if magnesium is adequate, langbeinite (18 percent magnesium oxide) might be a poor choice. Greensand would make more sense. If, however, too much potassium is added, it could result in a deficiency of magnesium and the trace mineral boron.

Some soil-testing laboratories endeavor to take into account the mineral balance of the soil in making recommendations. Certainly, anyone who is spreading soil amendments for the first time should be wary of trying to compensate too radically for soil deficiencies. Organic matter is a great healer and buffer, and a gentle way to restore soil health. Consequently, the application of composted manure or legume hay is a sound way to adjust potassium.

Wood ashes are another source of potas-

sium, but they too must be used with caution. Wood ashes also will boost soil pH. The danger is that wood ashes are easily overused, resulting in excess potassium and soil that is too alkaline for most soil life. Even if wood ashes are used in moderation, the potassium in these can be leached away by rain. To offset that, a split application is advised, half in fall and half in spring. Wood ashes should not be added when crops are growing, since the strongly alkaline ashes can kill seedlings if the ashes touch the seedling roots.

pH

Soil pH – is it acid or alkaline? – is the final indicator that a test will provide. Acid soil, usually a result of insufficient calcium, is a common problem in the East. In many parts of the West, just the opposite: alkalinity is the villain. Any soil test shows the pH; the lower the number, the higher the acidity. A neutral soil is 7, and as noted earlier, most vegetables do best in the range of pH 6.5 to 6.8, the range within which soil organisms are at their liveliest and the full spectrum of minerals is most readily available to plants.

To raise the pH of an acid soil, add calcium, usually in the form of ground limestone. Dolomitic lime is often recommended because of its high magnesium content. That is valuable because acid soils are also commonly deficient in magnesium. Remember, though, that too much magnesium will throw off the mineral balance.

If magnesium is not needed, calcitic lime would be the right choice.

For a 1,000-square-foot plot that is highly acidic (pH 5), about 100 pounds of limestone spread in the spring before planting will raise the pH above 6. These figures are approximations: light, sandy soils respond more to additions of lime than do heavy, clay soils.

For those who heat with wood, a partial substitute for limestone is wood ashes – if potassium is also lacking. Thinly spread about 25 pounds of wood ashes over a 1,000-square-foot plot, just before the first snowfall (to reduce leaching), and repeat the following spring, plus add 50 pounds of limestone.

One soil-testing laboratory reports that soil samples from rural areas frequently come in with the soil pH in the optimum range, yet the soil still has a calcium deficiency. Often this imbalance is caused by a reliance on wood ashes alone, and no calcium-bearing limestone, to modify soil acidity.

Alkaline soils – with a pH above 7 – make life difficult for organic gardeners. Such soils commonly contain lethal amounts of minerals

RICHARD W. BROWN

The Superphosphate Debate

AN ORGANIC GROWER ARGUES IN ITS FAVOR

There probably will always be passionate disagreement about what constitutes true organic practice. At one extreme are those – mostly but not exclusively gardeners – for whom the word "organic" evokes ideological overtones: if it's synthetic, it's *bad*. At the other extreme are those – almost exclusively commercial growers – for whom the question is economic: don't confuse the consumer, or the consumer might go away. Between those two extremes is the central question: "Does this represent good farming or gardening practice?" In other words, is this *enhancing* soil life, or is it *destroying* it?

A case in point: should an organic gardener/farmer use superphosphate?

Superphosphate is, without question, synthetic. Superphosphate is rock phosphate that has been doused with sulfuric acid. That leaves a concentrated, soluble phosphorus that is immediately available to the plants, in contrast to the natural rock or colloidal phosphate, which releases its phosphorus slowly. It is important to note that there is nothing to indicate that superphosphate is anything but benign as far as soil organisms are concerned.

Much of the rock phosphate now used in the U.S. for direct application – almost exclusively by organic gardeners and farmers – comes from huge open-pit mines in Florida. Colloidal phosphate is dug in Tennessee. Either material is costly to transport; most of what growers pay for it serves just to move the stuff. Great quantities of a nonrenewable resource – oil – are consumed to do that.

At its 1985 annual summer conference, the National Organic Farmers Association (NOFA), which has a membership of some 1,500 home gardeners and small-scale organic farmers in the Northeast, staged a debate on organic standards. The debate centered principally on superphosphates. Robert Houriet, former city editor of the Newark, New Jersey, *Star-Ledger*, helped organize NOFA and was its president in its formative years. In 1985, he was cropping a 14-acre market garden in northern Vermont. During the debate, he fervently argued that the moderate use of superphosphate should be permitted on grounds that it does not harm the soil in any way and, since it makes phosphorus immediately available to the plants, is superior to "natural" sources of phosphate.

Market gardener Robert Houriet believes organic standards should be relaxed.

Arguing on the opposite side was Bart Hall-Beyer, a Canadian farmer and co-author of *Ecological Farming in the North.* Hall-Beyer adamantly favored the no-synthetics position. He argued that there is no need for synthetics and that, in any case, the issue comes down to a *marketing* question. The consumer has come to expect that the word "organic" on the label means absolutely no synthetics have been applied, whether they be pesticides, herbicides, fertilizers or whatever. To try to explain on a label that certain synthetics are okay under certain conditions but not others would be absurd.

"The crux of this debate about organic certification standards and enforcement," he declared, "is whether or not we want the word 'organic' to have any credibility in the marketplace; whether we want the term 'organic' to have the same credibility as the word 'natural' – which is virtually none."

Houriet replied: "We have different philosophies here. Bart is arguing from the point of view of the consumer. I am arguing from the point of view of the farmer. The perpetuation of this either/or dichotomy can only lead to a redefinition of organic food as that which can only be produced by the very few and eaten by the very few."

Houriet's arguments did not prevail. Consider, however, the Maine fish story:

The basic material that makes up fish emulsion is cannery waste. The material has been found most useful as a foliar treatment. But bits and pieces of fish obviously are difficult to apply with a sprayer. They clog. The problem is eliminated by treating the material with phosphoric acid to break down the lumps. But now you've got fish plus at least half again as much phosphorus as was there naturally. Fish emulsion, therefore, is a processed – synthetic – amendment.

Yet the added phosphorus is not harmful to plants or soil life; in fact, it is beneficial. For some time, fish waste treated with phosphoric acid was not allowed under Maine's organic-standards law, even though that state is a leading producer of fish emulsion and ships it all over the country. The law, after no little hassle, was finally amended. Maine's commercial organic growers can now use processed fish emulsion.

—J.C.

RICHARD W. BROWN   OVERLEAF RICHARD W. BROWN

What's Wrong with Synthetic Fertilizers?

LISTEN TO THE EARTHWORMS

Soil scientists have often remarked that plants don't distinguish between nutrients from natural sources and those from synthetic fertilizers, so why should the gardener?

Now, it is demonstrably true that the plants don't care whether they get their nutrients from, let's say, anhydrous ammonia or from an organic substance, such as horse manure. But the billions of organisms that live in the soil do care. The worms abhor synthetic fertilizers, which can damage and alter soil life. Organic matter feeds soil organisms lavishly. Without that soil life, the soil cannot restore nutrients that are lost as crops are taken off.

Moreover, organic matter invariably contains trace minerals—micronutrients like zinc, molybdenum, manganese, iron, copper, boron—that are crucial, in tiny amounts, for plant health. They are broken down from complex organic compounds by the soil organisms and eventually find their way to the plants. Synthetic fertilizers generally do not contain trace minerals.

Fertilizers typically are measured by three numbers, say 10-10-10, which are the percentages of nitrogen, phosphorus and potassium compounds in the fertilizer. A synthetic 10-10-10 fertilizer might appear more potent than a 3-2-3 organic blend, but the synthetic compounds are volatile—they can gas off or leach out in water—meaning the crucial elements may be available for only a short period of time. Synthetic fertilizers, in effect, force-feed the plant, promoting quick growth and high yield. Organic blends, however, because they are made of rock powders, plant and animal meals and, in some cases, composted materials, continue to furnish modest levels of balanced nutrients for years.

Then, too, there is a philosophical issue: anyone who tills the soil has a responsibility to take care of it. Synthetic fertilizers do not foster soil health. They merely satisfy in the short term a particular plant's cultural needs. And a one-time reliance on synthetic fertilizers can, because it ignores the soil's needs, lead to long-term dependence on such fertilizers. But tend to the soil, and the plants can take care of themselves.

Ultimately, it becomes apparent that synthetic fertilizers are not only potentially damaging, they are also unnecessary.

Eliot Coleman, farm manager at the Mountain School in Vershire, Vermont, and long-time advocate of the organic approach on purely practical grounds, puts it this way: "Look, I'm too dumb to know how to feed plants; it's a very complex business. But feeding the soil is easy. Soil consists of just two things: ground rock particles and organic matter. The fact is that if you have plenty of good compost, you can get anything to grow. And what is compost? Ground rock particles and organic matter."

—J.C.

like selenium and sodium, suffer from surface salt and consequent soil crusting, and contain insufficient amounts of many important nutrients. Correcting alkaline soil is more difficult than correcting acid soil. Sulfur is the common amendment for alkaline soil—adding one pound of sulfur dust per 100 square feet will reduce pH by one point—but is both temporary and expensive.

Sulfur is often lacking in soil with insufficient humus. But almost any good source of organic nitrogen contains sulfates. Sulfur, incidentally, is a major component of acid rain.

Micronutrients

A number of trace elements, also called micronutrients, are needed by plants. Among them are iron, copper, boron, molybdenum, manganese, iodine and zinc. Deficiencies of these are usually avoided if, once again, the soil is well supplied with organic matter, with the resulting biological activity it supports. One gardening technique to ensure that there are adequate micronutrients in the soil is to plant deep-rooted cover crops, like alfalfa and sweet clover, which bring up trace elements from the subsoil. Plowing in the cover crops adds organic matter to the soil, returning nutrients and stimulating biological activity.

Simply put, soil life is what supports plant life. In crucial respects, the soil's appetite is easy to satisfy; if an earthworm won't savor it, it doesn't belong in the ground. Feed your soil at least as much organic matter—aged manure, rich compost—as you remove when you harvest the crops. Consider also modest mineral amendments; the names are a bit exotic, but the practice is straightforward. Your garden may not be absolutely natural, but by working with natural materials in harmony with natural processes, you will assure yourself the best chance of producing a healthy harvest of healthful crops. 🌱

SOURCES

Bountiful Gardens (Ecology Action)
19550 Walker Rd.
Willits, California 95490
Soy meal, phosphate, greensand, hoof and horn meal, bone meal, fish meal, worm castings, kelp. Catalogue free.

Dirt Cheap Organics
5645 Paradise Drive
Corte Madera, California 94925
Individual amendments and Erth-Rite (see Erth-Rite). Price list free.

Erth-Rite, Inc.
RD 1, Box 243
Gap, Pennsylvania 17527
Makes Erth-Rite, a composted fertilizer composed of rotted manure, greensand, colloidal and rock phosphates, seaweed meal and a bacterial "starter." Offers several different formulations. Catalogue free.

Farm Tech Service Inc.
365 W. Bainbridge St.
Elizabethtown, Pennsylvania 17022
Blends of organic fertilizers suited to specific crops and locations. Price list free.

Fertrell Co.
P.O. Box 265
Bainbridge, Pennsylvania 17502
Makes organic fertilizer blends containing rock powders, bean meal, cocoa hulls, sea products, leather tankage, poultry waste, greensand and agricultural slag. Brochure free.

Gardener's Supply
128 Intervale Road
Burlington, Vermont 05401
Greensand, kelp, Sul-Po-Mag, Fertrell and other blends. Catalogue free.

Necessary Trading Co.
614 P Salem Ave., P.O. Box 305
New Castle, Virginia 24127
Individual soil amendments, Fertrell and other blends, kelp and compost. Catalogue $2.

Nitron Industries, Inc.
4605 Johnson Road, P.O. Box 1447
Fayetteville, Arkansas 72702-0400
Earthworm castings, greensand, compost, limestone, rock phosphate, bone meal, kelp, cottonseed meal, trace elements and fertilizer blends. Catalogue free.

Peaceful Valley Farm Supply
P.O. Box 2209
110 Springhill Blvd.
Grass Valley, CA 95945
A wide range of individual amendments, from chicken manure to cocoa bean hulls, rock powders and compost-fertilizer blends. Catalogue $2.

Summertime Lettuce

FIVE RULES TO COMBAT BOLTING & BITTERNESS

BY PATRICK LIMA

O f all the vegetables my friend and I cultivate in our central Ontario garden, lettuce is the one most often gathered. Leafy exotica may come and go – we may forgo mache in favor of mustard greens one season, or replace a row of radicchio with rocket – but lettuce remains the salad maker's standby. Indeed, despite shifting trends, one corn-fed neighbor of ours steadfastly states a preference for what he calls (at every opportunity) "a honeymoon salad – lettuce alone."

But even if a salad bowl is filled with only lettuce, it need not lack variety. With the exception of squashes and perhaps peppers, lettuce crops up in more shapes, shades, sizes and textures than any other vegetable. While seed sellers have recently been offering new varieties of unusual salad greens – longer lists of endives and chicories and an enhanced selection of herbs and edible flowers – the lettuce lists, too, have branched out, a fact that this gardener appreciates. From our garden come apple-green, soft-leaved Boston (or butterhead) lettuces; tall, crisp, emerald Romaine (or cos) lettuces, and frilly burgundy rosettes, the red-leaf lettuces, which look like overgrown flowers. Loosely folded heads tinted copper and green with creamy centers belong to 'Merveille de Quatre Saisons,' and tight cones of crimped, crackling leaves grow from seeds of 'Green Ice.'

Such an array is not difficult to achieve. Even novice gardeners usually have something to show in the lettuce row; with attention to spacing and soil fertility, it is entirely possible to bring in picture-perfect heads. Give some thought to timing as well, and you can reasonably expect to continue picking fresh lettuce for almost half a year, from mid-May through October.

The late sowings, however, need special at- tention. Lettuce, generally one of the easiest vegetables to grow, luxuriates under cool, moist conditions of both earth and air, and sails through light frosts unscathed. It does well, then, in spring. But if a blazing sun beats down from a cloudless sky for weeks on end, conditions quite likely in summer, this crop tends to turn bitter and shrivel or run to seed.

For lettuce that will last into late summer, there are some things to avoid. Here is a recipe – based on experience – for failure in the lettuce patch: take a piece of sun-baked clay or parched sand, add nothing in the way of organic matter, and sow a packet of lettuce seeds as thickly as carrots. Don't thin. Count on rain to do the necessary watering. Even with such an approach, the result will likely be an apparently prosperous row of greens (or reds) – for a few weeks. Soon, however, leaves will turn bitter, and the heat-stressed, starved, cramped plants will bolt to seed as soon as they can muster the strength. As in life, so in the garden: there is no point in repeating mistakes.

T he alternative approach – also based on experience – produces lush, sweet lettuce through fall. Theoretically, September and October days – a kind of spring encore in reverse – should see homegrown lettuces at their prime. But hot, dry weather does have to be endured at the outset. Last year, I set out to test the reverse-spring theory. I discovered that there are five key ways to circumvent the stress of hot weather: one, choose bolt-resistant cultivars; two, transplant carefully; three, water, water and water again; four, provide shade; five, apply an organic mulch.

Durable cultivars are worth seeking out. We keep in mind the advice offered in Johnny's Selected Seeds' catalogue that "a careful variety selection is important for hot-weather crops,"

Each summer, the author grows five favorite, proven lettuce varieties and samples four or five new culti- vars. Last season's crop included right, clockwise from lower left, *'Parris Island Cos,' 'Four Sea- sons,' 'Green Ice,' 'Canasta,' 'Crispy Sweet,' 'Red Sails,' and 'Esmeralda.'*

As the author's garden shows, lettuce cultivars offer a wide range of shapes, shades, and textures. Even if a salad bowl is filled with only lettuce, it need not lack variety.

loose leaf, and to be "fast growing and vigorous"; and 'Canasta,' a French crisp or Batavian lettuce, which Johnny's describes as "bolt resistant, for spring, summer and fall," and "too good to pass up." We would see. For fall harvest, we omitted both 'Ithaca' (an iceberg type) and 'Buttercrunch,' for lack of space.

For me, late-season salads start sometime in July. Last summer, it was July 6, to be precise, when I filled two 12-by-16-inch flats, 2½ inches deep, with a seed-starting blend of sandy garden loam, peat moss, sifted compost and a dash of bone meal. I then made a geometric pattern of little thumbprint hollows spaced 2½ inches apart across and down the flat, and dropped several seeds onto the surface of each depression. Since lettuce seeds germinate poorly if the mercury rises much above 75 degrees F, make provisions to keep them relatively cool and moist during midsummer's heat. My seeded boxes sat in a slat-covered cold frame — any lightly shaded spot would do — and were watered as necessary.

About 10 days after the seedlings appeared, I thinned them to the sturdiest single plant in each spot. Three weeks later, after dousing the seedlings with a half-strength solution of fish emulsion, I sliced the earth in the flats into squares — just like cutting a tray of brownies — each with a young lettuce at its center. I then eased the earth cubes out of the flats with a narrow spatula and set the young lettuces, again a foot apart, in a bed that had been recently cleared of withered pea vines, seedy radishes and passé spinach. Because this intensive bed had benefited from a generous dressing of decayed manure the previous fall (and almost every fall for a decade), only a shallow scuffling with a hoe and rake was necessary in order to ready the earth for transplants.

In gardens where the earth needs more immediate help, spot enriching will boost fertility around each lettuce transplant. Here is how to do it: in a wheelbarrow, stir together equal parts of old manure, rotted almost to the topsoil stage — bagged, commercial manure is sometimes handy — and dampened peat moss. Other sources of both humus and nutrients are finely textured compost, perhaps shredded or sifted, and thoroughly rotted leaves. To a wheelbarrow load of humus I like to add a shovelful of bone meal for phosphorus and half as much wood ash. Blend the works thoroughly. Two or three double handfuls of this mix stirred into each transplanting hole will feed each lettuce plant during its days in the garden.

and heed Stokes' suggestion that "leaf and cos lettuce are both more suitable for warmer regions." In other words, steer away from the icebergs in summer.

A quick check of seed catalogues reveals scores of enticing lettuce cultivars, many with such late-season commendations as "slow to bolt," "heat resistant" or "reliable and well adapted to growing through the season." We get around the dilemma of choice by consistently planting five proven favorites, and experimenting with four or five new sorts each season.

In spring, we always grow 'Green Ice,' 'Ithaca M1,' 'Red Sails,' 'Parris Island Cos' and 'Buttercrunch,' each quite different from the next in form, color and texture. Last year's trial cultivars were 'Esmeralda,' a green Boston type just released from Royal Sluis of Holland, who describes it as "very slow bolting in warmer climates"; 'Merveille de Quatre Saisons' (often called 'Four Seasons'), a green and wine-red butterhead back for a repeat trial and, according to the Shepherd's Garden Seeds catalogue, capable of being grown "quite late in the spring season as well as late summer and in the fall"; 'Crispy Sweet,' said by Park Seeds to combine the best qualities of butterhead and

JOHN SCANLAN

Lettuce Man

In less than 10 years, The Cook's Garden has grown from a roadside vegetable cart into a seed company with a national following. "We're still very small, but we're the only seed firm that is owned and run by market gardeners," remarks owner Shepherd Ogden, "and that makes us special." The Cook's Garden not only sells seeds, it grows them. That combination has earned the Ogdens one of the American Horticultural Society's most prestigious prizes, the G.B. Gunlogson Award.

What also makes The Cook's Garden special is the quantity and variety of salad seeds they grow and sell. This year's catalogue offers 50 kinds of lettuce, as well as another 50 varieties of salad greens, nearly half of which are imported. Lettuce was Shep and Ellen Ogden's first crop and is still the mainstay of both their farm market and seed business. "I'm a lettuce nut," Ogden admits.

At Looseleaf Farm—an allusion to lettuce and notebooks, for the Ogdens are also writers (*The Cook's Garden* by Shepherd and Ellen Ogden, © 1989. Rodale Press. Emmaus, PA)—they test new varieties and grow produce for their Londonderry, Vermont, farm market. "Basically, I grow the varieties that please me," Ogden says, "and it happened that many foreign varieties, which weren't available here, had wonderful forms and colors. I also wanted to grow and sell different types of lettuce—looseleaf, butterhead, crisphead, Romaine and intermediate kinds." For the farm market, the Ogdens cultivate large amounts of 18 varieties, including 'Little Gem,' 'Lollo Rossa,' 'Red Salad Bowl,' 'Salad Bowl,' 'Royal Oak Leaf,' 'Reine des Glaces,' 'Rouge d'Hiver,' 'Orfeo' and 'Four Seasons.'

Each year, they also test another 20 to 30 varieties, growing small amounts that they and their ardent farm-market customers evaluate. Ogden admits he often can't make distinctions based on taste, but he is a keen judge of visual and cultural qualities.

The geographic and horticultural origins of The Cook's Garden belong to Shep Ogden's side of the family. His grandfather was author Samuel Ogden, one of the pioneers of organic gardening. Shep and Ellen carry on Samuel Ogden's commitment: seeds from The Cook's Garden are untreated, and the Ogdens' produce is raised free of chemical insecticides or fungicides.

Looseleaf Farm's three acres have all the unyielding features of a typical Vermont homestead: hilly terrain, rocky soil and a growing season so brief that it serves chiefly to punctuate the long winters.

The Ogdens subscribe to the French intensive method, an approach that includes double-digging of the soil, the repeated addition of organic matter and the creation of raised beds. Each bed, Ogden explains, "catches more sun and gets better drainage because it is raised and sloped, and we never walk on the beds." Because of the short growing season, nearly all crops are begun indoors, on propagating mats, then moved to unheated greenhouses or transplanted outside. Ogden stresses the importance of not crowding plants. Local cow "slurry" is used to enrich the soil in the gardens and in the five greenhouses; seedlings and plants are sprayed with a solution of fish emulsion and seaweed.

This year's best-selling lettuce seeds were the looseleaf 'Red Grenoble'; 'Matchless,' an heirloom buttercrunch also known as 'Deertongue'; 'Little Gem,' a heat-resistant summer variety; 'Rosy,' a red iceberg type; and 'St. Blaise,' a small-headed Romaine, excellent for early planting.

'Little Gem' (or 'Sugar Cos') is also one of Ogden's favorites. "It's heat resistant and doesn't bolt, and it is small—perfect for the intensive garden, ideal for a single salad serving. When cut lengthwise, it looks like a miniature Romaine." Other favorites are 'Reine des Glaces,' a frost-green crisphead with notched leaves, and 'Lollo Rossa,' a pale green, deeply curled looseleaf with red margins.

'Little Gem,' Ogden warns, is not a good candidate for midsummer planting: "Moisture collects in the plant and causes stem rot." He recommends avoiding late crops of most standard head types for the same reason. Ogden's last yield of lettuce, planted at the end of July, matures in early October, though he overwinters some varieties under floating row covers of spun polyester, mainly to test their hardiness.

"In general, the cutting or leaf lettuces are best suited for planting late in the season, best able to withstand early frosts and short-day conditions." Ogden advises gardeners to try 'Salad Bowl,' 'Red Salad Bowl,' 'Royal Oak Leaf' or 'Black-Seeded Simpson.' "The right variety is important," Ogden continues. "It should be one that won't bolt or catch water and rot . . . one that will germinate in late-summer conditions and will resist frost and hold its quality until picked. And a variety which will mature despite low light. In northern latitudes, day length is what really matters."

—*Karan Davis Cutler*

As I mentioned, the second way to overcome the stress of high summer is to transplant carefully—as carefully as one would handle transplants of cucumbers or squash. In August, I take special care in transplanting to disturb roots as little as possible. When temperatures are high and the air is dry, plants need intact root systems more than ever. Otherwise, wilting and even death can occur.

I expect that the trauma of an August transplanting is not quickly reversed. In fact, next time I'll be even more careful by seeding into small plastic pots and tipping the plants out to prevent root disturbance entirely. As part of my ongoing experiments, I also plan to sow lettuce seeds directly in the open garden some time during the last half of July. Trials at Wisley Garden, showplace of Britain's august Royal Horticultural Society, provide a precedent. In their newsletter, *The Garden,* Patrick Walker reports on an early August planting: "After ensuring that the soil is thoroughly moist, seed is sown in clusters . . . spaced 8½ inches apart each way. After germination, eliminate all but the most robust specimen at each station. Visual comparison at Wisley between trial plants sown in this way and those subsequently transplanted is invariably in favor of the lettuces which are sown in situ and then singled." Although I would stay with a 1 foot spacing between the seed clusters, the method and timing sound promising.

The third priority in hot weather is water. My seedlings in their little soil cubes were set firmly in the earth and watered twice in a saucer-shaped well around each. Thereafter, I watered them about every two days during rain-free periods, always by filling up the well around each plant. Once a month, I gave the plants a drink of fish emulsion. I don't think lettuce can be overwatered in the days when it is becoming established, especially in the heat of summer. If plants wilt, do water—but you have already let them go too long. Any kind of setback, such as root disturbance or wilting, will trigger bolting and cause bitterness. This early flowering is a survival mechanism for the plant. Proper spacing along with adequate watering are the secrets

to the formation of full-sized lettuces packed with nicely blanched inner leaves. Our transplants sit a full foot apart, but they are not long in filling the gaps.

The fourth priority is shade. Temperatures in full sun may be more than 10 degrees higher than those in deep shade. Partial shade is the rule for lettuces, because they do need sunlight. Planting the lettuces where they will be shaded from the noon sun by corn, staked tomatoes or asparagus will help them endure the hot weather. Alternatively, a cover of laths nailed an inch apart to crosspieces can be placed over the young lettuces and moved away as they mature and the season cools toward autumn. I often scatter a handful of straw over August transplants to filter out the sun.

The fifth priority, mulch, also lowers temperatures. An organic mulch keeps the ground relatively cool. Soil temperatures under a hay or straw mulch can be more than 5 degrees cooler than those in bare soil nearby. Since lettuce thrives in cooler ground, a mulch of straw, compost or what have you is always a help. After that, routine weeding should do it.

In my experience, lettuces are virtually immune to plant diseases—I expect that generous organic treatment keeps them hale and hearty—and are only occasionally bothered by bugs. Earwigs and slugs are the worst offenders in my garden, and both feel the pinch during flash-lit 11 o'clock tours. Insecticidal soap is the only effective way I know to cope organically with more earwigs than I care to hand-pick. "At least they die clean," quipped one visitor.

And the results? An unidentified creature ate almost all of the 'Four Seasons' lettuces, so I have little to report this time around. Our ever-useful garden record from several years back says, however, that this cultivar, seeded in spring, matured by July into attractive copper-and-green, tender-leaved heads. Shepherd Ogden, master salad grower and seedsman in Vermont (see box, page 121), concurs. " 'Four Seasons' wins the color contest hands down," he writes. "It is not just beautiful, though. I have been able to get good stands from first planting to last, and have had very little trouble with bolting."

'Parris Island Cos' bolted to seed in August, providing only a little edible greenery on the way, but this one has grown well for us on a spring/summer schedule since we started to garden, so it stays. 'Crispy Sweet' was not far behind in the race to produce seed. 'Red Sails' and 'Green Ice' grew nicely. They seemed to shrink a little from the August heat, but still provided lots of leaves for the September salad bowl. My gardening intuition says that these quick-growing cultivars would fare better with an even later start, perhaps during the last week of July. They would then be garden-ready just as cooler September days were approaching.

'Esmeralda,' our second runner-up, matured into elegant, light green heads. As befits a Boston lettuce, the texture was tender, the taste gentle.

And best of all was – the envelope, please – 'Canasta,' a lettuce both lovely to look at and exceptionally fine to eat. Its waved and glossy outer leaves were tinted the green of 'Granny Smith' apples, shading to purple-red at the edges; hearts continued to fill with light-green-to-creamy-yellow leaves. The texture was crisp but tender. Indeed, "too good to pass up." In one season, 'Canasta' joined our list of "old" favorites.

Incidentally, centuries-old gardening books not only provide fascinating reading, but may often yield a practical tip or two. John Evelyn was a popular English garden writer during the seventeenth century. In 1699, he wrote *Acetaria, A Discourse on Salletts.* His suggestions for preparing a salad begin, "Let your Herbe ingredients be exquisitely cull'd and cleansed . . . and rather discreetly sprinkled than over much sob'd in water . . . especially lettuce. After washing let them remain a while in the cullender to drain the superfluous moisture and lastly swing them all together gently in a clean coarse napkin."

A cotton pillowcase is a perfect alternative to a napkin or, for that matter, a plastic salad spinner, when quantities of greens must be dried for a feast for many or a meal for two or three avid salad eaters. I dump washed leaves in a pillowcase and swing it, outdoors, in vigorous, arm's-length circles; I shake the bag to redistribute the contents and swing it again. This is rather rough handling for soft butterheads, but works well with other sorts.

Over the years, I have come to expect a salad a day from the garden throughout the growing season, and lettuce is usually among the ingredients. Any gardener who plans and plants for successive lettuce crops will have the basis for colorful, interesting salads spring, summer and fall. 🌢

SOURCES

The Cook's Garden
Box 65
Londonderry, Vermont 05148
'Buttercrunch,' 'Ithaca,' 'Red Sails,' 'Royal Oakleaf,' 'Curly Oakleaf,' 'Salad Bowl,' 'Red Salad Bowl,' 'Little Gem,' many others. Catalogue $1.

Johnny's Selected Seeds
Foss Hill Road
Albion, Maine 04910
'Buttercrunch,' 'Canasta,' 'Oakleaf,' 'Parris Island Cos,' 'Red Sails.' Catalogue free.

Park Seed Co., Inc.
Cokesbury Rd.
Greenwood, South Carolina 29647-0001
'Salad Bowl,' 'Green Ice,' 'Selma Lollo,' 'Red Sails.' Catalogue free.

Shepherd's Garden Seeds
30 Irene St.
Torrington, CT 06790-6657
'Lollo Rossa,' 'Merveille de Quatre Saisons,' 'Red Oakleaf.' Catalogue $1.

Stokes Seeds Inc.
Box 548
Buffalo, New York 14240
'Buttercrunch,' 'Parris Island Cos,' 'Red Sails.' Catalogue free.

Steadfast Perennials

A GARDENER'S PALETTE OF BLOOMS THAT STAY THE COURSE

BY ALLEN LACY

To the disciples of St. Gertrude of Jekyll, there is more to gardening than growing a profusion of healthy plants and much more to creating a perennial border than simply assembling a hodgepodge of favorite specimens. Jekyll (1843-1932), the prolific British garden writer, admonished us all to consider the individual plant not only as a solo performer, but also as a player in an ensemble of other plants. Her passion for painting hampered by impaired vision, Jekyll reputedly viewed her gardens as blurs of color, composing them in the manner of an Impressionist painter working a canvas. She called her gardens "living pictures" and is remembered for having audaciously planted an entirely white-blooming garden and an all-pink garden.

Inspired by Jekyll or not, thoughtful gardeners will take care to see that their borders include perennials that vary in size. Thus they may grow *Hosta venusta,* a dainty little charmer, but also make room – considerable room – for *Helianthus angustifolius,* surely the noblest of our native perennial sunflowers. They will also see to it that there is a good succession of bloom during the growing season. They may sigh a bit when the Oriental poppies and the peonies begin their spectacular show in late spring, knowing that it will soon be over, but they will take consolation in the assurance that a succession of other perennials will follow, each one in its own season. The peonies will cease their bloom in late spring, but delphiniums will bloom in early summer, and in September, there will be the pink and silvery-white elegance of Japanese anemones to look forward to.

Peonies and other perennials with a brief and showy season have had their share of praise, and they deserve it. But I would like to single out, somewhat at random, another class of perennials that is sometimes overlooked and to put in an appreciative word on their behalf. These are the perennials that stay the course, that come into bloom and then stay in bloom through the summer and well into fall.

Highest on my list, partly because it's utterly new to me, partly because it's really wonderful, partly perhaps because we both are natives of Texas, is *Gaura lindheimeri.* I am so enthusiastic about it that a friend has accused me of plotting to start up The American Gaura Society and have annual conventions. I saw my first *Gaura* last June when visiting the sandy garden of fellow garden writer Pamela Harper in the tidewater of Virginia, and was completely struck by it, especially after she told me that its season of bloom began in late spring and would continue well into the fall. It bears small, rather whiskered-looking pinkish-white flowers on tough and airy stems which eventually reach six feet. When I saw it in the Harper garden, it was backlit by the early morning sunshine, making a fine accent among some lower-growing perennials. A week later, while visiting a promising new nursery, Holbrook Farm and Nursery in western North Carolina, I bought three small plants, which I set out in my garden when I got home. I didn't expect much from them the first year, but they took hold immediately, and by the first frost, they had made heavy clumps almost six feet high. With their wiry stems, they make fine cut flowers for lightening an informal bouquet.

As for the several cultivars of the hardy fuchsia (*Fuchsia magellanica*) I've grown the past three years, I must confess that before I actually ordered some from Lamb Nurseries in Spokane, Washington (the only source I know), I had grave doubts that these smaller cousins of the large-flowered tender fuchsias would actually be hardy, even though I knew

A classic perennial border, left, demonstrating a gardener's orchestration of colors, sizes, and species.

Top, **Verbena rigida canadensis,** *the perfect edging plant;* bottom, **Geranium sanguineum,** *a white cranesbill;* right, *the new long-blooming day lily 'Stella de Oro.'*

that they had naturalized themselves in parts of Scotland. The sturdy potted plants I received in late April grew rapidly, becoming bushy specimens two feet high by Memorial Day. They started blooming in early June and kept at it until frost. The flowers were tiny, but so abundant that the plants fairly glowed with deep red and purple throughout the season. I mulched them after the ground froze, but didn't really expect them to return, despite having read reports of their survival well up into Ontario. I decided that it didn't matter; if need be, I'd just order new ones each spring and treat them as annuals. The ones I had planted in a sunny spot (contrary to the orthodox advice) survived one of the worst winters in years. (Those planted in the shade bloomed poorly and didn't live through the winter.) The survivors were a little slow in sending up new shoots, and the first blooms didn't appear until the middle of June, but from then on my fuchsias were little fountains of ruby and amethyst from summer to late fall.

No one doubts the hardiness of a clematis, but most clematis are vines, and the one I like best is *Clematis integrifolia,* which displays no aerial ambitions. It's a very weak-stemmed bushy perennial which sprawls and hugs the ground under the burden of its abundant, nodding, bell-shaped flowers, which are a radiant metallic blue. It blooms heavily for several weeks in early summer, then sporadically, but the flowers are followed by pinwheel-like, silvery seed heads, themselves as striking as any blossom.

If I had to make do with just one daisy or rayed flower in my garden it would be *Coreopsis verticillata,* the threadleaf coreopsis. One of its relatives, *C. grandiflora,* is a glory of the summer roadside, but its season of bloom is brief, and in the garden, it tends to fall over in a very untidy way. The threadleaf coreopsis has better posture, handsome ferny foliage,

and a wealth of small blossoms smothering the plant from early summer almost until frost, if it is lightly sheared in late August when the bloom begins to wane. The cultivar 'Golden Shower' is aptly named; 'Moonbeam' is a soft and creamy light yellow.

It seems a bit strange to include a day lily in this account of perennials that stay the course. Any given day lily or hemerocallis will remain in bloom, on average, something between two and three weeks, but since day lilies vary over a month in initiating bloom, according to the kind, the day lily season lasts about two months starting in early summer. But there is one day lily that is different, one that sends up one set of scapes after another, over a period of some four months. Bred by Walter Jablonski, a former butcher and farmer in Indiana who is now 90, it is called 'Stella de Oro' (though one catalogue has it as 'Stella de Oreo'!). The blossoms are under three inches across, classifying it as a miniature. It grows only 22 inches high. The winner last year of the Stout Medal, the highest honor bestowed by The American Hemerocallis Society, 'Stella de Oro' is one of those rare day lilies that will be a staple of the general nursery trade, not just an item in a specialty catalogue. It will take its place alongside 'Hyperion' as a day lily that everyone knows and grows.

Sedum maximum 'Atropurpureum' is perhaps the most arresting of all the sedums, a genus filled with garden-worthy plants. Its season of bloom is brief, a mere two weeks in early autumn, but the pink flowers are cheering. The main feature of this plant, however, is that its leaves are purple-bronze, its stems so dour a shade of purple they seem black. Growing about 30 inches tall, this fine succulent looks especially fetching when planted alongside artemesias, lamb's ears, or anything else with gray foliage.

I should also take note of salvias, though not of the low-growing, torrid red annuals that

Pamela Harper *top left.* Derek Fell *bottom left.* Courtesy Wayside Gardens S.C. 29695-0001, *bottom right*

bloom so unstintingly all summer, including its hottest weeks. There are a good many perennial salvias that produce large plants and bloom over a long season, with blossoms in the blue-to-purple end of the spectrum. *S. pitcheri* is among the best of these, standing four to five feet high with deep azure-blue flowers—a cooling sight in the depths of August.

Other torrid red summer annuals, such verbenas as the hybrid appropriately called 'Blaze,' have their cooler counterparts in hardy perennial species which tend toward purple.

I have great admiration for *Verbena rigida canadensis*, sometimes listed as *Verbena venosa canadensis*. This diminutive charmer stays low but spreads wide, covering itself with lovely, somewhat soft-spoken mauve-pink flower clusters throughout the summer and fall. It is a perfect plant to edge a long section of a perennial border or to line a sunny pathway.

I mustn't overlook geraniums, of course, by which I do not mean the plants that are properly called pelargoniums, though American gardeners will probably use the word "geranium" until the crack of doom in referring to

True geraniums, the tall purple cranesbills, are hardy and trouble-free.

Not quite stead-fast, **Helianthus angustifolius** *is a prolific autumn bloomer.*

the bright red and pink and white bedding and windowbox plants sold by the millions each spring. Pelargoniums are gaudy and fun, but they are not hardy. True geraniums, commonly called cranesbills, are more subtle in their beauty, and they are bone-hardy and trouble-free. Many species and selected cultivars are sold commercially. Some bloom heavily for a few weeks and then call it quits, but *Geranium endressii* 'Wargrave Pink,' *G. sanguineum, G.* x 'Johnson's Blue,' and some others stay in bloom throughout the summer.

Those with room to spare may want to include the robust *Helianthus angustifolius.* In her classic book *A Southern Garden,* originally published in 1942 by the University of

North Carolina Press and still in print today, the late Elizabeth Lawrence called this plant "the best and latest of the perennial sunflowers," dazzling in its furious bloom throughout October. She also complained that it was hard to find; she got hers from a Mr. Tong, who got it from a Mrs. Mitchener, "who had it from some other gardener." It is still difficult, but not impossible, to find. It also requires careful placement, since it ranges in height anywhere from five to eight feet and grows four feet across.

Finally, there are two long-flowering ground covers that I suspect would look stunning grown together, although I've only seen them separately. *Ceratostigma plumbaginoides,* commonly called leadwort and generally sold under the incorrect scientific name *Plumbago larpentae,* grows about eight inches high. The green and glossy foliage turns a brownish-maroon in the fall, with a solid mass of intense blue flowers in August and September. Since *C. plumbaginoides* is slow to break dormancy in the spring, it seems a good idea to combine it with an American native called green-and-gold (*Chrysogonum virginianum*), which has attractive light green leaves and appealing golden blossoms appearing sporadically from late March well into September.

Should we gardeners forgo iris, peonies, Japanese anemones, and anything else with a brief but spectacular season to fill our home grounds with *Chrysogonum virginianum, Gaura lindheimeri* and other perennials which bloom over the long haul? I think not. A blaze of poppies, even though brief, is still a blaze, something to be looked forward to, to be remembered when it is swiftly past, and to be held in memory for the next year. None of the plants I have celebrated here could be called spectacular, except perhaps *Clematis integrifolia,* if planted in sufficient quantity. (Two dozen plants would be about right.) But together they lend continuity to the perennial border, being constant presences that serve as a foil to other, briefer and more pyrotechnic displays. ❧

SOURCES

Busse Gardens
Rt. 2, Box 238
Cokato, Minnesota 55321
Catalogue $2: Hemerocallis 'Stella de Oro,' Salvia pitcheri.

Carroll Gardens
P.O. Box 310
444 East Main Street
Westminster, Maryland 21157
Catalogue $2: Ceratostigma plumbaginoides *(listed as* Plumbago larpentae), Clematis integrifolia.

Holbrook Farm & Nursery
Rt. 2, Box 223B
Fletcher, North Carolina 28732
Catalogue $2: Gaura lindheimeri, Chrysogonum virginianum, Helianthus angustifolius.

Lamb Nurseries
101 Sharp Avenue
Spokane, Washington 99202
Catalogue $1: Fuchsia magellanica.

Viette Farm & Nursery
Rt. 1, Box 16
Fishersville, Virginia 22939
Catalogue $2: Chrysognum virginianum, Coreopsis verticillata, *hemerocallis 'Stella de Oro.'*

Wayside Gardens
P.O. Box 1
Hodges, South Carolina 29695
Catalogue $1: Ceratostigma plumbaginoides, Coreopsis verticillata, *hemerocallis 'Stella de Oro,' true* Geranium *species.*

Salvia pitcheri,
a cooling sight in August.

Insect Wars

RECRUITING ALLIES FOR NATURAL PEST CONTROL

BY LINDA GILKESON

As soon as a new acquaintance finds out that I am an entomologist, the questions start to fly—what to do about caterpillars on the broccoli, insects on the roses, worms in the apples, fleas on the dog and beetles under the house. Every week, I am sent plastic bags or vials of insect specimens, usually rather the worse for their travels, for identification and recommendations. Not long ago, a huge assassin bug was brought in on suspicion of being a cockroach—luckily, this beautiful beneficial predator was unscathed by its capture and was released to resume its life as a paladin in the garden.

In dealing with people's various entomological queries, I am often struck by two things—first, the general distrust, even fear, with which people view insects (some of the most fascinating creatures on Earth) and second, the widespread desire of people to avoid using dangerous chemicals in controlling them. Many gardeners have heard of biological control, which is the use of natural enemies (predators, parasites, disease organisms) to combat pests. They like the idea of biological control, which is gentle on the environment, employing, as it does, nature's own methods of limiting insect populations. Also, where biocontrol programs have been sufficiently developed, they have saved growers time and money. Biological control is increasingly popular in the confined spaces of commercial greenhouses, and for home gardeners, an array of effective biological methods of pest management is available.

The key idea behind biological control is that pest populations need not be eradicated—just reduced to an acceptably low level. I like the term "pest management" because it implies finding a balanced population level for the pest in question. That level depends on the crop: a few holes in the outer leaves of a cab-

bage are fine, but a few holes in a tomato are not. If pests aren't gnawing the part of the plant you plan to eat, then it is often surprising how much damage can be tolerated, especially by root crops. More than half of the foliage of potatoes and turnips can be chewed up before yields start to decline.

The most sensible (and easiest and least expensive) pest management strategy for the home gardener is to *attract* and *protect* the native predatory insects and mites—not to buy them. Although gardeners can buy some beneficial insects (which I will discuss shortly), the selection that can be purchased is nothing like the huge variety available in nature. In every area of the country, thousands of indigenous species are consuming pests—for the most part unnoticed. These cheap and hardy natives make much more sense for a home garden than costly imports.

Take the example of insects that attack aphids (which I know better than others because biological control of aphids is my main area of research). Common predators of aphids include the sluglike larvae of flower flies, which are beautiful black-and-white or black-and-yellow flies that hover, like helicopters, over flowers. The small, bright orange larvae of predatory midges feed on aphids, as do ladybugs and their larvae. Aphids occasionally fall victim to the ferocious larvae of the delicate green lacewings and to such general predators as assassin bugs, minute pirate bugs, dance flies and big-eyed bugs (really!). Tiny parasitic wasps that inject an egg into each aphid are common and widespread. The parasitized aphids are easy to find because they turn into black or silvery brown, rigid mummies as the young wasps develop inside.

Of course, there are many pests in the garden besides aphids, and fortunately, there are many more native predators and parasites

Right, **Cecropia, or silk moth caterpillar, and Cabbage butterfly larvae,** *inset.* **Both are pests that can be controlled by natural methods.**

DOROTHY S. LONG/PHOTO/NATS

*Top to bottom: **Predators of various leaf-eating pests include ladybugs, clustering in winter; tiger beetle, feeding on pill bug; praying mantid, dining on grasshopper; lacewing larva, attacking aphid.***

as well, nine of which are described on pages 136-137. In addition, predatory midges (related to spiders, not insects) prey on plant-feeding mites and small insects. In the upper layers of the soil, predatory mites feed on fly larvae and the eggs of many insects and nematodes. Important predatory beetles include not only the large ground beetles and rove beetles, but also the small hemispherical hister beetles; the ferocious, iridescently marked tiger beetles; fireflies (really beetles), of which both larvae and adults feed mostly on snails, slugs and insect larvae; and the leathery-winged soldier beetles that eat aphids, caterpillars and other small larvae.

There is no way a gardener can purchase such an insectivorous menagerie – the task is to create an inviting environment. And the first step in enticing insect predators to your garden is to stop using pesticides. Period.

The next step is to lay out and plant the garden so that it contains perennial beds or areas that remain undisturbed each year. An ideal approach is to garden in permanent beds with sod or mulched paths between them that are not cultivated. The perennial beds and paths give refuge to ground-dwelling predators and provide a stable habitat from year to year so their populations can build up.

A profusion of flowering plants, especially those with small flowers, rich in nectar, is necessary to attract many beneficial flies and wasps to the garden. It is the larvae of most beneficial species that are predators, not the adults. The adults need pollen and

nectar to sustain them and enable them to lay the maximum number of eggs. Particularly attractive to these adults are mint family herbs (lemon balm, pennyroyal, thyme), carrot family plants (dill, parsley) and cabbage family plants (radishes, mustard, broccoli) that have been allowed to bolt. I am always astonished at the insect activity in the few parsley plants I leave to flower every year – on a warm day, the plants literally hum with hundreds of visitors. Many weeds are also attractive to predatory insects: Queen-Anne's-lace, or wild carrot, is one of the most important nectar plants for native parasitic wasps.

I think the attractiveness of certain plants to insects may be the most important effect of companion planting. Herbs interplanted among the vegetables do not particularly repel pests (many pests have incredibly sophisticated sensory equipment for locating their host plants and aren't a bit confused by interplanting), but the herbs attract the pests' natural enemies to the garden.

Providing a stable habitat from year to year and an attractive food supply for adults will entice many beneficial insects, and most people will be happy to leave it at that. There is, however, one more touch that you may want to add: an "insect bath." In one garden I had with a friend, we set up a small birdbath in the garden. We built up gravel islands in the water, so insects could drink without drowning during the hot, dry summer days. An enormous variety of insects frequented the watering hole, with honeybees and parasitic wasps the most numerous. I have discovered in my own research that providing drinking water for female aphid midges causes them to lay nearly twice as many eggs as they do when they have ample food (honeydew) but no water.

Buying Predators

After taking all the appropriate steps to attract beneficial insects naturally, you still might want to weigh the virtues of buying some predators for your garden. Ladybugs are the classic biological control agent advertised for use in gardens, but they are a bad buy for the home gardener. The species usually sold, *Hippodamia convergens,* is collected from its overwintering sites in the Sierra Mountains, where beetles congregate and can be easily scooped up. When they are sent to a customer, their hibernation is broken by their being warmed up; then their instinct tells them to fly away. When they are released in a garden, they disperse to distant pastures, although they can be useful in a greenhouse if the vents are screened to keep them in. Probably the

FROM TOP TO BOTTOM: KEVIN SCHAFFER/TOM STACK & ASSOCIATES. DR. E.R. DEGGINGER. DWIGHT KUHN. DWIGHT KUHN.

greatest benefit of buying ladybugs is that their presence will discourage you from using pesticides, thereby encouraging local species to move in. In a study done several years ago, marked ladybugs were released in a garden to control aphids. When samples were later checked, aphids were indeed being eaten by ladybugs – unmarked ones. A home gardener probably would have given the credit to purchased beetles.

Praying mantids are enormously entertaining as pets, but do not invest in them for pest control. They eat any insect they catch, beneficial or not, and because 9 out of 10 insects around are not pests, their indiscriminate gorging makes them outlaws in the garden. Also, according to a recent review, most of the young nymphs die upon emerging from the egg cases unless there is a continuous food supply for them. In addition, because mantids only have one or two generations per year, their populations do not increase along with prey numbers, as do populations of predators with short life cycles.

Well then, you say, what should I buy? For aphid control, a small order of the aphid midge (*Aphidoletes aphidimyza*) is probably useful to supplement native aphid predators, particularly in early spring before the native midge populations have built up. This midge is now being used commercially to control aphids in greenhouse peppers and experimentally in apple orchards. It is a hardy, native species, whose small orange larvae have a voracious appetite for many species of aphids. The midges are sold in the pupal stage; when the adults emerge, the females lay about 250 eggs each among aphids on leaves. Their life cycle takes about 3 weeks in the summer, and they increase quickly.

Green lacewings (*Chrysopa carnea*) are also for sale, and being hardy, they can become established in a garden. The larvae are active predators of many soft-bodied insects, including each other if their numbers are too high. As with the aphid midge, a small order will supplement the native species in the garden. Lacewings lay each egg at the end of a long stalk; larvae resemble ladybug larvae.

Additional predatory insect species are being used commercially in strawberries and citrus crops and are being tested experimentally on field corn and other crops. For a home gardener, however, they are most effective if confined in a greenhouse or on interior plantings. There is a predatory mite (*Phytoseiulus persimilis*) to control two-spotted mites, a parasite (*Encarsia formosa*) for greenhouse whitefly, and a predatory mite (*Amblyseius cucumeris*) that controls western flower thrips.

Australian ladybugs (*Cryptolaemus montrouzieri*) to control mealybugs are occasionally available, as are *Chilocorus* beetles, to control scale insects.

BT and Doom

Even in a garden with a full complement of beneficial insects, there may still be one or two species that cause damage every year or every second or third year. It may be cabbage butterflies or potato beetles. Another biological control – the introduction of specific disease organisms – may offer a solution.

Bacillus thuringiensis, or BT, is an insect-infecting bacteria that kills cabbage loopers, cabbageworms, tomato hornworms and corn earworms. BT is widely available in both liquid and powder formulations (under the brand names Thuricide and Dipel), which are mixed with water and sprayed on plants. When an insect eats the sprayed leaf, the BT spores germinate and grow inside its gut until they infect the blood. BT does not last long in the environment in direct sunlight, and it is most effective if used when the caterpillars have grown large enough to bite a hole in the leaf, thus ensuring that they will eat enough spores to be poisoned. Caterpillars stop feeding immediately after eating BT, but they may not die for several days, so wait a few days to assess the effectiveness of the spray.

As a result of extensive research, USDA scientists have found 72 new varieties of BT in soil samples from such disparate places as caves in West Virginia, the Himalayas, a car bumper in Iceland, and the bottom of a cat's foot (that strain is *B.t. fluffiensis*). New commercial formulations of BT are targeted at specific pests such as locusts (*B.t. kurstaki*), blackflies and mosquitoes (*B.t. israelensis,* sold as Teknar, Bactimos and Vectobac), wax moth larvae in beehives (*B.t. aizawai*), and Colorado potato beetles (*B.t. San Diego,* sold as M-One, a recent discovery now being test marketed). And researchers are even incorporating BT into the genetic makeup of vegetables (see page 137).

Because BT kills caterpillars only when it is eaten, not by skin contact, it does not infect humans, animals and most other arthropods. Because it is so safe, it can be used on food crops up until harvest. I have found that, even in areas where cabbage butterflies are severe pests, only two or three sprays were needed during the summer to control them.

Another microbial insecticide that has been available for years is the milky bacterial disease (sold as Doom and Japidemic) that infects larvae of the highly destructive Japanese

beetle. The larvae feed on roots of grasses in turf, so it is simple and effective to treat the lawn with the bacterial solution. Other microbial insecticides, including a virus that infects codling moth (Decyde) and a virus that infects corn earworm (Elcar), have been registered.

Beyond the arsenal of biological controls is a whole range of traditional techniques of managing pests, from carrot rust flies to cutworms. Here are some to consider:

Other pesticides: There are four main botanical insecticides on the market for food crops: pyrethrins, rotenone, ryania and sabadilla. They are poisons that occur naturally in plants, and their main advantage over synthetic pesticides is that they quickly break down into harmless compounds once they are used in the environment. They also have relatively little effect on the natural enemies of pest species because they poison only the leaf-chewing insects. Pyrethrins and rotenone are readily available; ryania and sabadilla are more difficult to find.

Pyrethrins are extracted from the pyrethrum daisy; they will kill a wide range of pests. The botanical insecticide should not be confused with synthetic pyrethrins, like allethrin, or with the synthetic pyrethroids, an altogether more complex and persistent set of chemicals that are devastating to beneficial insects as well as pests.

Rotenone is a favorite insecticide of some organic gardeners, because it is obtained from the roots of certain tropical plants, and because it breaks down in a few days and is not passed on or concentrated in the food web. I am, however, cautious about recommending it. As measured by oral toxicity (how much a laboratory rat has to eat to be poisoned), rotenone is more toxic than such chemicals as dimethoate and 2,4-D. It is lethal to birds, fish and pigs, and there is evidence that it can stop cell development. Serious questions about its safety persist. If you use rotenone, which is effective on leaf-chewing beetles and caterpillars, use the wettable-powder formulation, rather than the dust. The spray will cover the same area as the dust, using less of the active ingredient, and the risk of breathing in dust is reduced. Users should take the same precautions required for the application of chemicals classed as moderately toxic: use good skin protection and wear a face mask.

The least toxic spray of all is a strong stream of water from a garden hose. This is effective against aphids and spider mites. Water containing a small amount of pure soap like Ivory or a commercial insecticidal soap like Safer's will knock back aphids and a variety of other insects, although not bees. The fatty acids in

Praying mantids should not be imported to the garden. They indiscriminately feed on beneficial insects, like this monarch butterfly, as well as on pests.

Nine Predators

A GALLERY OF BENEFICIAL INSECTS

HERBERT B. PARSONS/PHOTO/NATS

LADYBUGS: Although there are about 3,000 species of ladybugs of all sizes, varying from white through yellow to red and black, the convergent ladybug, *Hippodamia convergens*, is the best known in most North American gardens. This species has black underparts, a head and thorax of black marked with pale yellow, and an orange-red back, usually spotted. In all species, both adults and their larvae, which look like tiny alligators, will eat soft-bodied plant pests such as aphids, scale and mealybugs.

ROBERT C. SIMPSON/TOM STACK & ASSOCIATES

YELLOW JACKETS AND HORNETS: Members of the family Vespidae, these social creatures make nests with a pasty pulp formed from saliva and macerated wood. The bald-faced hornet makes a big gray nest, the European hornet a brown or yellow one, often in a protected place, and the smaller yellow jackets make nests either near or under the ground. All feed mostly on animal matter, although they also take some honey and pollen. They may not be welcomed by most people, but they do carry off a

lot of caterpillars. They are especially active feeders on plants growing in full sun.

TACHINID FLIES: Scarcely noticeable, these common, bristly, brown or gray flies, which resemble large houseflies in appearance and sound, are most active in sunshine. They are important parasites of cutworms, armyworms, tent caterpillars, corn borers, stinkbugs and beetle larvae. The tachinid larvae burrow through the skin when they hatch, then breathe by leaving an opening in the host's body or attaching to its respiratory system. Last fall, nearly every tent caterpillar I saw had at least one, and often a dozen, white tachinid eggs laid on it, most just behind the head where the caterpillar couldn't dislodge them. Leland Howard wrote in *The Insect Book* of 1908 that "one great outbreak of armyworm in northern Alabama in the early summer of 1881 was completely frustrated by the tachina flies."

FLOWER FLIES are beautiful black-and-white or black-and-yellow flies that hover, like helicopters, over flowers. Also known as hover flies or syrphus flies, they feed on aphids and mealybugs in the larval stage and help pollinate plants as adults. Furthermore, they are fascinating examples of insect mimicry. In appearance, sound and habit, the smooth species resemble wasps; the hairy ones, honeybees. None can sting, however. The adults are frequently seen feeding on nectar and pollen and are especially visible around midday on sunny days.

HERBERT B. PARSONS/PHOTO/NATS

PARASITIC WASPS: These come mostly from three main groups, chalcids, braconids and ichneumonids. They come in all sizes from pinpoint-small chalcids to ichneumonids up to 2 inches long, with their narrow waists and long ovipositors, often mistaken for stingers, trailing behind. The female wasps inject their eggs into other insects, and the resulting larvae literally mine the innards of their hosts. H.E. Jacques in 1947 wrote in *How to Know the Insects* that he had "counted over 500 braconid larvae within the body of what appeared to be a fairly healthy tomato worm." Some

DOROTHY S. LONG/PHOTO/NATS

under stones, boards, loose bark and other debris, but they become active at night, killing all sorts of pests, including gypsy moth larvae, cankerworms, snail and slug eggs, onion root maggots, small potato beetle larvae and cutworms. They can also chase prey in trees, like armyworms and tent caterpillars. The larvae, which live in burrows in the ground, feed on the soft-bodied larvae of other insects. Black is the most common color, but some ground beetles are beautifully marked.

DWIGHT KUHN

species live in their host and leave to pupate just before the host dies. Others enter aphids to pupate, then cut a neat hole to emerge.

ROVE BEETLES: These common scavengers, members of the family Staphylinidae, are so long and slender that they are easily confused with earwigs, although rove beetles lack pincers. Most are black, and most of the abdomen is exposed because the elytra, or top wings, are short. Many species are abundant in decaying organic matter, excrement and fungi, and some, when disturbed, will run around with the tip of the abdomen up as if they are about to sting, which they cannot do. One species parasitizes pupae of cabbage maggots and can kill up to 80 percent of the maggots in a field, provided pesticides are not applied. Rove beetles are among the garden's recyclers, turning organic matter into a form that can be utilized by plants.

GROUND BEETLES belong to one of the largest insect families, Carabidae, which has members throughout the world. During the day, they are likely to be found hiding

ASSASSIN BUGS: Described by one author as "bloodthirsty pirates," these predaceous beetles feed mostly on the juices of other insects, which they pierce with a strong, sharp beak. Usually fairly large, sometimes brightly colored, assassin bugs have a distinct neck and a head that is pointed in front. They kill many kinds of caterpillars, aphids, leaf-eating beetles and, from time to time, other garden benefactors.

DAMSEL BUGS: More vicious than their name implies, damsel bugs should not be confused with damselflies, which, though also predatory, look like small versions of dragonflies. Damsel bugs, members of the family Nabidae, are rather flattened, black or yellowish bugs; they have front legs modified for grasping and fitted with fine spines for catching small prey like aphids, leafhoppers and caterpillars.

—L.G.

Breeding for Self-Defense

Soon you may not ever have to spray another drop of BT to control leaf-eating pests. Scientists at Monsanto Company have successfully bred tomato plants that contain their own natural pest deterrent, and the technology is likely to work on other vegetables.

Explained in simplified terms, the researchers used genetic-engineering techniques to splice the effective ingredient from BT into the tomato plant. As a result, mature plants were able to withstand attack by tomato hornworms and other caterpillars. The insects that were controlled by

the engineered tomato plants are the same as those that can be controlled by BT when sprayed on leaves. The experiments were done on only one type of tomato, a commercial variety, but scientists say the technique could be applied to any variety and can be adapted to other crops. No such genetically engineered vegetables are on the market yet— and nothing has been said about their flavor—but plants with inbred defenses against pests may be available to home growers within the next five years.

—Rick Boling

The larvae, eggs and adults of the potato beetle can now be controlled with a new strain of Bacillus thuringiensis.

the soaps are the active ingredients; they penetrate the bodies of insects and cause them to become dehydrated. The effectiveness of Safer's soap seems to be related to the pH of the water used to dilute it, so it works better in some places than others. An improved formulation is expected.

Another spray with a long and effective history is nicotine water—cigarette butts soaked in water to brew a toxic tea. Nicotine is a potent insecticide, and when sprayed on plants, it controls leaf-chewing species.

Diatomaceous earth (sometimes sold under the brand name Fossil Flower) is a soft white powder mined from geological deposits of fossilized marine diatoms and other algae. When crushed, the fragments break into microscopic, sharp pieces that scratch the protective layer of wax on insects. Insects are susceptible to drying out, and DE causes them to lose water and die. It is an excellent, safe pesticide for use in stored grain, on pets to kill fleas and, because it is a physical rather than a chemical control, in houses to control insect invasions. It is not selective, however. It kills any insect, so I never use it in a garden. A garden powdered with DE would be just as lethal to the insect community as one dosed with DDT. With care, DE could be used selectively, around the roots of cabbage plants to deter cabbage maggots, for example.

Additional promising insecticides are under development. Products made from the neem tree, *Azadirachta indica,* have been used in some tropical countries for centuries to control pests. The main active ingredient, azadiractin, is extracted from neem seeds. It is a powerful feeding deterrent and also disrupts growth in a wide range of species, yet seems to show low toxicity in mammals.

Although most of the pesticides I have described are more specific, less toxic and less persistent than synthetic chemicals, regular and widespread application of these organic controls will have some of the same side effects as a reliance on stronger chemicals. Pests can become resistant to them and nontarget organisms are also harmed. Therefore, the application of a pesticide should be viewed as a treatment of last resort, a practice that may be used in conjunction with other tactics to restore a long-term balance in the garden.

Resistant varieties. One line of defense is to choose resistant varieties. Disease resistance is often listed in seed-catalogue descriptions, but there are also some insect-resistant varieties. For sweet corn that resists corn earworm, look for a description that includes the phrase "good husk cover." The 'Illini' hybrids and some others with this characteristic have husks that make it difficult for the insects to get into the ear. To avoid cabbage butterfly damage, try purple cabbage varieties. They are much less attractive to the butterfly than green varieties; when the butterfly is ready to lay eggs, it finds yellow attractive.

Traps. Sticky yellow traps, made of Stikum or Tanglefoot spread on bright yellow cardboard, plastic or wood, attract cabbage butterflies, winged aphids and other pests. You can make your own traps or buy them. Japanese beetle traps are also available. I imagine everyone has heard of the slug trap made of a saucer of beer set out in the garden—I can't honestly say I have had any luck with this, but there are people who swear by it.

Timing plantings. Major damage from some pests can be avoided by shifting planting dates. For example, in most northern regions, cabbage-root maggots have two generations each year, the first in April-May, the second in August. Brassicas planted after May are too big to be seriously harmed by the time the late-summer brood hatches, and midseason radishes avoid the problem altogether.

Hand picking. This is a tedious and often repellent method of curbing pests—but it does work on invaders that are slow enough to be caught. In areas where leaf miners are a problem on leafy greens like chard for a few weeks in summer, it isn't much trouble to remove and destroy the mined leaves containing larvae and pupae. I remember, years ago, attempting to control potato beetles in my garden in Prince Edward Island by crushing the larvae on the leaves. It seemed an endless job, but I was cheered by the arrival of many large wasps, attracted, perhaps, by the odor of mashed larvae.

Physical barriers. Cutworm collars have been used for years to protect transplanted seedlings in early spring. The collars are made of 2-inch-wide strips of light cardboard, taped or stapled into a ring around the stem of the plant, and set half above and half below the soil line. Early cabbage seedlings can be protected from root maggots by planting the seedlings through a cut in a square of heavy paper (thin paper rots too quickly; tar paper lasts for several seasons). The paper is pressed flat against the soil and as tight to the stem as possible to prevent flies from laying their eggs around the roots. Covering seedlings with a fine-mesh cloth or one of the new spun polypropylene row-cover fabrics (Reemay, for example) works even better. These fabrics can be tacked over a wire or wooden frame and are perfect for covering carrots to keep out carrot rust flies. The flies lay their eggs, which hatch into maggots that bore deep into the roots. The spun-bonded fabric lets in sun and rain and has the advantage of raising temperatures under the covering as well as reducing evaporation.

Small World

Of course, none of these substances or methods will be of much use unless the gardener can identify the pests. Correct identification is essential in using biological controls because most of them are specific. To identify specimens, you can take advantage of professionals in your area, extension agents and entomologists at universities and research stations, and you can turn to experienced gardeners and the many good insect identification guides available. Also invest in a hand lens with magnification of 10 to 16 times. A magnifying lens is great, not just because it enables you to see insect life in amazing detail, but also because you can catch insect damage in the early stages, while the pests are still small. Typically, gardeners are not attuned to such a diminutive world, so they usually don't notice leaf damage until after the offending caterpillars have left to spin their cocoons elsewhere. With aphid infestations, gardeners usually feel compelled to spray when the pest populations reach a noticeable level, at which time the populations of attacking native ladybugs, midges, flower flies, wasps, lacewings and others have also peaked. At that stage, spraying is hardly wise.

With the aid of a hand lens, you will be able to determine the pest/predator balance before you act. And aided by insect guides, you will be able to ensure that what you think is a pest truly is one and not a helpful predator.

I remember that once, just before I gave a talk on biological control to a garden club, a keen gardener told me that, luckily, she had many ladybeetles in her garden that year and few potato beetles, which she had persistently caught and killed. I was encouraged by her enthusiasm and her diligent hand picking. My smile froze, however, when she described the striped "ladybeetles" and the spotted "potato beetles." She spared the pests but had killed the beneficial ladybugs. The moral is, identify before you act.

Just don't send your specimens to me!

SOURCES

Harmony Farm Supply
P.O. Box 451
3320 Gravenstein Highway North (Sebastopol)
Graton, California 95444
Ecological pest controls, organic fertilizers, farm and garden equipment. Their catalogue is packed with information. $2, refundable with first order.

The IPM Practitioner
Bio-Integral Resource Center
P.O. Box 7414
Berkeley, California 94707
The latest on "integrated pest management" and biocontrol information. Comes out monthly and covers every conceivable aspect of pest management. One-year subscription $25.

Natural Gardening Research Center
Highway 48
P.O. Box 149
Sunman, Indiana 47041
Publishes an annual "Newsletter and Guide to Natural Control of Garden Insects, Diseases and Animal Pests," which is both a catalogue and reference for pest-control information and products. Catalogue free.

Necessary Trading Co.
614 P Salem Avenue
P.O. Box 305
New Castle, Virginia 24127
Organic soil amendments and biological pest-control agents. Catalogue $2.

Peaceful Valley Farm Supply
110 Springhill Boulevard
Grass Valley, CA 95945
Extensive list of beneficial organisms for biological pest control, organic fertilizers, seeds, bulbs, nursery stock, farm tools. Catalogue $2, refundable with first order.

Rincon Vitova
P.O. Box 95
Oakview, California 93022
A large selection of beneficial insects, including lacewings, fly parasites, predatory mites, Encarsia formosa, parasitic wasps and many others. Catalogue free.

Stalwart Herbs

TEN CULINARY PERENNIALS THAT BELONG IN YOUR GARDEN

BY PATRICK LIMA WITH ILLUSTRATIONS BY TURID FORSYTH

Soon after the snow disappears from our garden, I begin to harvest fresh perennial herbs for the kitchen. The chives have been busy sprouting since winter's end, and thyme and sage will be in good condition. (If they haven't been protected by a natural covering of snow, which is common at my Ontario homestead, I come to their aid with a blanket of evergreen boughs.) Lovage is one of the first herbs to stir, with sorrel and then tarragon and oregano not far behind. These are the stalwarts capable of surviving most northern winters.

With various plantings—including annuals in summer—our garden provides fresh herbs of one sort or another for a good eight months, from April through November; many can be harvested year-round in balmier regions. And favorites are easily dried for winter use.

When it comes to choosing which culinary herbs to grow, I encourage cooks who garden simply to check their spice racks and see which herbs they use most. That jar of Italian Seasoning, so useful for spiking spaghetti sauce and chili or for sprinkling over pizza, is likely to be a blend of perennials—oregano, thyme, rosemary—and the annual, basil. The list is started. The cook may notice, too, that garlic powder, parsley flakes and chives are depleted in short order and are expensive to boot. So grow them.

What would I grow if pressed to choose just a half dozen herbs? Not an easy decision. Of the annuals, I would not like to do without basil, summer savory or dill; among perennials, I use lovage at least once a day, as long as it is green and growing. Nor could I cook without garlic. Just one more? Let it be the biennial parsley— but I would miss tarragon and chives. A silly game—but a way to discover the essentials.

Where should one grow the kitchen herbs? In theory, the answer is easy: grow herbs as close as possible to the door nearest the kitchen—nothing encourages use as much as accessibility. In a country garden, it is a mistake to hide the herbs at the bottom of the vegetable garden. Although a special bed or even a garden of herbs is always a pleasant feature in the landscape, herbs do not need that sort of splendid isolation. There are many nooks in the landscape where they are at home: annuals at the edges of vegetable garden beds, chervil under shrubs, dwarfs in a rock garden, others among the flowers. We edge our perennial flower beds with different thymes, and the likes of lemon balm and lovage rub shoulders with poppies and delphiniums.

Chives
Allium schoenoprasum

The genus *Allium* is a vast and varied race of more than 300 species, and throughout the temperate regions of the northern hemisphere, alliums of one sort or another flourish. Among them are some of the best seasoning herbs: shallots, garlic and some of spring's first edible greens—Welsh and Egyptian onions and the native wild leeks.

And chives.

Chives are anyone's herb in perpetuity for the mere sowing of a few seeds in a sunny, fertile place. Better, however, to start seeds in spring in a small pot of good loam and wait until the stripling onions have grown a bit before setting them outdoors. The six fat clumps in our garden are descendants of skinny seedlings started 12 years ago and 200 miles away—chives are among the more portable of plants. Alternatively, buy nursery-grown plants, or divide an outside bit of an established garden clump, pulling away five or six of the thin, tightly packed bulbs in spring.

Once in the garden, the indestructible chives, "a good sawce and pot-herb," as early English herbalist John Gerard wrote, will be in constant demand for flavoring any dish improved by a mild tang of onion. "In the Ukraine," Ontario

MELVIN GREY/OCTOPUS GROUP LTD

gardener Mary-Ann Robinson told me, "the appearance of dill seedlings and the first shoots of chives signal spring—just like the first robin here; we sauté minced dill and chives in butter very briefly and pour the sauce over everything." I envision pasta, asparagus, boiled potatoes and baked fish. Along with chervil, parsley and tarragon, chives are a fourth constituent of the classic French *fines herbes* so good for omelets. Snip small bundles of chives to flavor cream or cottage cheese, salad dressings (especially yogurt-based), green or grain salads, herbed butter, hot or cold soups or eggs or potatoes in any guise.

Spiky-leaved mauve-flowering chives are also pretty enough to edge a bed of flowers or decorate a rock garden. Always, there is a drone of honeybees and a flutter of butterflies around the nectar-rich flowers. Pink vinegar tasting mildly of onions is easily made by steep-

ing a handful of chive blossoms in a quart of white vinegar, with a sprig of tarragon or lovage for extra flavor. We give the chives a close shearing each year after flowering is past to encourage a new crop of tender leaves.

Chives freeze well, dry poorly; but since this is the earliest herb to rise in spring and one of the last to retire in fall, we enjoy the extended fresh-from-the-garden season.

Garlic
Allium sativum

For many years, we grew no garlic, assuming that this Mediterranean native needed a long, hot season to mature. Instead, we made do with store-bought bulbs. Then, one propitious September day, a friend brought some bulbs of the best garlic I had ever seen and surprised us with the news that they had been grown not in California but by a market

The gardener who grows herbs has the edge at mealtimes. Nothing so simply sparks up most foods as fresh herbs: they elevate everyday fare magically.

Garlic

gardener only a few miles south. We have been reveling in the "reeking rose" ever since.

Garlic is as hardy and as easy to grow as any allium. I am always surprised at the generous return for so little work – plant one clove, harvest ten. Garlic is one of the few crops that is best planted in the fall. Sometime in mid-September, perhaps after the beans have been blackened by frost, I turn a 6-inch dressing of old cow manure and a dusting of bone meal into the garlic bed, which is in full sun, rake the ground to a fine tilth, and push the largest cloves saved from that season's crop several inches deep into the loose earth. (In heavy ground, trowel out a little planting hole.) I set the cloves 6 inches apart in rows 8 to 12 inches apart. Soon, thin blades of garlic grass emerge and continue to grow into fall, until checked by severe cold. One garlic grower who contends with fickle winter weather suggests mulching the garlic beds with straw at that time to prevent repeated freezes and thaws from heaving the bulbs, but consistent snow cover is the winter rule here so I skip that step. As soon as the snow has receded in the spring, the flat, arching garlic foliage begins to grow strongly – several visitors have looked at the garlic beds in June and wondered why the "corn" was so far advanced. Some attention to weeding and a deep drink of fish emulsion in a droughty season are all that garlic requires for good growth. Needless to say, insects give the bed of garlic, which has pesticidal properties, a wide berth.

As its foliage begins to ripen in August, I harvest the bulbs as needed to blend with basil, olive oil or butter as a sauce for pasta or rice; to mince with summer savory and toss with buttered green beans; to slice, sweet and raw, on buttered dark bread; or to sauté with yellow crookneck squash seasoned with tarragon, lemon thyme and fresh tomatoes. The abundant use of fresh green herbs, especially lovage, parsley or celery leaves, helps mute the "sulfurous stink" that is garlic's chief virtue in the kitchen but a liability in some company.

By late August, after most of the leaves have yellowed, I harvest the crop; bulbs left in the ground much later, especially in a wet fall, will continue to fatten and are apt to split their protective husks. Bulbs are dried in an airy, rain-free place for a week or so, soil brushed off, the roots and tops trimmed, and the cache stored someplace dry and cool in open baskets – I have yet to learn how to turn out those decorative braids. Thus treated, garden-grown garlic keeps firm and fresh all winter long.

Lovage
Levisticum officinale

Best of the essential culinary herbs, at least to my taste, is lovage. Many other gardener-cooks agree, but I know one who has taken lovage out of her herb bed entirely. "Too strong," she says, "and takes up too much space." Lovage certainly is the green giant among herbs: a clump will grow over five feet tall and widen eventually to several feet around. But it is handsome enough to be planted at the back of a flower bed or stand sentry by the kitchen door, and is also well placed in a bed of strong-growing perennial vegetables and herbs – horseradish, rhubarb, Jerusalem artichokes and asparagus. One of our plants competes with raspberries and does just fine. Locate this heavyweight carefully; it is not easy to move once established.

Lovage is the preeminent soup herb, just the thing to simmer in chicken broth with the usual onions and carrots. But I like to flavor almost any savory dish with these dark green leaves, which taste sharply of celery and parsley with a spicy depth. Use lovage – sparingly at first – to season all hot dishes including bean, pea and lentil soups, slow-cooking chili and beef stews, chicken pies or tuna casseroles. The taste of lovage does not dissipate with cooking. A snippet in an omelet is good, and I like the tenderest leaves raw in a sandwich or finely chopped into green, grain or potato salads. With garlic and ginger, lovage deliciously flavors stir-fried vegetables, especially bland summer squash.

Fresh leaves are traditionally used with potatoes in all forms – mixed with sour cream to spoon onto baked potatoes, added with marjoram to potato soup, or sprinkled on buttery mashed potatoes or in a white sauce for boiled potatoes.

Lovage grows easily from seeds sown in late summer or fall; freeze and thaw the seed to break dormancy. The plant takes a full season to fatten up, but returns faithfully every year thereafter. Divisions may be cut from the outside of an established plant and set out in nourishing soil. Lovage flourishes in damp ground but does not demand it. A single plant supplies an eight-month harvest of leaves, and a few branches hung in an airy, shaded place become crisp in a few days and stay nicely aromatic for winter.

Lovage flowers are typical wasp flowers, attracting hosts of the tiny, beneficial social and parasitic wasps that prey on garden pests such as cutworms and tent caterpillars. Organic gardeners often send for *Trichogramma* wasp eggs without realizing that, unless the emerging young wasps have access to certain kinds of nectar in the garden, they will either starve or head for the fields in search of Queen Anne's lace. So let the six-foot flowering stocks of lovage stand. But just before the seed ripens, cut them back to avoid having to root out a small forest of lovage that springs up all around the mother plant. If seed heads are hung to dry, seed may be harvested as a celery seed substitute.

Oregano
Origanum spp

There is no such thing as oregano, pure and simple. One catalogue lists Greek, wild Greek, Italian, golden showy, beautiful, woolly and white oreganos. Another assures the reader that theirs is the "true oregano collected wild in the mountains of Greece." Other catalogues list oreganos under marjoram. Few plants, herbs or otherwise, suffer such a confusion of Latin and common names. Let me spare you the tangled taxonomic details and say, first, that oregano grown from seed labeled *Origanum vulgare*, wild oregano, is likely to be a sprawling, scentless disappointment. Better to pick up plants in person. Here is an herb, like lemon thyme, that ought to be pinched, sniffed and nibbled if possible, so that you can be sure of its potency.

Currently, in our garden we have – or rather had, because one is now gone – four plants labeled oregano. "Showy oregano" (*O. pulchellum*) looks more like thyme than oregano, has pretty magenta tubes for flowers and no scent. "Golden oregano" ('Aureum') looked sickly, as do many yellow-leaved plants, and sat absolutely still one season and the next until it was finally shown the garden gate – well, in truth, dumped without ceremony or regret in the compost heap. The Italian oregano (*O. onites*) resembles the Greek, but the former has a scent and flavor that are mild to the vanishing point. Laurels go, finally, to the herb variously labeled *Origanum dictamnus* or *O. heracleoticum* (or, mysteriously, *Origanum* sp). This is

Greek oregano, properly pungent smelling and peppery on the tongue.

Greek oregano is said to be only half-hardy, needing pampering in a flowerpot indoors over winter, but ours has lived outdoors for four seasons in a gravelly pocket of a stone patio. The secret may be to situate this sun- and stone-loving herb where conditions are appropriate to its Mediterranean origins: in the hottest, driest corner. Mulch it with gravel or small pebbles, and if during winter it lacks a snow cover, protect it with evergreen boughs.

So much for rules and botanical confusions. Oregano supplies fresh leaves for tomato sauce, salad dressings of olive oil and lemon juice, sautéed summer squash (with tarragon and lovage), chili and hamburgers through the summer, and dries in a twinkling for winter pizza, meat loaf or thick soup. This is one herb I use more of dried than fresh, the robust flavor being more appropriate to fall and winter dishes. The dried branches with their gray-white flowers are woven into herbal wreaths by a neighbor, who also uses silvery artemisias, branches of thyme and a

Lovage

few pink strawflowers to create decorations that are as useful as they are beautiful over the winter.

Rosemary

Rosemary
Rosmarinus officinalis

Neither a hardy perennial nor a tender annual, but rather a tender perennial shrub that can overwinter only in zone 6 and south, rosemary fortunately adapts well to pot culture. I know several gardeners who go to great trouble to transplant it from an indoor pot to an outdoor garden bed each spring, then back again in fall. But it is far easier to set a small starter plant directly into an oversized pot – 12 inches in diameter is good, but no less – of nourishing soil, and leave it there. Winter the potted rosemary in a sunny but not overly warm place indoors – given its seaside origins, it likes a biweekly misting – and set it outside

in good sun from mid-May to October. It withstands light frosts, but must not be frozen hard. If you find that a potted rosemary on the patio or porch dries out too quickly, sink plant, pot and all, into the ground up to the pot rim. An annual pruning, just before rosemary goes out for the summer, keeps the shrub shapely and leafy; shorten the winter-spindly stems by at least one-half. I like to wait until flowering is over before pruning any plant, just because it seems a considerate thing to do.

After three or four seasons, I usually find it necessary to start again with a new small plant; the "mother" rosemary has grown lanky and woody and often leafless along the lower part of the stems. Cuttings are a sure and simple means of renewal. Snip a 3-inch piece from the tops of several branches, remove the lower few leaves, and dip the ends of the cuttings in a rooting hormone powder sold for softwood cuttings. Plant three to six cuttings firmly in a 4-inch pot of very light soil, then slip a clear plastic bag, punctured with a few tiny holes, over the pot, fastening it with an elastic band. Keep the pot in a bright place out of direct sun; the roots should form within three weeks, after which the new plants can be potted singly.

The scent of narrow, gray-green rosemary foliage is cool and resinous, a little piny or camphoric – I find it invigorating just to tousle a bush and breathe deeply. My favorite way to use rosemary in the kitchen is this: sprinkle halved or quartered potatoes generously with rosemary leaves, either dried or fresh, drizzle potatoes with olive oil and roast until done. Rosemary is a natural for other oven-cooked foods, too – chicken, roasts and the like.

Sage
Salvia officinalis

All herbal literature holds sage in highest esteem as a medicinal plant. The name salvia is derived from the Latin verb *salvere,* to heal, the root of our words salve, salutory, salvation, sage (wise) and the French toast *salut,* "to your health." The sagacious Chinese once valued the herb so highly that they willingly exchanged three pounds of black tea for a pound of sage from Dutch traders.

Today, the plant is better known in cooking, especially for its starring role in the festive turkey – sage seems a necessary complement to fatty poultry and other meats. Unlike mild-mannered basil or dill, sage is too potent to be used with a lavish hand. But I like to tear a leaf into bean soup or minestrone; a little goes a long way in cream cheese. Fresh sage tastes balsamic and slightly bitter (but much less so than the dried, powdered herb), making a pleasant spring tea when blended with milder

Sage

Sage

lemon balm and spearmint.

At one time, English peasants ate fresh sage with their bread, butter and cheese. This is, in fact, a simple way to get to know the flavor of many culinary herbs. Spread sweet butter on some good bread and lay on a few leaves or a sprinkling of herbs. Or melt cheese over bread under the broiler and press fresh herbs onto the top. One garden writer passed along a suggestion that sage leaves be dipped in a flour and egg batter and deep fried: "These are gobbled up when served with drinks, and people rarely guess what the crusty tidbits are."

Sun and well-drained soil are all sage needs for good growth, but it responds best to the shelter and warmth of a house wall, to the north if possible. With its gray-green pebbled foliage and spikes of lavender bloom, it can decorate a sunny corner of a flower bed or rockery. At the top of a dry wall, "where it can indulge in a tendency to lounge," wrote an old-time gardener, "the slurred softness of gray-green leaves and violet flowers makes sage an herb of real beauty."

An easy plant to grow from spring-sown seed – an indoor start is best – sage can also be propagated from cuttings, but the half-shrubby bushes do not divide well. Fortunately, if local nurseries have few other herbs, most do sell sage plants in spring. And occasionally a "lounging" branch will root where it touches the ground. To hasten this process, called layering, anchor branches to the ground with stones or hairpins and toss a few handfuls of earth over them. Allow at least a month for roots to form.

In early spring, we clip the straggling, winter-worn branches back by about half (but not to the woody portions); new growth soon sprouts and the plants stay compact. Even given this treatment, sage may need replacing after three or four seasons. In our garden, the bushes seem to become overly woody and then succumb to a hard winter. Other gardeners tell me that sage goes on and on for them. They must be living right; legend says that sage follows the fortunes of the house, dwindling during evil days and reviving miraculously when things are bright again.

Salad Burnet

Sanguisorba minor or *Poterium sanguisorba*

A perennial pretty enough to edge a flower bed or decorate a rock garden with its low rosettes of lacy blue-green foliage, salad burnet, or pimpinella, remains evergreen over a snowless winter. Only the youngest leaves go into salads or "green sauce," a German specialty that is served over boiled potatoes and hard-cooked eggs for a nourishing lunch. These young leaves have a subtle flavor, reminiscent of cucumber, a little tart, a little hot. Older leaves are as stringy as grass and taste about the same. In early summer, up come slender reddish stems topped by a small ball of crimson bloom that make decent cut flowers; cutting the flowering stalks encourages new leafy growth.

Burnet does not transplant well, so the seeds are best sown in the open garden in spring around the last frost date, and the seedlings thinned to six inches apart. Alternatively, start them a few weeks earlier indoors in 3-inch peat pots or the equivalent. This elegant little herb tolerates dry ground, but like most things, grows better with a bit of fertility, moisture and sunshine. If it is left to seed itself, little burnets are sure to appear.

Burnet is one salad herb that seems to have been passed by in the current interest in unusual greens. Even in 1934, Mrs. Grieve (in *Culinary Herbs and Condiments*) noted that "burnet, once in every herb garden of older days, has now gone out of fashion and as a kitchen herb is much neglected." But, as an Italian proverb says, "L'insalata non è buona ne bella, ove non è la Pimpinella." ("The salad is neither good nor fair, if pimpinella is not there.")

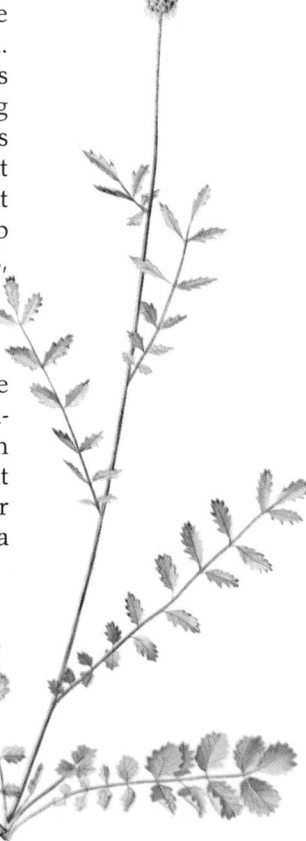

Salad Burnet

Sorrel
Rumex acetosa

Two culinary herbs adopted by the French as their own are perennial essentials. The first is sorrel *(Rumex acetosa)*.

The species name tells of the acid bite of this herb, called Sauerampfer by the Germans, sourgrass by the English. Now that it has scaled the heights of *haute cuisine,* it is known as French sorrel, with cultivars such as 'Blonde de Lyon' and 'Nobel' available. Easily grown from seeds sown outdoors a month before the last spring frost, or indoors about four weeks earlier than that, a few plants provide a long harvest of young leaves. It is recommended that flower stalks be removed to prevent seeding and encourage tender basal growth. In any case, sorrel is at its best in spring or early summer and again during the moist days of fall, but it becomes stringy and less flavorful during summer heat. Space the plants 8 inches apart in peat-enriched soil in a sunny corner where they can remain undisturbed for some years. Like tarragon, the same sorrel plants return year after year in this garden, but one writer says it is "grown as a hardy annual throughout most of the North." Experimentation is the essence of good gardening; I say, try and see.

Besides giving a tang to the soup that bears its name, sorrel tarts up a lettuce salad or seasons a cream sauce for poached fish, with a bit of lovage and fennel added. It is also good finely chopped with lovage and stirred into sour cream or thick yogurt to dress boiled or baked potatoes.

Tarragon
Artemisia dracunculus sativa

French tarragon *(A. dracunculus sativa)* – "little dragon" – is the second of the essential French herbs. Tarragon seed is always suspect, producing a tasteless sprawler of no use in the kitchen or garden. True French tarragon, with more moderate growth and simple linear habit, has a sweet taste of anise and a brief analgesic (numbing) effect on the tongue if nibbled alone. A clump in the garden keeps a cook in fresh tarragon for more than half a year, and the branches freeze or dry easily for winter.

Tarragon responds to sun, warmth and ordinary garden soil that does not stay wet for long periods. This herb has lived in our garden for many winters without any problem, but others say its hardiness is not ironclad. No doubt the persistent snow here protects it; often snow arrives so early that the ground beneath never freezes. Each spring, just as the tips of tarragon are showing aboveground, we take a morning to divide the clumps (for sell-

ing). A plant is pried out of the ground with a spading fork and the spaghettilike runners are split by hand or with a small knife into three-to-five-shoot rooted divisions. The roots are trimmed a bit to fit 6-inch pots without bending, and the divisions are planted firmly in a mixture of sandy loam flecked with peat moss and bone meal; the pots are then well soaked, and fresh green soon sprouts. But except for propagation, tarragon need not be divided.

The taste of tarragon is featured in: tarragon chicken, eggs *a l'estragon,* omelets, tarragon mayonnaise, hollandaise and tartar sauce. Tarragon vinegar is a pricey but delicious culinary cliché easily concocted by anyone with a plant in the garden. Push a little bundle of fresh tarragon tops into a bottle of cider, wine or white vinegar and leave it to steep, in the sun if possible, for a week or so – that's all. Forget the instructions that call for heating the vinegar, shaking the bottle twice daily or straining out the herbs – but a few cloves and a bit of lemon peel can be added for élan.

This vinegar, with oil, salt and pepper, pro-

Tarragon

duces the simplest of elegant salad dressings. More elaborate is tarragon vinegar added to a mixture of half sour cream or yogurt and half mayonnaise, with plenty of chopped chives; a pressed clove of garlic is optional. Spread this over slices of cooked beets, hard-boiled eggs and still-warm boiled potatoes arranged on a bed of lettuce and garnished with tarragon leaves. Such a salad might well include cooked, chilled green beans, chickpeas and crunchy steamed cauliflower.

Tarragon butter seasons vegetables wonderfully. And a nice change from regular tomato juice is this: to every pint of fresh or canned juice, add a teaspoon each of minced tarragon, chives and basil, one-half teaspoon of lemon thyme, the juice of half a lemon and a dash of cayenne pepper (and a pinch of salt if starting with fresh juice). Allow the mixture to stand for an hour or two in a cool, not cold, place, and strain before serving.

Thyme

Last spring, a friend handed me a catalogue listing no fewer than 27 variations on the theme of thyme. No child in a candy store ever surveyed an inventory as eagerly: there were orange-balsam, lemon and lavender thyme; 'Moonlight' and 'Silver Needles' thyme; thymes flowering pink, crimson and white. Fruity or medicinal, sweet or savory, tall or short, thymes are friendly, lovely plants that fit well in any garden and add their distinctive flavors to all kinds of cooking.

Nor do these treasures gobble up garden space in the manner of mints. At present, 21 species and varieties of thyme grow in our garden. Home for 10 of them is a narrow raised bed, 10 feet long and a foot and a half wide. But thymes need not be in a special herb garden—they easily spill over the limestone rocks that edge flower beds, creep between paving stones or carpet the ground around a garden bench. These accommodating plants are tiny, in scale with the smallest garden.

When it comes to knowing which thymes are which, botanists are hard to pin down. Even England's august Royal Horticultural Society, champion of botanical clarity, concedes that thymes are "notoriously difficult to classify and identify; and as specific limits are not well defined and local variants are numerous, accounts by botanists disagree widely."

For the garden, it is enough to know if the thyme in question is good to eat—all thymes are edible, but some are delectable—and how it will grow. Thymes grow in one of three ways. Some hug the ground closely and send out little searching shoots that root as they go—these are the creeping thymes. Others, lemon

Lemon Thyme

thyme for one, form small mounds of wiry, procumbent branches clothed with larger, shining green or variegated leaves. Several of these, the mound-makers, mimic the fragrance of lemon, lavender, camphor or oregano. A third group grows into small upright shrubs, 10 to 15 inches tall, that eventually develop a woody central trunk and side branches that rarely root unless held to the ground.

Whatever their size, thymes cannot cope with crowding—pressed by pushy neighbors, they either die or send some stringy runners into the light in an effort to survive. That new corner of herbs that looks so well ordered in May—everything in its place, given plenty of space—can grow rather tangled later on. By July, the thymes will be scrambling for their little lives to get out from under a shoving sage or toppling tarragon. If possible, give thymes a place of their own—a rock garden in full sun is just their notion of home—but take care, in any case, that neighboring plants are in scale.

LEMON THYME
Thymus x citriodorus

Lemon thyme is at its best only when fresh. The delicate bouquet of citrus and spice is lost through drying or anything more than the briefest cooking. Our garden grows three variants of this species: lemon thyme (*T. x citriodorus*) is upright and bushy, with uniformly green leaves and a sprinkling of lavender flowers well into September; varie-

Volunteers

THREE THAT SELF-SEED FOR FRESH CROPS EACH SEASON

Caraway
Carum carvi

Caraway is a hardy biennial that grows a leafy rosette the first season and runs to flower and seeds the next. In fact, as much as I appreciate its delicious seeds, I am always tempted to banish caraway from the garden entirely. Every last seed left unharvested falls, sprouts and grows into a well-anchored rosette of carrotlike foliage and yet another crop of seeds. "Weed," I say, extracting the competitive volunteers.

The only trick to growing eager caraway is getting it started in the first place. Typical of umbelliferous plants (dill, carrots, parsley and others), caraway produces seed that is viable for a short time only; by spring, it may not sprout if it has been badly stored over winter. Putting seeds in the freezer for a few days before sowing may wake them up. The hardy seeds are sown in spring at the same time as lettuce and radishes. Three or four plants will be enough. To harvest, cut the heads when the first seeds turn brown and hang the stalks upside down over newspaper or a dishpan, or enclose the seed heads in a paper bag. Any seeds that do not fall are easily rubbed off. Be sure the seeds are thoroughly dry before storing them in jars. Leave one or two unharvested seed heads in the garden to perpetuate the crop.

I like to use caraway in split pea or lentil soups, in creamed cabbage or ground with wheat kernels into flour for homemade crackers.

Parsley
Petroselinum spp

Intensely green, always vigorous, parsley looks every bit the nutritional powerhouse it is. It is a mistake to relegate this plant to the side of the plate as a garnish alone. Eat it.

There are several types of parsley. Italian, or flat-leaved, parsley looks more like a small-leaved celery, but has the same flavor as the curly-leaved, which is the most common type. Many food snobs extol the flat-leaved parsley, but I prefer the tightly curled, jewel-green mossy sort – more my idea of what parsley should be. Nonetheless, Italian parsley is full of flavor and as easily grown. I have noticed, however, that some years it bolts to seed in midsummer, especially if dry or crowded, while curly parsley is always biennial.

Hamburg-rooted parsley supplies flat leaves all summer and a storage crop of white roots, like skinny parsnips, that are just the thing to flavor any soup or stew. This delicious dual-purpose vegetable and herb ought to be more generally known and grown; it is especially suited to small gardens because it takes up little space – thin the seedlings to 6 or 8 inches apart – and is usable from leaf top to root tip from midsummer until well into winter if stored or mulched in the garden. We keep a sharp eye on the fragile seedlings, a favorite food of earwigs.

All parsley is notoriously slow to germinate. Some gardeners suggest soaking the seed in water overnight, but one author notes, "You end up with a gelatinous mess that sticks to fingers and everything else and is impossible to sow properly." Briefly freezing the seed helps to break dormancy. Another approach that results in an even stand of seedlings is to soak the seeded flat or furrow with a kettleful of boiling water. And then there is always patience: I generally seed a 4-inch-deep flat indoors around April 10 and leave it in the vicinity of the wood stove for the few weeks it takes the tiny green backs to show through. In mid-May, parsley goes into our garden; light frosts leave it unharmed.

Parsley stays green and usable late into the fall; the wise gardener leaves the parsley row undisturbed during the October cleanup. Often the hardy plants survive the winter and resprout at spring's first encouragement. If left to flower and set seed, parsley perpetuates itself, but the original plant disappears after seeding, proving that this is a biennial plant that only seems perennial when it is allowed to complete its life cycle.

There are many ways to carry the goodness of parsley to the table. The easiest is to mince a half cup or so and toss it into any and all mixed salads, coleslaws and potato salads. Tabouli, a cold Lebanese salad that starts with cooked bulgur wheat, is green with parsley; egg or tuna salads can be well flecked, and simple white sauces are always improved with parsley, a little lovage and chervil. Stir sweet butter, minced parsley and chervil (or basil) into plain cooked rice, and season the mixture with plenty of fresh-ground pepper and Parmesan cheese. A garnish of sweet red pepper and slivered almonds makes this easy dish festive. I sprinkle almost every soup generously with parsley just before serving.

Dill
Anethum graveolens

There is never enough dill. Some gardeners will disagree as a tide of green and yellow sweeps over the garden, but even though dill sows its hardy seed everywhere, the plants insist on running right back to seed in short order, producing on the way only a few sparse leaves. And it is the leaves I want. Others may prize the flowers and seed heads for pickles, but it is the cool, aromatic dill foliage, often called dillweed, that is among my favorite fresh herbs.

For its own perverse reasons, dill is always better if left to find its own way around the garden. Year after year, we seed a careful patch, usually the improved 'Aroma,' in hopes of having a dense harvest in one spot. But each year, half-wild dill appears in outlying corners of the garden, while the planted seeds, for all their extra breeding, often come to nothing.

I serve finely chopped dillweed in tossed salads or coleslaw; with lovage and Spanish onions for potato salads dressed with yogurt; with parsley over buttered new potatoes; blended with lemon thyme and chives into cream cheese to spread on homemade crackers; added to any recipe for stuffed, baked fish; or tossed by the handful into traditional Greek tadziki, a summer salad of cucumber, yogurt, pressed garlic, olive oil, lemon juice, salt, pepper and a pinch of cayenne, the whole left to marry until it is redolent of garlic and green with dill.

—P.L.

gated lemon thyme (*T. x citriodorus* 'Aureus') is shorter, has leaves flecked along the edges with cream and is more prone to sprawl in a small way; and nicest of all is 'Doone Valley' thyme, shorter yet, with small, green leaves marbled with yellow, cream and red, especially in spring. Seeds will not produce lemon thyme, and I have even seen plants tagged with the name that gave no hint of the plant's notable citrus tang, so although several mail-order nurseries list this herb, it is best, if possible, to let the nose judge for sure.

Lemon thymes are perfect small plants for a sunny spot among rocks, along the edge of a flower bed, or spilling over the sides of a raised bed. Once settled in the garden and sprawling nicely, lemon thyme is easy to increase. Often, the plant does the preliminary work: side-shoots that touch the ground send out tentative roots, and these branches may be snipped off and planted elsewhere.

Lemon thyme grows more compactly and winters better if sheared back by at least half – but not to the woody framework – in mid-August, in time to allow the plant to make new growth during fall's cooler weeks. Use sharp scissors rather than garden shears.

Like parsley, chives and chervil, fresh lemon thyme is a pleasantly mild herb that can safely season most foods. All summer and well into fall, we harvest lemon thyme, and I encourage experimentation.

COOKING THYME
Thymus vulgaris

The taller, shrubby thymes include the common cooking thyme (*Thymus vulgaris*) of spice racks and supermarket shelves. Usually the first of the tribe to find a place in a garden, cooking thyme grows easily from seed started indoors about a month before the last frost date; set out a month later, the herb becomes a usable little bush by midsummer the first season. A fortunate occurrence, because this Mediterranean native, safe only in very well drained or gravelly ground, does not winter as well here as other thymes. Gardeners in milder areas, however, will have little trouble keeping cooking thyme flourishing all year long.

Rodale's *Encyclopedia of Organic Gardening* calls cooking thyme "the universal herb" and suggests its use with fish, poultry and meats, vegetables, egg dishes, soups, stuffings, cheese sauce and chowders. The small, arrow-shaped thyme leaves are pungent and peppery, not unlike but milder than oregano. Sprigs tied together with parsley and bay leaf (and I would add lovage) form a classic *bouquet garni* to simmer in soup stock and stews. This herb dries easily, but the flavor becomes more pronounced as the moisture evaporates, leaving only the aromatic oils. I like to be lavish with fresh herbs all summer, but with dried herbs it is easy to tip the balance from pleasant to overpowering.

There are other thymes to explore, thymes for cooking, thymes for garden decoration. Few plants are as friendly or as easy, given their modest demands of full sun, well-drained soil, light winter protection and the occasional cutting back. Theirs is the charm of fragrance, persistent green, gray or golden foliage, a gently spreading habit and tiny abundant flowers buzzing with bees in the summer sun. ❧

Excerpted from The Harrowsmith Illustrated Book of Herbs *by Patrick Lima. Camden House Publishing, 1986.*

SOURCES

Plants and Seeds

Companion Plants
7247 N. Coolville Ridge Road
Athens, Ohio 45701
Herb seeds and plants for over 500 varieties, including 25 kinds of thyme and 12 kinds of rosemary. Catalogue $2.

Kingfisher Inc.
P.O. Box 75
Wexford, Pennsylvania 15090
Herb seeds. Catalogue $1, not refundable.

Meadowbrook Herb Garden
Route 138
Wyoming, Rhode Island 02898
More than 250 varieties of herb seeds. Seed list 50¢.

Sandy Mush Herb Nursery
Route 2, Surrett Cove Road
Leicester, North Carolina 28748
Herb plants and seeds, as well as an extensive list of many varieties of sage, mint, thyme, oregano and rosemary. Catalogue $4, deductible from first order.

Publications

The Business of Herbs
Northwind Farm
Route 2, Box 246
Shevlin, Minnesota 56676
A bi-monthly journal of international news and resource services for herb businesses and serious herb hobbyists. $20 per year (6 issues).

The Herb Quarterly
Long Mountain Press
1271 Kuhn Road
Boiling Springs, Pennsylvania 17007
Elegant magazine for herb fanciers. $24 per year.

Devil Root

Horseradish Offers Subterranean Heat and Other Sinful Delights

By John J. Pullen

Mark Twain once said of the Devil that he is the spiritual head of four-fifths of the human race and the political head of all of it. He may also be responsible for that perennial herb, *Armoracia rusticana*, or horseradish, the roots of which make one of the hottest of the world's hot sauces.

Certainly horseradish has some characteristics in common with sin: it's delicious, but there are side effects. And like sin it's easy to start. Horseradish is propagated not by seeds but by root cuttings taken from old plants in someone's garden or ordered from a catalogue. These are pieces of root typically 8 to 12 inches long and perhaps as thick as a pencil. Dig a trench and place the cuttings in the ground at an angle with the tops 2 to 4 inches below the surface. (A supplier will usually send them to you with the intended tops cut square across and the bottoms cut slanted so you won't get them in upside down.) The cuttings should be spaced 18 to 24 inches apart in rows 3 to 4 feet apart. Then replace the soil in the trench and firm it down with a roller or press it down with a board.

Horseradish will grow in almost any type of soil except light sand or heavy clay, but it does best in deep, rich, moist soil of a medium texture, easily penetrated by the roots. It is generally adapted to the northern temperate regions of the United States, but not to the South. Horseradish likes a long growing season that is followed by a cold winter, and it is hardy to Zone 4.

Plant the cuttings in March or April, and in May you will see crowns, which are like tight rosettes of buds, emerging from the ground; from these will grow the stems of wide, dark green leaves to make a plant 1 to 3 feet tall. Commercial growers use the process of "lifting" or "stripping" to grow larger and more uniform roots. They remove the soil from around the original root cutting without disturbing the new roots around the lower end. Then they raise the crown end to strip off excess shoots and rub off small side roots from the upper part of the main root. The soil is then replaced. The earlier in the season this is done, the less it affects the growth of the plant. The best growth occurs in autumn. In October or November, you should be able to harvest roots from cuttings planted in spring of the same year. Or, in some locations, roots can be left in the ground and taken as needed during the winter.

I usually dig horseradish from my Connecticut garden in November, just before the ground freezes. In soil of favorable quality and texture, the roots of a horseradish plant may go as deep as 14 feet, although they rarely spread more than 18 inches. I dig so deeply – 18 inches down – that I leave a large crater in the garden, and I take all the fragments of root I can find, yet I have never been able to recover every piece. From the small remnants, the horseradish bed arises luxuriantly again the following spring.

This brings us to one of the devilish features of horseradish – the difficulty of eradicating or containing it. I planted a few root cuttings in the south end of my garden about 20 years ago. Within a few years, the horseradish had gone far beyond its original bed, at least in scattered outposts. First, a plant appeared 18 feet away in a northwesterly direction. Later, 25 feet farther on to the north, two or three plants came up in the middle of the rose garden. (The roses hate them.) About 40 feet from there, on a northeasterly bearing, plants have recently appeared around the compost heap. Moles could have been responsible for transporting small pieces of root that later took hold, but I suspect that these colonists came from crowns and other waste pieces of root

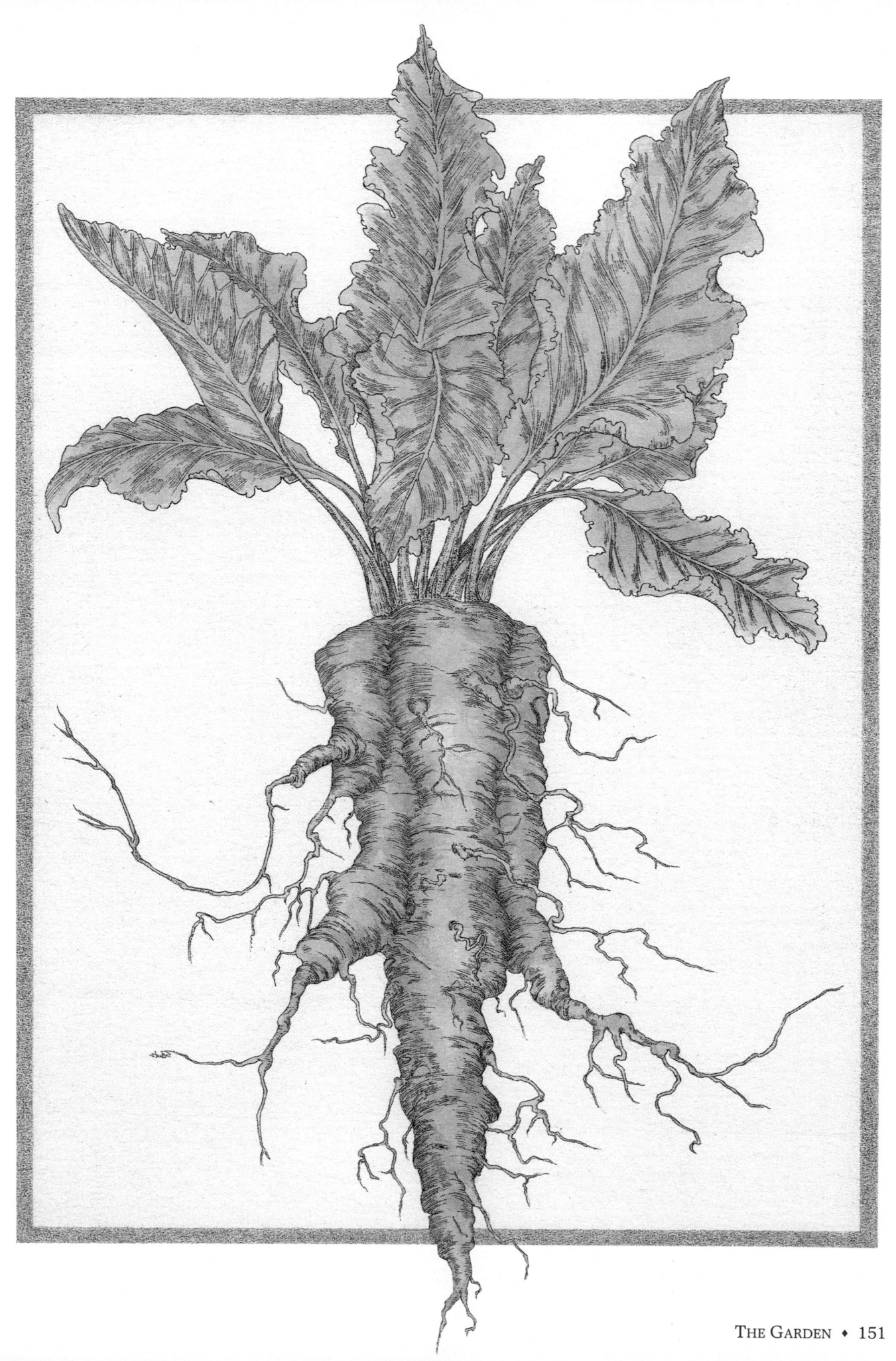

Horseradish roots may go down 14 feet, but rarely spread more than 18 inches.

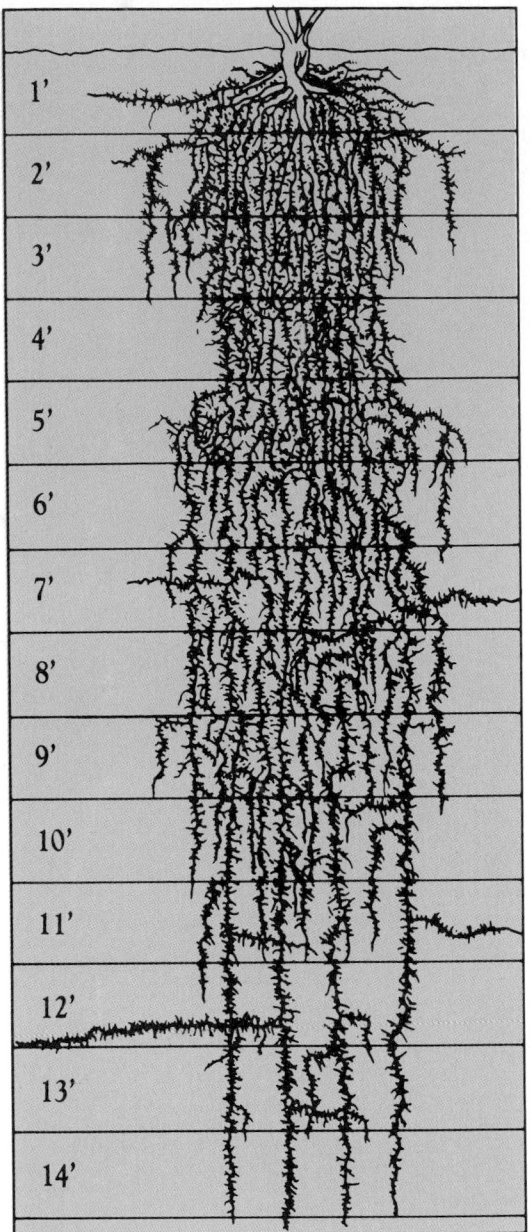

1'
2'
3'
4'
5'
6'
7'
8'
9'
10'
11'
12'
13'
14'

ing you to weep uncontrollably. I have noticed something strange, though: you can cut up the root with a sharp knife and remain relatively dry-eyed. It is only when you start grating the root that the air is filled with an invisible eye irritant and the tears begin to fall.

To discover the reason for that, I called on Professor Jack Juvik at the University of Illinois, perhaps the only place in the country where horseradish has been seriously studied. (Most of the nation's commercially grown horseradish comes from 1,400 acres of Mississippi Valley bottomland in two counties in southwestern Illinois.) Professor Juvik explained that horseradish contains two substances, sinigrin and myrosin, which are normally separated from one another in different compartments in the tissues of the root. The root can be cut without greatly disturbing its constituents. Grating is something else again; it destroys the membranes that usually keep sinigrin and myrosin apart, and they combine to produce a volatile oil, allyl isothiocyanate. This oil is primarily responsible for the irritating odor and hot taste. You can't escape from it when you grate horseradish, but you can mitigate its effects by always performing this chore outdoors, preferably when a strong breeze is blowing.

Horseradish has yet another devilish trick; after grating, its taste and aroma will quickly escape if you don't watch out. One evening several years ago, I was preparing horseradish sauce and had grated up a large bowlful of the roots. The next step is to salt the grated horseradish to taste and mix it with white vinegar until it reaches a pasty consistency. (White vinegar preserves the natural white color of the root. Cider vinegar would taste just as good but give the sauce a yellowish cast.) On this occasion, when I looked into the cupboard I found there was no white vinegar, so I left the grated horseradish uncovered until I could go to market the next day and buy white vinegar. That was a calamitous mistake. When I returned to the grated root, I found that it had lost most of its flavor and aroma and was little better than sawdust. That crucial oil, allyl isothiocyanate, is so volatile that it can be lost in just a few hours.

After that experience, I always make the sauce as rapidly as possible, sealing it up in jars. When using the horseradish, I never leave a jar open any longer than is necessary. It's a good idea to put up horseradish in several small jars rather than a single larger one; then each portion can be kept sealed until needed. The containers should be refrigerated. Even so, the horseradish slowly loses pungency and becomes darker. Keeping it in the freezer pre-

that were scattering during harvest or thrown out at the time of the annual horseradish grating. (Horseradish seldom grows from seed.)

I haven't heard of any way to eliminate horseradish short of killing the unwanted plants with herbicide, which obviously would pose some problems in the vegetable garden. I suppose there may be circumstances in which the plant could be isolated and controlled, but judging from my own experience, when you plant horseradish, you're forever in bed with it.

And horseradish isn't only tough; it turns downright nasty when you take a grater to it. I don't wish to imply that you were ever part of an unruly mob, but have you ever had a whiff of tear gas? When you grate horseradish, you are immediately enveloped by a vaporous emanation that produces a similar result, caus-

ILLUSTRATION BY ALEXANDRA SCHULZ

serves the tang longer, but some darkening still occurs. Adding dairy cream to the prepared horseradish improves retention of pungency and whiteness.

There are, however, some true delights in having fresh horseradish always on hand. And the suffering during preparation can be greatly reduced by grinding the roots in a blender rather than grating them by hand. Just dice them in small pieces with a sharp knife and put these into the blender along with the vinegar to make the process go more smoothly (perhaps a quarter-cup of white vinegar to a cup of diced horseradish). Grind it or grate it as fine as you can, because the finer it is the more flavor it has. Even chewing horseradish, Professor Juvik told me, enhances the flavor; several components are activated when enzymes and other substances not normally associated are released by the crushing of plant cells.

By Jewish tradition, horseradish is one of the "bitter herbs" served on the seder plate at the Passover meal, but bitter does not describe its taste. The only word to describe it is hot.

The basic sauce — just the grated horseradish mixed with white vinegar and a little salt — makes a zingy condiment to spread on boiled or roast beef, roast pork or other meats and fishes, and a little dab will be enough to electrify your taste buds. If the bite is too fierce for you, it can be toned down by adding grated turnip to the sauce.

A superb seafood sauce can be made by adding grated horseradish or the basic sauce to ketchup with a little lemon juice and a dash of Tabasco. With some shrimp to dip in this, or a dozen oysters on the half shell, you're in gustatory paradise. Wasabi, the pungent green sauce served with sushi, is made from Japanese horseradish, which is a different species. Other tasty sauces can be made by mixing grated horseradish into mayonnaise, sour cream or cream cheese, with the extra flavor of dill seed, if you wish, or the added color of parsley or grated beets. Horseradish is also sometimes combined with mustard — a natural enough combination, because this herb is part of the mustard family.

You might think that after 20 years of crying my eyes out and otherwise suffering the

insults of this strong-natured plant — which I am now unable to get rid of — I would regret having become involved with it. Not so. When I slather an oyster with a savory horseradish sauce, or spread a little on a slice of cold roast beef, I realize I've sold my soul to that ol' devil horseradish. But I just don't care. ❧

Horseradish grows best from root cuttings. Harvest in fall before the ground freezes.

SOURCES

Ahrens Nursery & Plant Labs
R.R. 1, Box 351
Huntingburg, Indiana 47542-9589
Horseradish crowns. Catalogue free.

Gurney Seed & Nursery Co.
2751 Page Street
Yankton, South Dakota 57079
Hybrid horseradish and 'Bohemian.' Catalogue free.

Nourse Farms, Inc.
Box 485, RFD
So. Deerfield, Massachusetts 01373
'Big Top,' roots or crowns. Catalogue free.

Ground Rules for Planting Trees

All New Guidelines to Get Your Sapling Off to a Healthy Start

By Robert Kourik with Illustrations by Maia Farrell

Planting a shade tree seems easy enough to most people. Just dig a big hole, throw in lots of compost and fertilizer, tie the trunk to a stake, water like there's no tomorrow, then sit back and wait for the shade. And this approach works nicely—for a while. But ultimately, a pampered tree may be as much trouble as a spoiled child.

When I first became a gardening enthusiast, compost was the garden god—the panacea. One could never have enough of this sacred material. In the early days of my landscaping career, I used barrows full of compost and buckets full of fertilizers when planting trees, the bigger the hole the better. And the trees grew fantastically—for a few years, that is. After that, they would just putter along, with noticeably less yearly growth.

Over time, I was amazed to notice that the trees that had been nurtured with the most soil amendments were the most likely to blow over. Also, perfectly good-looking small perennial shrubs could be pulled right out of the ground years after planting, their roots still conforming to the shape of the planting hole.

Now, thanks to the research of horticultural scientists and my own mistakes, I know that many of the ways I learned to plant and stake trees, ornamental and fruitful, were less than ideal. And the myths begin from the ground up.

Digging a hole in the ground seems like a simple task. Yet, improperly dug, a hole has a detrimental effect on the tree for many years. In fact, a poor hole can kill your tree.

Don't dig if the soil is too wet: that's the worst thing you can do in clayey soil. The act of turning over a shovelful of wet clay soil causes the platelike structure of the clay to compress on impact, excluding air and destroying what little tilth (loose structure) the soil had. The result is a clay soil that is even stickier than usual and is lacking in oxygen. Both conditions are tough on young root hairs. The sandier the soil, the wetter it can be when you work it.

The right time to dig is when a shovelful of soil will crumble if tapped slightly with the back of the shovel. After digging the hole, you should be certain to finish it off by using a spading fork to fracture its sides and bottom. When you dig with a shovel or spade, the back of the blade "slicks" any clay particles on the side of the hole, producing what I call the "flowerpot effect." The heavier the soil, the more this slicked surface acts like a buried clay pot—impeding growing roots, as though they have hit the pot's sides.

You only need to dig a hole slightly bigger than the spread of the roots of your bare-root tree or shrub. The standard guideline calling for "a $50 hole for a $25 tree" is mostly, I now think, a marketing device for retail nurseries and the manufacturers of soil amendments. (A larger hole is necessary in the case of balled-and-burlapped plants, where you need plenty of room to pack the soil around the ball.) You do not need a vast planting hole because the roots of the tree or shrub must eventually fend for themselves well beyond the walls of any hole you are likely to excavate.

It is, however, a good idea to heave and break up the soil surface beyond the planting hole. This aerates the soil and aids root penetration. The roots of most trees and shrubs will, if unrestricted, grow well beyond the outer edge of the foliage, or dripline. In clayey soil, the spread of the roots will measure 1½ times the diameter of the crown of the tree; in sandy soil, the spread of the roots will measure 3 times the spread of the foliage. For a wonderful shade tree like a pin oak (*Quercus palustris*) with a 50-to-80-foot spread, that means roots 75 feet across in clay soil and 240 feet across in sandy soil. The task in planting a tree or shrub is to encourage its roots to grow beyond the planting hole into the surrounding soil as quickly as possible.

Since the plant's success depends on its ability to thrive in your yard's native soil, choose plants that are compatible with the ground they will go in. Where nearly all trees are concerned, most gardening books will say: "prefers a rich, deep soil." And I prefer lobster with every salad. But I don't get it—nor do the majority of trees get planted in ideal soil.

The traditional approach to planting in poor soil is to improve the soil in the planting hole. There are many amendments suited to the job. Familiar amendments (as distinct from fertilizers) are materials like sand, peat moss and compost that are added to the hole to improve drainage and keep the soil loose and friable. Fertilizers, such as blood meal, cottonseed meal, greensand and wood ashes, are added to provide nutrients. Some amendments, like compost, also act as mild fertilizers. But it turns out that adding such richness to the planting hole is wrongheaded.

One of the best studies on the effect of amendments and fertilizers was done at Oklahoma State University at Stillwater by Joseph Schulte and Carl Whitcomb. They planted 108 silver maple trees in holes with 11 different soil treatments, and they included controls (trees planted in untreated planting holes). Among their conclusions: "No benefit was derived from the use of soil amendments either with a good clay loam soil or a very poor

silt loam subsoil." They found that the control plantings with no additional fertilizer generally outperformed the plantings with amendments for drainage and fertility.

As a result of this and other studies, there is a new planting guideline, one that is hard for me to get used to: do not amend the soil in the planting hole. Not in clay, not in sand. According to Schulte and Whitcomb, this is another way of avoiding the flowerpot effect. To make a healthy tree, the roots must get out of the hole, and initially coddling the roots with lots of amendments only leaves them unprepared for the shock of what lies beyond the enriched area. Often the roots fail to make it out of the well-amended hole and merely circle around in the loose planting medium, rendering the tree likely to blow over during a storm.

The trees best able to stand up to wind are those with the most extensive root systems. Except for some nut trees, such as pecan and walnut, and some oak trees, most ornamental trees and all fruit trees have a fibrous root system; that is, they lack a central taproot, but they have large horizontal roots from which substantial sinker roots descend at many intervals. These sinker roots act like underground guy wires to anchor the tree away from the trunk. Confining the root system to an area near the trunk prevents these sinker roots from forming at a distance sufficient to support the tree.

Fertilizers also encourage the tree's roots to stay in the planting hole. Roots are relatively lazy; they feed where it's easiest. Compost, especially in quantity, turns out to be one of the worst additions when planting trees, because it is both an amendment and a fertilizer.

You should, however, fertilize. But fertilize *beyond* the planting hole. This practice encourages the roots to spread into the native, unamended soils. On older trees, the roots nearest the trunk acquire a barklike covering and actually stop absorbing water and nutrients. As the tree grows, I water and spread fertilizers beyond the dripline of the tree's foliage to stimulate the smaller, outward-reaching roots.

You may want to scuff the soil lightly to work the fertilizer into the ground, but do not dig it in. The tree's feeder roots come right to the soil surface, and digging will damage those delicate roots.

The spring of 1985 in our part of northern California was an educational one for tree-planters, especially orchardists. Unusually late rains in April and May caught our ornamental and fruit trees in full leaf. Many of the trees died of crown rot (*Phytophthora*

The roots of most trees grow 1½ to 3 times wider than the crown; deep sinker roots anchor the tree.

spp), including up to 25 percent of those planted in some orchards on clayey soils. Crown rot is a fungal disease of the upper portion of the roots, near the soil surface. The fungus damages the sapwood of the tree, either stunting growth or killing it. Once the telltale symptoms (pale, wilted leaves) appear, it is too late to do anything. Observant horticulturists noticed that the trees that survived were either in well-drained soil or planted on high spots or small mounds.

Since that gloomy but instructive spring, I've been planting all trees on small mounds 8 to 18 inches high and 3 to 4 feet wide. (The heavier the soil, the higher the mound. Sandy soils don't require a mound, since they are naturally well drained.) This mounding technique is especially important as preventive medicine in climates where it rains during the summer, because the crown-rot fungus thrives in damp warmth.

If the final mound is to be 18 inches high, and I'm planting a one-year-old bare-root tree, a planting hole isn't even required. The whole time I'm preparing the mound, I soak the roots in water. This counteracts any dehydration and helps wash off any sawdust (used to keep roots moist during shipping).

(If gophers are a problem, I bury a wire basket below the ground. I use ½-inch aviary wire to fashion a cylinder with a closed bottom. Then I dig out enough soil to bury all but the top 6 to 8 inches of the basket, place the basket in the hole and refill.)

To prepare the ground, all the grass and weeds are removed from an area 3 to 4 feet in diameter. Then, with a spading fork, I heave and crack the native soil within the entire circle, not bothering to turn it. Next, I scrape up good topsoil from the surrounding area (after the weeds have been skimmed off) and make a small cone of soil, 10 to 18 inches wide, in the center of the circle. Then I spread the roots of the bare-root tree over the top of this cone of soil. If I'm planting container-grown plants, I tear apart the root ball, knock off most of the planting mix and spread out any circling roots on the mound's cone of soil. I make sure that some of the exposed roots are tucked into the native soil that was fractured open with the spading fork. After the roots of the tree are spread out evenly on the cone of soil, I gather plenty of topsoil to make the rest of the mound, covering the tree's trunk to the same depth as it was in the nursery. This line is easily spotted as a marked change in color, usually from orange or amber to dark orange or brown, depending on the tree. I tamp the soil with my feet several times to eliminate air pockets that can desiccate young root hairs.

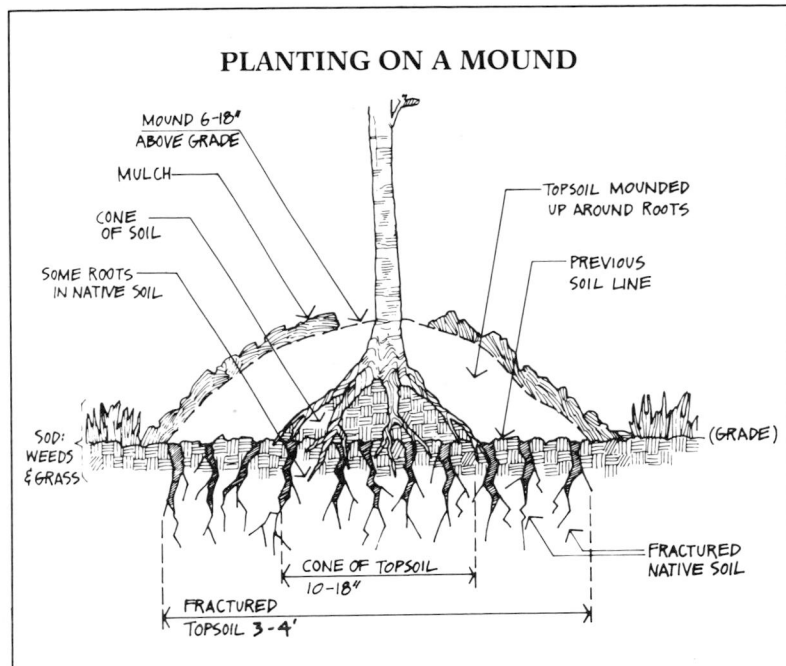

PLANTING ON A MOUND

MOUND 6-18" ABOVE GRADE

MULCH

CONE OF SOIL

SOME ROOTS IN NATIVE SOIL

TOPSOIL MOUNDED UP AROUND ROOTS

PREVIOUS SOIL LINE

(GRADE)

SOD: WEEDS & GRASS

CONE OF TOPSOIL 10-18"

FRACTURED NATIVE SOIL

FRACTURED TOPSOIL 3-4'

Many people remain suspicious about the mounding method, even though I've used it successfully with ornamentals and edibles for nearly four years. But I have found support among the experts. Alex Shigo, a pioneering tree pathologist formerly with the U.S. Forest Service, says of planting on mounds: "I'm all for it. The best botanical gardens in England and Australia have *all* their trees planted on small mounds. It's easier to regulate watering from a position of dryness than from wetness." When I asked him why this technique has not caught on in America, he answered, "Our pioneering spirit still prevails. It's easier to treat trees as expendable than to show them the respect they deserve. Now that we've run out of land and we're trying to plant in tougher settings, like the prairies, we're finding out how important techniques like this one are."

Many people, upon viewing one of my mounds, worry about the dryness of the mound hurting or killing the tree. Remember, though, that, unimpeded, the roots will grow to be much wider than the canopy. Within a month or two, the majority of the feeding roots will be beyond the mound, deep into the native soil—providing that water and fertilizers are kept *away* from the trunk area and are used to lure the roots farther into the peripheral soil. Continual watering in a basin near the trunk, however, will discourage the roots from spreading, leaving them vulnerable to drought.

After planting, I water the tree generously and soak the entire mound once or twice. Then I mulch the whole mound about 6 inches deep, making sure that the mulch doesn't pile

Instead of planting trees and shrubs in holes, set them on mounds. The author recommends this method for establishing trees in poorly drained soils.

The right way to plant a tree: dig a hole only slightly larger than the spread of the tree's roots. Use a spading fork to fracture the sides and bottom, and break up the surface beyond the hole to improve aeration and aid root penetration. Set the tree in the hole on a mound of un-amended topsoil. Spread out the tree's roots to encourage them to grow into the surrounding soil, and backfill with soil that was removed from the hole. This method is recommended for planting in well-drained soils.

up against the trunk. All further waterings are done at the edge of the mound, not on top of it. Give the tree enough water to keep it from losing its leaves; they supply the energy to the plant's roots.

To prevent sunscald, paint the trunk with white or light beige latex up to the first branches. Once the tree's trunk is painted, there are a number of strategies to protect new trees from rabbits, mice, bobcats, deer, children and other varmints.

A cylinder of ¼-inch wire hardware cloth extending from several inches below the ground to 18 or more inches above the ground (depending upon the average snow depth) will prevent rabbits and mice from chewing on the bark. A pile of small crushed rock reaching from several inches below the soil to 4 inches up the trunk will also help prevent most mouse damage.

I once lost a tree to bobcats, who so severely scratched the bark while sharpening their claws that the tree died. Now, I protect trees with a white plastic collar; a spiral slit up the length of the cylinder allows you to wrap the trunk. This collar, cut to the right length, will prevent sunscald, stop rabbit damage and prevent domestic and wild cats from scratching the trunk.

Deer should be fenced out with either a perimeter fence or individual wire cylinders until the tree is over 8 feet tall. Fencing is also the solution to young tree climbers of the *Homo sapiens* persuasion. Either fence the trees in or the kids out.

If people did to their animals what they do to their trees, they'd be picketed by animal-rights activists. The ways many people stake and tie their trees appear to be some peculiar brand of horticultural torture.

I once took over a landscape maintenance job after a landscaper had dug some large holes in a heavy clay soil for several eucalyptus trees. The trees were tall and spindly when they were planted on this windy hilltop. After two years, even with repeated pruning to lessen the sail effect of the canopy, they were flopping over with each windstorm. The clients were too attached to the trees to let the wind defeat them. So I was forced to cement three 4-inch galvanized iron pipes into the ground for each tree and use heavy-gauge wire to lash each tree to its three posts. If trees are planted properly, however, the least amount of "bondage" is the best for them.

You need to stake a newly planted tree so that it will not simply blow over, but will be allowed to sway in the wind. The more a tree flexes, the stronger it gets. Trees with stakes tied tightly to their trunks will have smaller, weaker trunks than those tied loosely and low. Trees staked properly will develop more girth as they flex in the wind.

Never tie the tree directly to a stake. The best support comes from two wooden stakes, each 2 to 3 inches in diameter, placed 8 to 10 inches away from the trunk. Andrew Leiser, environmental horticulturist at the University of California at Davis, recommends that the stakes "should be placed so that the tree doesn't hit the stake when it blows and so that the stakes don't hit the roots or root ball when they're pounded in place. If you're planting a large balled-and-burlapped tree, you may have to drive the stakes through the root ball, but carefully avoid any noticeably large roots." In windy areas, place the stakes so that a line drawn between them is perpendicular to the direction of the strongest winds.

The lower you tie the tree, the more flexing you'll allow. To find the best spot for tying a spindly or relatively weak tree, Leiser recommends that you "grab the tree with your right hand near the top and bend over the top with your left hand. You'll notice that the tree is able to return to an upright position. Move your right hand down the trunk and try bending and releasing the top with your left hand. At a certain point, the top will stay flopped over and not regain its upright position. Tie the tree to the stakes at a point 6 inches higher than the last position of your right hand."

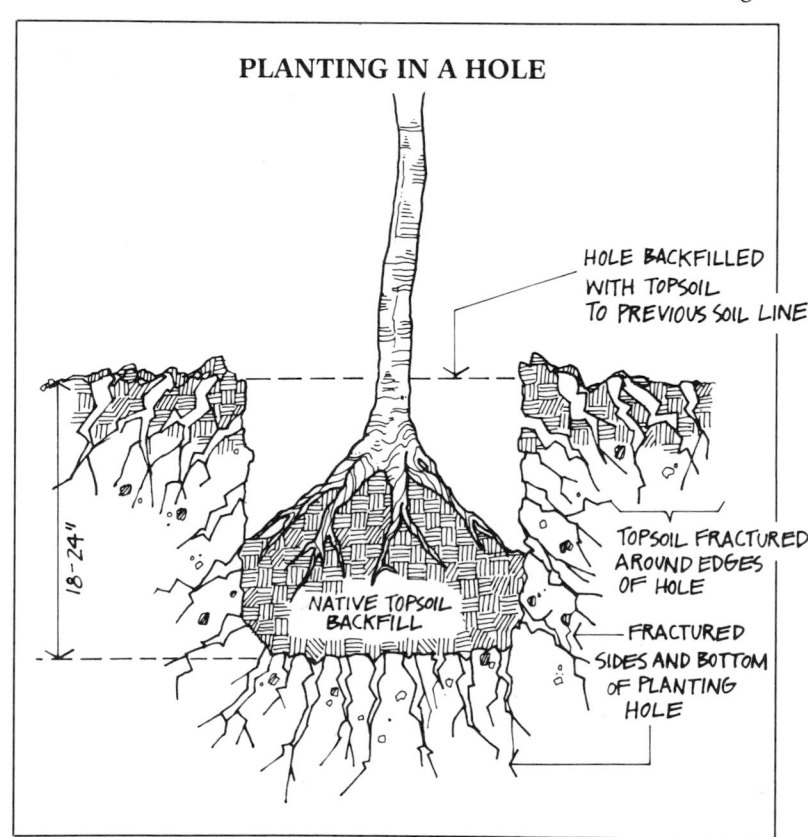

PLANTING IN A HOLE

HOLE BACKFILLED WITH TOPSOIL TO PREVIOUS SOIL LINE

18–24"

NATIVE TOPSOIL BACKFILL

TOPSOIL FRACTURED AROUND EDGES OF HOLE

FRACTURED SIDES AND BOTTOM OF PLANTING HOLE

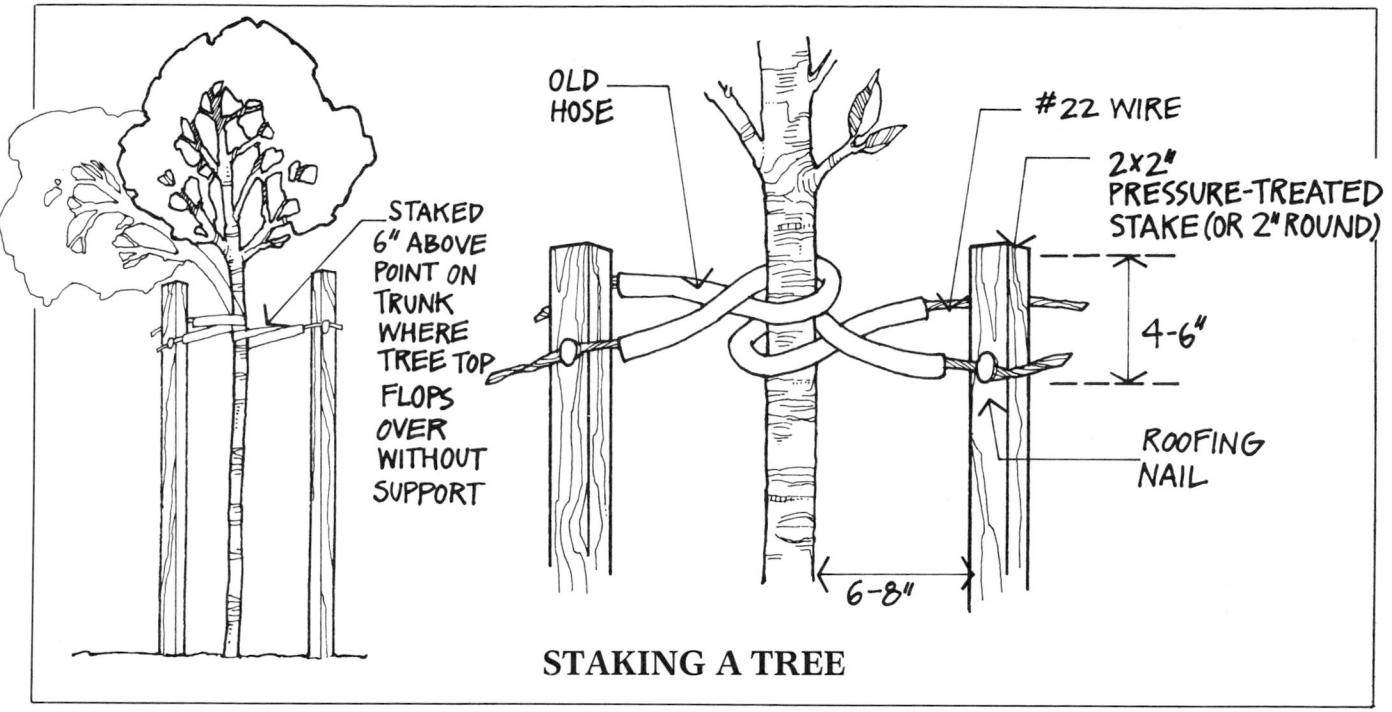

STAKING A TREE

Labels on figure:
- OLD HOSE
- STAKED 6" ABOVE POINT ON TRUNK WHERE TREE TOP FLOPS OVER WITHOUT SUPPORT
- #22 WIRE
- 2×2" PRESSURE-TREATED STAKE (OR 2" ROUND)
- 4-6"
- ROOFING NAIL
- 6-8"

Sometimes this can be as low to the ground as 18 inches. This method of staking allows for the most flexing above and below the ties and allows the trunk to develop a thick, strong stem.

(On poorly formed trees, where the top is disproportionately bigger than the root ball and the trunk is too spindly to withstand wind, Leiser also urges the planter to thin the tree's top selectively by up to 50 percent after planting. The thinning will help reduce the sail effect and allow for a better proportion between roots and top.)

Run a small-gauge (#22) 6- or 10-strand wire in a figure-8 loop from each stake around the trunk. The loop of wire should pass through a piece of old garden hose or such to keep it from damaging the trunk. Make sure the combination of wires allows the trunk to sway 6 to 8 inches.

For windy spots, the smallest seedlings ultimately make for the most wind-resistant trees. I have clients who own the last house on the road, some 500 yards from the Pacific Ocean. They transplanted some 6-foot-tall Monterey cypress trees (*Cupressus macrocarpa*) from 15-gallon containers. The trees had been cramped in their containers for several years after purchase, but my clients wanted to save money by not getting newer trees. The first winter the trees started blowing over. By the third winter, the owners had pruned the tops to reduce the wind exposure.

They wanted a windbreak on the west side of the property, so I convinced them to allow me to plant some fast-growing shrubs and small trees along with some small Monterey cypress. The cypress were planted as 1-foot-tall, 1-gallon container trees among the border planting of ornamental shrubs and small trees. Because they were so small, the 1-gallon Monterey cypress trees needed no staking. The 1-gallon trees cost $4.95, in contrast to the original $65 cost of the 15-gallon trees.

The border of fast-growing shrubs and trees acted as a "nurse planting," helping to break the wind for the newly planted cypress. Thus, the cypress trees were sheltered from storms, but able to bend and flex in the buffered wind.

Within four years, the 1-gallon, unstaked trees were taller than half of the 15-gallon, 9-year-old trees. And I suspect that they will show even more impressive growth rates in the next several years, far surpassing the more expensive trees in height and sturdiness.

So when planting trees and shrubs, forgo the amendments and fertilizers, plant high but plant small, and avoid the perversion of tree bondage. 🌱

The proper way to stake a tree: run a thin wire in a figure-8 loop around the trunk from each of two wooden stakes. Pass the wire through a piece of old garden hose to protect the tree. Allow the tree some flexibility; this will encourage the development of a thick, strong stem.

Flowers That Bloom In the Night

WITH A SCENT THAT HINTS OF PARADISE

BY ADRIAN FORSYTH

Arriving home late one summer night, I had the sensation of falling into a perfume bottle. As I stepped out of my truck, I was enveloped by a thick cloud of sweet and intoxicating scent. It was exotic and tropical in the manner of jasmine or vanilla, and unexpected in a northern garden. Ahead of me by the house, I could see the source – a large trumpet-like blossom tilted skyward and shining in the starlight. The first flower of the sacred datura had opened.

Until that night, it had been hard for me to imagine why anyone would want to grow a flower that blooms after dark and begins wilting as soon as the sun rises. Conventional wisdom has it that the purpose of planting flowers is to provide color and beauty that one can appreciate by day. But that spectacular datura showed me that the night flowers have their own gifts. Their pale or white moonlight-reflecting shades and their sweet fragrances enhance the lingering twilight that is such a pleasant aspect of a climate otherwise fraught with obstacles. At sundown, most gardeners, too busy to enjoy their handiwork during the day, can finally trade hoe and hose for a chair or hammock and enjoy the evening flowers. Night bloomers have even been planted directly under bedroom windows, thus granting dreamers the illusion of sleeping in paradise. The flowers can also be cut as buds just before sunset and brought inside. They will open just after dark and release perfume all night.

The qualities that make the night flowers so appealing are, for them, simply efficient survival mechanisms. Nocturnal bloomers have a natural history that makes sense of their special size, shape, smell and color. I hadn't expected the daturas to set seeds, believing that far from their native habitat, they would not be pollinated. But they soon began producing large, well-filled seedpods. Watching them one evening, I learned the reason. Large sphinx moths were hovering around and diving into the flowers, searching for the pools of nectar inside. In the morning, their dustlike scales could be seen streaked down the inside of the corolla, the tube made by the flower's petals.

Daturas, like many night-flowering plants, are designed to be pollinated by moths, and coadaptation between many night flowers and moths explains some of the characteristics of the flowers. They are usually white or some light shade that renders them visible at night; they have a long tubular structure that excludes most insects except long-tongued moths, and they have a powerful fragrance. The strength of the fragrance seems necessary to draw the long-tongued moths, which are not as abundant and as available for pollen transfer as are day-flying bees and flies. Day-flowering relatives of the datura, such as tomatoes, have abundant accessible flowers that many kinds of bees compete for. Moth flowers, in contrast, must compete to attract pollinators distributed over a wide area, and they do so using a powerful aromatic beacon. The advantage of this system for the plant is long-distance gene transport. Many of the pollinating moths, such as the sphinx moths, can fly miles in a single evening, carrying pollen from one plant to another. That attribute is particularly useful for rare plants that are widely dispersed in nature. When a night flower comes into bloom, we are witnessing a special evolutionary confluence of plant and

'Queen of the Night,' right: The luminous flowers of the night-blooming cereus appear only after sunset, opening so fast that one can see their movement; and then the blossoms drop off before morning.

COURTESY OF THE HUNT INSTITUTE FOR BOTANICAL DOCUMENTATION, CARNEGIE MELLON UNIVERSITY, PITTSBURGH, PA

pollinator life histories.

Incidentally, the tomato hornworm is the larva of a species of sphinx moth, and it is conceivable that night flowers could attract egg-laying females into the garden, to the detriment of tomato plants. We have never suffered this problem, however, and since the vast majority of sphinx moth species are attractive, beneficial insects useful for pollinating native plant species, encouraging them seems to be a worthwhile endeavor.

Excellent examples of successful datura are to be had in the two species suitable for cultivation as annuals in northern gardens. The sacred datura (*D. meteloides,* also known as *D. inoxia*), named for its religious use by American Indians in the Southwest, flowers easily in its first summer, especially when grown in a large container. *Datura fastuosa* (also known as a variety of *D. metel*) is another that will flower during the northern gardening season. Simply grow them as you would peppers or tomatoes, with full sun and a well-drained soil.

Several years ago, in the Canyonlands of southern Utah, my wife and I collected the seeds of *Datura meteloides*. The plant had no flowers, only an array of stout, bristly, attractive seedpods reminiscent of sea urchins or the heads of medieval maces. At home, the seed remained unused for several years until we decided to see what a desert native might yield in a northern garden. We started the seeds in peat pots in March, along with our peppers, eggplants and tomatoes, all nightshades, members of the family Solanaceae, to which datura belongs. In June, after the threat of frost had abated, we transplanted them in their peat pots into a half whiskey barrel full of light, sandy, desertlike soil. The daturas thrived, but their sprawling foliage was not promising, the slightest touch producing a rank smell with the pungency of tomato leaves.

The flowers came as a surprise. They were totally unlike those of the plant's vegetable relatives. Peppers, tomatoes and potatoes have small blossoms that are buzzed by a wide range of bees, but produce little smell or nectar. The daturas, however, had massive, deep flowers the better part of a foot long, flooded with nectar, and their scent was stronger and richer than that of almost any flower. Later in July, when several flowers had opened, their cloud of scent could be detected more than 50 yards away.

Also in the nightshade family is another night bloomer, nicotiana. A more familiar group of plants, the nicotiana genus includes the infamous tobacco (*Nicotiana tabacum*), source of nicotine (a potent insecticide that is, in effect, able to parasitize the human nervous system and force large numbers of humans to devote vast resources to the welfare of this weedy plant). A more benign species of this genus is the jasmine tobacco or flowering tobacco, *N. alata* or *N. affinis*, which is well-suited to the night garden. It is a tall, upright plant growing a yard or more high, with long, narrow, white tubular flowers up to six inches long. Its shape makes it a fine background plant to stand behind lower and more colorful flowers.

All nicotianas like full sun and a light, well-drained soil, and they are sensitive to frost. Their seeds are as fine as dust and accordingly require careful attention when being started in flats indoors. They must be dusted on the surface, preferably in a mix of finely pulverized peat, pressed flat with a board or glass sheet to ensure firm contact with the soil and kept constantly moist by misting frequently until germination. Covering the flat with plastic or a glass sheet is one method to prevent drying, but mildew and fungus are always a threat under these conditions. Peat moss in the mix will alleviate some of the threat. The easiest way to get fine nicotiana seedlings is to do as I do: visit your local greenhouse. Almost every seedling operation sells nicotianas, but ask for the white night-bloomers, not the brightly colored selections bred for pigment rather than odor.

Another night bloomer is the moonflower, *Ipomoea alba,* which produces fragrant four- to six-inch blooms similar to morning glories. The large seeds have hard coats and so should be soaked for a day in a wet paper towel or nicked with a sharp knife to encourage germination. They should be planted one-quarter inch deep in sandy soil about two weeks after the last frost date, as soon as the weather is dependably warm. Plant them close to a trellis, fence or stakes, because they are vining plants that can grow about 15 feet tall.

When working with any of the nightshades, including the vegetables, one should be aware that nightshade foliage is well defended by chemical alkaloids, many of which are commercially extracted for medicine. One product of the Solanaceae – scopolamine – is used in sleeping prescriptions, while many tropical cultures use extracts as hallucinogens and intoxicants. The smell of the crushed foliage is so fetid that I cannot imagine anyone chewing on a leaf absentmindedly with unanticipated ill effects. But it is conceivable that relatively mindless creatures such as cows might damage themselves by eating the foliage.

The daturas, nicotianas, jasmines and other nightshades are a largely tropical group, usually grown as annuals in the north or grown in

*Redolent of tropical summer evenings, the sacred datura, left, displays voluptuous, perfumed flowers in its first summer.
Overleaf: the night-blooming cereus, a cactus.*

Adrian and Turid Forsyth *Overleaf* Robert C. Simpson/Valan Photos

The gumbo lily, despite its delicate appearance, thrives in heavy soil.

containers wintered indoors if treated as perennials. The ipomoeas, also tropical natives, love warmth too.

But not all night flowers are from the tropics. Many of the evening primroses are hardy night-flowering biennials and perennials. The most widely distributed species is the weedy evening primrose, *Oenothera biennis.* In our garden, this plant is a weed that self-sows in any spot with heavy soil. Most of the seedlings are culled, but sometimes a dense aggregation is worth leaving. Individual plants look ungainly and spindly, but a mass of spires decked out in lemon yellow blossoms is attractive in a group of mixed flowers. The plants vary in size, and the flowers pop out erratically, the hallmark of a wild species. Around our house, and I expect elsewhere, they have the virtue of attracting rosy maple moths, robust moths of delicate yellow, banded with pink. In the morning, these attractive insects can be found in the flowers, apparently sleeping off a binge of rich nectar and intoxicating perfume.

A far more attractive wild evening primrose, one that looks as though it had been bred for beauty, is the gumbo lily, *Oenothera caespitosa.* It gets its common name from its ability to thrive in the gumbo clay of prairie regions. I have seen this plant flowering in the badlands of southwestern Saskatchewan, where the soil is an incredibly greasy expanse of clay that swells when wet and then cracks into polygons when dry. The volatile character of the soil makes it difficult for most other plants to survive, so entire areas of the badlands are composed of nothing but large bare swaths of soil dotted with nothing but gumbo lilies. This freedom from tall shading competitors may be what allows these gumbo lilies to grow no more than six inches tall, as low rosettes instead of the spires of the evening primrose, which grows in thick, tall meadows. In any case, gumbo lilies are able to build four-inch-wide white blossoms that seem highly ambitious in relation to the size of the plant that produces them. In the early morning, as the first low rays of sun flare on the translucent blossoms, the low badland gullies seem to be sprouting giant blossoms directly from the soil. Then, as the day progresses, the flowers turn pink. By noon, they fall limp, and the gully regains its eroded and barren atmosphere. But in the moonlight, a swath of gumbo lilies must be a powerful and ghostly vision.

These flowers can also be cut as buds just before sunset and brought inside as cut flowers. They will open just after dark and begin emitting perfume for a night-long olfactory experience.

One can get the same effect with certain houseplants. One of the most spectacular of all houseplant flowers erupts from the commonly cultivated cereus and hylocereus cacti. I don't grow cacti, but I have watched these in action in their desert and tropical forest habitats. Some of them have flowers that are a foot long and weigh a quarter pound each.

Louise Wilder Beebe, author of a wonderful old gardening book, *The Fragrant Garden*, remembers "being allowed to 'sit up' when a little girl to witness the flowering of this strange plant in a neighbor's greenhouse. The huge flower began to unfold at about eight o'clock and at eleven was fully blown, its rich perfume seeming to fill the world. The calyx of the flower when fully expanded is nearly a foot across, brownish in color without and bright yellow on the upper side, having the appearance of a great gilded star. The petals, snowy white and of a high luster, gleam against this golden background and the vast number of stamens at the heart add to the splendid appearance of this flower; probably no other flower equals it in sheer magnificence. But its hour of triumph is short. Before the cock crows, the drama is played out and the beautiful blossoms fallen into decay." In nature, they are even more spectacular, being attended by swarms of sphinx moths, diving and hovering like nocturnal hummingbirds.

A more delicate, if less spectacular, flower and night fragrance can be had by growing citrus indoors. We once bought a dwarf 'Meyer' lemon from the type of mail-order firm with a catalogue of retouched photographs of fruit trees bearing several tons of monstrous colorful fruits. What arrived was a pathetic seedling with scarcely a root on it. To our surprise, it grew into a sturdy shrub that blossomed and fruited in its second season, producing not only high-quality lemons but a long-lasting crop of nocturnal flowers that have the virtue of giving off their scent during cloudy days.

My favorite night flower, however, is the evening-scented stock, *Matthiola bicornis*. It is an unassuming low-growing plant rarely more than 18 inches high, with a pale bluish green foliage that blends into mixed plantings. The tiny seeds of this plant can be sown here and there in gaps among other more showy flowers, and by day the plants will go almost unnoticed, especially since their small purple flowers fold up.

For myself, evening-scented stock is linked with all the pleasurable sensations of the growing season; high summer arrives on the first July night when their odor fills the darkness. Humans are usually said to be a highly visual species, with excellent eyesight but noses of slight acumen. We still retain, however, the mammalian legacy in which smell and memory are strongly linked. Almost everyone has had the experience of detecting a particular smell that suddenly elicits a memory of a time and place in vivid detail. I associate the smell of evening-scented stock with the first blinking displays of fireflies, the whisper of hunting bats and all the sensations of summer at its fullest.

The night fragrance of these plants lasts all summer long. Only a hard frost will put an end to their durable flowers. As the gardening season progresses and evenings arrive earlier and become cooler, the smell of the evening stock becomes tinged with nostalgia, the memory of lingering northern twilight and warm summer nights redolent with their own sweet fragrances. ❧

SOURCES

The seeds of nicotiana and night-scented plants are available from most all-purpose seed houses.

Four Winds Growers
Box 3538
Fremont, California 94539
True dwarf lemons and other citrus suitable for indoor culture. Send a self-addressed, stamped envelope for free catalogue.

J.L. Hudson, Seedsman
P.O. Box 1058
Redwood City, California 94064
Seeds of six species of datura including D. meteloides; *several species of* Ipomoea; Matthiola bicornis; Nicotiana alata; Oenothera biennis. *Catalogue $1.*

K & L Cactus Nursery
12712 Stockton Boulevard
Galt, California 95632
Cereus cactus plants and seeds. Catalogue $2.

Thompson & Morgan
P.O. Box 1308
Jackson, New Jersey 08527
Seeds of three species of datura; Ipomoea alba. *Catalogue free.*

A Moment in the Sun

PREPARING GARDEN PRODUCE FOR WINTER STORAGE

BY JENNIFER BENNETT

My first garlic harvest produced a wonder of fat, juicy bulbs redolent with the scent of Italian markets. I had purchased garlic "seeds"—the bulbils produced on the top of the plant—planted them the previous fall and harvested them that summer after the foliage died. All I had to do now, I thought, was to store them for about three months until late fall, when they could be divided into cloves and replanted to produce full-sized bulbs next year. Delighted with the first whiffs of success, I brought the bulbs indoors and put them in a plastic pail where, in the heat and humidity of summer, they sat and quietly rotted into a sort of garlic stew for the next few weeks. By the time I spotted the spoilage, I had lost half of my coveted harvest, but fortunately I still had enough to plant—although somewhat earlier than I had planned. I was lucky, for ignoring the needs of vegetables at harvest time can result in no usable produce at all.

Because I was planning to keep the bulbs for a relatively short time, I had not bothered to prepare them for their indoor stay. I knew that the bulbs were reputed to be long keepers. But, like several other vegetables, garlic will keep well only if it is first cured. The term "curing," or preparing for keeping, embraces such processes as the drying of tobacco, the brining and sugaring of corned beef and hams, and the treatment of vegetables so that they will store well. This use of the word "cure" was once more popular than it is now: Daniel Defoe, for instance, wrote in *Robinson Crusoe* in 1719 that he had picked enough grapes "to have cured into raisins," though who he was going to have them cured *by* remained a mystery. Properly cured, garlic can last about a year, even under less than perfect storage conditions; my homegrown garlic now resides all winter, sound and dry, in a paper shopping bag on an upstairs landing. Without curing, however, it would remain crisp for only a couple of weeks.

Curing enables certain vegetables—not just garlic but also onions, potatoes, carrots, beets, parsnips, rutabagas, winter squashes and pumpkins—to develop a slightly thickened dry skin that will resist molding. It also heals small abrasions that would otherwise provide entry places for fungi and bacteria. Some water content is also lost, leaving the vegetable better able to remain free of mold in a damp root cellar. Leafy greens and vegetables lacking distinct "skins" do not require curing, nor do tree fruits. And the only candidates suited to the process are those being considered for storage other than freezing, canning, pickling or drying. Cured produce is intended to be kept in the open air, in bags or boxes or on shelves.

Whether cured or not, only sound, fully mature produce is appropriate for such storage. Defective or immature vegetables should be eaten as soon as possible or perhaps trimmed and then frozen, canned or dried. Undersized vegetables, too, are best put in the eat-first category; they may become excessively dry and withered in curing. For storage, choose vegetables bred for long keeping: potatoes such as 'Netted Gem' and 'Kennebec'; carrots such as 'Danvers' and 'Chantenay'; onions such as 'Canada Maple,' 'Downing Yellow Globe' and 'Sweet Sandwich.'

Putting Potatoes By

Potatoes are among the vegetables that benefit most from curing. The objective is to improve their storage properties by making their skins firmer and tougher. This reduces

Before being stored, thick-skinned vegetables should be "cured": left in the sun for a day or so to toughen their skins, right.

RICHARD W. BROWN

subsequent moisture loss, increases resistance to disease and aids in recovery from injury. The commercial curing of potatoes requires 10 to 14 days of storage at 56 to 60 degrees F and very high humidity. During this process, the potatoes will not sprout because, for about two weeks after harvesting, they are in a state of rest.

Such long-term conditions are not easily met by the home gardener, nor are they necessary; homegrown potatoes will not have to endure shipping to packagers and distributors and storage in a warm supermarket until they are sold. Just a day of exposure to sunny weather will cure potatoes well enough to allow them to be kept indoors in a cool basement or root cellar until the following spring. Eugene H. Grubb described this less sophisticated curing process in his 1912 book, *The Potato:* "An essential in digging potatoes is to let the tubers lie on top of the ground for two to six hours to dry out any dirt clinging to them and to toughen the skin. In this way, the potato is less liable to bruise in the after-handling and much less dirt is carried from the field."

If possible, do not harvest the tubers until at least two weeks after the tops have died. This allows the skins to "set" so that they will be less likely to suffer harvest damage. A potato mature enough for storage should have a skin that cannot be rubbed off with the thumb. Choose a clear or, at least, rainless day for harvesting, and dig early in the morning so that you can allow the potatoes about six hours of exposure to the open air. Immediately after the harvest, gently remove clumps of dirt and leave the tubers in a single layer, not touching one another, on a dry surface like mulch, newspaper, a path or patio. After about two hours, check that the potatoes are thoroughly dry on the tops, and then turn them over to expose the bottoms. Late in the day, pack them loosely in boxes, feed sacks or paper bags that will admit air but exclude light in cool, slightly moist, storage. As Catherine Parr Traill aptly observed in 1855, "A vast deal of loss, both in quantity and quality, is caused by storing potatoes wet."

Beets, Carrots, Rutabagas, Parsnips

Commercial growers harvest these root vegetables, wash them and put them immediately in cold, humid storage. At home, however, storing directly after washing would almost certainly result in moldy produce within a few weeks; in early fall, few basements can offer the optimal temperature – exactly 32 degrees F – these vegetables require to stay crisp. In the warmer environment of most home root cellars, roots will last longer if cured. I have had uncured carrots settle into an unpalatable brown mush by midwinter; but cured ones, simply stored in plain plastic bags in the basement, stay crisp and delicious until spring.

Save a sunny morning for harvesting these vegetables. They will need at least a day of curing, because the roots, especially those raised in a clay soil, need a light wash before they are cured; dirty vegetables become muddy if they sweat and can develop an off taste in storage. After harvesting, twist off the tops. Fill a pail with cool water, and rinse each root, gently

Garlic bulbs should be dried in sun until their skins turn brittle and necks shrink. Store in a dry place.

rubbing off clumps of soil; then place the wet roots in a single layer on mulch, newspaper or a patio to dry, turning them after three or four hours. If necessary, bring them in overnight and spread them outdoors again the next sunny day. Store in plastic bags (if the storage temperature will not drop below freezing) or in boxes packed with peat moss or straw, in a very cool, slightly moist, place.

Squash, Pumpkins

Harvest squash and pumpkins when they are fully mature; that is, when the color is bright and the skin is difficult to break with a fingernail. Curing for two weeks at 80 to 85 degrees F is recommended for commercial growers of these related vegetables, but this can be difficult at home. Exposure to fall sunshine in the field for just two days, however, produces a skin hard enough to withstand any minor damage the fruit is likely to receive away from the marketplace. Before frost has damaged the fruits but after they are full-sized and mature, cut them from the plant, leaving a piece of stem intact. Gently rub adhering soil from the underside and place upside down (or as near to it as possible) in a sunny, dry spot for a day, turning once. Cover them or bring them indoors overnight and spread them out again on the next sunny day, turning them once after a few hours in the sun. Store in a single layer in a cool or warm, relatively dry place. Among the best keeping squash are buttercup and Hubbard.

Onions, Garlic, Shallots

Commercial North American onion growers usually cure their produce in a special temperature-controlled room, where it is treated to forced air for about two weeks before it is moved to storage at freezing temperatures. "About 5 percent of the onion weight has to be evaporated," notes one agricultural bulletin, "and completion of curing is indicated by a well-contracted neck and brittle skin. Overcuring causes loss of skin. Excessive humidity or high temperatures cause staining of the skin. The latter effect may also result from moisture condensation on the surface of the bulbs, as sometimes happens when outside air on a warm day is brought into contact with onions at a lower temperature; that is, when the onion temperature is below the dew point of the outside air."

All this may be a bit daunting to gardeners. Nevertheless, simpler means are effective at home, where onion consumers are unlikely to be concerned about problems as minor as stained skins. In the English magazine *Prac-*

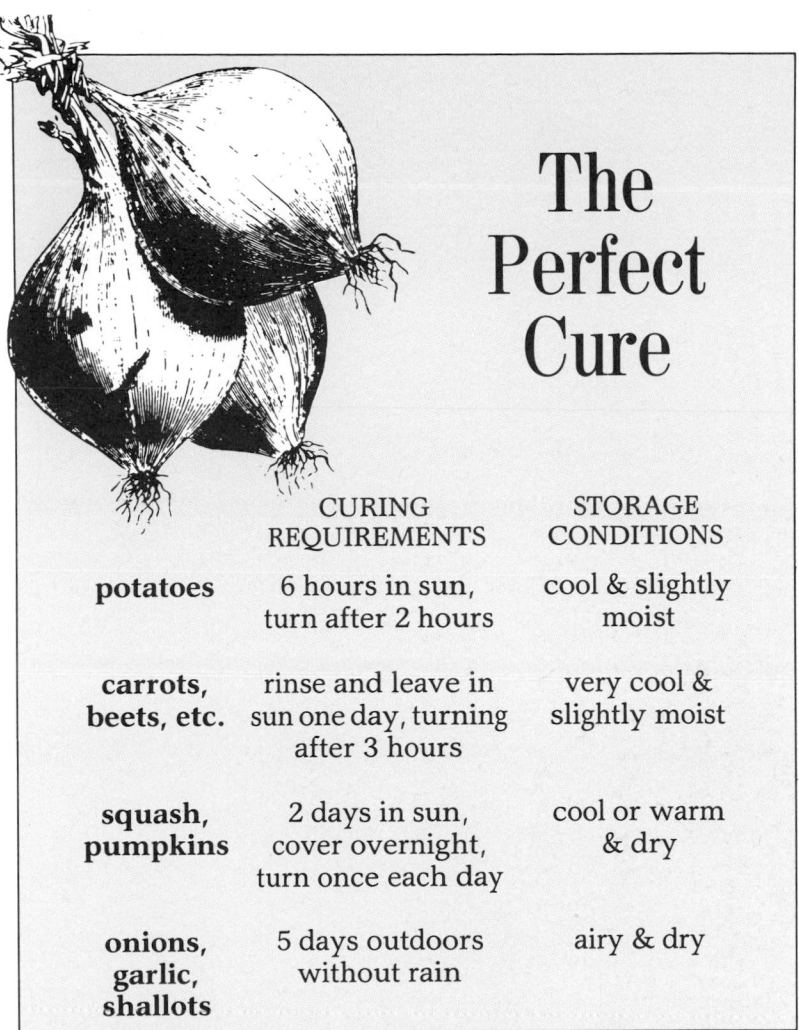

The Perfect Cure

	CURING REQUIREMENTS	STORAGE CONDITIONS
potatoes	6 hours in sun, turn after 2 hours	cool & slightly moist
carrots, beets, etc.	rinse and leave in sun one day, turning after 3 hours	very cool & slightly moist
squash, pumpkins	2 days in sun, cover overnight, turn once each day	cool or warm & dry
onions, garlic, shallots	5 days outdoors without rain	airy & dry

tical Gardening, Geoff Hamilton wrote that in Ireland, where frequent rains make onion curing difficult, one gardener had "hung her bulbs on the clothesline when it was dry and sunny outside and brought them in at night. She still had very good onions in July." (This innovation gives new meaning to Hugh Kingsmill's sober words: "Bacon's not the only thing/That's cured by hanging from a string.")

A few days of sun have given me onions that stayed firm until summer—even without a clothesline. Harvest the bulbs on a rainless day before the first fall frost, when they are full-sized and at least half the tops have died or bent over. Garlic and shallot tops should be almost entirely brown. Cut the tops off, leaving about an inch of stem above the bulb (unless you wish to braid the garlic, in which case the foliage should be left intact). Lightly brush off only the outermost, dirty layer of skin, and place the bulbs in a sunny place on newspapers, mulch or on a patio. Bring them indoors overnight and return them outdoors for about five sunny—or at least rainless—days. Brittleness of skin and contraction of the neck indicate complete curing. Store in paper bags, boxes, braids or nylon stockings in an

airy, relatively dry place.

Whatever the vegetable, there are few rules for proper curing; it is an easy, essentially passive job that is worth the small effort involved. Just remember to be gentle in all handling of vegetables prior to storage – bruising or cutting them at this point will make them more vulnerable to molds and bacteria. And with all vegetables, exposure to rain or dew will mean that curing must be repeated or prolonged, thus lowering the food's quality. If harvesting on a day that threatens rain is unavoidable, bring the produce indoors at the outset or cover it until the weather improves. Vegetables can be brought in during inclement weather and taken out during good weather for several days without damage. Never leave curing produce outdoors overnight unless it is covered with something water-repellent. Remember that the object is to dry and harden the items, preparing them to hold up during a long, dark winter. To prevent the problems that can occur during storage, we have, happily, an easy cure. ❧

Rural Arts

Border Lines

STENCILED DESIGNS FOR LOW-COST, HANDMADE WALL DECORATIONS

ARTICLE AND ILLUSTRATIONS BY SANDRA BUCKINGHAM

My first encounter with painted wall decoration was in 1974, when I spent a year working in Schloss Laxenburg in Austria. My office was in the belvedere, an enclosed lookout above the roof of the schloss, in part of what used to be the nursery for the Empress Maria Theresa's children. The walls were decorated with painted latticework, arbors and mountainscapes, the overall effect of which was so delightful that I decided if I ever had children, I would create a similarly imaginative space for them.

The memory of that decorative artistry stayed with me long after I returned to Canada, and when I eventually did have children, it should have inspired a nursery brimming with fantasy. Instead, I wallpapered the baby's room. And with stripes, no less, because that way, I would not have to line up repeats in the pattern. It was not that I didn't want to carry out my noble decorative intentions; it was just that I didn't know how, and I was too intimidated to think that I, without any formal artistic training, could actually figure out what to do. Part of what kept me from pouring my mental images onto walls was the fear of making a mistake.

Then, without knowing exactly what stenciling really was, I signed up for a two-hour course on the subject. I stenciled two teddy bears and a heart on a piece of fabric and was promptly hooked. Stenciling, I discovered, makes creativity almost idiot-proof. I could plan everything ahead of time, make drafts and corrections in pencil, then when the design was just the way I wanted it, I could cut a stencil and use it as a template to paint the image. As long as I used a stencil, the shape of the image would be exactly as planned, and unless I made some gross error when applying the paint, so would the color and shading.

Boiled down to its essentials, stenciling is nothing more than cutting a shaped hole in some material and using the cutout as a template for applying color. The design might be inspired by wallpaper, textiles, cross-stitch patterns, children's books, chinaware, inlaid wood patterns — the list is endless.

My own sources of inspiration have been many and varied, some obscure and some very common. Often the resulting designs will recall memories just as effectively as a photograph album. An art nouveau rose stenciled on a scarf reminds me of an 80-year-old cousin who gave me the brooch that suggested the

design. A swag stencil on a bedroom wall was inspired by a label on a bottle of wine that was part of a dinner shared with friends. And so on.

The first step in stenciling is creating the stencil. You can buy ready-made stencils, but part of the pleasure of this form of decoration is making it unique and individual. You can start your stencil design by making pencil sketches or by tracing the outline of the object of your inspiration; don't worry about size at first – you can adjust that on a photocopier later. From this point, there are two approaches to completing the design. The first is to give it a straightforward, honest stencil style with obvious bridges, or "ties" – the gaps between stenciled elements. This kind of image will always be more or less stylized. The second approach is to aim for a more naturalistic image by trying to hide or eliminate the bridges and to make subtle use of shading and color to give the image shape and structure. This approach always involves many more stencils and very close registration, so it is best left to experienced stencilers.

The number of stencils you need for any given design will depend on the number of colors, the amount of shading detail and whether or not you want the bridges to be obvious. You need to work all this out on paper by marking up your design with pencil crayons to help you decide which parts of the pattern will go on each stencil unit. For instance, a simple flower would need two stencils, one for the green leaves and stems and one for the red blossoms. An elaborate bouquet might need a dozen stencils.

Once you have the basic motifs, you can play around with them to create borders or overall patterns. At this stage, I often cut a temporary stencil of the basic motif, print a dozen copies on paper, then turn the stencil over and print a dozen mirror images. Next, I cut out this collection of prints and start arranging and rearranging them on a large sheet of paper over which I have drawn a rough grid – a roll of newsprint, shelf paper or recycled computer paper works well.

For a border, I might try a straight line of repeats, an undulating wave of repeats or a combination of the motif and its mirror image. When I am happy with the layout, I tape down all my little paper proofs, put tracing paper over them and trace a clean outline of one repeat of the whole pattern. For a border, I make two copies, then position them in sequence to make sure that the repeats match properly.

With a simple border, once you have drawn a guideline on the wall that ensures the border will be straight and parallel to the floor or ceiling, you just start stenciling at one end and keep going until you reach the other end of the wall or arrive back where you started. You might fudge the spacing a bit in an ad hoc fashion as you go so that you don't end with half a leaf, but it is nothing to worry about. Minor changes in spacing will not be noticed.

This is not the case with borders that have more obvious repeats, like swags or bows. With such designs, you need to calculate how many complete repeats will fit into each section of border space, then determine how large a space to leave between the repeats. The spacing may not be the same for each wall, but as long as the differences are small, they will not be noticed. Suppose the room measures 12 feet by 14 feet. If you want to do a swag border with 2-foot-long swags, you can fit exactly 6 swags on the 12-foot side and 7 swags on the 14-foot side.

If the room measures 12 by 15 feet, however, you are stuck with 7½ swags on the long side of the room, which will really spoil the effect. A better solution is to use the 24-inch swag on the short walls and cut a second stencil with the swag stretched out to 25.7 inches for the long wall. This will again give you 6 complete swags on one side and 7 on the other. If the stencil design is a loosely connected undulating vine or rosette with large gaps be-

empty space with a corner motif. Then there is the mitered corner: Cut a triangular piece of stencil material, and use it as a mask, taping it on the surface before you stencil to create a clean 45-degree edge. Finally, you can fiddle with the pattern and design a corner piece that makes it look as though the border is wrapping around the corner.

The main difference between borders on walls and borders on napkins, tablecloths or Christmas cards is that you will eventually need to repaint the wall, and you may want to avoid redoing all the stenciled borders. The best way to accomplish this is to use some sort of physical or visual device that completely separates the border design from the rest of the wall. For example, a frieze around the top of the walls might be physically divided from the lower part of the walls by a picture rail, a strip of molding fastened high on the wall from which paintings can be hung. A visual separation – a border edged with a painted stripe or with some form of uninterrupted stenciled edging – can be just as effective.

These devices work best if the background of the stenciled border is a different color from the rest of the wall. Then, when you repaint the plain part of the wall, you need not worry about the new paint matching the old; all you need to do is repaint up to the edge of the border background.

Once you have chosen a border design and figured out its placement on the wall, you will need to cut a separate stencil for each color. Almost any material that is flat, can be cut and is impervious to paint can be used for stencils, but I prefer 5-mil clear Mylar because it is durable, easy to clean and transparent, and thus simplifies the stenciling process.

The floral border design illustrated in the registration diagram requires two stencils – one for the green leaves and another for the red blossom. It can be enlarged for use as a wall border or reduced to border stationery or bookmarks. The following directions are for a wall border, but they hold true for most stenciling projects. After you enlarge the design, put the photocopy on the cutting board, or whatever you use to protect the table, and place a sheet of Mylar on top. Make sure the Mylar is positioned so that there is a border of an inch or more around the edge of the design, then tape the Mylar to the photocopy – but not to the board. Now you are ready to cut.

Stencil cutting is easier than most people think, but it sometimes takes a little practice to become really good at it. All you need is a sharp blade – a utility or an X-acto knife – and a good eye. Holding the knife as you

Use a sharp blade to cut the stencil, *top left,* **holding the Mylar with one hand and turning it slowly so that you are always cutting toward yourself. Arrange the paints and solvents on a tray,** *top right,* **and make several paper proofs,** *above,* **to perfect your technique and finalize the color scheme before beginning a project.**

tween the elements, instead of a continuous swag, you may not have to cut a different stencil for the problem wall. You may be able to get away with simply adding a 1½-inch gap between each stencil repeat. Sketch a master plan to guide you as you paint, and test the design on a paper proof before tackling the wall.

If you plan to put a border around a window frame, a tablecloth, notepaper or anything else that involves a sharp angle, you have to decide how to get the pattern around the corner. If you have ever done any quilting, some of the turning techniques will sound familiar. Doing a square-cut corner is just like doing a log-cabin quilt. Stencil the first section, stopping at the inner edge of the turn. Use masking tape or a piece of straight-cut paper to get a clean edge. Stencil the second section at right angles to the first, starting at the outside edge. Alternatively, you can stop the first section and begin the second at the inside edge, filling the

would a pencil, begin cutting along the outline of the design. Keep your other hand firmly on the stencil material, and turn it as you cut so that you are always cutting toward yourself. This provides the best control. If the blade starts slipping or if your knuckles turn white from pressing too hard, then you need a fresh blade. The cut pieces should pop out easily. If a piece hangs on in one spot, trim it off carefully — don't try to tear it. To get a smooth curve, try to cut without lifting the blade. To cut a sharp corner cleanly, make two separate cuts from opposite directions, overcutting the corner a little on each side. In case you slip, always cut away from areas where there is only a narrow bridge of stencil material between the cutouts. Do the smallest cutouts first and the largest last. To get a perfectly straight line, use a metal-edged ruler to guide the knife. Make sure you press down very hard on the ruler to keep it from slipping.

Before you untape the Mylar from the pattern, use the blade to scratch on registration marks that will help you position the stencil when you are painting the wall. You will need three different types of registration marks:

• *Guidelines* to position the stencil with respect to features of the surface you're painting; for example, lining up a frieze six inches below the ceiling.

• *Repeat registration marks* to position the stencil with respect to the previous print in the design, as in a repeating floral print.

• *Color registration marks* to position the second or third stencil with respect to the part of the motif already printed; for example, a red tulip among green leaves.

It is best to put all three types of registration marks on the stencil when you are cutting it out. The original design should have a guideline and repeats drawn on it. Trace the outlines of the repeats in the design with the cutting knife — do not cut all the way through — and scratch a line on the Mylar to indicate the guideline. This design requires more than one stencil, so use the knife to trace the outside edges of the parts that will be painted with the other stencil. You do not need to redraw the whole design — just enough so that you can position the stencil accurately with respect to the other color.

Now you have to mark the wall so that you will know where to put the stencils. Use a chalk line if there is someone to help; otherwise, use a ruler and a soft pencil, chalk or small pieces of masking tape. (Be sure that whatever you use is removable.) With the ruler method, you don't need to mark solid, continuous lines. Small dashes or dots at intervals appropriate to the length of the stencil will

give you a workable guideline. Remember, this line will coincide with the guideline on the stencil, not with the edge of the stencil itself, so measure accordingly. Realize also that walls are seldom perfectly vertical, floors and ceilings hardly ever horizontal and corners rarely square. This is especially true of old houses. As far as your guidelines are concerned, this means that you need to make a careful trade-off between true horizontal or vertical and the visual references in the room. For example, you do not want a horizontal border near a sloping ceiling or a vertical border near an off-kilter corner.

For simple repeating borders — probably the most common stenciled decoration for walls — one guideline is usually all you need. Just start at one end and keep going, repeat after repeat. When you get back to where you started, the end of the border will likely not match up exactly with the beginning. (This is a good reason for starting the border in an inconspicuous place.) Sometimes you can adjust the spacing between the last few prints to balance the alignment. Otherwise, try to fill the gap between the first and last prints with selected parts of the stencil so that the two blend seamlessly. I find the easiest way to turn a corner on a wall is to use another stencil cut out of Mactac. It is flexible enough to fit snugly into the corner, and its adhesive backing holds it there nicely. For more complex designs where the exact placement of each repeat is important, mark each stencil position on the guideline using the master plan as a guide.

The next step is to start stenciling. If you are nervous, start behind a door or a bookcase,

Although the stencils are usually associated with borders, they can also be used to produce elaborate overall patterns such as fake tiles.

Techniques

Overpainting

Stenciling details or highlights on top of previously stenciled areas usually works very well if the top color is either brighter or darker than the one underneath and if the two colors together do not produce some ghastly hue. For tiny details such as flower stamens and leaf veins, I use thin stencil material that is easy to cut, like paper or Mactac. These stencils do not need to be robust, and they are very finicky to cut out otherwise.

Strawberry: Stencil the stem and sepals of the berry in green and the general form of the berry in red. The outer edges should be crisp and dark and the inside shaded lighter to suggest roundness. Now, stencil the berry details in dark, unshaded red on top of the first red.

Peach: Sometimes you can use overpainting to suggest shape. The peach example uses two colors, one for the undertone and one for the shading. Start by painting the first stencil of the peach a golden yellow, shading it darker around the outside and quite light at the center. Now, stipple a blush of pink or red around part of the outside. Lift the first stencil, position the second one, and stipple the same blush along its edge to define the crease of the peach.

Shading

Shading lends a more three-dimensional effect to an image, which is useful if you are using stencils for trompe l'oeils or murals. For period decoration, make sure the shading is appropriate, for in most cases, stenciled images were painted quite flat, with little definition. When you are painting the examples illustrated, it is important that the brush be quite dry. These examples are also good exercises for stencil work done with metallic powders instead of paints, since it is almost always shaded.

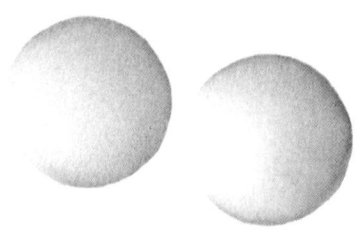

Sphere: To shade a round object, start by working the brush around the edge, trying to get an even color. Gradually work inward with an ever lighter touch so that the color fades to almost nothing in the center. Use the same technique for anything round — balloons, apples, teddy-bear tummies, fat geese.

Leaf: This two-part stencil lets you show something of the structure of a leaf without actually painting any veins. Paint the bottom half of the leaf, making the lower edge darker than the top (the top is really the center of the leaf). Now paint the top half of the leaf, again making the lower edge darker than the top (this time, the lower edge is the center of the leaf).

Two Stencils, One Color

Sometimes you need to use two or more stencils for a single design, even if only one color is used. This is the case with designs that have bridges so narrow that the Mylar is unlikely to survive multiple prints – for example, a chessboard or checkered border with squares and rectangles of color that almost touch. You will also need two stencils for designs with overlapping parts that eliminate bridges altogether – as in the petals of an opening rosebud. Using two stencils also allows you to give the impression of structure by overprinting certain parts, such as the veins on a leaf or the grooves on a scallop shell.

Flowers: Flowers with overlapping petals are done the same way, except that you must be careful not to make either print too dark; otherwise, you will not be able to see the overlap. The two stencils for this type of design are sometimes identical except for the registration marks. Print the first stencil lightly but with well-defined edges. Position the second stencil and apply paint, again using a light touch and making sure that the edges are crisp. It is very easy to make one of the prints too dark, which spoils the translucent effect of the overlapping petals. This technique works best with paint that is more transparent, such as japan or fabric paint.

—SB

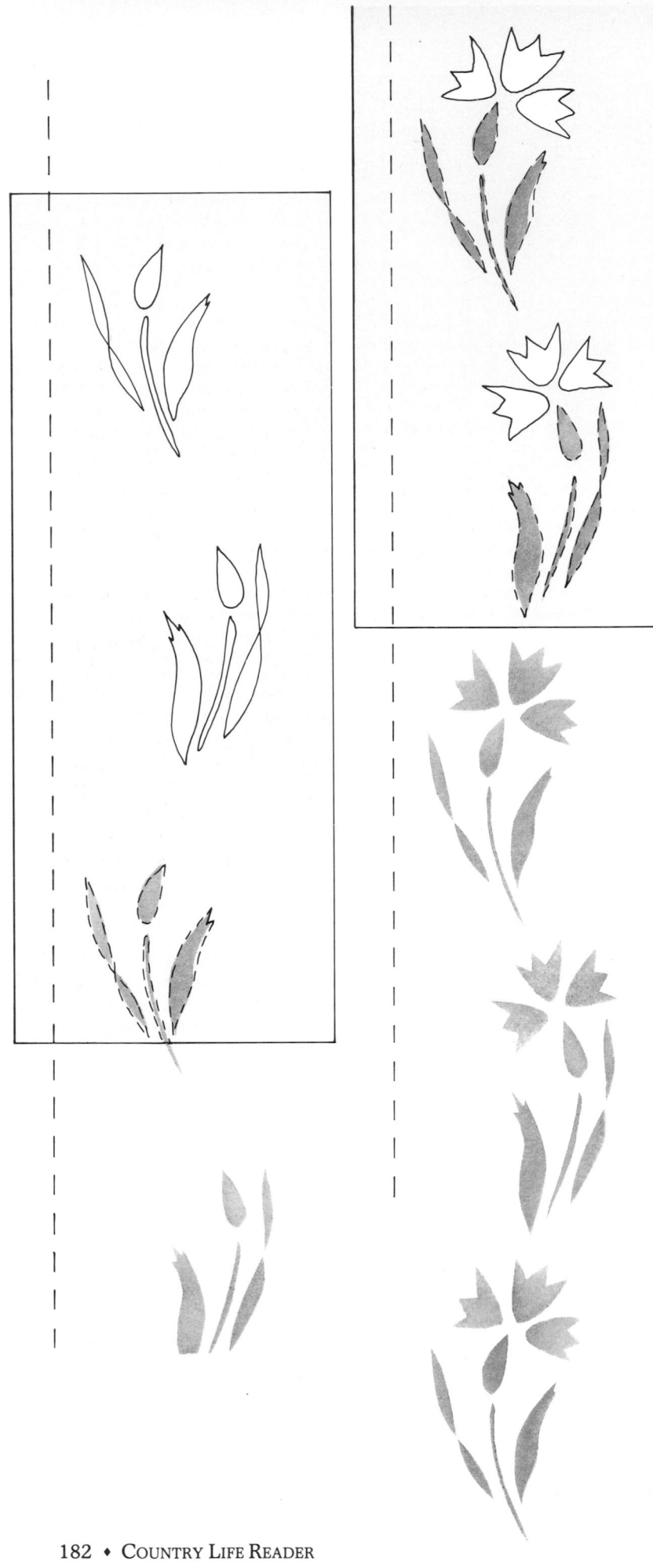

where mistakes will be less obvious, and take the time to make lots of paper proofs first. If there is carpet underfoot, move it or make sure it is well protected. Assemble all your supplies on a tray or cookie sheet so they can be moved around easily. If you are working above floor level, put the cookie sheet on a wheeled trolley to save yourself a lot of bending.

There are two ways of applying paint to a stencil: one is to use a circular rubbing movement, and the other is to stipple, making short, dabbing pounces with the brush. The major disadvantages of stippling are that it is both tiring and noisy, especially if you're pounding out a wall border – the hollow spaces between wall studs amplify the sound like a drum. Nevertheless, experiment on scrap paper with both methods because they produce different effects.

For both, the procedure is the same: put about half a teaspoon of japan paint onto a glass plate or a disposable palette sheet. (For wall borders, I prefer japan paints to acrylics unless I am stenciling a light color on a dark background. Special paints are available for fabrics.) Holding the brush perpendicular to the plate, dip the bristles into the paint. You should have only a tiny dab of paint on the ends of the bristles. Distribute the paint evenly by working the bristles in a circular motion in a clear spot on the plate, being careful not to add any more paint to the brush in the process. Now use the same circular motion on a dry paper towel to remove most of the paint from the brush. (I know this sounds ridiculous, but stenciling is essentially a "dry-brush" technique; the most common mistake for a beginner is to have too much paint on the brush, which produces a blotchy or smudged print.) Apply the paint around the edges of the stencil cutout first, gradually working toward the center. Of course, if the stencil openings are quite small, you will probably end up coloring the whole design at once.

Don't try to produce a dark print all at once. You will get much better results if you build up the color gradually by going over it several times. Before it becomes too dark, lift a corner of the stencil and check the print. It will always be darker than it looks with the stencil still in place.

Once you are satisfied with the print of the first stencil, untape it, and using the registration marks as a guide, position and tape the second stencil in place. Paint it, and the first print of the design is complete. You will be amazed at how many imperfections vanish when the stencil is lifted.

When the prints start looking very faint and dry, you need to dampen the bristles with solvent, but only slightly. Keep a folded paper towel moistened with solvent on the side of your supply tray. Dab the end of the brush onto the paper towel, then work the bristles around on a clean corner of the plate before recharging the brush with paint. If paint starts to accumulate around the edge of the brush, wipe the sides of the bristles with the damp paper towel. Do not immerse the brush in solvent until you have finished painting – it will become too wet for stenciling, and you will have to clean it and let it dry before you can continue. If the paint on the plate starts to dry, add a drop of solvent.

I prefer to print the stencil with the largest part of the design first – in this case, the one for the leaves. Usually it is best to finish all the repeats of the first color before going on to the second. This avoids problems with paint drying on the brush, the palette and the stencil while you are switching colors. It also prevents you from accidentally putting the green brush into the red paint. But what is a rule without exceptions? I often find that I am so eager to see what the completed design looks like that I do both colors in parallel.

Borders are among the simplest wall decorations. A single motif can also be stenciled at regular intervals over the entire wall surface – an approximation of wallpaper – or the space between borders can be filled with large, complex designs such as baskets of fruit or flowers. I sometimes use stencils to help create murals, for example, to paint flowers, foliage, the fabric pattern of draperies or anything that is symmetrical, such as urns, balustrades or architectural details.

Such ambitious trompe l'oeil projects may be beyond the scope of the novice stenciler, but with the help of stencils, you can achieve other surprising effects. One of these is fake tiles, which you create by stenciling traditional tile patterns on a suitably colored background. First, draw up a master plan on graph paper, showing the dimensions of the space and indicating tile placement (including any "cut" tiles). Refer to books or magazines for inspiration. Remember that some of the tiles can be plain ones, that you can have border tiles and that different arrangements of a single tile pattern can yield secondary patterns where the corners meet.

You need a smooth surface to begin with. To get a clean edge around your "tiled" space, mask it off from its surroundings with strips of masking tape. Paint the area to be decorated with two coats of flat (latex or alkyd) paint in the background color. With the master plan as a guide, lightly mark a reference grid on the wall to show where each fake tile will go. Use

a sharp pencil and a set square for accuracy. Stencil the designs with a circular motion and a minimum of shading. Now take a warm grey felt pen, and remaining as relaxed as possible, draw freehand grout lines over the penciled grid lines. Draw toward yourself, resting your baby finger against the wall for support and greater control. If the thought of doing anything freehand makes you tense, then use a ruler to guide the pen. If you need to use a ruler but don't want perfectly straight lines, a piece of wood will produce a less rigid effect. You can also use the pen to make tile corners look slightly rounded. Examine some real tiles to see how they look.

Let everything dry for two or three days before "glazing" with a coat of polyurethane. If the grouting shows any tendency to run (test the marker in an inconspicuous spot), then give it a coat of spray varnish first, use an acrylic varnish, or coat it with shellac before applying the varnish. The same method can be used to create stenciled tile floors and tabletops.

There is more than one right way to stencil and more than one way to go wrong. If you have never stenciled before, following proven methods will certainly save you a lot of frustration. But once you have the hang of it, feel free to experiment and to invent your own variations and shortcuts. I've described what works best for me, but there are other ways that work, too. My own motto is: "If it works, it's the right way." 🌿

The key to stenciling success is good registration. The first stencil for the two-color border, far left, is scratched with a dashed guideline laid directly over the guideline drawn on the wall and a dashed-line motif that covers the last painted print to ensure accurate spacing between repeats. For correct positioning, the second stencil, near left, has the guideline and green part of the design scratched on the Mylar. Above, borders are among the simplest wall decorations. A single motif can be stenciled at regular intervals as an approximation of wallpaper.

Excerpted from Stencilling: A Harrowsmith Guide *by Sandra Buckingham. Camden House Publishing, 1989.*

Ernie Sparks

Elementary, My Dear Chandler

HOME CANDLEMAKING MADE SIMPLE

EDITED BY CHERYL DORSCHNER

"The making of so many candles involved an amount of disagreeable particulars hard to conceive in our days, when gas and kerosene make the lighting of houses one of the least of our cares.

"In the times we speak of, candlemaking for a large household was a serious undertaking, and the day devoted to it was one that any child would remember as an unlucky one for childish purposes of enjoyment, sevenfold worse in its way even than washing day."

— **Poganuc People: Their Loves & Lives**
Harriet Beecher Stowe, 1878

Pity our ancestors' children: the weeks of late fall inevitably found them lugging buckets of fat from freshly butchered beef, sheep and wild game to the family's cast-iron rendering cauldron. For days, the outdoor fire needed feeding, and with each load of wood carried, the helpers found themselves bending close to the black pot of simmering grease from which emanated a stomach-wrenching cloud of vapor. Each batch had to be skimmed repeatedly to remove impurities and the shriveled bits of flesh known as cracklings—to produce unclean tallow was to risk spending the coming winter with a supply of sputtering, smoky, evil-smelling candles all too reminiscent of the rendering cauldron.

Home chandlers endeavored to make a supply that would last for many months, and it was a sign of good household management to put away a stock of candles that would last the year. In addition to the convenience, candles stored safely from heat and vermin for several months could be counted upon to burn better and longer than unaged tapers. Nonetheless,

the repetitious dipping of the wicks into the tallow – up to 40 layers for each candle – made for a seemingly endless day of tedious, messy and not altogether safe work. Little wonder that the nation's candleholders were gleefully abandoned almost overnight when the kerosene lamp made its appearance.

Today, candlemaking is no longer "unlucky for childish purposes of enjoyment." It has all the rewards of doing something uncommonly tied to the past, but the back-bowing chores and odors of colonial times have given way to more manageable ingredients and methods and the honey-sweet smell of beeswax. Surprising to some, homemade candles today are not only easier to make but in almost every way superior to those of our pioneering forebears.

Candlemaking can be a snowy winter afternoon's project – there will be no shortage of volunteers these days if children are about – and the results will have special appeal to all who harbor a spirit of frugality and a love for the handmade.

Now that candles burn more dependably and brightly, it is ironic that they are burned much less frequently. But it is still the candle we reach for when the power lines go down or the flashlight dies. A properly made candle is a simple, reliable and elegant piece of equipment, both fuel and support for the flame it provides. Some believe that candlemaking's most bizarre turn came some years ago, when wax creations shaped like Buddhas, toadstools, frogs and bad dreams sputtered and died in legions as overtaxed wicks drowned in rainbow pools of colored wax. The candle market is only now recovering its senses as a generation rediscovers the practicality and simple charm of classic tapers.

It need hardly be said that candlelight always provides much more than illumination. Candles are mood makers, adding an extra glow to festive meals, friendly gatherings and religious holidays. Bringing a pair of candlesticks out of the cupboard announces that a special occasion is at hand. "Candlelight is one of the best methods I know of getting people relaxed and talkative," says an acquaintance whose home is a favorite gathering place for friends. "It may be our fascination with an open flame or it may just be the flattering quality of the light, but it works."

Another friend says that she makes a point of serving at least one family meal a week by candlelight. "It's a great way to remind your kids that life can go on without electricity."

Such habits, our friend is also quick to point out, can become costly, especially if one succumbs to the aesthetics of good-quality dinner candles, a pair of which can easily melt through a few dollars in the course of an evening. Homemade candles of comparable size and quality can be made for a fraction of this, and a single day's efforts can easily meet the annual candleburning requirements of a modern household – with a number of pairs of handsome tapers left over for gift giving.

Tallow to Paraffin

Most 19th-century New Englanders used their candles frugally, lighting them only a few hours at night and going about in what, by today's standards, would be dim light. These people were just as thrifty in their choice of candle ingredients. Tallow candles – from the hardened fat of beef and mutton – were considered the best, while the fat of bear, moose, deer and elk was preferred over the too-soft lard of the pig.

There were sweet-smelling alternatives to tallow candles, but it is believed that candlemakers of the early 19th century did not seek scents or colors to improve their candles. An exception was the pale green, fragrant, semi-transparent wax made by boiling and repeatedly skimming the silver-gray fruit of the bayberry bush.

Spermaceti, an oily substance from the head of the sperm whale, was used for candles and lamp oil in America beginning around 1750. One Boston chandler, touting this new use for the even-then beleaguered beast, said that spermaceti candles exceeded "all others for Beauty; Sweetness of Scent when extinguished; Duration, being more than double Tallow Candles of equal size; Dimension of Flame, nearly four Times more, emitting a fast easy-expanding Light." By 1761, there were eight spermaceti candle factories in New England and one in Philadelphia. The candles became a major export item from New England to other American colonies and to the West Indies.

Paraffin, a petroleum product, revolutionized candlemaking in the 1860s. The first paraffin had a low melting point of just 120 degrees F, but today's many grades of paraffin range up to a 162-degree melting point and make for high-quality candles. Inexpensive, clean burning, odorless and easy to work with, paraffin became and has remained the material of choice for most candlemakers. The addition of stearic acid or stearine, a purified form of tallow, makes paraffin candles pleasantly opaque and improves their burning quality.

Minding the Beeswax

Among the most coveted and richest of all candlemaking ingredients in burnability, aroma and historical associations, is beeswax. The beautiful, sweet-smelling candles it produces were made wherever beehives were plundered or tended, but it was a precious commodity, to be bartered or sold for articles beekeepers needed more urgently than quality candles. For centuries, Roman Catholic churches have burned beeswax, even when the common householder was more likely to opt for simple rushlights, common rushes peeled and dipped in animal fat, then set on an angle in special holders and burned. If most 18th- and 19th-century farmers did not have the luxury of burning beeswax candles, many strived to add at least a small quantity to make tallow candles harder and clearer.

Most beeswax used in candlemaking comes from cappings that beekeepers scrape from their combs each year before extracting the honey. Capping wax is white or yellow. Brood comb wax, used in the hive for about four or five years, is quite dark – from a butterscotch color to dark brown. This dark wax contains more impurities and will produce a lower-quality candle; any honey and visible contaminants must be removed from brood comb wax before it is used for candles.

The chore of separating honey from such wax was recorded in 1833 with the publication of *The American Frugal Housewife, Dedicated to Those Who Are Not Ashamed of Economy:*

"The neatest way to separate wax from honey-comb is to tie the comb up in a linen or woollen bag; place it in a kettle of cold water,

and hang it over the fire. As the water heats, the wax melts and rises to the surface, while all the impurities remain in the bag. It is well to put a few pebbles in the bag, to keep it from floating."

Foolproof Tapers

Fortunately for today's home candlemakers, beeswax is no longer so prohibitively expensive, partly owing to the increased competition that has grown up abroad, most notably from the honey producers of China. Although beeswax may cost three to ten times the price of paraffin, it is seldom used alone, although not just for economic reasons. Unless mixed with other ingredients, beeswax is extremely difficult to mold. Canadian candlemaker William Nelson maintains that the perfect candle consists of 51 percent beeswax, 10 percent stearic acid—less than this can produce a mottled candle—and 39 percent paraffin. Hobby chandlers often find that 10 percent beeswax is enough to give a candle its char-

acteristic aroma without adding substantially to the price, while more than 51 percent beeswax yields a candle that is tacky to the touch and difficult to remove from a mold.

By far the most easily made candles—and, some contend, among the most elegant—consist of sheets of beeswax rolled around wicks. The wax appears very similar to the stamped wax foundations used by beekeepers—an overall honeycomb pattern that makes for a most unusual candle, and one that catches and reflects rays of its own light.

These rolled beeswax candles are child's play to make once one has located a supply of wicking and beeswax sheets. (See *Sources.*) The quality of these sheets and the beeswax content vary considerably from supplier to supplier, and some are called craft wax and consist mostly of paraffin.

The beeswax or craft wax sheets can be purchased in a variety of colors from hobby shops or apiary supply houses; some suppliers sell wax and wicks together as kits. One sheet of about 8 inches by 16 inches will produce four

*Left, **sheets of beeswax can be left whole or cut into triangles and rolled into straight or tapered candles.** Right, **a juice can in boiling water holds a beeswax mixture for dipped tapers.***

Candlemaking: the rewards of doing something uncommonly tied to the past.

tapers eight inches tall or two 16-inch diagonally rolled tapers.

Jean Siegchrist of Jericho, Vermont, who started making the diagonal tapers as a hobby a little over a year ago, has turned the craft into a small cottage business. "You just need wax and wicks," says Siegchrist, who stresses that candle rolling "is very simple." She points out that some suppliers sell softer wax sheets than others and that more malleable material "is much harder to get started, but easier to roll once you have it going." Siegchrist has also found that the same-sized wax sheets sold as foundation wax to beekeepers "would not hold together. They tried to unroll by themselves."

The wax sheets can be cut to various sizes and rolled into straight-ended cylinders or into cylinders with the top end pointed (resembling a crayon). The wax can also be cut into triangles and rolled to form a spiral edge winding down the exterior of the candle. Here is the spiraling method:

Cut the 8-inch-by-16-inch sheet of wax crosswise into two equal squares by putting it on a cutting board, placing a ruler against the line to be cut and pressing along the line with a sharp knife. Then cut each square diagonally. Place a 9-inch length of square-braided wick (size 30 or 40 is good) on one triangle a quarter-inch from the longest edge of the "L" and parallel to it so that the wick meets the bottom corner (the right angle) and extends beyond the top. The wick now looks like a flagpole, with the piece of wax as a pennant. Using the warmth of your hands to soften the wax and to prevent it from cracking, work very gradually and gently up and down the edge of the pennant, pushing the wax up against the length of the wick and over it, then slowly and carefully rolling the wax around the wick, always moving back and forth. The tighter the candle is rolled, the better it will burn. As the candle becomes fatter and the wax pennant narrower, it will become easier to roll. Finally, press the spiraled wax edges in toward the candle, or flute them slightly outward.

Antique Candles

Graduating beyond rolled candles, the next logical step is the making of molded tapers, which burn longer and are less vulnerable to the dents and disfigurements that sometimes befall sheets of beeswax.

Candlemaking supply houses and craft shops have all manner of candle molds into which one inserts braided wicking and pours melted wax. The process is simple, and most beginners meet with quick success, provided they use a reasonable wax mixture. Suppliers offer blends of paraffin and stearic acid in the right proportion, some premixed with dyes (warm white to cranberry red and even black) and fragrances (bayberry and balsam to French vanilla).

The least expensive molds available are made of acrylic and generally last through thousands of uses. The clear plastic models allow the candle maker to watch as the wax cools and solidifies within the mold. Acrylic candle molds are available in many sizes.

Once initiated, many neophyte chandlers are tempted to put an antique tin or pewter mold back into service. While most of these have been relegated to the mantelpiece or pioneer village, many are still suitable for active use. Tom Weekly, author of *How to Make Candles* (The Candle Mill), says to check antique molds for rusted or pitted tubes, which will allow the wax to trap itself. "Boy, I'll tell you, you can't pull it out with a team of oxen," says Weekly.

"You're not going to harm a good antique mold by making candles in it if it's tin," says Weekly. He advises cleaning molds with a bottle or coffee-percolator brush and hot water. "Hot water does wonders for wax," he says, adding that stubborn wax can be removed with rubber-cement thinner.

Antique candle molds, especially rare ones, can be expensive. A valuable mold would probably have some sort of wooden ornamental framing. "You could pour wax into one or two of those tubes in the middle, but I sure wouldn't want to put any wax near the edges where that beautiful wood is," says Weekly. He has accumulated what is now one of the country's largest candle mold collections. "One time a woman from Manchester [Vermont] gave me a 24-tube antique mold that was unused. It was still in the tinsmith's paper," Weekly says. "It was just a beautiful mold. We named it after her."

Weekly offers tin reproductions of antique molds in his own candlemaking museum; an 8-tube model will turn out 8-inch dinner tapers.

Paraffin is the main ingredient in molded candles, and it is sold in blocks, chunks, flakes or sheets. A pound of paraffin will make seven or eight 8-inch tapers.

The general procedure is to melt the wax over water in a double boiler. Set the wicks through the centers of the molds. Place the mold on some newspapers and then pour the wax slowly so that no air bubbles form. Allow the wax to cool at room temperature, which will take several hours.

When the candle is cold—some chandlers leave their work in the molds overnight to be sure—remove it by freeing the wick from the outside of the mold base and turning it upside down. If the candle does not drop out readily, tap the mold gently or place it in the refrigerator for half an hour before trying to remove it. A mold that still will not release the candle can be doused with hot water, which will loosen the candle but will also soften it and mar the finish.

Hand-Dipped Candles

Those who want to dabble in candlemaking without acquiring the molding paraphernalia may enjoy making hand-dipped tapers. The smooth layers and the natural tapering shape caused by repeatedly dipping wicks in hot wax cannot be achieved by any other method.

Hand-dipped candles are easy to make but tricky to make well: even in experienced hands, they tend to have quirky shapes and uneven finishes, which some find appealing. The dipping is time-consuming and requires the use of a pot at least an inch deeper than the desired length of the candle and plenty of wax—the supply has to be kept topped up even as the candles increase in size.

Virtually any wax can be used, even pure beeswax. To make dipped tapers, loop lengths of small-sized wicking about a foot longer than the length of two candles over a board that is wide enough to keep the candles separated by two or three inches. Each pair should be separated from other pairs by two or three inches along the length of the board. Heat the wax as usual, and dip the hanging lengths of wick in the wax to the depth of the desired length of candle for about five seconds. The board is then suspended between two chairs for the adhering wax to cool, while excess wax drips onto newspapers. When the wax layer is cool, the process is repeated. Dipping time and wax temperature are critical, with the best temperature usually in the range of 160 to 170 degrees F. If the wax is too hot, previously accumulated layers will melt away; if too cool, the new layers will be lumpy. Expect about 40 dips to produce a candle something less than an inch across at the base.

An alternative way to make tapers, also practiced by the pioneers, circumvents the need for a very deep pot and a large supply of wax. Hot wax is poured from a pitcher over the wicks into a waiting pot, the wax again accumulating in layers. This method makes the production of a fairly even candle more difficult. With either process, after the first few layers have collected, the candles are straight-

Most 19th-century New Englanders used their candles frugally, lighting them only a few hours at night and going about in what, by today's standards, would be dim light.

ened by hand, and when finished, their bases are snipped off straight. These candles will always be slightly uneven.

The Cautious Chandler

Whether one makes candles by pouring wax into molds or by dipping the wicks into hot wax, a few cautions are in order. Because wax ignites at about 400 degrees F, it should always be melted in a double boiler. Over boiling water, it cannot heat beyond 212 degrees. Candle wax is usually poured at 160 to 195 degrees, and a candy thermometer is handy to

keep an eye on temperatures. Wax must never be poured over an open flame or stove. Keep a box of baking soda within reach in case of accidental fire. Never try to use water to extinguish a wax fire. Wear old clothing and keep potholders nearby.

Do not use containers that could melt at temperatures lower than wax. It is best to use melting pots set aside for candlemaking purposes only. Large tin cans and old cookware work well. If using a tin can, crimp one edge into a pour spout. Good pots and thermometers can be cleaned by pouring out as much wax as possible, then heating just until the wax melts and wiping the surfaces with paper towels or newspapers. Follow up with a soapy hot-water wash.

If wax splatters, let it cool, then scrape it off with a knife or cover with layers of paper towel or other paper and press with a hot iron. Send unwashable fabric to the dry cleaner. Remove wax from skin by running it under cold water, peeling the wax, then washing with warm, soapy water.

Frugality

When the spirit of chandlery really takes hold, candlemakers rather quickly realize that an economical supply of paraffin and stearic acid can drastically reduce the cost of a candle. Buying bulk wax will save 25 percent or more. Tom Weekly warns his customers that "the freight costs on paraffin are *high*" and advises that serious candlemakers seek out a local supplier, sometimes found in the Yellow Pages under "Wax."

Today, small-scale candlemakers can render crude beeswax in a stainless steel, aluminum or ceramic pot (copper, iron, zinc or brass may discolor the wax). The melting vessel is filled about one-quarter full with water and a slow heat is applied. As the wax melts, the honey and solids dissolve or sink to the bottom. The clean wax is decanted, then ladled into containers or allowed to cool and harden in the pot.

By obtaining crude beeswax from a local beekeeper and using this simple process, one can also realize considerable savings over retail candlemaking supply prices. Depending on how refined the beeswax is, it costs from 3 to 10 times the price of paraffin. The price beekeepers receive for crude wax varies with demand during the year.

Dick Kaehl of A.I. Root Company in Medina, Ohio, one of the country's oldest apiary outfitters, notes that suppliers no longer bleach beeswax from its natural honey color to white. From the supplier's point of view, bleaching "cost too much money." Moreover, "people prefer the natural look." ❧

SOURCES

Candle Mill Village
P.O. Box 248
East Arlington, Vermont 05252
Candlemaking supplies for retail and mail order, including antique reproduction tin molds. Owner Tom Weekly is happy to offer advice on making antique candles. Free catalogue.

Illuminee du Monde
22 Main Street
Bristol, Vermont 05443
Rolled candles. Send a #10 self-addressed stamped envelope for brochure.

Knorr Beeswax Products Inc.
14906 Via de la Valle
Delmar, California 92014
A wholesale, retail and mail-order supplier of 100% beeswax sheets and candles in 31 different colors.

Pourette Manufacturing Co.
6910 Roosevelt Way N.E.
Seattle, Washington 98115
Pourette, the largest candlemaking supplier in the United States, offers wholesale, retail and mail-order goods via an extensive 70-page listing of molds and other equipment, including wicking, beeswax sheets and waxes by the pound. This catalogue is available for $2, refundable with the first order, but Pourette also offers a small $1 catalogue that describes its most popular items. For 50 cents, one can order a 16-page instruction booklet. And for a #10 self-addressed stamped envelope, the company will send a yard of wicking and information sheets on the basics of candlemaking, making candles and other items out of remnants and making wax items to sell at bazaars.

A.I. Root Company
P.O. Box 706
Medina, Ohio 44256
One of the oldest apiary suppliers in the country, Root offers all manner of beekeeping paraphernalia, various grades of beeswax and sheets of craft wax for rolled candles. The 48-page catalogue is free.

Sitting Pretty

BUILD AN ADIRONDACK CHAIR – SIMPLE COMFORT FOR SUMMERTIME LOUNGING

BY LEIGH SEDDON

The Adirondack chair is a camp classic. With a pair of wide, flat arms and a gently sloping seat, it is the picture of rustic repose – just add a summer day and an extra-large serving of your favorite drink.

The chair has held its ground against newcomers on the yard-furniture scene for nearly a century, outlasting the rest with its sturdy elegance. Today, Adirondack chairs are a fixture at north-country camps from the White Mountains to the Sierras. They have also begun to show up in less expected places, such as Manhattan penthouses and Malibu bungalows. What was once a regional novelty has become a nationally recognized style. An architect may wish to expound on how the chair's design is a perfect example of form following function, but it's really just unadorned practicality at its best.

The Original Adirondack

The Adirondack chair was not always known by that name. According to Craig Gilborn, director of the Adirondack Museum in Blue Mountain Lake, New York, it started its life as the Westport chair, named after a small town close by the Adirondack Mountains on the edge of Lake Champlain.

As the story goes, a gentleman named Thomas Lee first worked out the design of the chair around 1900. Vacationing at his family's house, Stony Sides, along with some 22 relatives, he set about designing a truly comfortable outdoor chair.

Nailing boards together on the front lawn, he asked other members of the family to test his prototypes and tell him which were the most comfortable. With this research as a guide, he built a chair with a sloping seat and back, each made from a single pine board, and with the wide armrests that became a hallmark of the Adirondack style. His chair was an immediate success with the family, who promptly hired a carpenter to build several more just like it.

Thomas Lee's only intention was to furnish his summer home with a few comfortable lawn chairs. His creation might never have become famous, except that Lee offered the design to a friend in Westport who was in dire need of a source of winter income. The friend, Harry Bunnell, had a small carpentry shop. He quickly realized that Lee's chair was just the thing to sell to summer residents, to resorts, and especially to the sanatoriums that were springing up around nearby Saranac Lake for the treatment of tuberculosis patients.

Without asking Lee's permission, Bunnell filed for a patent on the Westport chair in 1904, and received it in July of 1905. In his patent application, Bunnell wrote that "the object of this invention is a chair of the bungalow type adapted for use on porches, lawns, at camps, and also adapted to be converted into an invalid's chair." After describing the 11 pieces of wood that make up the invention, he concluded, "From the above description, it is thought that the advantages of this construction will be obvious."

Thomas Lee never disputed Bunnell's patent. He was probably happy to have provided his friend with a livelihood and the town of Westport with a steady supply of lawn chairs. For the next 20 years, Bunnell manufactured the original Westport chair and several variations, such as a child's chair and a tandem chair with a shared armrest in the middle, selling them throughout the region.

Reconstructing the Westport

Several of Bunnell's original chairs are now housed in the collection of the Adirondack Museum. The wide white pine boards from

The Adirondack chair, right, is a folk design that seems ideally suited for the short summers of a cold-weather climate. Although the garden may need attention, the chair entices its occupant to relax and enjoy the hot weather while it lasts.

Left, a floral motif suits both this setting and the chair's history of improvised design. Right, Beeken and Parson's elegant adaptation of the original Westport chair.

which the chairs were made attest to the magnificent virgin timber that once graced the Adirondack region.

Because of growing interest in Adirondack-style chairs, the Adirondack Museum recently prepared a construction blueprint of the Westport chair. With only 11 pieces to cut and fasten together, it seemed like an ideal weekend project for someone, like myself, who possesses modest carpentry skills and only the basic hand and power tools.

After studying the blueprint and reading a little about chair design, however, I began to wonder about Thomas Lee's creation. Comparing the Westport's dimensions and angles with guidelines suggested by modern ergonomic research, which focuses on the design of tools and furnishings for optimum human efficiency, I concluded that I'd be far more comfortable next summer if I made some changes.

The most important relationship in a lounge chair, I learned, is the angle formed by the seat and back. Too steep an angle (less than 95 degrees) is uncomfortable for the lower back, while an angle greater than 120 degrees makes the chair feel like a recliner. The back of the original Westport chair angled sharply from the seat – almost 90 degrees. I decided 105 degrees would be a more leisurely angle for my chair.

A related problem was the angle of the seat in relation to the ground. In the original design, the seat angles steeply backward, making the chair difficult to climb out of. I decided on a less precipitous angle of 15 degrees for my design.

The Westport's armrests were also abnormally high, pushing your elbows practically up to your ears. I decided to keep the arm-

rests about 10 inches above the seat, and to tilt them slightly toward the back of the chair – not enough to spill a drink, but enough to keep them more nearly parallel with the seat.

When I began to look at the pieces the original Westport was made of, I realized I had another problem. The back is a single piece of 1¼-inch-thick pine, a full 13¾ inches wide. I haven't seen boards that wide in 20 years. And even if I found one and could afford it, the thought of its splitting and checking drove me to consider alternatives. Forming a slatted back out of narrow boards seemed the most sensible solution. I knew historical purists would wince, but making the back and the seat out of several narrow slats would eliminate splitting and warping, and also help reduce material costs.

The use of the slatted back cleared up another problem. A comfortable lounge chair should be at least 18 inches wide, and the Westport was not even 14 inches wide at the rear. The front was 25 inches wide, with the result that the seat was somewhat wedge-shaped. Aesthetically, this was pleasing, but it made for several nasty bevel cuts on the legs, arms and seat so all the pieces would join securely. I decided to make my seat square – 20 inches at the front, 20 inches at the back. Again, practicality and limited woodworking skills won the day.

The Museum's blueprints call for the use of ⁵/₄-inch white pine boards. Five-quarters material is actually 1¹/₁₆ inch thick, making it considerably stronger than nominal 1-inch stock, which is only ¾-inch thick. A better choice than pine, however, if it is locally available, is redwood or white cedar. Both are rot-resistant species that are better suited for outdoor furniture than pine, though they are considerably more expensive.

To help protect the wood, I applied a finish of tung oil. Unlike polyurethane or varnish, which dry to a hard surface coat that deteriorates with exposure to the sun, tung oil penetrates and seals the wood below its surface. Any finish, whether varnish, polyurethane or tung oil, will have to be re-applied each year in order to protect the wood. Varnished or polyurethaned surfaces, however, must be scraped or sanded before recoating, while a new coat of tung oil can simply be brushed over the old coat – a 15-minute job. It is not as weatherproof a finish as polyurethane or paint, but three coats followed by a yearly reapplication will provide reasonable protection with a minimal amount of work.

By the time I had finished making changes to the Westport, my version hardly resembled its namesake. But I felt that even if Thomas Lee wouldn't have approved of my changes, he would at least have understood my motives. For about $50 in materials and several afternoons of work, I had my own custom-fitted Adirondack. (Plans and construction steps appear on pages 196 to 199.)

Building on Tradition

If you don't have the time or inclination to build your own Westport chair, but are nonetheless attracted by its charms, you may be interested in a version of the chair built by two craftsmen who work just across Lake Champlain from where Thomas Lee designed the original.

Bruce Beeken and Jeff Parsons are partners in a woodworking shop in Shelburne, Vermont. Several years ago, while searching for a production item to make, they were inspired by a painting of two old Adirondack chairs done by Janet Fredericks, a local artist. After studying the design of the original chairs and that of factory-built models on the market, they concluded that there was plenty of room for improvement, in both comfort and quality.

By raising the seat height, introducing a gentle curve to the seat and making the back somewhat less bolt-upright, Beeken and Parsons designed a chair that was easy to get in and out of, as well as comfortable for hours of lounging. They also modified the horizontal armrests of the original, making a curved arm with a moderate backward slope.

Next, they considered the problem of how to make a wooden chair that would withstand the elements. The least durable parts of the traditional Adirondack chair were its fasteners—usually galvanized nails and screws. These allowed water to penetrate the wood,

causing rot. The liberal application of paint, building up year after year to a formidable crust, can slow this process, but not by much. Eventually, the moment arrives when chair, occupant and drink collapse to the ground without warning.

Beeken and Parsons decided that their chair would have no metal fasteners, but would rely instead on dovetail and mortise-and-tenon joints, held together with shipbuilders' "trenails" (wooden pegs) and epoxy glue. Most of the chair's pieces are tapered, leaving the area around the joints full-thickness for strength, but giving the chair a graceful, sculptured appearance.

A final departure from tradition was to make the chairs from Atlantic white cedar from North Carolina, a wood prized for its resistance to rot. To highlight the beauty of the wood, they decided to leave the chairs unfinished, allowing them to weather to a natural gray patina.

To date, Parsons and Beeken have produced about 75 of these chairs, selling them directly from their shop. By reworking Thomas Lee's original design with craftsmanship and style, they have created what is perhaps the ultimate Adirondack.

A Folding Version

Another imaginative and stylish takeoff of Lee's original chair is made by Willsboro

Our chair, while departing from the original for greater comfort and ease of construction, retains the classic lines.

Build Your Own Adirondack-Style Chair

1. Cut all pieces of ⁵/₄-inch material to length as indicated. Carefully select and mark each piece so its best face is the one that will be most visible (for example, the top of the arms and seat slats). Cut the front of both stringers to a 75-degree angle and cut the arms and arm braces to the shapes shown in the plans. With a jigsaw or scroll saw, cut the indicated radius bends on the stringers and the arms. (The radius on the top of the back slats will be cut after the back is assembled.)

2. Sand off all square edges, clean all exposed faces and smooth off the radius cuts using a belt or orbital sander (if available; if not, sand by hand). Do not sand edges that are to be joined, such as the front of the stringers, the ends of the bottom back brace and the front leg brace, or the inside edge of the arm braces.

3. Assemble the back slats using the three braces as shown in the back detail drawing (opposite). Position the braces on the slats so that the braces are the specified distance apart (and the bottom brace is flush with the bottom of the slats), and so that the slats are spaced equally. Depending on the exact width of the slats, there should be about ¾ inch between each of them. Use a framing square to make sure the braces are square to the slats. Then attach the braces to the slats using two #8 x 1½-inch wood screws per slat. Use a #8 counterbore drill bit to predrill and countersink the screw hole. The screws should be slightly offset from the center of the slats to avoid possible splitting. When all the braces are attached, use a string and pencil to draw a 24-inch radius across the top of the slats, and cut with a scroll saw or jigsaw.

4. Assemble the two stringers and the front brace, using three screws in each stringer. Square up the stringers and attach the seat slats using one screw on each side of all five slats. The front seat slat should overhang the front brace by ¼ inch, and the remaining slats should be spaced about ⅛ inch apart. The entire seat should measure 17½ inches, front to back.

5. To attach the back of the chair, first mark the lines where the bottom back brace will hit the inside of the stringers. To do this, mark the top of each stringer 20 inches from the front edge of the front brace. Then, on the bottom of each stringer, make a mark 16¼ inches from the front face of the leg brace. Connect these marks. The resulting line should form a 105-degree angle with the seat, and can be checked with a simple plastic protractor. Predrill three screw holes in each stringer ½ inch forward of the line. The assembled chair back can now be positioned and screwed in place. For maximum strength, the joint between the chair back and stringers should be glued with epoxy or plastic resin glue.

6. The front legs can now be attached to the chair assembly, using six screws for each leg. Three of these six screws secure each leg to the front brace; the other three secure each leg to its adjacent stringer. The legs should be positioned so they are flush with the front of the chair and the top of the seat is 16½ inches from the bottom of the leg. Remember, there is a bevel cut on the top of each leg that must slope toward the back of the chair. Also, when drilling into the side of the front brace, be sure to avoid hitting the three screws attaching the brace to the stringers. This joint should also be glued.

7. Attach the arm braces to the outside of the legs, and perpendicular to them, using three screws. The top of the braces should have a slight bevel corresponding to the bevel on the top of the front legs. These bevels will permit the arms to slope slightly toward the back of the chair.

8. With a chisel, make a beveled notch on the ends of the middle back brace where it supports each arm. The notch should start about ½ inch out from the back slats. Bevel the notch at an angle so the arms will rest flush on top of it. The arms can now be attached, leaving a 1-inch overhang on the back and ½-inch overhang on the inside of the front leg. Use two screws in front, one into the leg and one into the arm brace. In back, secure the arms with two screws going into the middle back brace.

9. The screw holes can now be plugged. Use a ⅜-inch plug cutter and a drill to cut about 80 plugs from scraps of ⁵/₄-inch material. Make up a small pot of epoxy or plastic resin glue and dip each plug in the glue, then gently hammer the plug in place. When the glue has dried, cut the top of each plug with a sharp chisel, and sand off any excess glue.

10. The chair can now be given its final sanding. Take care to remove any pencil marks, glue lines or rough edges. Start with 120-grit paper and finish with 220-grit to bring out the grain in the wood.

11. Unless you are using redwood or cedar, some type of protective finish is recommended. Three coats of tung oil will seal the wood and give a semi-weatherproof finish that is easy to maintain.

—L.S.

(See lumber, materials, and tools lists, page 198)

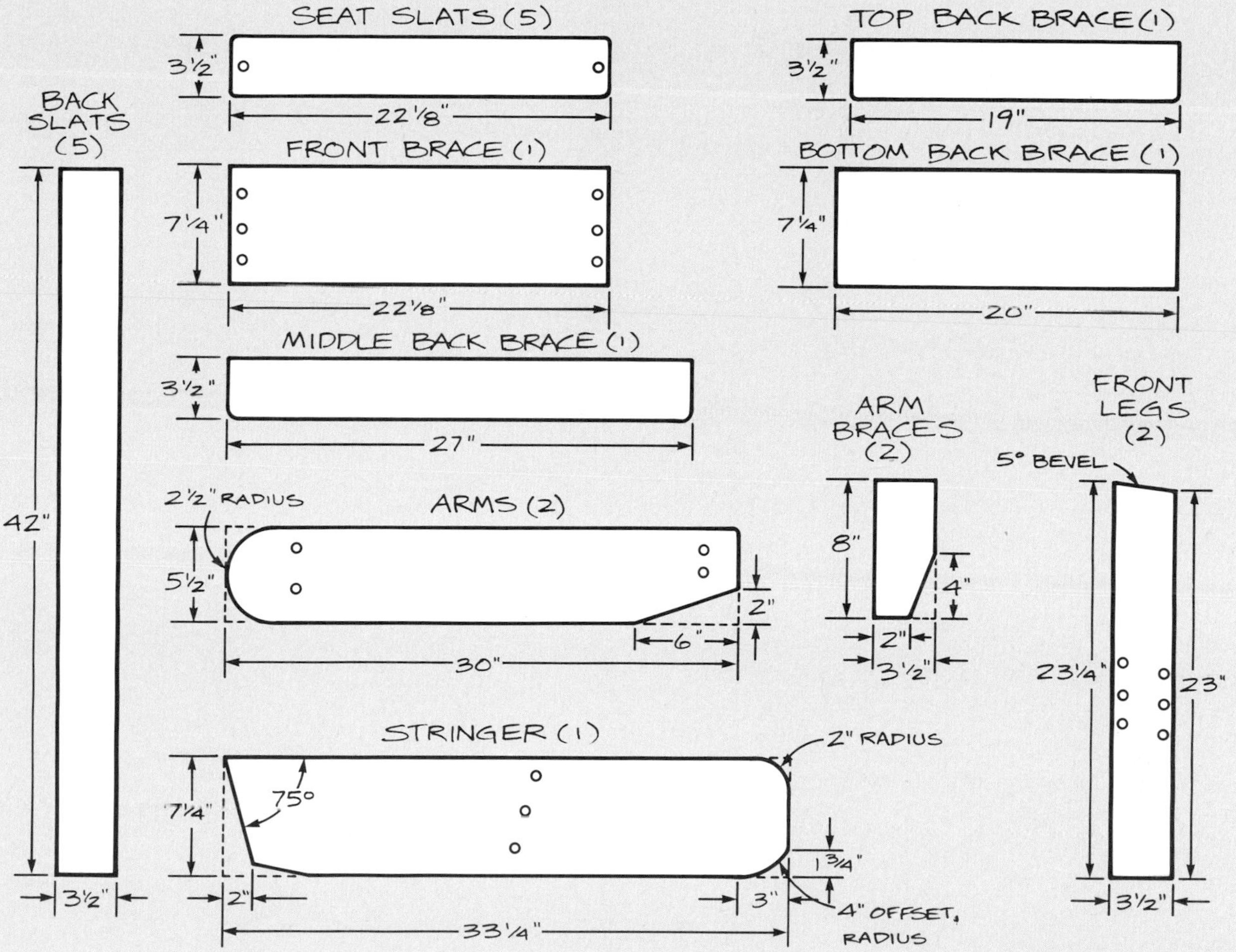

SEAT SLATS (5)

3½" ⊢ 22⅛" ⊣

TOP BACK BRACE (1)

3½" ⊢ 19" ⊣

BACK SLATS (5)

42"

3½"

FRONT BRACE (1)

7¼" ⊢ 22⅛" ⊣

BOTTOM BACK BRACE (1)

7¼" ⊢ 20" ⊣

MIDDLE BACK BRACE (1)

3½" ⊢ 27" ⊣

ARM BRACES (2)

8" 4" 2" 3½"

FRONT LEGS (2)

5° BEVEL

23¼" 23"

3½"

ARMS (2)

2½" RADIUS

5½" 2" ⊢ 6" ⊣ ⊢ 30" ⊣

STRINGER (1)

2" RADIUS

7¼" 75°

3½" 2" 1¾" 3" 4" OFFSET, RADIUS

⊢ 33¼" ⊣

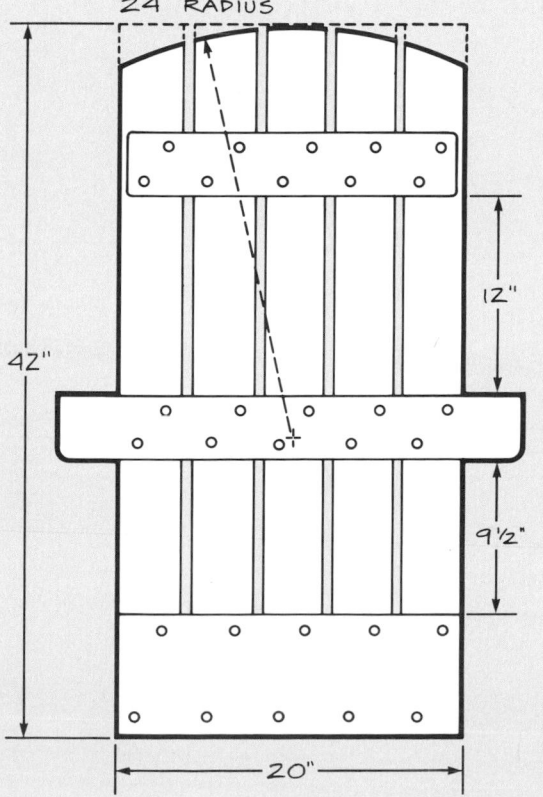

24" RADIUS

42"

12"

9½"

⊢ 20" ⊣

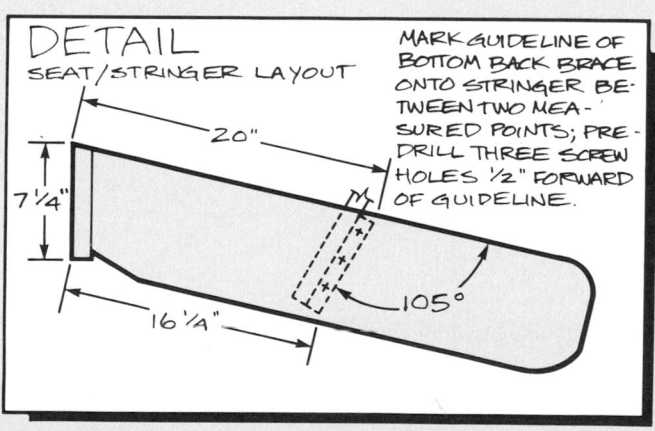

DETAIL
SEAT/STRINGER LAYOUT

MARK GUIDELINE OF BOTTOM BACK BRACE ONTO STRINGER BETWEEN TWO MEASURED POINTS; PREDRILL THREE SCREW HOLES ½" FORWARD OF GUIDELINE.

20"

7¼"

16¼"

105°

The cutting diagram, top, *shows the dimensions and shapes of all the pieces needed to make our version of the Adirondack chair. Cut the pieces from the boards specified in the Lumber List and Cut List (page 198). The back assembly,* left, *should look like this upon the completion of step 3. The seat-stringer detail,* above, *shows how to lay out the angle for the chair's back, as described in step 5.*

MATERIALS LIST

(78) #8 x 1½″ flat-head wood screws
  (zinc-coated)
Epoxy or plastic resin glue (a few ounces will do)
Tung oil (one pint)
(3) #120 sandpaper sheets (or 2 sheets and 1 belt,
  if a belt sander is available)
(1) #220 sandpaper sheet

TOOLS LIST

Circular saw or table saw
Scroll saw or jigsaw
Variable speed drill
#8 counterbore drill bit
⅜″ plug cutting bit
Screwdriver or flathead
  drill bit
Wood chisel

Framing square
Protractor or
  "Speed Square"
  to mark angles
  and bevels
Hammer
Belt sander or
  orbital sander

LUMBER LIST   CUT LIST

Note: All lumber ⁵/₄″ select pine (cedar or redwood
can be substituted)

Lumber	Cut
(1) 10-ft. ⁵/₄ x 8	(2) stringers, 33¼″
	(1) front brace, 22⅛″
	(1) back brace, 20″
(1) 5-ft. ⁵/₄ x 6	(2) arms, 30″
(5) 8-ft. ⁵/₄ x 4	(5) back slats, 42″
	(5) seat slats, 22⅛″
	(2) front legs, 23¼″
	(1) back brace, 27″
	(1) top back brace, 19″
	(2) arm braces, 8″

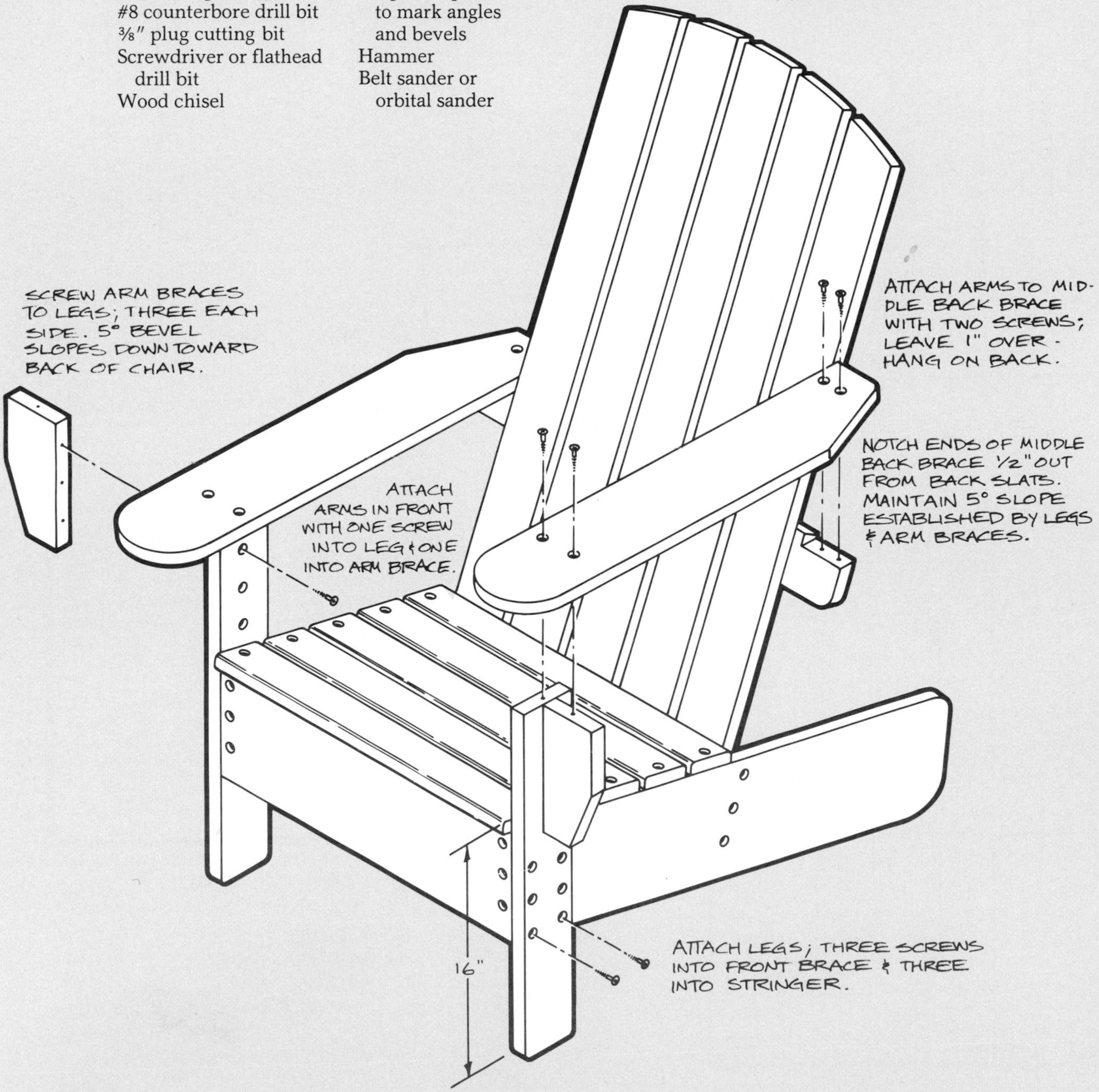

SCREW ARM BRACES TO LEGS; THREE EACH SIDE. 5° BEVEL SLOPES DOWN TOWARD BACK OF CHAIR.

ATTACH ARMS IN FRONT WITH ONE SCREW INTO LEG & ONE INTO ARM BRACE.

ATTACH ARMS TO MIDDLE BACK BRACE WITH TWO SCREWS; LEAVE 1″ OVERHANG ON BACK.

NOTCH ENDS OF MIDDLE BACK BRACE ½″ OUT FROM BACK SLATS. MAINTAIN 5° SLOPE ESTABLISHED BY LEGS & ARM BRACES.

ATTACH LEGS; THREE SCREWS INTO FRONT BRACE & THREE INTO STRINGER.

16″

ILLUSTRATION BY EUGENE MARINO III

Wood Products, in Willsboro, New York, just a few miles north of Westport. The Westport Foldaway Adirondack Chair collapses into a slim 10-inch bundle for easy storage and carrying.

To increase the durability of its folding model, Willsboro Wood Products uses rock maple rather than a softwood such as cedar or pine. Like the Beeken-Parsons chair, it is fastened together with hardwood pegs instead of metal fasteners. Protected by a urethane finish, the chair is designed to weather the elements with little maintenance.

Willsboro also makes an Adirondack settee, which is a double-seated bench, perfect for gardens and porches. Along with its Adirondack chair and bench, the company offers two sizes of Adirondack tables. Although the tables appear more Scandinavian than Adirondack, I'm sure Thomas Lee would still approve. Anything to add to the enjoyment of country leisure. ❧

SOURCES

Adirondack Museum
Blue Mountain Lake, New York 12812
Westport chair blueprint, $6 postpaid. Free catalogue of publications.

The Bear Chair Co.
RR 1
Magnetawan, Ontario P0A 1P0
(705) 387-4466
Ready-to-assemble pine chair, $95 plus $10 shipping; matching ottoman, $25 plus $5 shipping.

Beeken-Parsons
Shelburne Farms
Shelburne, Vermont 05482
Adirondack chair.

Lee Valley Tools Ltd.
Box 6295, Station J
Ottawa, Ontario K2A 1T4
(613) 596-0350
Full-scale plans, $7.95.

Weall & Cullen Gardeners Supply Inc.
400 Alden Road
Markham, Ontario L3R 4C1
(800) 387-9777 (Canada)
(416) 479-9111 (U.S.)
"Sundowner Chair," unfinished and disassembled, $99 plus $8.50 shipping.

Willsboro Wood Products
P.O. Box 509
Keeseville, NY 12944
Westport Foldaway Adirondack Chair, $140 plus shipping. Free catalogue.

There are as many styles of Adirondack chair as there are lakes they sit beside.

ILLUSTRATION BY JOHN BIANCHI

Getting the Hang of It

How to Build a Patent Rail Fence

By Charles Long

Almost as an afterthought, Glen Switzer waves out the truck window at the sturdy rail fence that has tracked us for a mile or more along the narrow Ontario sideroad. "My grandfather built that fence," he says, "more than 60 years ago."

It is not a boast, but it should be. This land is not easily reconciled to farms and fences. The rocky, untillable roadside is

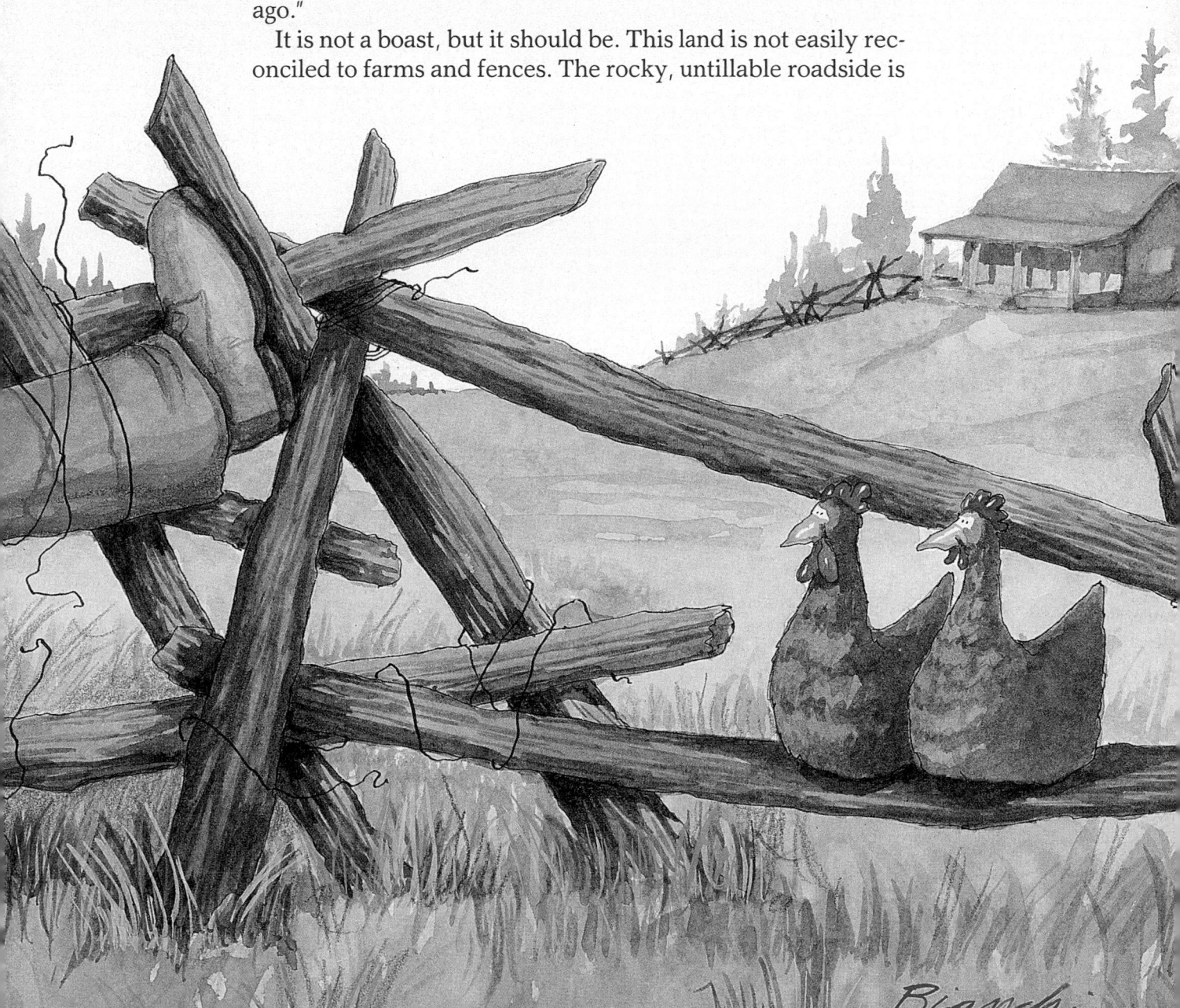

Bianchi

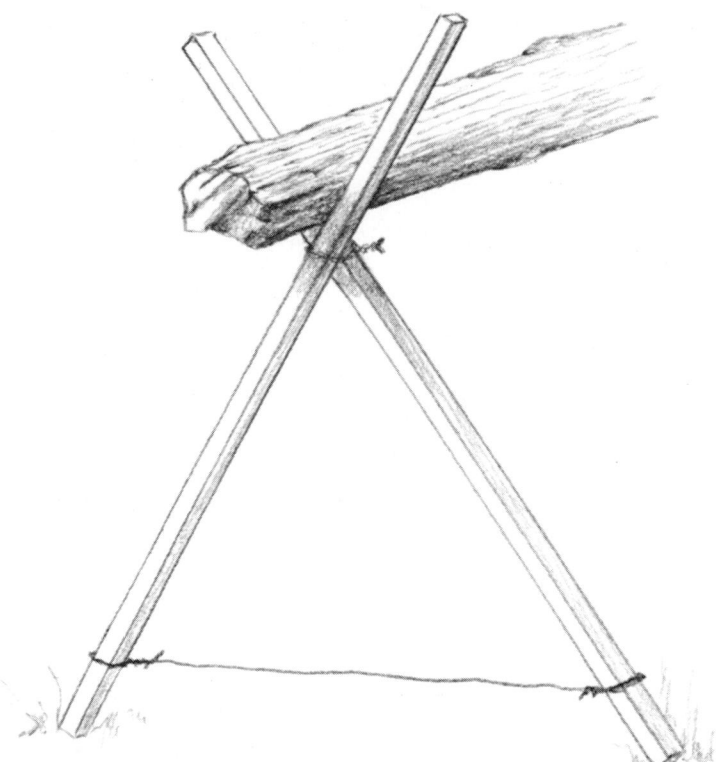

Acting as the fencer's skyhook, a homemade jack suspends the bench rails in mid-air at about hip height while the fence is built around them.

Gerald Switzer wires upright stakes to a pair of bench rails supported by a jack.

choked with juniper and grape that grapple with fences until they pull them down. Dying elms drop limbs from above. Wind and snow-plows take their toll. And you don't dig post-holes in this inhospitable shield—you prospect for them.

A fence that would stand at all in such conditions is a rarity. Sixty years is a wonder. Consider this: machines were making barbed wire as early as 1874, and by 1899, a farmer could fence with good-quality woven wire for as little as 25¢ a rod (about 1½¢ a foot). When Glen Switzer's grandfather built this fence in the 1920s, progressive farmers were already plugging in electric fences and burning their old rails in maple-syrup evaporators. Yet, in modest defiance of the industrial revolution, the humble rail fence is not only still standing, it is being built anew—often in preference to more "progressive" alternatives.

To contain curious livestock, wire fences must be strung banjo-tight, and they rely on sturdy posts and well-anchored corners to maintain that tension over long spans. Even then, a single failure—a fallen limb or a broken post—can break the tension and spoil an entire length of wire fence. If a tree falls on a rail fence, one panel may have to be rebuilt; if it falls on a wire fence, the whole fence may have to be replaced. And a rail fence will never short-circuit on a weed.

Glen Switzer and his three sons, Gerald, Peter and Mark, work full-time at the fencing business. Gerald holds the franchise for an electric-fencing outfit, but "if you can get the rails," he says, "there's no better fence for rough ground and bush pasture. Last year, we fenced every day and only had three little wire jobs. All the rest was rails."

If you can get the rails. Ah, there's the rub. Half the secret of the 60-year fence is arbor vitae, better known as cedar. Eastern white cedar grows from Manitoba to the Maritimes, western red cedar in British Columbia. Both species are light and easily split; both have natural resistance to rot.

Cedar is the farmer's consolation prize. Tenacious and shallow-rooted, it sprouts in thickets in swamps and on dry rocky land. It seems to thrive on the very kind of ground that would drive a posthole-and-wire fencer to tears. If the ground is too mean to yield a decent posthole, chances are there is cedar around.

Glen and his boys find different species in the old fences—pine, white ash, even iron-wood—but they have to be thrown aside when the fence is rebuilt. Only cedar rails last long enough for salvage and reuse.

"In fact," says Gerald, "we'd rather use old cedar rails than new ones." Early settlers split the original rails from the heartwood of large primary-growth trees. The old heartwood rails

ILLUSTRATION BY JOHN BIANCHI   PHOTOGRAPHY BY JIM MERRITHEW

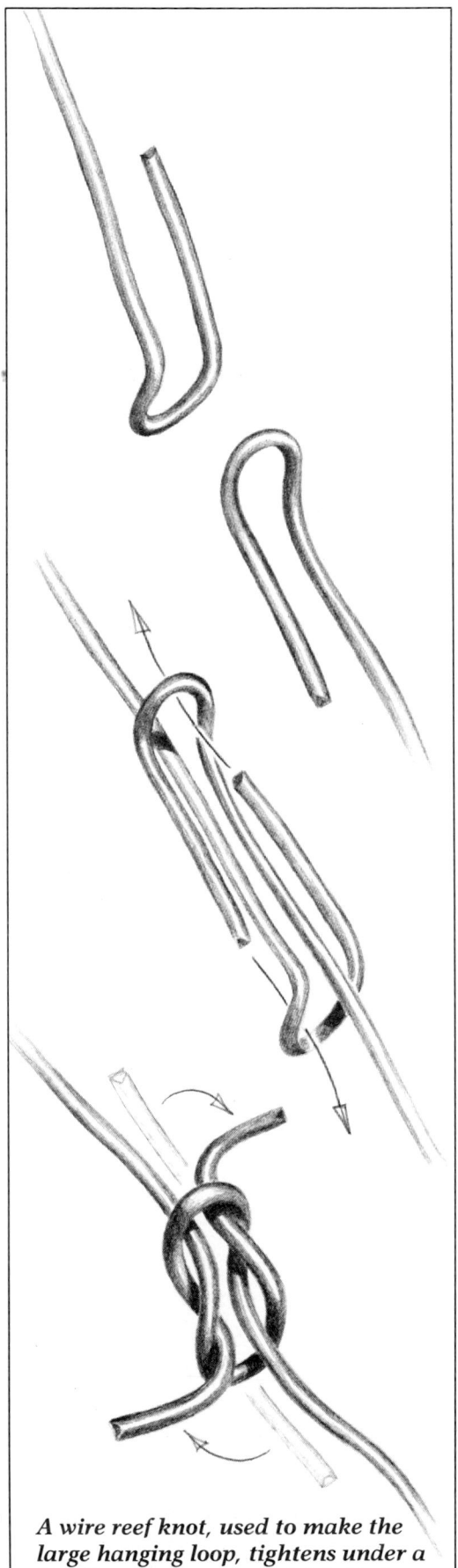

ILLUSTRATIONS BY JOHN BIANCHI   PHOTOGRAPHY BY JIM MERRITHEW

A wire reef knot, used to make the large hanging loop, tightens under a load but does not put a kink in the wire.

The wire figure eight that holds the bench rails under the crossed stakes is the key to the fence's strength. The hanging loop will hold the bottom rails.

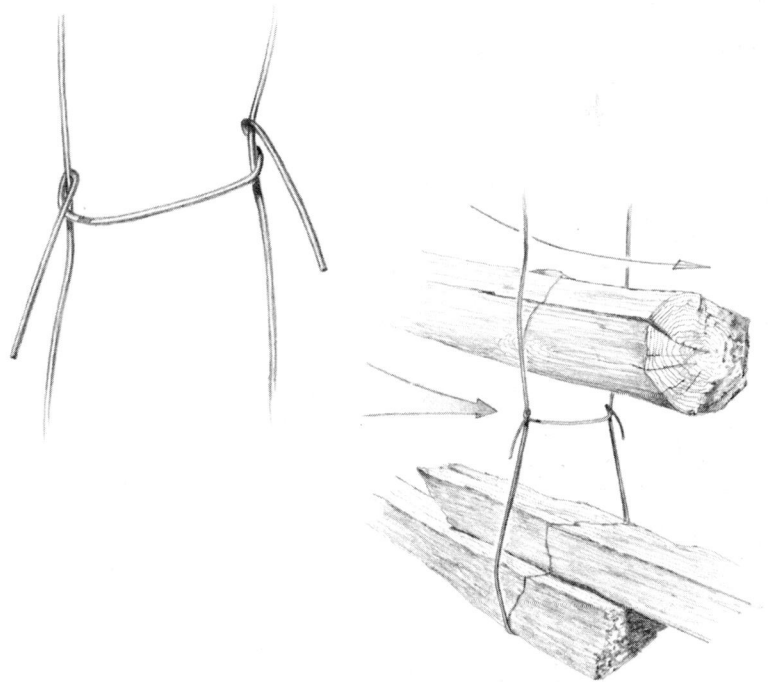

The weight of heavy bottom rails strengthens the fence by tightening the joint. If a fourth rail is desired, wire across the loop to support it.

For a binder fence, put the small end of the brace into the top of a loop of wire set around the stakes, and pull it down. This twists the wire tight, and when the brace is wired to the bottom rails, it provides longitudinal support.

A center brace. Note that it is wired to the rails "the long way round," or through the narrow angles. This resists the tendency of the rails to sag closer together.

For a patent fence, wire the stakes together and twist the wire tight with the handle of the fencing pliers.

are hard and uniform, with little taper from end to end. A new rail is likely to be a smaller unsplit pole with an awkward taper and a sheath of sapwood that is prone to rot.

If old cedar is half the secret, the other half is a near alchemy of folk art and family tradition. The rail fence evolved as a North American frontier skill. It is unknown in Europe. Here, settlers began to fence as they cleared the land, using oxen to drag big stumps into a solid barrier around a small garden or grain patch.

Stump fences eventually gave way to the snake fence. Farmers stacked rails or whole logs in zigzag fashion with overlapping ends. It was quick and easy to build, and it could be moved as new ground was cleared. But the snake fence made extravagant use of both timber and land: a mile of fence might take 4,000 rails and sit on an acre of land. Worse still, livestock could push off the top rails one at a time until the barrier was low enough to jump.

Homestead tinkerers gradually developed a series of improved fences, registering at least nine patents on rail-fence design between 1825 and 1872. In many rural areas, a straight rail fence is still called a "patent" fence, but asking a dozen builders to erect one will produce a dozen different configurations. Possibly, the variety stems from the fact that the patents required payment of a fee to copy the design exactly. The Switzers build three different styles of rail fence, including one they call a patent fence, but they admit only to the most picayune differences between the styles. Durability and ease of construction are common to all.

The important question in terms of function is, what is the fence intended to keep out? Or in? The best fence, in rural tradition, is horse-high, bullstrong and sheep-tight—in imperial measure, that converts to about six feet high for horses, five feet for cattle and at least four feet for sheep. The size of the rails determines the size of the escape gaps between them, but on average, sheep need a five-rail fence, horses and cattle three or four. A five-foot-high four-rail fence is standard.

Those blessed with an old rail fence that merely needs propping up already have the materials at hand. If it is necessary to cut new rails, peel the poles and look for the smallest taper from butt to top. Substitute for cedar at your peril; birch, for example, will rot after a heavy dew and a fog. Rails should be at least 12 feet long and as straight as possible. They will overlap at the ends, so 12-foot rails make fence sections, or panels, about 10 feet long.

Stakes (the upright braces, or legs) should be about seven feet long for the usual five-foot-high fence. Lengths vary as the fence goes uphill and down, but the standard practice is to cut them seven feet long and then trim off any excess tops at job's end. Unlike rails, stakes need not be uniform or straight, and taper is not a problem. Use the heavier stakes for main supports and the lighter ones for binders and braces.

When salvaging an existing fence, resist the temptation to cut up old rails to make new stakes. It is easier to buy two new stakes than one new rail, so when you have more good rails than you need, hoard them rather than cut them. You may eventually need them to repair the fence. If you don't, someone else will.

Old rails can still be purchased from farmers who have switched to wire or from landowners who have given up farming. The market is regional and a slave to the law of supply and demand: *the more you need it, the more it costs.*

The total quantity of material required depends on the fence style. A patent fence à la Switzer takes three stakes per panel (two supports and a brace). Their "binder" fence uses 3½ stakes per panel. And the "four-stake" fence . . . well, you figure it out. The number of rails per panel depends on the disposition of the livestock and the greenness of the grass on the other side.

Fencing one side of an acre (approximately 210 feet) requires 21 panels. Thus a four-rail patent style fence will consume 84 rails (21 times 4) and 63 stakes (21 times 3). Add an extra set of stakes at each end of the fence and two extra sets to incorporate a gate. Fence wire comes by the pound or the roll—the usual type is 12-gauge "black" wire. Galvanized wire is also available; it is slower to rust but too brittle to take much twisting and tightening. You will also need a good pair of fencing pliers, a saw for trimming the stake tops and a couple of homemade fence jacks.

A jack is the fencer's skyhook, the thing that holds the first rails up in the air while the support is built around them. To make one, take two sticks about four feet long and cross them near the top. Put a twist of wire around the intersection, then spread the feet outward and connect them at the bottom with a long wire. This should result in a triangle, with a wire for the bottom side and a notch at the top—about hip-high for a five-foot fence.

Clear the fence line of brush, vines and entanglements. Don't worry about rocks and stumps—the rails can accommodate those. The chief concerns are to make some working room and then to clear away those things that will grow up and strangle the fence the moment your back is turned.

The first rail laid is the bench rail. Like a keystone, it holds the whole assembly together and so should be the strongest and soundest rail in the panel, although not necessarily the biggest. When the fence is complete, the bench rail will be second from the top. A broken top

The extra stakes in a four-stake fence are set in place, then wired to the fence.

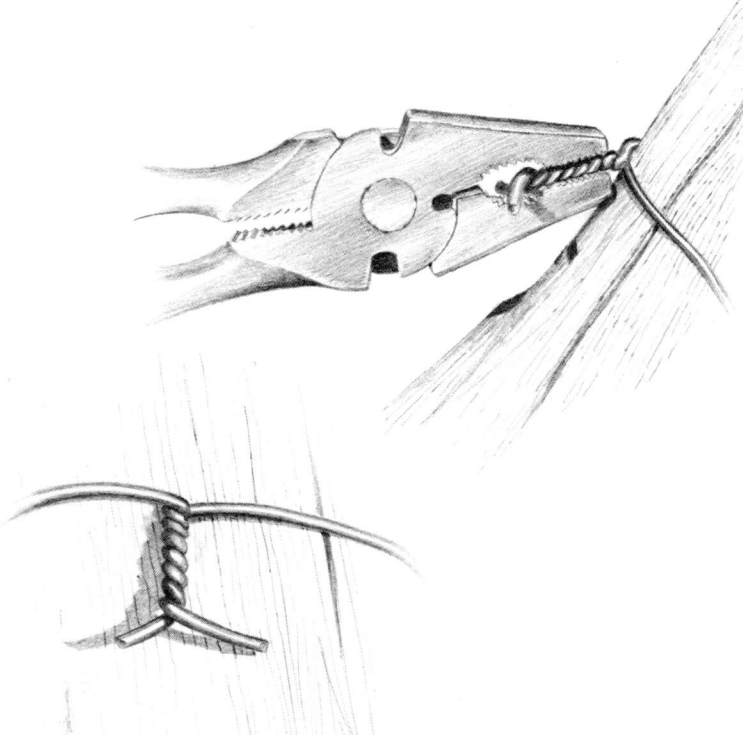

Cross the ends of each wire, then twist them together tightly enough to bite into the wood. Finish the job neatly, bending the ends flat against the wood.

rail or bottom rail can be replaced easily; if the bench rail breaks, the whole section has to be taken down and rebuilt.

Set up the first jack about 10 feet down the fencerow, then lay the first bench rail in the notch at the top, and wire the other end to the building or other fence that marks the start of this section. Set the second jack about 10 feet away, and place the next bench rail across both jacks. The first jack is now holding the over-lapped ends of both rails. Build the first support at this spot.

Cross two stout stakes *above* the overlapped rails—the stakes lean against the rails, and the rails rest on the jack. Set the bottoms of the two stakes about five feet apart, and heel them firmly into the ground.

Now wire the two stakes together *beneath* the two bench rails. Stand on one side of the fence and pass the end of the wire under the bench rails, between the two stakes, around the far stake, back between the two stakes again—so the wire crosses itself beneath the bench rail—and around the near stake. Cut off the wire, cross the free ends, and twist them tight. The wire forms a figure eight, a sling that holds the bench rails up under the crotch of the crossed stakes. Wriggle the jack out from under the permanent support and leapfrog it 20 feet ahead, 10 feet beyond the second jack.

With the first jack out of the way, hang a big loop of wire from the overlapping bench rails to carry the bottom rail. The length of the loop depends on both the girth of the bottom rail and the desired ground clearance. Place the bottom rail high enough to keep it out of the mud and damp weeds yet low enough to block nosy calves or adventurous sheep.

Cut the wire to length, and bend each end back on itself, forming two long, flat hooks. Turn one hook to the right and the other to the left, then bend the curve of one hook up and the curve of the other hook down. Pass the wire around the bench rails, slip the two hooks together in reef-knot fashion, and bend the free ends aside. This forms a self-tightening knot that joins the big loop at the top.

Rest the bottom rail in the loop. Its weight will tighten the loop and pull down on the bench rails, which will in turn tighten the first key joint at the top, the one that holds the bench rails to the stakes. For this reason, the bottom rail should be the heaviest one in the panel, pulling the whole assembly together. The bench rail, remember, was the strong-est—the bottom rail is the heaviest.

Some builders form an upright triangle by joining the two supporting stakes with a cross-member on which they rest the bottom rails instead of using a wire loop. There are pros and cons to the crosspiece design. It does help to keep the feet of the fence from spreading;

on the other hand, it requires one more stake, provides another lever for the cattle to work at and takes away some useful tension from the critical intersection at the top. For these reasons, the Switzers prefer to sling the bottom rail in a wire loop. For a three-rail fence, they set the loop so that the bottom rail rests halfway between the bench and the ground. For a four-rail fence, the loop is longer, leaving a wide gap between the bottom rail and the bench. The fourth rail (fourth in terms of design but the third to be put in the fence) goes in this gap.

Fix a short length of wire across the loop, just above the overlapping bottom rails, by wrapping each end around the vertical sides of the hanging loop. Lay the fourth rail on the cross wire.

Set the top rail in the V of the stakes. Now, all the rails are in place, and the two main supports are up. The only remaining weakness is a tendency toward longitudinal collapse – a slow shift along the length of the fence that lets the whole thing sag to its knees like a centipede lying down in its tracks. The solution is to add a diagonal brace against that longitudinal movement. The variety of styles in rail fencing stems largely from differences in how the diagonal brace is added. The Switzers use three styles: binder, patent and four-stake.

To build the binder fence, loop a wire around the tops of the two stakes above the top rail. Twist the ends together, closing the loop without tightening it. Now, take a third stake, and push one end of it into the loop *from above*. Pull down on the free end of the stake, as if it were a pump handle, thus twisting the wire and binding the junction tightly. Lower the free end of the stake all the way to the ground, then wire it to the two bottom rails. The Switzers put one binder stake at each set of supports in alternating directions: they twist one stake forward into the next panel, and at the next support they twist the binder back into the panel just completed. Again, the following binder twists forward, and the next one twists back. The result is two binders at opposite slants within a single panel and no binders in alternate panels. Finally, they add a simple diagonal brace to the open panel.

The Switzer version of the patent fence begins with the same givens as the binder fence; that is, with four rails and two supporting stakes already in place. Again, put a loop of wire around the tops of the stakes above the top rails. This time, however, flip the loop once to make a figure eight, then stick something short and sturdy, like the handle of the fencing pliers, between the two wires, and twist the whole thing tight. Now, the support is secure, but the fence can still sag lengthwise. To prevent this, the Switzers wire a diagonal

ILLUSTRATIONS BY JOHN BIANCHI   PHOTOGRAPHY BY JIM MERRITHEW

Farmers in wet or windy areas sometimes weight the stakes with rocks. This allows the bottom rails to move freely but prevents the fence from being carried off.

A gate without a gatepost is made by moving the stakes back two feet, wiring on a pair of vertical braces and sliding the gate bars in place.

FOUR-STAKE FENCE

PATENT FENCE

BINDER FENCE

brace in the center of every panel, alternating the slope and the side each time: in one panel, the brace slopes back and hangs on the inside of the rails; in the next panel, it slopes forward and is on the outside of the rails. Wire each brace to all four rails.

The four-stake fence has two diagonal braces at each support, making a four-legged pyramid. It is possible to hang the bottom rails in the wire loop as before and then to add the last two braces to the pyramid. In that case, the third and fourth stakes serve only to brace against longitudinal sag.

The more common approach is to start with the first two stakes, add the bench rails and top rails and then wire the third and fourth stakes to the pyramid. As before, one stake goes inside the rails and the other outside, each sloping away from the other. Finally, without hanging a large loop, wire the bottom rails to the third and fourth stakes. This is a good design for using up short rails because the bottom rails are wired to the longitudinal braces, so they do not need to overlap as they would in a hanging loop.

Wherever rails are wired to stakes or braces, one little secret will help to beat the sags: wire the long way around the intersection, not the short way. In other words, wire through the narrow angles, not the wide ones. More mindful of the cost of the wire than the mechanics, apprentice fence builders may be tempted to wire around the shorter circuit. Don't. As the fence begins to sag, the rail and the stake will align themselves in closer parallel, which will loosen the wire. If the rails are wired through the narrow angles instead, the wire will tighten when the two pieces try to settle in parallel and will resist any such movement.

And while we are looking at wire, note the way professionals finish a wire fastening. They grip the crossed wires with pliers and twist them tight—the wire should be tight enough to bite into the surface of the wood—then they bend the snag ends flat against the wood, out of harm's way.

Like most folk arts, rail fences evolved with personal touches and custom refinements that will never be hammered or twisted into anything like a standard. In the usual course of events, a special improvement is invented on the spot to meet a special problem. Farmers with particularly pushy livestock may attach barbed wire to the stakes. Where fields flood,

ILLUSTRATION BY JOHN BIANCHI

builders may add a twist to the hanging loop so the bottom rail can float free without floating away; other wetland farmers may weight the fence with rocks. The Switzers use rocks to brace a fence in especially windy spots: they place two crosspieces at the bottom of the support, wire them to the stakes and then pile stones on them.

Where the fence crosses a slope, take care to keep the rails plumb, not leaning out over the hill. This means using a longer support stake on the downhill side and a shorter one on the uphill side. Where the fence climbs or descends a hill, it is the longitudinal braces that will have to be adjusted to the slope. Steep fences are just contrary enough to fall uphill, so be sure to pay attention to the uphill brace.

A gate hangs on a gatepost. Everybody knows that. But a rail fence is the natural child of terrain too rocky to take a post. The answer is a sliding-bar gate. Set the jack and the bench rail as if you were adding another ordinary panel. Cross support stakes over the bench rail in the usual way, but place them two feet closer to the previous supports. In other words, the final panel will be an 8-footer instead of the usual 10-footer. The rails, however, are standard length; consequently, the ends of the rails project about three feet beyond the last supports. Sandwich the project-ing ends between two vertical stakes, and wire the uprights to each rail. Do the same thing on the other side of the gate opening, then cut four bars, each a couple of feet longer than the opening. The bars slide onto the rails, and the uprights keep them from rolling off. The eight-foot panels on either side of the opening need extra bracing: use two diagonals in each panel, slant them in opposite directions, and fix them on opposite sides of the fence.

As with farming and child rearing, fencing with rails is not quite as simple as it appears from the other side of the fence. A fence is an integrated thing that rests on all its parts, and one subtle misstep may lead to grief three panels hence. Gerald Switzer and a partner once fenced a building lot while the owner studied every step. It took them two hours to build 25 panels. Only four panels remained unfinished when the owner sent them home. "Don't worry about the rest," he said. "I've been watching you guys, and I'm sure I can do it myself." He did, but it took him eight hours to finish those last four panels.

The Switzers build 600 to 700 feet of fence on an average day. On a really good day, they have done twice that much. They will keep on doing it as long as they can get the rails. And when their grown-up grandchildren drive down the road, chances are those fences will still be there. ❧

Woodlot Wizardry

Common-Sense Silviculture That Works Like Magic

By Des Kennedy

Even-aged stands must be thinned to promote rapid growth, which peaks when the branches have touched for two years.

Those who have tried their hand at it agree: few aspects of rural living demand as wide a range of skill and insight as the successful management of a woodlot. Poor choices can ruin a forest. Mistakes take decades to set right again. In the bush, even doing nothing has its consequences. There is, the adage goes, no forest management without the ax.

"If you want a healthy, sound stand of timber," says Oregon forester Dick Smith, "you'd better get in there." Even sitting behind a desk in the downtown Portland office of his forestry consulting firm, Smith is clearly a passionate advocate of enlightened woodland management. "You can't hold living plants in one position," he argues. "Change is going to take place whether you make it happen or not." What a good steward of the land should do, he says, is direct the growth of living trees so that the stand is better than it would be if left to its own devices.

The son of a Quaker minister, Smith, now 78 and slowed by a recent stroke, works with an almost evangelical zeal to convince others that they can harvest the timber but conserve the forest. "What you're attempting to do," he says, "is help the forest reach maturity. You're trying to grow small trees into big trees, and you're doing that without destroying the plant-succession process."

Plunging into the bush with ax and chain saw, most greenhorns know enough to take out the dead, diseased and malformed stems; but after that, what should be cut and what left to enhance the beauty and vigor of the woodlot? Because clear-cutting dominates the forest industry — and therefore the schools of forestry — there are few experts who can answer that question. Smith, who has been developing and perfecting the art of individual tree selection (ITS) for 34 years, is one of the few. At no point in his selection system is an entire stand of trees removed. Rather, his strategy is to keep as many trees growing as possible, encouraging their growth by the periodic removal of large, merchantable trees.

At the heart of the system are the two Rs: release and regeneration. By carefully and continually removing a few large trees, the forester creates openings into which new trees will naturally seed and into which smaller trees will expand and become large in their turn. The system was first articulated in the late 18th century by a Danish forester named Reventlow in response to the German practice of a series of thinnings followed by a final clear-cut. Such an approach, Reventlow calculated, cuts the profitability of a forest in half. "Instead of using a few periodic thinnings in order to remove suppressed trees," he argued, "thin all those trees which by unfortunate placement prevent their neighboring trees from making rapid growth."

Smith says there are two fundamental principles that determine what trees should be selected for harvest: "First, the removal of a designated tree should enhance the growing conditions of the remaining trees. Second, the tree being harvested has to have grown to a size that will give the owner maximum dollar return." The rules apply even to the part-time woodlot owner whose only dollar return is a heating bill reduced by the amount of firewood he or she cuts. "You harvest the mature trees. It doesn't matter if you have half a dozen trees or a thousand — the principles are the same. The harvest *benefits* the forest."

Over the years, I have heard foresters claiming to be "benefiting the forest" with industrial harvests that border on holocaust, so I was anxious to see firsthand the results of Smith's selection system. Roaring out of Portland in a pickup truck driven by his young partner Scott Ferguson, we crossed the fertile Willamette Valley, climbed into the Yamhill County hills on the eastern side of the coast mountains and stopped in a small valley of woodlands and pasture. Here, rising from the stony banks of Willamina Creek, is the Brown Tract, 272 acres of wooded hillsides that Smith's firm, Individual Tree Selection Management, Inc., has been overseeing for two dozen years.

The tract is like a wild park. Great stout firs are scattered throughout, and their robust offspring thrive on old skid trails and landings. Shade-loving hemlock and grand fir crowd together in the darker places. Broad-leaved maples spread themselves lazily in sunny spots, and down in the wet hollows, alders stretch slender white limbs like young bathers. In the dappled sunlight of the understory, lacy ocean spray and hazel bushes weep down to olive-green sword ferns. A flock of jays chatters noisily, harassing a busy squirrel. In a thick stand of oak and fir, we hear the telltale thumps of a deer bounding away from us.

Smith's selection system goes beyond aesthetic sensibility. Its more profound beauty is that it maintains a continuous forest, protecting herbs, shrubs, wildlife — including microorganisms in the soil — and the genetic pool of all the tree species which have adapted themselves over centuries to a particular site. It means, Smith says, "being aware of the total environment." Ferguson calls it "looking at forests as diverse ecosystems, not as agricultural crops." In addition, the system makes sound economic sense. In 1964, when Smith began managing the property, a timber cruise showed that it held a little less than two million board feet of conifers and alders. By 1985, the tract had undergone 14 harvesting operations yielding 4.3 million board feet of wood worth more than $500,000 — and there were *still* two million board feet remaining. Although this was somewhat shy of Reventlow's prediction of doubling the forest's production, an independent analysis of the Brown Tract concluded that after 21 years, selection cutting had already earned $200,000 more than clear-cutting would have.

Slice of Life

"People who come from the town to the country," says Peter Sanders, "often buy a piece of property because they feel good about it. Then they either destroy it in trying to develop it or get disillusioned because they have great plans and the forest system itself is limiting what they can do with it." A soft-spoken Englishman, Sanders is the resident silviculturist at the sprawling research forest run by the University of British Columbia (UBC) in the Fraser Valley hills east of Vancouver. Like Smith, he is a resolute believer in forest management.

"The first question you should ask yourself," he says, "is this: 'Why do I own land?' There are any number of reasons. It can be the straight satisfaction of working on it or the enjoyment it will give you in retirement. Some people want a steady or periodic income from it. Some want to enhance it for their kids, to create an inheritance. Some, of course, just want to sell all the timber and subdivide it. The first step is to determine exactly why you own it. Then you can set up a series of goals and objectives."

Before coming to UBC, Sanders worked for the Scottish Woodland Owners Association, and since his arrival, he has helped organize the Fraser Valley Woodlot Owners Association. "I think the key to successful management of a small area," he says, "is a rolling, or evergreen, plan that you update every year and that always lays out your next 5 to 10 years of work." Such a plan saves time by helping the landowner schedule work in the woodlot, it provides a continuity of intent, and it protects the forest from what Sanders calls

Whether interested in harvest or regeneration, woodlot owners must decide which trees to cut.

"bright-idea management." Because a forest's evolution is measured in decades, perhaps even centuries, an overview is critical.

On any piece of land, there is a natural progression of plants, from the pioneers that reclaim disturbed soil through the rapid successional changes of a young forest to the maturity of the climax species that eventually dominate the site. "When you walk into a stand of trees," says Ferguson, "you're looking at a very narrow slice of what *has* happened and what *will* happen. The history of the forest is probably the most important thing for any owner to know."

Sanders concurs. "Identify the trees you've got," he advises, then go to a good textbook on silviculture. There, the woodlot owner can learn what climate and soil conditions each tree species prefers, its life history, reproductive pattern and other information, such as what species it is associated with. After studying the silvics, Sanders says, "go and see it demonstrated in front of you on the ground. Look at the tree, and try to understand its characteristics. Recognize that it's at a particular stage. See how it is influencing and being influenced by peripheral trees. If something is not exactly as the book says it should be,

reason out *why* it's not, because nothing happens by accident. When you understand all that – when it's no longer a mystery – then you can project what will happen in the next stage. And it's that projection that allows you to plan."

Take advantage of resource people, whether longtime residents or professionals, to learn about forest ecosystems. Many areas have local foresters who will visit woodlots. Extension services staffed by experienced foresters and technicians will also offer on-site advice even to owners of small properties. If there is a woodlot owners' association in the vicinity, it can be a source of valuable silvicultural information. Also, many universities, community colleges and school districts offer courses in land management and forestry.

Another visit that Sanders advises is to the local government agent's office. Maps and aerial photographs obtained there can help enormously in getting an overview – literally – of the woodlot. "If you've got 10 acres," he says, "then for $10, you can get a set of photographs that will cover the whole block in stereo." From these, the owner can draw a detailed map showing property lines – always know exactly where your boundaries are, and have them well flagged before beginning any woodlot work – fences, buildings, wet areas, steep slopes, drainage and access. "That's your data base," Sanders says. "It's what you've got." Even a rudimentary grasp of the principles of plant ecology will help one understand the biological limitations of the forest. The small-holder needs to establish and consider his or her objectives. Some may be unrealistic; others, such as cultivating wildlife habitat while earning a steady woodlot income, are compatible only with careful planning.

For many people, the production of wood fiber is not the primary aim. They expect their wooded acres to supply firewood, fence posts and an occasional building pole, but they also want shelter for plants and wildlife, protection for watercourses and a beautiful, peaceful place to wander about in. Rather than asking, "How can I derive the maximum dollar return from this woodlot?" they want to know, "What must I do to keep this forest the healthiest and most attractive that it can be?" In any forest, growth is regulated by the nutrient content of the soil, the availability of water and the amount of sunlight reaching the trees. A mixed-age forest contains a variety of tree species, ages and sizes intermingled throughout the stand. Normally, there is a scattering of old veterans, the dominants, which receive light from above and on all sides; below them are the codominants, which receive light from above and on two sides; and below them, the intermediates receive light only from above. Lower still, the trees under the canopy receive no sunlight and are spindly and suppressed.

Determining which trees to cut in order to let the others develop is not a facile matter of "taking a few trees out." Each big tree must be carefully studied for the effect it has on its neighbors, where it could be felled, how it could be yarded out without damage to the understory and, finally, what its current value is in the wildly fluctuating timber market. Surprisingly, other than diseased or dangerous trees, the ITS system does not advocate removing anything just to clean up the place. Old snags are left for woodpeckers and cavity nesters. Small dead trees remain to rot back into humus. Even severely suppressed or damaged trees are left alone.

"The small farmer tends to want to have everything neat and clean on the property," Ferguson says, "because the neighbors will come in and see it. But if your forest looks neat, if it has only good, beautiful trees growing, that may represent an opportunity you've lost. One of the biggest things I've learned from Dick is that if the growth process will correct a problem and you're not giving any-thing up by leaving it there, why not leave the tree and let it improve?" Trees with broken-off tops, he says, can throw out new leaders and become merchantable in time – the Brown Tract has a number of such rehabilitated trunks, with large new trees growing from the old breakage.

The standard wisdom is that severely suppressed understory trees, particularly shade-intolerant species like Douglas fir, will never grow properly. But with ITS, managers regularly release young firs that have been badly suppressed for as long as 15 years, and Smith claims he has successfully released some that have been partially suppressed for 80 years or more. Such a tree, according to Ferguson, has simply proven itself to be a lot more resilient and adaptable than it was believed to be. "The only time we would cut small trees to release others," he explains, "is if nothing was growing and you had a truly stagnant stand, which does happen once in a while." But the classic mistake small farmers make, he says, is to throw away what's growing naturally and then spend money to get something else growing in its stead.

The guiding principle of the release process is one of gradual introduction of sunlight. "If you go out all day on a sandy beach on the first day of summer without any clothes on, you're in trouble," says Smith. "And it's the same with trees. You have to open up the stand gradually, leaving enough shade for the plants to adapt themselves to the new environment." Growth spurts begin when a tree has at least two sides free to grow and can get a good share of sunlight. It might take several successive thinnings around some trees before they are eventually released.

"Now there's what we're shooting for!" Smith is standing in the Brown Tract, pointing to a grove of several dozen large, widely spaced Douglas firs. With straight, clear stems and bushy tops, they rise 100 feet toward the sun. Beneath them, hundreds of small trees jostle together. "We've harvested 30,000 board feet in this one little area," he says. "Now just look at that reproduction. Look at those cones." He picks up a slice of trunk left over from a logging operation. At the core of the sample, the growth rings crowd together, small and tight, almost indistinguishable. Nearer the perimeter, they become dramatically larger – the tree, released from shade, had entered a period of rapid growth with tremendous increments in wood production. We count the rings: harvested when 30 years old, it had a 20-inch diameter, three rings to the inch in its latter days.

Farther on, we look at two Douglas fir trees

growing cheek by jowl. The bigger one is perhaps two feet in diameter, the smaller one about half that and two-thirds as tall. My instinct would be to remove the smaller, less imposing tree and give the big one room to spread out. "But look at the crowns," Smith insists. New growth tips on the larger tree are quite small and anemic. The younger tree, even though partially shaded by its neighbor, is bristling with strong, vigorous leaders — the "bottle brush" effect of a fir in its growing prime. ITS would have us remove the larger tree, which is no longer growing much and has achieved its market value, and let the younger, stronger tree occupy the full space.

Harvesting big trees in a mixed-age forest requires forethought as well as skill in felling and yarding. Since the whole idea is to enhance growth on understory trees, it is essential not to damage small stems in the felling process. Where possible, casualties are minimized by dropping trees in the direction they will be pulled out of the woods. On hillsides, timber is felled either up or down the slope. "You can do a lot of damage trying to go crossways on steep slopes," Ferguson says.

Smith maintains a steady crew of contract loggers, some of whom have worked with him for years and who are highly skilled in the system. "You have to know what the logger can do," Ferguson says. "You have what you'd like to do, and you have what's possible. If you mark a tree that's impossible to fell, maybe the logger will cut down another tree to get the first one out. So then you've got two down where it would have been better to mark the outside tree and leave the first one standing. You have to learn the interactions between the tree and everything around it."

Once down, the tree is limbed and the slash spread around to put nutrients back into the soil. "The closer it is to the ground," Ferguson says, "the more quickly it decomposes. Getting light and temperature in there helps that process. Five years later, you can walk right over it." On the Brown Tract, logs to be sold for telephone poles are skidded out whole; the rest are bucked into shorter sections that can be moved with minimal damage to other trees. The skid trails lead from one felled tree to the next and, to avoid compaction, are generally used only once, then allowed to reseed. Here, fast-moving skidders minimize the need for roads and landings. With a different yarding system or in hardwood stands in flat terrain, things would be done differently. "But," says Smith, "the principles are the same."

How readily can an amateur adapt the ITS system to a small woodlot, I ask. "It's easier to make mistakes," Ferguson answers, "and

selection is more of an art. But if you work slowly, do light thinnings and only thin after the trees have grown back up and have replaced the volume of wood you removed by distributing it to other trees — if you do that in a natural sequence, it can be done."

Field and Forest

Of course, not all landowners begin with an established woodlot. For those starting with fields or a logged-off acreage, an even-aged forest is the only option for at least several decades. Sanders offers a word of caution to anyone planning to develop a woodlot on abandoned farmland. Especially in the east, many old fields are impoverished by a chronic lack of fertilization, and repeated plowings have created a hardpan that is impermeable to tree roots. In a dry summer, when the water table drops below the pan, young trees planted in such soil will die. "I suggest ripping the field with a tine ripper," he says, "to break any pan that may have built up. Plant the trees along the ripped part, so the roots have access to that break in the pan."

What species to plant? The local extension forester will probably be helpful here, but the abiding principle is diversity of species. "Have an intimate mixture," Sanders advises. "It makes a beautiful forest to look at, and every owner should look on the forest as a thing of beauty." And forests grow better in mixture — for example, leaf litter from a variety of trees can balance soil pH, thus raising microorganism activity and enhancing nutrient cycling for improved tree growth. "In central Canada," he adds, "I'd suggest the person with a small piece of land have a scattering of the more valuable hardwoods all through the stand. Make sure you have a few walnuts, cherries and hickories — not just birch and maple." Where acid rain is taking its toll, planters should explore which species best resist the stresses it imposes — early research indicates the sycamore is one.

Intensive management of an even-aged stand requires a series of cultural operations, the first of which is a thorough weeding and thinning when the trees are 6 to 12 feet tall. Using an ax or power saw, the operator removes diseased and malformed trees and unwanted species, leaving the best stems about eight feet apart. This improves the growth of the remaining trees, stabilizes the species mix and produces a better quality of wood. Repeat the operation when the trees are at the "pole stage" — about 20 feet tall — and salvage the wood for fuel or fence posts. In this and any subsequent thinnings, the spacing between the stems varies with the species, height and intended use of the trees. Allow one foot between trees for every inch of diameter at chest height for softwoods, 1½ feet for hardwoods.

Thinning mixed hardwood stands is a far trickier business than working with softwoods. Hardwoods are generally slower-growing, they are prone to epicormal branching (multiple forks) and crooked stems if thinned excessively, and they are harder to thin without damaging their neighbors. Normally, hardwoods need no thinning until they are three or four inches in diameter and about 25 years old — adolescent crowding helps them grow straighter. After that, a light thinning every 10 years or so is all that is needed. With young trees, the rule of thumb is to create about five feet of new growing space between crowns at each 10-year thinning. To avoid damaging the remaining trees, do the work in winter, when the sap is down and the bark is tight. With a mixture of softwoods and hardwoods, most managers favor retaining the more valuable hardwoods, letting them coexist with such shade-tolerant softwoods as white pine, red spruce and hemlock.

Pruning is an option rather than a necessity. "If you want quality timber in a hurry, though," says Sanders, "you've pretty well got to prune. Locally, we cut off everything up to about six or seven feet when the trees are 11 or 12 years old. This lets you walk through the stand, and it gets rid of a lot of the bridge fuel so that if you have a fire, it won't ladder up into the crown. Then we go back in four or five years and take another lift, maybe up to 15 feet, following the live crown up the tree. The final lift is to about 25 feet." He cautions that branches need to be cut off flush with the trunk to avoid bleeding and says the best tools for the job are still a ladder and a handsaw.

"If you look at the growth curve of a stand of trees," says Sanders, "you see that it starts off very slowly and reaches a maximum gradient for a period of about 20 years, which is called the period of grand growth. The sooner you can get onto the curve, the faster you'll have a stand in full productivity. That happens when the trees have touched for maybe two years, when they've got their maximum foliage-to-stem-size ratio. Once the branches overlap, they create an air cushion to the ground that ameliorates the extremes of temperature, so the roots actually have a longer growing season. In this area, they can grow for 300 days a year." Plainly, pruning and thinning programs should be planned to take full advantage of such vigorous growth.

"A lot of these things are wrapped in mystery," he adds, "but it's really just common

sense. For example, if you're thinning, you can look up and estimate the time it will take for the branches to touch again. You want them to touch in about four years, so don't isolate them so much that they aren't touching again by then." Since excessive thinning can expose a stand to wind and sun damage, foresters suggest protecting exposed or wet sites with an unthinned buffer zone. Sanders recommends a systematic thinning even to those not planning to sell any logs. "It will produce a more attractive and more vigorous forest. You'll begin to see development of individual trees. You get to recognize them as they develop, and they become, well, friends. But that won't happen if you don't give them room to develop."

Sanders pauses for a moment, lost in thought. "The forest," he says finally, "is like a huge book. All you have to do" — and here he smiles — "is learn how to read it." ❦

SOURCES

American Forestry Association
P.O. Box 2000
Washington, D.C. 20013

American Tree Farm System
American Forest Council
1250 Connecticut Ave., NW
Washington, D.C. 20036

Forest Engineering Institute of Canada
2601 East Mall
Vancouver, British Columbia V6T 1W5

Forest Extension Service
Box 6000
Fredericton, New Brunswick E3B 5H1

Forestry Canada
Place Vincent Massey
351 St. Joseph Blvd.
Hull, Quebec K1A 1G5

U.S.D.A. Forest Service
P.O. Box 96090
Washington, D.C. 20014-6090

Publications

Managing Your Woodland: A nonforester's guide to small-scale forestry in British Columbia; no charge. Forestry Canada, Pacific Forestry Center, 506 West Burnside Road, Victoria, British Columbia V8Z 1M5.

The Forestry Handbook by K.F. Wenger (John Wiley & Sons, 1984). Hardcover; $59.95.

The Practice of Silviculture by D.M. Smith (John Wiley & Sons, 1986). Hardcover; $55.50.

Secrets of the Hearth

THE RUMFORD RESCUES THE FIRESIDE ROMANCE

BY MAX BURNS

A Rumford is the most beautiful, aesthetic fireplace you can have," says Cliff Walker. "It has the best draw you have ever seen. It is like a blowtorch roaring up the chimney, the flames leaping high and the smoke curling back into the fireplace. To hear it crackling—it is the merriest fireplace there is."

Walker, a timbersmith by trade, is a romantic in spirit. After carefully crafting his log house in a small town in Ontario near the southern shore of Georgian Bay, he could not bring himself to install a squat, glass-fronted fireplace in the massive stone wall that was the centerpiece of the main floor. Instead, he searched for a fireplace better attuned to the proportions of his early-Ontario house, and he eventually found it in the Rumford, a 200-year-old fireplace design with an opening as high and wide as full-length cordwood. Walker built the fireplace himself, shaping the shallow, sloped walls of the firebox to Count Rumford's archaic specifications to recreate a design that had long since fallen into disuse.

At first glance, the gaping maw of Walker's Rumford does little to gladden the heart of an energy conservationist. Fireplaces in general have earned a reputation for wasting energy— they suck heat out of the house when the grate is cold and return little warmth to the room even when the fire is lit—and the size of Walker's Rumford suggests these drawbacks would only be magnified. In fact, this venerable fireplace has recently proved to be more than twice as energy-efficient as the stunted fireplaces that grace modern living rooms and dens. Although it cannot match the heat output of a furnace or an airtight wood stove, the Rumford, developed in Napoleonic Europe as a fuel-saving, smoke-free heating device, is by far the best fireplace for energy-conscious people who are loath to relinquish the pleasures of the open flame.

Poets wax eloquent on the magic of fireside encounters, but the human attraction to fire was initially more physical than romantic. Intent on getting maximum heat from the flame, our earliest ancestors built their fire smack in the middle of the cave or tent, where it was also convenient for cooking. Smoke-filled rooms were considered an inevitable consequence of keeping warm until the 14th century, when house builders moved the fire to an outside wall and capped it with a hood in an attempt to direct the smoke out through a designated hole in the wall or ceiling. Stunted columns, narrow pilasters and dwarf caryatids were dragged out of the archives of ancestral decor to grace the sides of this wall fire, lending visual as well as structural support to

A soldier, statesman, scientist, and man of letters, Count Rumford, left, *is best remembered for the cheery, efficient fireplace,* far left, *that bears his name.*

the hood. By the height of the Renaissance, the fire was countersunk into the wall where it burned in a walk-in cavern of brick or stone that was as high and wide as a man is tall and deep enough to accommodate at least one cauldron suspended over unsplit cord-length logs laid on sturdy andirons. The walls of this gargantuan fireplace rose vertically to meet the flue, a hole with a diameter determined less by science than by the size of the local chimney sweep. Consequently, most of the heat shot straight up the chimney to greet the stars, and what began as an effort to guide smoke out of the house ended by containing the fire so completely that little of its warmth radiated back into the room. What was worse, smoke still found its way past the lintel and into the eyes and lungs of the occupants.

Although much reduced in size, the contemporary fireplace has a great deal in common with this fuelwood fiend of the past: it will not heat a room, let alone a house, and it still smokes. The only advantage that the current incarnation holds over fireplaces of yore is that the shrunken opening is more easily plugged with a fireplace insert or enclosed behind glass doors. While such drastic measures may convert an energy loss into a moderate gain, they also tend to melt the wax of poets, stifling the romantic flicker and castanet crackle of the fire behind a curtain of efficiency. Buckminster Fuller referred to wood burning as "sunlight unwinding from a log," and the pleasure of witnessing that event firsthand is strong enough to make the fireplace a fixture in numerous homes. We now know that this hearth-to-heart communiqué costs us dearly, and there is talk among bureaucrats of banning open fireplaces altogether. It need not be so: the Rumford lets us have our magic and heat the room too.

The Rumford fireplace was the brainchild of Benjamin Thompson, man of letters, diplomat and scientist, born in North Woburn, Massachusetts, in 1753. Thompson was a Loyalist and left America for England when Boston was abandoned to the Revolutionaries in 1776. He eventually rose to the rank of colonel in the British army, received a knighthood and moved to Bavaria, where he became the Minister of War, the Minister of Police, and a Count of the Holy Roman Empire.

Count Rumford – the name he took in honor of the New Hampshire hamlet where his first wife had been born – is remembered today neither as a German soldier nor a British patriot but as one of the fathers of thermodynamics. As a scientist, he was fascinated by light and heat and was the first researcher to recognize the existence of radiant heat energy. A practical man, Rumford applied his theories to the stuff of everyday life: for instance, after studying the insulative qualities of various drygoods, he redesigned his soldiers' uniforms to make them warmer. It was radiant heat, however – a term he coined – that most intrigued the Count. His discovery that radiant heat travels in straight lines and that air is largely unaffected by its passage revolutionized domestic heating systems. It is only when the heat waves from a fire strike a solid object – the room's walls, ceiling and floor or its furniture – that the heat is transferred to the air through conduction and convection. "One must never forget that it is the room that heats the air," wrote Rumford, "and not the air which heats the room."

The traditional source of heat in late-18th-century Europe and North America was the fireplace, and like Benjamin Franklin, Rumford was bothered by the inefficiency and smokiness of this household fixture. Both men realized that the problem lay in the fireplace's proportions. Franklin's solution was to take the fireplace out of the wall and combine the flue and firebox innovations of several earlier inventors into a freestanding metal enclosure – the precursor of the modern wood stove. He used baffles and doors to control heat and smoke. Rumford, on the other hand, chose to redesign the masonry fireplace so that it effectively siphoned smoke out of the house without sacrificing the warmth and beauty of the flames. His theories received widespread acceptance at the time: his own crew of masons built more than 500 Rumford fireplaces, and he became as famous in Europe and England as Franklin and his stove were in the United States.

Both men had their names affixed to their wood-burning inventions, but although the Franklin stove is still produced today, the Rumford fireplace has, for the most part, been forgotten. Vrest Orton, author of *The Forgotten Art of Building a Good Fireplace*, claims that "liberal revisionists" have written Rumford out of history and that, had Rumford's notes for his autobiography not been stolen during a trip to England in 1795, he would surely have gained a historical stature equal to that of Franklin. As it was, his theories on fireplace design crossed the ocean and countless Rumfords were built in North America in the 19th century, but the unique design disappeared when fireplaces in general were replaced by central heating systems.

To the uninitiated, a dormant Rumford fireplace looks more like a place to store the card table than a hearth on which to start a roaring

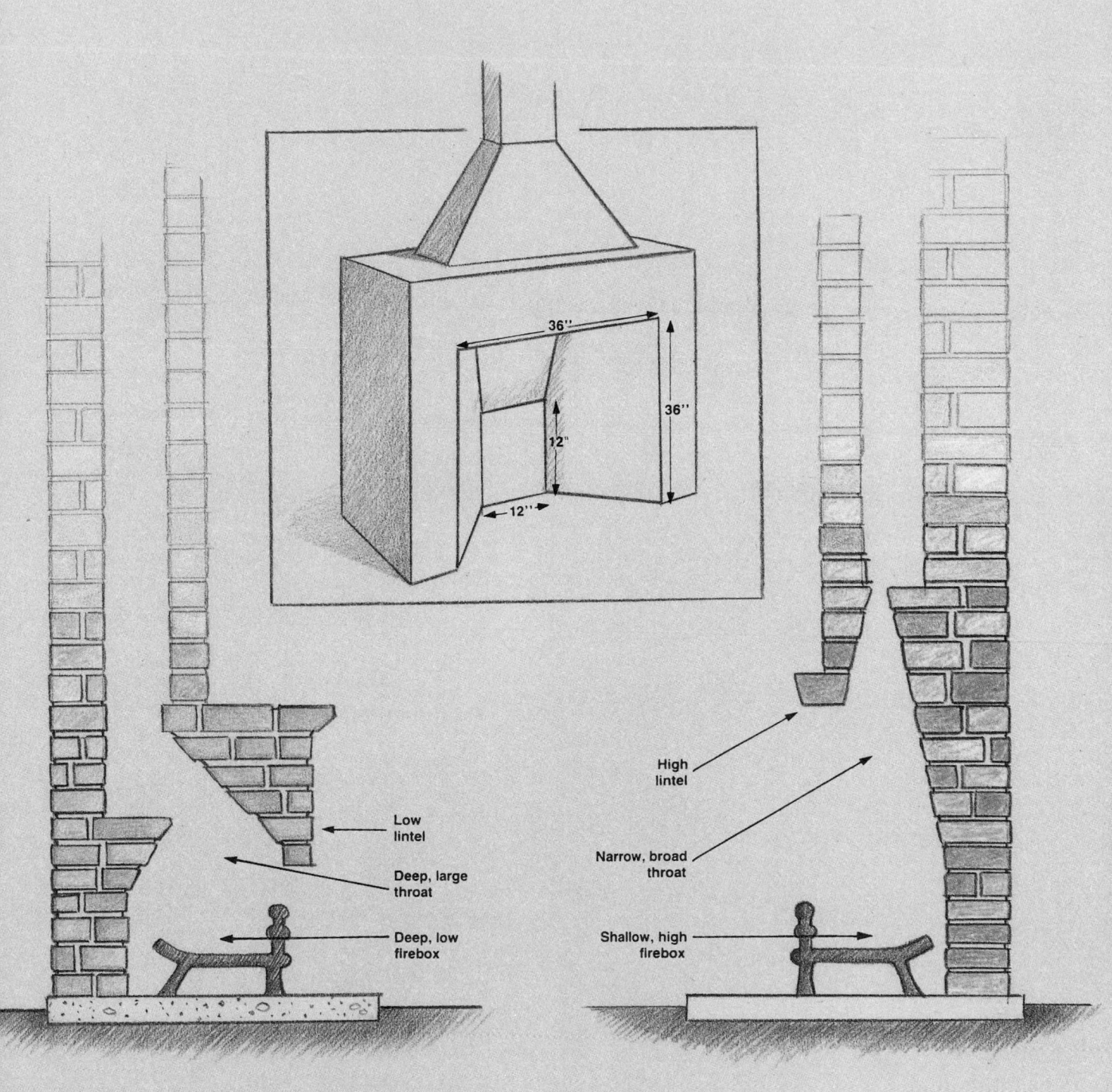

A standard contemporary fireplace, *left,* differs markedly from a Rumford, *right.* Most fireplaces built today have a low square opening and a relatively deep hearth. The fire enclosure is basically a box with vertical square sides and a back wall that is as high as the front opening. The Rumford, on the other hand, has a shallow hearth that is set directly below the throat and chimney. The back wall is only one-third as high and wide as the front opening, so the sides and top slope toward the front, creating a funnel-shaped firebox, *center,* that reradiates heat absorbed in the masonry back into the room and down onto the flames. Therefore, the fire burns hotter and cleaner. Recent tests confirm Rumford's efficiency claims.

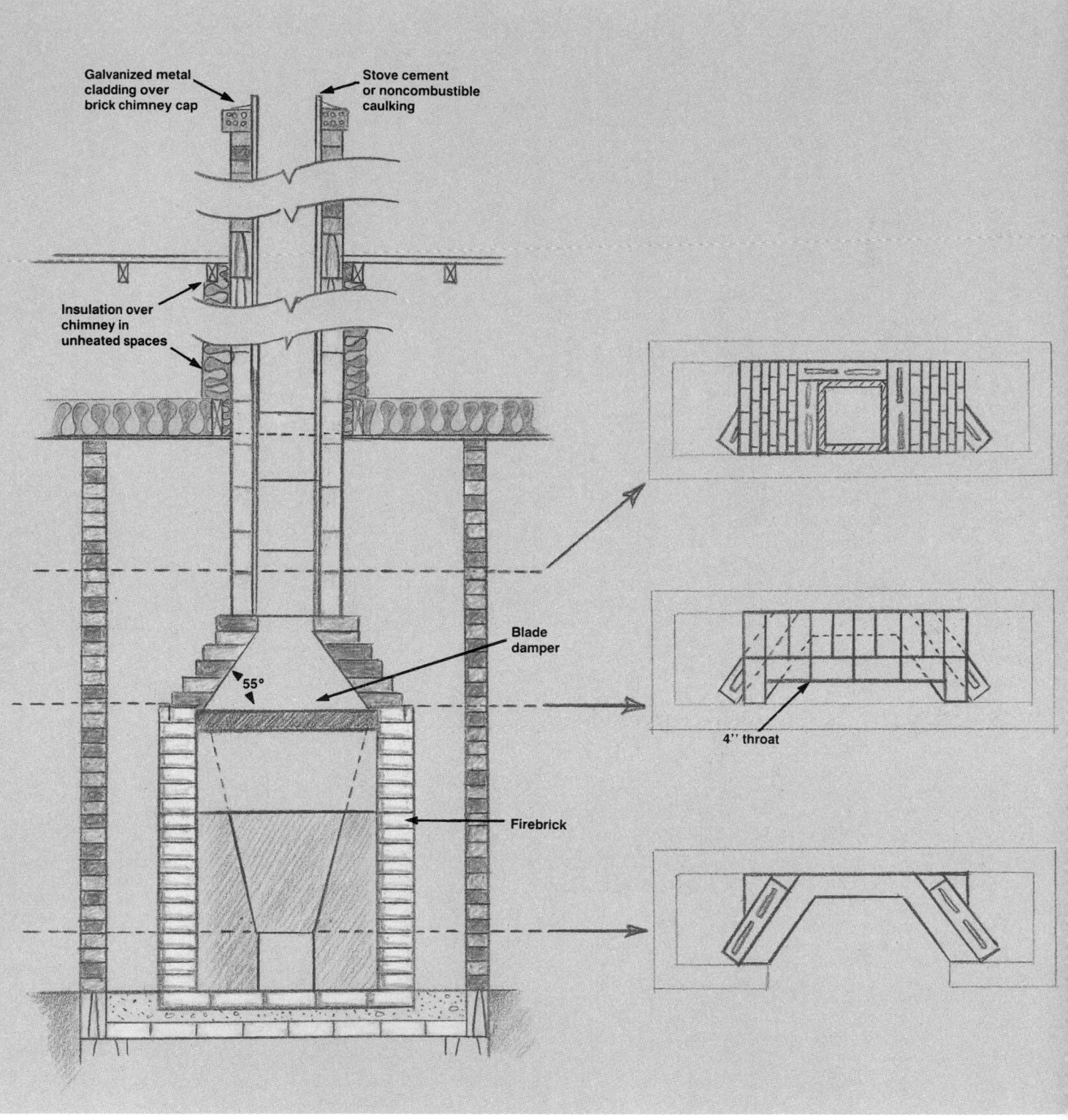

Galvanized metal cladding over brick chimney cap

Stove cement or noncombustible caulking

Insulation over chimney in unheated spaces

Blade damper

55°

Firebrick

4'' throat

A Rumford is no harder to build than a conventional fireplace. The sloped walls require more cutting of the brick, but this will be less arduous if the bricks are laid flat rather than on edge. Ragged edges can be hidden under a thin coat of refractory mortar, which also helps guide the smoke smoothly up the throat. For fire safety, extend the hearth 2 feet into the room, and do not mount wooden mantels or other combustibles in the area of the throat. For maximum efficiency, build the fireplace inside the heated envelope of the house, and insulate the chimney where it extends through unheated attic spaces.

fire. It has a large, square opening at least 3 feet wide but is only half as deep as a conventional fireplace. Most fireplaces built today are rectangular boxes; a Rumford looks more like a cubist funnel: the vertical part of the back wall – commonly called the fireback – is only a third as high and wide as the front, so the top and sides of the firebox fan out toward the opening at an angle that ensures maximum benefit from the heat absorbed by the masonry. In a traditional fireplace, the high vertical fireback reradiates heat horizontally into the room where it may or may not strike a solid object within effective range. The sloped top and short vertical back section of the Rumford, however, cast re-emitted radiation onto the floor in front of the fireplace, where it rises to heat the room. Instead of bouncing off the back log in the fire, re-emitted radiation in a Rumford beams down on the flames, heating both the wood and the gases above so that there is more complete combustion and a hotter, cleaner fire. The narrow back wall also means there is less heat loss to the outside, and the deeply splayed side walls ensure that heat is not simply reradiated horizontally across the burning wood but is deflected into the room.

A fireplace built to Rumford specifications is only as deep as the back wall is high – usually 12 inches. Because the firebox is so shallow, the hearth extends at least 2 feet in front of the opening. Instead of being entirely enclosed by the fireplace, the fire can be built as much as a foot into the room so that direct radiation emanates from three sides instead of just one. With the fire set so unnervingly far in front of its niche, one might expect smoke to permeate the room, but Rumford redesigned the firebox-chimney connection so that the fireplace draws smoke and combustion gases into the flue even from out in front of the lintel. Instead of rising directly up the chimney, smoke in a Rumford fireplace flows up the long, smooth slope above the fire to the funnel-shaped throat that connects the firebox to the smoke chamber at the bottom of the chimney. As Bernoulli demonstrated, gases flow faster when they move through a gradual constriction of their path, drawing the gases behind them rapidly through the stricture. Rumford positioned the throat close to the mantel side of the fireplace so that a plumb line dropped from its center would fall in the exact middle of the firebox floor. The chimney rises directly above the throat: Rumford insisted the mason should be able to see the sky when sighting straight up through the throat, which converges to a narrow opening no more than 4 inches deep. There, Rumford placed a trapdoor or damper that could be opened and shut with a pull chain to regulate the amount of air leaving the house. He designed the smoke shelf to be directly behind the damper, theorizing that warm smoke would necessarily rise close to the front wall of the chimney and downdrafting cool air would fall along the back, flow across the smoke shelf situated behind the narrow, funnel-shaped throat and be carried up the chimney with the exhaust from the fire.

Of the principles of fireplace design that Rumford published nearly 200 years ago, only the smoke shelf and the damper remain – and these only as permutations of his original designs. Yet ironically, the Rumford was the model for the contemporary fireplace. When fireplaces resurfaced after World War II as status symbols instead of as heaters, the designs were based on Rumfords still in use in old houses. However, since warmth was no longer the raison d'être of the fireplace, the angled walls were straightened, reducing the cutting and fitting of the firebrick and thus making the whole thing easier to build. The firebox was deepened to fit wood-frame construction, and the resulting smoke problems were solved by enlarging both the damper opening and the throat. By the end of the evolution, the fireplace resembled a squatter version of the early British fireplace, its Rumford roots apparent only in the damper and the smoke shelf.

Although the angled firebox requires a little extra cutting and fitting and the inside walls have to be carefully smoothed, the Rumford is not a complicated piece of brickwork. Finding a competent mason willing to build one, however, can involve almost as much work as the actual construction. "People who build fireplaces all the time just look at you like you're crazy when you give them Rumford dimensions," says Grant Williamson, owner of a Bracebridge, Ontario, construction company that specializes in post-and-beam houses of period design. Several years ago, Williamson designed a replica of a 19th-century farmhouse as a weekend retreat for Martin Belman, a Toronto dentist. The house is full of such down-home, friendly features as wainscoting and wraparound porches, and Belman wanted a Rumford to complete the rustic decor. However, his mason, Dan Boothby, did not think the fireplace would work and tried his best to talk Belman out of it.

"I would not have built that fireplace if he hadn't insisted," admits Boothby. "I'm in business in a small community: I can't afford to build something that reflects badly on my name, and I was unsure of what I was building. So many things about the Rumford were so different, so conflicting with the theories of the traditional fireplaces I've built, that I couldn't conceive that it would even work. Apparently it does, but I can't take credit for it."

The untraditional concepts of a Rumford gave Boothby more difficulty than the actual bricklaying. Belman's fireplace turned out to be a model of turn-of-the-century charm: reclaimed brick frames the opening and a swinging cook arm arches over the open flame, ready to suspend a pot of steaming après-ski stew. It is not a textbook Rumford, however. Its firebox is a little deeper than specified, not because of the mason's intransigence but because the plan did not fit the available space. Nevertheless, the Rumford "seems to be a very efficient fireplace," reports Belman. "I wanted to get some heat as well as enjoy the look of a fireplace, and this design has worked out really well, in both appearance and heat efficiency. The fireplace couldn't possibly heat the entire house, but when we have it on, the electric heat in the downstairs area is turned off."

As a house designer, Williamson practices what he preaches. His own house—a 2,400-square-foot, post-and-beam two-story building clad in grey wood siding—contains a Rumford: "It's an incredible source of heat. When you stand the wood up against the back wall like a tepee, the heat just pounces into the room," says Williamson. "You can pull the fire a foot out in front of the whole fireplace, and it will take the smoke off the flame and draw it back into the fireplace and up the flue." Williamson has built three Rumfords, all of which he claims have never smoked since the first fire was lit. He admits, however, to building the firebox a little deeper than Rumford recommends, "to save a bit of cutting in my firebrick."

In fact, in looking for contemporary Rumfords, it is difficult to find one built precisely as originally prescribed. This is partly Rumford's fault, since instead of giving specific dimensions he suggested relative proportions. Vrest Orton compares Rumford's rules to the immutable principles of Euclidean geometry: the fireback's height and width equal the distance from the lintel to the throat, which equals the depth of the firebox; the front opening's height and width equal three times that figure; and the area of the opening is 10 times the area of the flue. Tinkering with these proportions can have a marked effect on how well the Rumford works. For instance, as the 3:1 ratio of the height of the opening to the depth of the firebox decreases, so does the efficiency of the fireplace. Nevertheless, variations on the Rumford abound—some coming from late-night thought on the privy, others from well-educated, trained sources—and this may explain some of the negative responses the Rumford name draws.

Randy Jackson is the current owner of Cliff Walker's log house, but he does not share Walker's enthusiasm for the Rumford. "They're extremely inefficient from what we've found. When the fire was on, there wasn't a great amount of heat dispersing throughout the room, and there's an extreme heat loss afterwards. I felt there was a lot more heat going up the chimney than was actually being produced in the room for the amount of wood being burned."

The Jacksons do not build nearly as large a fire as Walker did, which may account for the difference of opinion on the heat output of the fireplace. The large opening and shallow firebox of a Rumford require a commensurately large and ongoing fire to offset its excellent draw and to gain full advantage of its radiant heat capabilities. The heat from a roaring blaze radiates into the room, while the heat from a small fire is lost up the chimney.

Both Walker and Jackson discovered that once the fire had died down to coals, the huge front opening sucked heat out of the interior, leaving the house frigid by morning. Although Walker was too much of a purist to consider glass doors across the firebox, the Jacksons promptly added them. The problem of excessive heat loss may be traced to Walker's own deviation from Rumford's rules. In extolling the virtues of his Rumford, Walker stresses the importance of a healthy and substantial draw, which he achieved by building a high chimney with a 20-inch-square flue. That flue measurement, in relation to his fireplace opening, is almost double Rumford's recommendation. Since this is the only report of such extreme heat loss, the logical conclusion is that the extra-large flue is the culprit.

Williamson adhered more closely to Rumford's specifications, but he also added a feature that helps solve the heat-loss problem. Sitting snug in the top flue tile of his chimney is a homemade damper, operated by pull chains running through standard copper plumbing pipe to the firebox. "Once the fire's going really hot and the flue is warm all the way up, you can virtually shut the thing down," says Williamson. "It's just like a wood stove."

Williamson would never claim that his Rumford has the heating capacity of a wood stove—he has an airtight stove in the basement that shoulders much of the space-heating load in winter—but it is clearly superior to a conventional fireplace. Rumford claimed

Rumford Rules

- The height and width of the fireback are the same dimension as the depth of the firebox at hearth level, usually 12 inches. The height and width of the fireplace opening are three times as long as the depth of the firebox at hearth level, usually 36 inches.

- The front wall of the lintel (the upper edge of the fireplace opening) is no more than 5 inches thick.

- The top of the throat to the bottom of the lintel is 12 inches.

- The throat is 3 to 4 inches deep and as wide as the fireplace opening at hearth level.

- A plumb line dropped from the exact centre of the throat will hit the middle of the firebox floor. Experts suggest that instead of a smoke shelf, the back wall of the smoke chamber behind the damper may be sloped with masonry and mortar so that the damper blade fits flush when fully open.

- The area of the flue should equal $1/19$ the area of the fireplace opening.

- The hearth extension should be at least 2 feet deep and as wide as the fireplace opening.

Room Heat Output of Conventional and Rumford-Designed Fireplaces

	Conventional	Rumford
Energy Lost in Incomplete Combustion	10%	7%
Direct Heat Loss Up Chimney	70%	53%
Loss of Warm Room Air Up Chimney	7%	5%
Net Heat Output to Room	13%	35%

(These numbers represent estimates for the average operation of typical fireplaces.)

Reprinted from The Energy-Efficient Rumford Fireplaces *by Jack C. Norman. University of Wisconsin Press, 1982.*

ILLUSTRATION BY JOHN BIANCHI

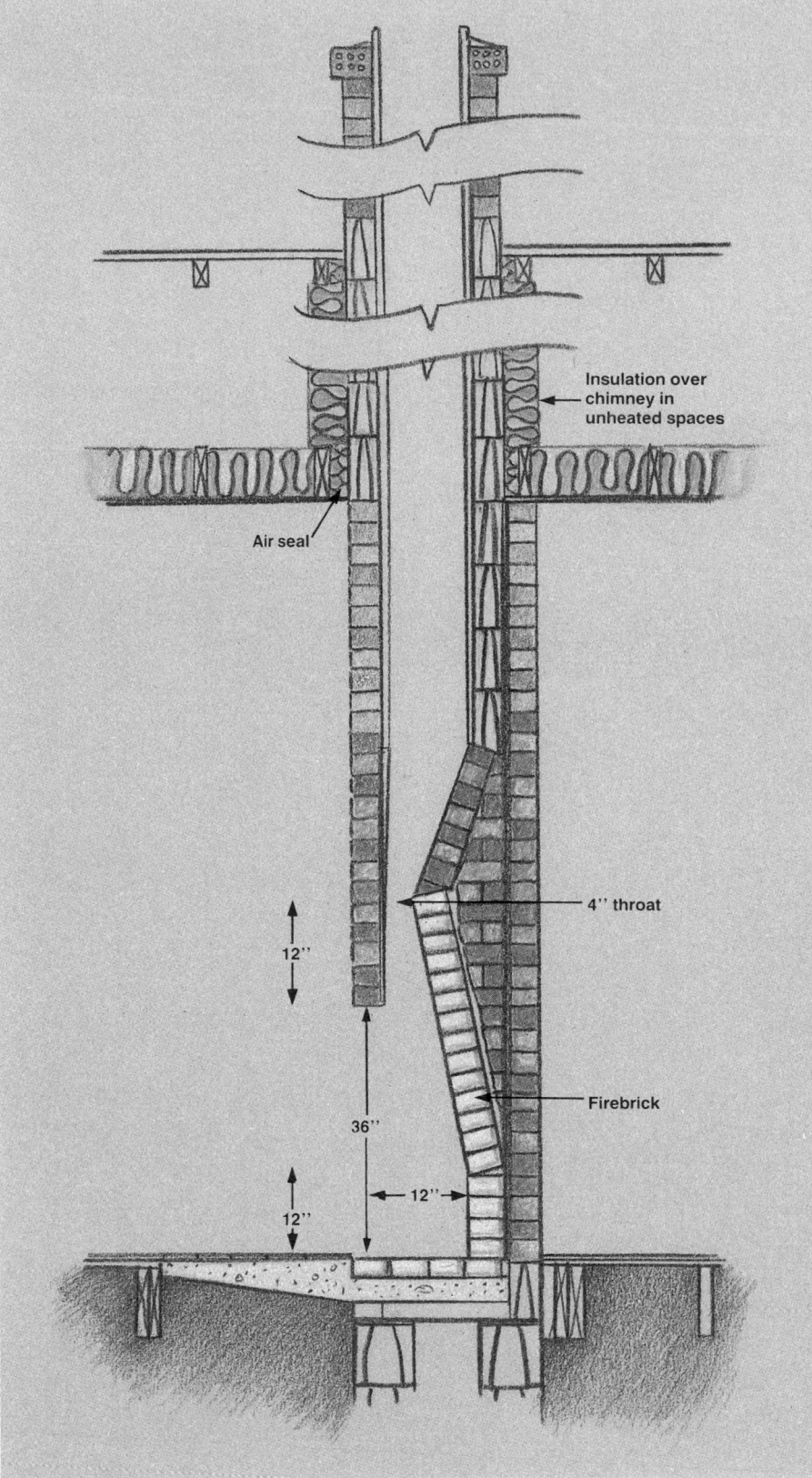

Instead of the smoke shelf advocated by Rumford, which can cause turbulence, the Centre for Research and Development in Masonry report recommends angling the back of the smoke chamber smoothly to meet the base of the chimney.

The Comforts of a Rumford Stove.

Count Rumford, born Benjamin Thompson, became famous — and the butt of more than one cartoonist's wit — for his revolutionary fireplace design. *Right, for those unwilling to relinquish the pleasure of the open flame, no fireplace has proved as efficient as a Rumford.*

that his design was at least twice as efficient as fireplaces of the time. In his essay, succinctly titled "Chimney Fireplaces With Proposals for Improving Them to Save Fuel, to Render Dwelling Houses More Comfortable and Salubrious, and Effectually to Prevent Chimneys From Smoking," Rumford reports that "by several experiments which have been made with great care, and with the assistance of thermometers, it has been demonstrated that the savings of fuels arising from these improvements of fireplaces amounts in all cases to more than half and, in many cases, to more than two-thirds of the quantity formerly consumed."

In 1980, the University of Wisconsin-Green Bay tested Rumford's claims with a computer simulation of conventional and Rumford fireplaces. The results confirmed that the Rum-

ford was two to three times more efficient than the kind of fireplace usually built today. According to Jack Norman, who wrote the study's final report, the Rumford would probably have scored even higher had the computer program taken into account such factors as the size of the throat and the lintel, the effect of reradiation on the fire and the flow of air into the fireplace and up the flue.

Throughout the early 1980s, two experimental fireplaces were monitored at the now defunct Center for Research and Development in Masonry (CRDM) in Calgary, Alberta. The model that adhered most closely to Rumford's principles was rated the best performer, showing considerable improvement over the standard fireplace. In the CRDM report, *Fireplace Technology in an Energy Conscious World* – without doubt the most extensive examination of fireplace theory to date – author Harry Morstead confirms that the shape of the Rumford firebox affects both the quantity of heat generated and the efficiency with which that heat warms the room.

Although Morstead laments the unscientific changes made to fireplaces since Rumford's time – "Open fireplaces have now reached the point where they have been totally replaced or fitted with costly heat-extracting devices that are less effective than a modest design change in the construction stage" – he also suggests some changes to Rumford's specifications. Testing at the CRDM confirmed that the smoke shelf, one of the few Rumford concepts carried over to modern fireplaces, serves no useful purpose and actually restricts the flow of smoke and gases in the chimney by creating turbulence. "It now appears that the entire smoke shelf should be done away with," writes Morstead. He suggests, instead, sloping the back of the smoke chamber up from the inner lip of the throat to meet the flue, thereby creating a smooth, uninterrupted passage for the smoke on its way up the chimney. It is surprising that Rumford himself did not think of this, since he was sufficiently concerned about turbulence to caution women against sashaying in front of his fireplaces. Their voluminous skirts, he wrote, "would cause eddies in the air by which puffs of smoke might easily be brought into the room."

The placement of the damper is also open to question. Most building codes require a damper installed at the throat, although some masons suggest that the optimum place for it is at the top of the chimney. The CRDM report recommends one each at the top and bottom of the flue, based on the belief that such a system traps a column of warm air in the flue and thereby prevents downdrafts. However, there

is no conclusive evidence to suggest that either location has a distinct advantage.

Although Count Rumford did not make a pronouncement on the subject, most informed masons and Rumford aficionados agree that the hearth should not be raised but should be built flush with the floor to avoid chilling drafts. As Orton points out, "One can see and enjoy the fire in tall, shallow fireplaces by leaving the hearth on the floor where it belongs." To gain maximum benefit from the flames' radiating warmth, the fire should sit in front of the fireplace opening by as much as a foot, which means the hearth should extend at least 2 feet into the room. A grate and its resident pile of ashes lying underneath do little more than block the reradiation benefits that otherwise reach the room from the full area of the fireback. Therefore, the fire can be laid directly on the hearth, with short, heavy logs at the rear and smaller logs or split wood in front, slightly staggered to reach from side to side so that it almost completely fills the firebed. A fire burns hottest when blazing, so it is a good idea to keep the Rumford well stoked.

When Rumford designed his fireplace, enough air leaked into the house through the walls, windows and doors that the fire was never starved, but in today's energy-efficient houses, every fireplace, including a Rumford, should have a source of outside air. In fact, this is now required by many local building codes. Providing the right amount of make-up air requires a delicate balance that can be easily upset by operating furnaces or air-greedy appliances like dryers and kitchen barbecue fans. Experimenting with the air-supply damper and controlling the use of exhaust fans will keep the problem in check.

The shallow Rumford also requires some changes to the framing around the masonry. Because the flue is adjacent to the inside wall of the fireplace, mantels, facings and surrounds should be built of noncombustible materials to avoid any fire hazard. The face veneer on a Rumford fireplace will also be subject to greater localized heat expansion. Morstead recommends that "no mortar stronger than Type N be used, with Type O being preferable. Parging mortar need also not be stronger than Type N, but it should be applied over moist surfaces."

Although current building codes allow firebox linings to be as thin as 2 inches, such a thin wall will not radiate heat as long. Morstead recommends that the firebrick be laid flat, rather than on edge. This will also make it easier to fit, given that a Rumford-style firebox requires more acute, delicate angles than a conventional fireplace. Even a careful mason may end up with a ragged-looking sloped wall, so Morstead suggests hiding it under a thin coat of high-temperature, air-setting refractory mortar applied over the entire surface of the firebox with a trowel. The trowel ridges can later be smoothed by lightly brushing the surface with a soft, dry brush.

Even Rumford's greatest admirer, Vrest Orton, admits that, measured in cold science, stoves and furnaces are undoubtedly more efficient today, but adds that "these modern contraptions produce no other kind of warmth. They never give forth the bright, cheery, happy qualities of high sparkling flames leaping up in a well-built fireplace, nor do they exert the almost hypnotic influence which drew the family together in a warm and intimate embrace to become the genuine foyer of the home."

For many people, ridding their homes of the open fireplace is a sacrifice too great to contemplate. Thanks to Count Rumford, the loss is unnecessary. "Just talking about it makes me want to run out and build a house with a Rumford in it," says Walker wistfully. "You'll never get that kind of fire in any other fireplace. It's a joy." ❧

SOURCES

The Forgotten Art of Building a Good Fireplace by Vrest Orton. Yankee Books, 1974.

Since the demise of the CRDM, copies of *Fireplace Technology in an Energy Conscious World* are available for $12.50 plus $3 shipping from the author:

Harry Morstead
6508 Laurentian Way SW
Calgary, Alberta T3E 5N3

Husbandry

The Natural Dog

HEALTHY AND INTELLIGENT, THE ALL-BREED MUTT IS THE IDEAL COMPANION

BY DR. MICHAEL W. FOX

Seven pairs of eyes stared at him—hopefully, plaintively. Six pairs were human: those of his wife and five children. The seventh pair belonged to the puppy. It was sitting forlornly on the shredded newspaper in a small cage in a pet store in a shopping center.

No one had to say anything. Dad had once told the kids he would buy them a dog, and everyone seemed to sense the weakness of his position at this moment. It was not as though the family had researched the breed of dog they wanted, had built an outdoor exercise pen in anticipation of its arrival, had talked with various breeders to find an animal that could handle a household of five children. It was simply that Dad's casual promise had suddenly taken physical shape in the form of this black-tan-and-white puppy. And the six pairs of eyes told him that he could bitterly disappoint his whole family or he could let them make a home for this instantly beloved animal.

"What could I do?" he asked the next day. His voice was tinged with exasperation, but mostly his tone was of resignation. Sooner or later, he was going to have to make good on his promise—why not sooner? The pet store made the purchase convenient; and the dog was a purebred—it came with papers and a stiff price tag—so it must be a first-rate animal. Besides, it was just a dog, nothing the kids . . . or Mom . . . or Dad . . . couldn't handle.

The dog has become an integral and significant member of the family of man. The average dog of today is perceived by millions of people as a companion and is treated as such—as a family member or friend worthy of equal and fair consideration. Deliberate cruelty toward a dog is now recognized as indicating emotional and psychological impairment, and to abuse or neglect a dog is a punishable offense. The social, moral and legal status of dogs has risen significantly as we ourselves have become more civilized. The dog, symbol of fidelity and devotion, has done much to awaken in us a sense of kinship with all living creatures. Certainly its place in the home today affirms the proclamation of St. Francis of Assisi that animals are our brothers and sisters.

But there is much to consider before bringing a dog into one's home, since many problems can arise if there is insufficient forethought and guidance. An estimated 4.3 million dogs are destroyed every year in municipal pounds across the U.S., indicating that something is amiss in the relationship between dogs and people. Further, over one million people receive dog bites every year, and purebred dogs suffer from over 170 inherited genetic defects. Many of these problems are preventable. A well-bred, properly raised and cared-for dog will be a healthy, trustworthy and fulfilling companion, and to this end the following details are given for the benefit of dogs and people alike.

Bringing a dog into your life, be it a puppy or an adult, is a responsibility. It is best to regard the new canine companion as an additional family member. Are you fully prepared to welcome someone into the family? Is your life compatible with keeping a dog? A dog is a highly social and dependent animal and won't do well if you're away at work all day and no one else is at home. Being left outdoors on a chain is no life for any creature. An outdoor enclosure with well-insulated kennel, plus plenty of human contact, is OK. But since dogs are "pack" animals, I am opposed to keeping one dog alone outdoors. Two dogs together—indoors or out—are usually happier and healthier than one alone. You cannot simply

allow a dog to roam; that is dangerous both to the animal and the community. Rural dogs roaming free often form packs and can cause havoc with local livestock and will also harass, injure and kill wildlife, especially deer.

Dogs not only need companionship, they also require regular exercise outdoors. Puppies and old dogs need to go out every 3 to 4 hours to evacuate, and a healthy adult dog should have a good 10-to-20 minute walk at least three times a day.

With these considerations in mind, the next step is to decide if your family is ready for a new puppy. The extra work may be more than you bargained for if you have a baby on the way or an infant under three years of age. If you have an older dog in the house, look out for jealousy and give your first dog extra attention.

You must also consider whether you want a purebred dog or a mixed breed, a male or a female. Gender is a matter of personal preference; I see no particular advantage in males or females. In either case, for many reasons, and particularly for health reasons, it's advisable to have the dog neutered at around 6 to 8 months of age. In females, neutering stops unwanted pregnancies and eliminates uterine disease and other diseases of the reproductive tract and ovaries and helps reduce the incidence of breast cancer. In males, neutering reduces the desire to roam, eliminates cancer of the testicle and reduces the likelihood of prostate disease and perianal hernia in old age.

When it comes to deciding upon a purebred dog or a mongrel, or mixed breed (the virtues of which will be elaborated shortly), there is, however, a lot to consider aside from price and pedigree. You need to think twice about keeping an activity-loving breed, like a husky, Afghan hound or Italian greyhound in a confined space. And a husky, with its thick coat, like a St. Bernard or Old English sheepdog, is not a sensible choice for hot and humid southern states. These are good dogs for colder climates. Most dogs are capable of handling the cold, but they will not adapt well to freezing temperatures if they are kept outdoors one night, then allowed indoors the next. Supplemental heat (a heat lamp or pad) is needed for kenneled outdoor dogs in very cold weather, especially if they are old. Old dogs feel the cold. And an Old English sheepdog or Afghan hound, like other long-haired individuals, isn't the right dog for anyone unprepared to groom the dog every day.

As should be evident from these remarks, the decision to buy a purebred dog is not one that should be made casually. The truth of that statement will become even more apparent a little later. First, though, let me tell you about the ideal country dog.

What is the best dog in the world? Most veterinarians and dog experts who don't have a bias for any particular breed will respond without hesitation: it's the mongrel.

If we were to take all the various breeds of dog and let them loose on an island with a plentiful supply of food and then were to come back 100 years later, we would probably have the best dog imaginable. It would probably resemble the so-called pariah dog, so common in the villages of Southeast Asia.

The pariah dog is a "super mutt," and the most natural dog around. It has never been to any extent subjected to artificial selective breeding to create local breeds with various unique traits, as happened in Europe where most purebred dogs originated. (In other regions too, dogs have been bred for specific purposes, such as for herding or guarding sheep, for draft work and hunting.)

The pariah dog, thanks to an absence of genetic interference by man, has been subjected to the most rigorous selection and survival pressures of nature, such that only the fittest survive. As a consequence, the average pariah dog is a highly intelligent, agile and well-proportioned animal, resistant to many endemic parasites and other diseases.

The pariah dogs of India are essentially a regional variety of what one might call the *natural* dog. This prototype dog of dogs is best regarded as an "all-breed." It is not simply a "mixed breed," with an ancestry of two or more pure breeds. The more the various pure breeds are crossed, the more the offspring come to resemble this prototypical dog. In every animal shelter, from Detroit to Delhi and from London to Rome, we can find dogs who are almost identical, yet they are not of any particular lineage. Often demeaned as "mongrels" and "bastard" dogs, they are regional replicas of the Asiatic pariah dogs. They are smart and adaptable, physically and mentally capable of living independent of man, but sufficiently domesticated to make life-long companions and loyal and affectionate members of a human family.

The natural dog possesses the following basic characteristics: medium build (35 to 55 pounds), a long, slightly upcurled tail, and long, straight legs. The head, body and limbs are beautifully proportioned and aligned, the ears erect or semi-erect, the muzzle of moderate length and the eyes oval or almond shaped.

The coat is short and may vary in color from black to white and piebald to brindle, the most common being basically light fawn or a darker reddish-brown. With proper care, these dogs enjoy a long lifetime well into their mid- and late teens and are virtually free of diseases of hereditary origin, which are so prevalent in pure breeds.

The Australian dingo is a somewhat larger type of pariah dog that has become feral (i.e., gone wild). The African basenji is one example of a local type of pariah dog that has been subjected to selective breeding to "fix" and exaggerate certain traits, such as the curled tail and wrinkled forehead.

After having spent time in Southwest India studying the village pariah dogs that live by their wits, scrounging food wherever they can, I became increasingly disturbed by the contrast between these superb animals and the relatively sickly and often deformed purebred dogs of the Western industrial world.

Dr. Wayne H. Riser, a veterinarian who has studied skeletal and other health problems that result from human interference with canine genetics, has emphasized that selective breeding to make dogs abnormally large or small results in disturbances in body metabolism and heat regulation. Toy breeds, like the poodle, because of their light body mass to surface area, are very susceptible to the cold and to hypoglycemia and tend toward hyperactivity. In contrast, giant breeds like the St. Bernard, with large body mass in proportion to the surface area of the body, tend toward hypoactivity, and especially in hot and humid weather, often pant continuously, have poor exercise tolerance and are susceptible to heatstroke.

My advice to anyone who is looking for a good dog and can't go to Southeast Asia to adopt one of the millions of homeless pariah dogs is to visit your local animal shelter. I will guarantee that there will be at least one natural dog waiting to be adopted into a good home. It's easy to choose a dog from the shelter, even if it is not a puppy of ideal age to be tested, because once fully developed, "what you see is what you have." You can quickly see how suitable the dog is for you by observing how it reacts to you and to other adults and children and by seeing how it behaves around other dogs. A good shelter should give you a few days "on approval"—after interviewing you to see if *you* are suitable for the dog.

If, despite the singular virtues of mutts, you are determined to have a purebred companion, you should proceed carefully. The best way to begin choosing the right breed for your family is to decide which overall canine type especially appeals to all of you. These types, or classes, are groups of breeds categorized by general characteristics and include: toys, terriers and hounds; working, sporting and herding breeds; and a class of miscellaneous breeds.

Lovable and cuddly miniature and toy breeds, like the poodle, Pomeranian and Chihuahua, are definitely indoor dogs, as are some of the smaller, feisty terriers. The biggest terrier is the Airedale and is a good, robust "country" dog.

The hounds, like the bloodhound and greyhound (you can adopt retired racing greyhounds), are very easygoing and great around children. Like the sporting breeds such as the various setters and pointers, they do well as either outdoor or indoor dogs. If kept indoors,

In choosing a purebred, make sure not only that the dog is right for your family, but also that your family can meet the dog's needs. Breeds like the Siberian husky, top, and the Rhodesian Ridgeback, bottom, require lots of exercise.

The Puppy Test

Knowing how to evaluate an animal's temperament can help you pick out the best puppy for you in a litter, since research has shown that by 6 to 10 weeks of age the animal's basic personality is already well formed.

These tests can be done on a puppy from 6 to 8 weeks of age onwards. In computing its rating, simply put down the appropriate score for each test and add them up. A very **high** score (above 70) means a strong-willed and outgoing animal, one that could be aggressive and difficult to control; a **low** score (below 40) means a shy, fearful animal that could become a fear-biter, be difficult to handle in unfamiliar surroundings and be hard to train later in life. A **mid to high** score (40-70) is probably the best, since such an animal would be outgoing, but at the same time cautious and not foolhardy.

A. When called, does the animal seek your attention (score **10**), approach you slowly and quietly greet you (**5**), or shy away (**2**)?

Keep track of your score as you continue with the other tests, noting down the appropriate number for the response that the animal gives to each.

B. If the puppy is with its littermates, does it push its way out first over its littermates to come to you (**10**), come up with one or two others to investigate you (**5**), or stay back and ignore you (**2**)?

C. When petted and/or picked up, does the puppy get overexcited (**10**), remain quiet and relaxed (**5**), or "freeze" fearfully, tremble or try to escape (**2**)?

D. When you quietly back away, does the puppy follow you immediately and solicit attention (**10**), pause and then follow you and solicit your attention less demonstratively (**5**), or go off and ignore you (**2**)?

E. Call the animal towards you and when it is beside you, clap your hands loudly twice over its head. Then call it to come to you. If it ignores the loud noise and continues to solicit your attention, score **10**; if it cowers or becomes passive but recovers quickly, score **5**; and if it freezes and will not approach even when you try to coax it, score **2**.

F. How does the animal respond to certain toys? Dogs are generally less playful as adults, so this test can give false measures with more inhibited or "cool" adults. Use three feet of string and a four-inch piece of towel or paper tied on the end. Drag it past the animal as though it were a mouse hopping by. Score **10** for an immediate response, **5** for one where the puppy paws tentatively or crouches and stalks first, and **2** for no response other than looking at the "prey" or simply ignoring it.

G. How does the animal respond when it is in an unfamiliar place, say, outside of its kennel or home, in a park or quiet yard. Does it run around wildly exploring things and not calm down quickly **10**, does it explore actively but with some caution **5**, or does it freeze, cower or attempt to hide somewhere **2**?

H. Since the above temperament tests involve the presence of a person, which could introduce a bias and lead to incorrect inferences, other tests without a person being present are essential. So repeat **G**, concealing yourself behind a blind or suitable screen. Next throw some large and unusual object near the animal, such as a ball of paper or cardboard box about the same size as the animal. This way you can test its reactions to surprising and novel stimuli.

I. Other set-ups include pulling a string that suddenly pops up a cardboard shape in front of the animal, or approaching the animal and opening up a large umbrella. Score **10** for an unhesitating approach, **5** for cautious approach or withdrawal then investigation, and **2** for flight with no investigation.

J. Also observe how the puppy reacts in your apparent absence to others that it lives with or its littermates. Score **10** if it is always number one when playing with others or in getting food, **5** if it is intermediate, and **2** if it is obviously the lowest one on the totem pole.

K. Since my research has shown a relationship between heart rate and temperament in pups, you may wish to try to detect a puppy's heart rate with a stethoscope. Pups with the highest resting heart rates in the litter tend to be the most assertive and outgoing, while those with the lowest rates are the most timid. Simply hold the animal in your lap and when it is quiet and not struggling, record its heartbeat for 15 seconds; multiply times four to find the rate per minute. Outgoing pups have rates of 200-240 beats/minute, while others in the same litter having rates as low as 160-180 beats/minute will, as adults, most likely be shy and easily scared by sudden or unfamiliar stimuli.

though, members of these vigorous breeds need to be given plenty of exercise and should have access to an enclosed yard for extended periods of activity. Members of the working breeds, like border collie and husky, also need ample opportunity to run around; it is a cruelty to have a dog bred for action and to stifle it indoors.

In the nonsporting class of miscellaneous breeds, we find a full spectrum of various sizes and temperaments, which would fill a book to detail.

If you are smitten by any particular breed, read up all you can about it first. And remember, many working, herding and sporting breeds like the German shepherd, collie, Irish setter and springer spaniel actually occur in two forms: a vigorous, robust type that is a carbon-copy physically and mentally of the original breed, and a more refined "show" type. Those bred for show are often, but not invariably, less robust, physically inferior and lacking the mental attributes of the original breed. Bird dogs selectively bred for show, for example, rarely do well in field trials, while a chunky, top-rank field-trial setter or slender retriever might be scorned in the show ring.

In my experience, if you want a purebred, it is essential to find a local breeder so you can visit and see one or both parents of the puppy you're thinking of buying. Since temperament is part heritable, you should think twice about having a puppy from parent dogs who are overly fearful, aggressive, lethargic and spiritless or uncontrollably hyperactive.

Never buy a purebred pup in a pet store. Resist the impulse no matter how appealing the "puppy in the window" is to you and your family. The pet store could have obtained the pup from a local breeder, but more likely, the animal came from a "puppy mill" – a commercial breeding farm of which there are hundreds, many located in the Midwest. Many of these dog factories have been investigated by the Humane Society of the United States, and often the sanitation, general care and quality of breeding stock have been atrocious. Since there are lots of good pups and adult dogs (for a fraction of the cost, too) awaiting adoption at your local shelters, please do not compound the problem of canine neglect by supporting callous operations.

There are several simple tests that can be conducted to help you choose the right puppy for you. One of these, the temperament and sociability test, is especially useful in helping to pick the most sociable and emotionally stable pup in the litter. This test should be conducted at around 6 to 8 weeks of age, which is also the best time to adopt a puppy. The test (see box on opposite page) will help you identify those pups that might be problem animals later in life. Unless you are an experienced handler, you may neither want one that is too outgoing and strong-willed, nor one that is very shy and that could be a poor learner and become a fear-biter.

One reason for going to a local breeder to choose a purebred and pedigreed dog is that if your pup develops a health problem – particularly a hereditary one – you can get back to the breeder for advice and possibly compensation. All reputable breeders should be able to give a clean bill of health to every puppy sold, but because of the multitude of genetic defects, few can offer long-term guarantees. Before buying a purebred dog, therefore, you should learn what the common genetic problems of the breed are and then ask if either of your prospective puppy's parents are afflicted. With large breeds, for example, hip dysplasia, a crippling genetic abnormality of the hip joints, is often a problem. Careful breeders will have the hips of prospective breeding animals X-rayed to make sure their hips are sound. If a breeder cannot assure you that the Orthopedic Foundation for Animals (OFA) has read as normal X-rays of the parents' hips, then you should avoid buying from that breeder. If the breeder is unaware of the OFA, that is a sure sign he or she is inexperienced and amateurish.

Conscientious breeders will also want to know if any defects show up, and one sign of a good dog breeder is that person's reluctance to let just anyone have a puppy: so be prepared for cross-examination to determine if you will be a responsible owner!

The 10 most popular breeds today, according to the American Kennel Club registry (in rank-order of numbers registered) are as follows: Cocker Spaniel, Labrador Retriever, Poodle, Golden Retriever, German Shepherd, Rottweiler, Chow Chow, Dachshund, Beagle, and Miniature Schnauzer. Remember, the more popular the breed (reflected by the numbers of each breed registered by the AKC) the greater is the incidence of genetic defects. This is due to excessive inbreeding and also to what I term "overbreeding," which means the production of lots of purebred pups without any careful selection or quality control both of parents and offspring.

Most of these breeds are afflicted by a variety of heritable diseases (which aren't usually apparent when dogs are young). The cocker spaniel, for one, has many genetically linked problems, including susceptibility to skin

even find them appealing. There are many health problems associated with these genetic deformations. So-called achondroplastic dwarfism in basset hounds results in lameness and arthritis. The brachycephalic pushed-in face of bulldogs and Pekingese can lead to breathing difficulties and increased susceptibility to heatstroke. And the giantism, or acromegaly, of breeds like the Great Dane and St. Bernard is linked with skeletal growth problems and bone cancer. Breeding for large heads and narrow hips, as in the bulldog, often necessitates cesarean deliveries. And breeding for facial skin folds in Shar-peis and other breeds can mean skin infections and turned-in eyelids (entropion), which can lead to blindness if not corrected surgically.

Even seemingly minor changes in body size can have a profound effect on a dog's overall health and well-being. Such changes, often compounded by other changes, such as the length of the back, legs and head, and the depth of the chest, can result in a variety of health problems in purebred dogs, and thus an increased probable risk of suffering sometime during the animals' lives.

Because of these conditions, you should think twice about buying any purebred dog, even from a reputable breeder. A reputable breeder, in my mind, is one who avoids inbreeding and overbreeding and has a progeny-testing program. This involves careful record keeping of how all the pups mature, so as to check for genetic defects that their parents might be passing on. Some reputable breeders also insist that any pups sold as "pet" rather than "show" quality be neutered, which is a good idea since many owners of not-so-sound purebred dogs go ahead and breed them when they mature. American Kennel Club registration "papers" are no guarantee of a sound animal. In reality, papers mean that a pup is more likely to have a disease of hereditary origin than would an all-American, "Heinz-57" mixed-breed dog.

The combination of domesticating dogs and of raising them in relatively unstimulating environments has, over generations, resulted in a reduction in the size of our pets' brains – and a reduction in their intelligence. The brain of a wolf is, on average, one-sixth larger than the brain of a wolf-sized dog.

While man has not, perhaps, deliberately attempted to lower canine intelligence while domesticating dogs, in selecting for more docile and easygoing animals, he has to a degree sacrificed canine alertness and curiosity. By breeding out or reducing "wild" traits, man has made domestic animals easier to handle and

Selective breeding produces traits like the broad heads of the bulldogs, top, *the large size of St. Bernards,* lower left, *and the excessively wrinkled skin of the Chinese Shar-Pei,* lower right, *that can lead to a variety of health problems.*

disease, ear infections, retinal dysplasia, glaucoma, cataracts, fear-biting, "cocker hysteria," hemophilia, tail-lessness, skull fissures, intervertebral disk degeneration, over- and undershot jaw, elbow dysplasia, congenital heart disease, cleft lip and palate, hydrocephalus, inguinal and umbilical hernias, skin neoplasms, malignant melanoma, oral fibrosarcoma and kidney disease.

There are many other diseases of cocker spaniels and other purebreds that may also be hereditary, and the list increases every year as careful study of breeding records and test-matings reveal their mode of inheritance.

Many purebred dogs are so deformed and dependent upon human care and veterinary attention that I see them as bonsai wolves: like crippled trees, often dwarfed and deformed so delicately that we

TOP & BOTTOM RIGHT: REYNOLDS PHOTOGRAPHY. BOTTOM LEFT: KENT & DONNA DANNEN

control, but those companionable creatures are not going to explore their environments with the intensity and thoroughness of their wild counterparts, and consequently, they will acquire less knowledge. Many domestic dogs learn little except when instructed or trained.

A second reason many pets have low IQs is that they are raised in a relatively bland, understimulating and monotonously predictable environment. Life in a small backyard can be so experientially depriving that the animal's potential is never fully developed.

Basic obedience training and field trials and also skilled performance trials (such as tracking, scenting and retrieving certain objects) play an important part in preserving and enhancing the intelligence and potential of purebred dogs. It is a pity that such competitions are not open to "mongrel" dogs, to encourage their owners to enjoy training and working with their animals. The elitist purebred dog show, where dogs are judged on their looks alone, is for people and not for dogs.

People who genuinely care for dogs will not find these views offensive. Those who do take offense have a different sensibility, one that is not offended by the sight of a sickly bulldog or fragile "toy" poodle. My sensibilities are offended, and it is not for want of loving these creatures, as many might conclude. I firmly believe that their propagation should be questioned and that firm steps should be taken to eliminate extreme deformities by phasing them out, simply by neutering afflicted dogs. "Love them but don't breed them" is my heartfelt conclusion.

Through selective breeding, the structure and overall health of all purebreds can be improved. Many show points of conformation (such as narrow and long or blunt muzzles, deep chests, and long or short backs or legs) need to be revised. Breeders should, through their breed clubs and associations, work closely with veterinary and medical genetic consultants to restore the natural beauty and vitality of the dog within a framework that preserves the diversity of various breeds without jeopardizing the fundamental soundness of any individual animal. 🌸

SOURCES

The Humane Society of the United States
2100 L Street N.W.
Washington, D.C. 20037

The American Kennel Club
51 Madison Avenue
New York, New York 10010

The Complete Dog Book: Official Publication of the American Kennel Club (Howell Book House Inc., New York, 1986).
Full descriptions of all AKC recognized breeds, with brief discussions of canine health, diseases and training.

How to Be Your Dog's Best Friend: A Training Manual for Dog Owners, Monks of New Skete (Little Brown and Co., Boston, 1978).
Sensible humane guide to the training and disciplining of puppies and dogs, including advice on how to deal with common behavioral problems.

How to Raise a Puppy You Can Live With, Clarice Rutherford and David H. Neil (Alpine Publications, P.O. Box 7027, Loveland, CO 80537, 1990).
Excellent puppy-training guide. Includes important discussion of dog's development during first 3 months of life.

Many hardy breeds come in two forms. Take the English setter, for example: those selectively bred for show often perform poorly in rigorous field trials where the original robust type excels.

The Hen-Pecked Homesteader

How to Enjoy the Company of a Small Poultry Flock

By Jake Chapline

My approach to poultry management is to make life comfortable and convenient for the chickens and myself, even if that means sacrificing some efficiency. My hen house is larger and (usually) cleaner than it has to be because I like it to look and smell nice. The chickens wander freely about the yard, which means they don't gain weight as quickly as they would if they were confined. I don't automatically cull hens that are taking a break between laying cycles, so I'm often feeding a few unproductive birds. Although I don't keep a close record of my expenses for feed and litter, my rough calculations suggest that I'm not quite breaking even. It would probably be cheaper for me to give up my flock and buy eggs and plastic-wrapped chicken at the supermarket.

It was exactly 10 years ago that I brought home my first flock of chickens — a half-dozen Brown Leghorn pullets and one cockerel purchased from a neighbor. The pullets were for eggs, of course; the cockerel was for entertainment. That flock set the pattern that my poultry enterprise has followed ever since: six parts practicality to one part whimsy.

There was a time when I thought my chickens should at least earn their keep. I read a lot of magazine articles and Cooperative Extension Service bulletins that explained how to increase the efficiency of my flock, operate more economically and maximize meat and egg production. Those publications made it clear that I was giving my chickens too much slack. I got the impression that if I didn't crack down and cull a few lackadaisical hens to set an example for the others, I would undoubtedly bankrupt myself and probably undermine the very foundations of American agriculture.

Eventually it occurred to me that the poultry management techniques recommended by the experts were designed for small commercial poultry farms, and they all went bankrupt 30 years ago. The fact is, almost anything I might do to increase the efficiency of my flock would make life more difficult for the chickens without making much difference to the household economy. When you work it all out, maximizing the productivity of a dozen or so hens doesn't amount to much. So I've abandoned any pretense of being an efficient poultry manager; I'm just a guy who enjoys the company of happy chickens and gives away a lot of eggs to his neighbors.

One of E.B. White's basic rules for keeping chickens was, "Don't try to convey your enthusiasm for chickens to anyone else." He didn't follow that advice, and I don't either. Admittedly, my proselytizing often falls on deaf ears. For example, I have a friend who loves fresh eggs and is always delighted when I have a dozen to spare. Since he lives in the country and has plenty of room, I once suggested that he should keep a flock of his own – an idea he immediately rejected. "I can't be bothered to feed anything dumber than a turnip," he said.

I'll admit that chickens are not bright, but they are companionable and entertaining, and many varieties are beautiful. (My wife regards our free-ranging New Hampshires as living lawn ornaments.) For those who find satisfaction in producing healthful food in their own yards, keeping a flock of chickens is a logical extension of gardening. They are certainly the easiest livestock to take care of, and if you find that chickens don't suit you, it's easy to close up shop. Just invite some friends over for a barbecue, and convert the hen coop into a toolshed.

Getting Started

If you would like to start a backyard flock, there are a few things you should know before going out to buy some chickens. First, let's get the terminology straight. A baby chicken of either sex is a chick. An immature female chicken is a pullet; she turns into a hen when she is a year old. An immature male chicken is a cockerel, and he turns into a cock, or in America, a rooster.

Chickens come in two sizes – bantam and large – and an incredible array of shapes, colors and plumage patterns. Bantams are about a quarter of the weight of large chickens, but some are good layers and their eggs are surprisingly large. The American Poultry Association recognizes 176 distinct varieties of large chickens and more than 200 bantam varieties. In addition, many types of hybrid or cross-bred chickens have been developed for rapid weight gain or exceptional efficiency as egg producers.

More than 95 percent of the chickens in America are hybrids. White Plymouth Rocks and White Leghorns – the two pure breeds most important to the egg and poultry industries – account for less than 3 percent. All other breeds combined make up only 1 to 3 percent of the total chicken population.

Large chickens are often divided into three categories: light, dual-purpose and heavy. The light breeds, like the Leghorns, are generally the best layers, but they are too small to be good meat birds. The dual-purpose birds include many old-fashioned American breeds, like Rhode Island Reds, New Hampshires, Plymouth Rocks and Wyandottes. They are reliable layers of large brown eggs, and they make good broilers and fryers. The heavy breeds, like Jersey Giants, Brahmas and Cochins, grow slowly and are poor layers, but they make wonderful roasting chickens, reaching weights of 10 pounds or more.

Now it's time to make your first crucial decision as a poultry manager. What kind or kinds of chickens do you want? There's no reason why you should be influenced by my biases, but I'll share them anyway. Personally, I wouldn't buy hybrid chickens, even though I know that some of the modern hybrid varieties are excellent for small flocks. Too many fine old breeds have become so rare that they are in danger of disappearing, and if small-flock owners don't preserve them, nobody will. So I recommend that you decide what you want from your flock – eggs, meat, or both – and select a traditional breed that suits your purpose and appeals to your eye.

Next you have to decide how many chickens to buy. A good dual-purpose hen should average four eggs a week, so a flock of ten or a dozen will produce more eggs than most families can use. Even if you plan to raise some chickens for meat, you should keep the enterprise small until you've gained some experience.

Most people start their first flock by ordering a batch of day-old chicks from a feed store in the spring. Usually you place an order for chicks about April 1 and pick them up when the shipment from the hatchery arrives in May. You can order straight-run (unsexed) chicks, which means they'll be more or less evenly divided between pullets and cockerels, or you can specify a certain number of either or both sexes.

Feed stores offer a convenient way to get your stock, but most don't provide much of a selection. They usually have hybrid broiler chicks, hybrid or White Leghorn layers, and possibly one or two of the more popular dual-purpose breeds. If you'd like to get a breed that the store isn't offering, ask the manager if he can put in a special order for you. Many commercial hatcheries carry a number of purebred varieties, and the hatchery that supplies your feed store might have the breed you want. The feed store I deal with has been cooperative in this regard.

An alternative is to order the birds you want directly from the hatchery. The chicks will be shipped to your post office on a prearranged date. They'll arrive peeping at full volume, and you'll get a call from a harried clerk asking you to pick them up as soon as possible, *please.* The hatchery should guarantee the safe arrival of the chicks, and you should open the carton at the post office to verify that they are in good condition.

Most hatcheries require a minimum order of 25 chicks, because a smaller group might not be able to keep warm in the shipping box. Some hatcheries insist that you buy at least 25 of the same breed, while others let you specify the combination of breeds you want, as long as the order totals at least 25 chicks. This may be more chicks than you want, but perhaps you can share an order with a neighbor.

You might well wonder how anything as tiny and delicate as a newly hatched chick can survive two days in a shipping crate without food or water. Here's the secret: just before it hatches, a chick absorbs the yolk of its egg, which provides all of the nourishment it needs for the first two or three days of its life. Nature provided this mechanism for the convenience of the chicken, not the hatchery. The incubation period for a chicken egg is not precise; it's 21 days plus or minus one day. So, suppose a hen is incubating a dozen eggs. The first chicks may hatch on day 20, but the hen can't get up and show them where breakfast is until the last chicks hatch, which could be two days later. So every chick starts life with emergency rations, just in case of an early arrival.

Food & Shelter

While you are waiting for your chicks to arrive, you can prepare some accommodations for them. For the first few weeks, they will probably live in your house, because it's essential that they be kept warm and away from drafts. The traditional chicken nursery, or brooder, is a large cardboard box with a heat lamp suspended inside. Cover the bottom of the box with a layer of newspapers or paper towels and a couple of inches of litter, like wood shavings or straw. Replace the litter frequently; the brooder should always be clean and dry.

The temperature under the heat lamp should be 90 degrees for the first 10 days. After that, gradually raise the lamp to reduce the temperature by about 5 degrees each week. If the chicks get cold, they will start to pile up under the lamp. If they are too warm, they will crowd to the edges of the box. As long as they move freely around the box, eating and drinking and exploring, they're comfortable.

Don't keep hybrid broiler chicks in a brooder with smaller chicks. Broiler chicks, usually produced by crossing a Cornish rooster and a White Rock hen, have the appetite and personality of a *Tyrannosaurus rex.* Chick suppliers call them a miracle of genetic science, but I call them chickens from hell. In high-production poultry factories, these chicks are kept closely confined, given appetite stimulants, and raised to market weight in only eight weeks. By that time, their weight has gotten so far ahead of their bone and muscle development that they may not be able to stand. In a home flock, they will quickly tower over other chicks their age, which are likely to get trampled and possibly eaten. The broilers will have to be kept in separate quarters throughout their brief lives.

Chicks must have access to fresh feed and clean water at all times. Your feed store will have inexpensive plastic or metal chick waterers that screw onto canning jars. These are excellent because the chicks can't fall into the water or spill it. You should also pick up a small chick feeder, which is designed to prevent the chicks from scattering feed all over their box. Give them a medicated, high-protein starter mash for the first six to eight weeks, then gradually shift over to an unmedicated grower feed. The medication in the starter mash protects the chicks from coccidiosis, a deadly disease to which they are particularly susceptible. They will build up a natural resistance to the disease if you get them off the medicated feed between 8 and 12 weeks of age. To accomplish a gradual transition, mix the starter and grower feeds together, increasing the proportion of grower feed over a period of a week or two.

Chickens that don't have access to the outdoors should have some fine gravel or grit included in their diet. The grit collects in their gizzards, where it grinds up grain so they can digest it. Even tiny chicks benefit from a little fine grit or coarse sand scattered on top of their feed.

By the time the chicks are a few weeks old, you can begin putting them outside in a portable coop on warm sunny days. Make certain they have food, water and some shade, and move the coop every day so they have a clean area to scratch up and explore. When they are pretty well feathered out, at the age of about six weeks, you can move them out to their permanent quarters, if the nights are warm enough. They might appreciate a heat lamp in a corner of their house for the first few nights.

The chicken house doesn't have to be elaborate. It could be just a corner of a barn or garage. It should be well ventilated, free of drafts and dry. There should be windows to let the sun shine in and a floor of wood or concrete; you can't keep a dirt floor clean, and it is likely to be too damp. Allow at least three square feet of floor space for each bird, and more if they are going to be confined in the chicken house all the time. In northern areas, chicken houses should be insulated, both for the comfort of the chickens and because extreme cold cuts egg production drastically. (For more information about chicken house design, see page 244.)

Essential chicken house furnishings include a feeder and waterer (the small ones you used for the chicks won't be adequate for larger birds) and roosts and nest boxes for laying hens (meat birds don't require either). The floor should be covered with wood shavings or some other absorbent litter. If the chickens will be confined indoors for more than a few days at a time, they should have a box full of fine dirt inside so they can take dust baths, which help to keep them clean and free of parasites.

Even if you plan to let the chickens run free most of the time, there will be days when you don't want to turn them loose. Therefore, every chicken coop should have an outside run. A run for large chickens should be enclosed by a chicken-wire fence six feet high. If you keep bantams, which are good fliers, you might need to cover the run with a top of chicken wire or netting.

A few chickens can convert a small run into a desert in no time at all. They'll find the area more interesting if you keep the bare ground covered with straw, grass clippings, leaves and other litter. My free-ranging chickens like to gather around the compost pile every afternoon for gossip and a snack. If I had to keep

Traditional dual-purpose chickens like this Silver Laced Wyandotte hen are reliable layers and good meat birds.

them confined, I'd put the compost pile in their run.

Most small-flock owners like the idea of free-ranging chickens, but in many locations it just doesn't make sense. I can let my chickens run loose because I live on an unmaintained and virtually untraveled road, with the nearest neighbor more than a half-mile away. Even so, the chickens cause some problems. They love to get in the garden, scratch up seedlings and compete to see who can excavate the largest hole before I notice what's going on. They hold community meetings in the equipment shed, leaving droppings and dust all over the tractor and other machinery. And I lose a few every year to a fox or coyote or goshawk. I've often considered confining them, but I haven't the heart to do it. They enjoy being out; I enjoy watching them go about their affairs with relatively little interference from me; and the fox enjoys giving her pups an occasional chicken dinner.

Tending the Flock

After your chickens are established in their coop, taking care of them will require only 15 or 20 minutes each day, with an extra half hour every few weeks for housecleaning. Never let the chickens run out of feed and

The backyard rooster is a mobile home-entertainment center. Crowing may be inspired by daybreak or anything else.

clean water. Check the supply at least twice a day, when you let the birds out in the morning and when you close them up at night. Feed goes through a chicken's digestive system in only two and a half hours, and it takes a lot of it to grow a chicken and make eggs, so they are hungry most of the time. If you supplement their regular rations with table scraps, greens (especially kale and comfrey) and gone-by vegetables and fruit, they'll be ecstatic. They also love scratch, an inexpensive mixture of grains that chickens consume like candy.

Given sufficient room to roam, chickens can do a good job of feeding themselves for much of the year. But providing them with the appropriate commercial ration is the easiest way to make certain that they are getting a balanced diet. A commercial mix is likely to include corn, soybean meal, alfalfa meal, bone meal, fish meal, salt and a long list of vitamins and minerals. Feed should always be stored in a cool place in rodent-proof containers (it can cost you as much to feed a rat as a chicken). Don't put out more feed than the chickens will eat in a few days, particularly in warm weather, or it could begin to spoil in the feeder.

Each time you tend the flock or gather eggs, take a few minutes to observe the chickens. If they are allowed to wander at will, do a quick head count and be alert for any changes in their mood or behavior. If a hen ever seems listless or uncomfortable, take the time to examine her, and if you suspect she might be sick, immediately isolate her from the rest of the flock. Disease is seldom a problem in a small flock that is well cared for. The most

common causes of health problems are overcrowding, inadequate attention to cleanliness, or a chicken house that is too damp or drafty.

Introducing new birds into the flock can also be a health risk. Buy chicks only from hatcheries that are participants in the National Poultry Improvement Plan; they are required to test their breeding stock for certain diseases. If you ever buy any adult birds, make sure that they come from a reliable source and quarantine them for at least a week or two before you let them join your flock.

Sometimes chickens might gang up on a particular bird and peck her to death. The target may be a hen who has suffered a cut or some other injury, or she may just be at the bottom of the pecking order. I've never had this problem in my own flock, and it is less likely to occur if the chickens have plenty of room. It is important, however, to remove any injured birds and keep them away from the rest of the flock until they have recovered fully. If you notice a hen who consistently goes after other members of the flock and pursues them when they try to get out of her way, fricassee her.

Meat & Eggs

If you are raising meat chickens, they will be ready to slaughter as broiler-fryers when they are 12 to 16 weeks old. Four pounds is considered the ideal slaughter weight for a broiler-fryer, eight pounds for a roaster. The younger the birds are, the more tender they'll be. Butchering chickens is not a complicated process, and most books on the subject of raising poultry provide step-by-step instructions.

Nobody who likes chickens can feel comfortable about killing them, but even if you raise only laying hens, you'll eventually find yourself at the chopping block with a chicken in one hand and an ax in the other. It's either that or run a retirement home for old hens; they won't lay many eggs after they are four years old, and they may live to be eight or older. Personally, I'd rather eat a chicken that I raised and killed with care and consideration than one that spent its brief and miserable life crammed into a tiny cage in an automated chicken factory.

Raising broilers is just a summertime project, but a laying flock is a year-round enterprise. Pullets that are hatched early in the spring start laying eggs in the fall when they are five or six months old, depending on the breed. When the first eggs appear, start switching the flock over to a layer ration, which contains the extra vitamin A and calcium that hens need to produce eggs. They will lay eggs without ever making the acquaint-

H. REINHARD/OKAPIA/PHOTO RESEARCHERS, INC.

ance of a rooster, but of course a rooster is necessary if the eggs are to be fertile. Fertile and unfertile eggs look and taste the same when they are fresh. Some poultry books say that unfertile eggs will keep better, but others say the opposite. I can't resolve the dispute; I've never kept eggs around long enough to find out.

If you appreciate pageantry, have a good sense of humor and don't mind sudden loud noises in the middle of the night, you have to have a rooster. They are more ornamental than hens, and if your flock is free-ranging, a rooster helps to keep the hens close to home. He also provides some protection against predators. A cat will think twice about stalking a chick if a rooster is on patrol. I've seen a rooster charge across the yard to slam full tilt into a fox that was pursuing a hen. He rescued the hen, I rescued him, and the fox went off in a huff. (I think the rooster still reminds the hens of that episode, without mentioning me.)

You'll notice that I'm talking about a single rooster. In a flock of a dozen hens, one rooster will fertilize as many eggs as twelve roosters would, with a lot less wear and tear on the hens. If you have a larger flock, you might assign the chief rooster a deputy, but keeping the ratio at ten or twelve to one will cut down on the number and intensity of barnyard showdowns.

Once the pullets get started, they'll keep laying for a year, although production may slow down during the coldest, darkest part of the winter. During their second autumn, when they are about 18 months old, they will stop laying and molt. Commercial egg producers sell the entire flock for soup or pet food at this point and start over with a new batch of pullets, but the keeper of a small flock can afford to give the hens a vacation. For a few weeks, they'll look pretty scruffy as their feathers fall out and new ones grow in. Some hens start laying again in just six to eight weeks; others might take most of the winter off. During the second laying cycle, the hens will lay larger eggs, but not quite as many of them.

Eggs should be gathered at least twice a day, and more often if the weather is particularly hot or below freezing. Keep plenty of fresh litter in the nest boxes and the eggs will stay cleaner and will be less likely to get broken. Hens like to eat broken eggs, and if circumstances encourage them, they can get into the habit of breaking their own.

Don't wash the eggs unless it's really necessary. They have a natural coating that retards spoilage, but it is removed by washing. If an egg is a little bit soiled, try to brush the dirt off or clean the egg with a damp cloth. An unwashed egg that is promptly cooled and stored at temperatures below 55 degrees will keep for several weeks at least. I always write the date on eggs when I gather them. That prevents confusion, and when I give some away, the recipients are delighted to see that the eggs are only a day or two old.

You can judge the freshness of an egg by how much it spreads when it's cracked into a bowl or pan. A fresh egg remains compact, with the yolk sitting up high. Incidentally, if you want hard-boiled eggs, use some that are at least a few days old. It's almost impossible to peel a farm-fresh egg without removing most of the white with the shell.

Broody Birds

Occasionally, a hen will take a notion to quit work and raise a family. She might hide a clutch of eggs in some out-of-the-way place, or she might just take over a nest box and defy anyone to remove eggs from it. Such a hen is said to be broody or setting. Left alone to follow her instincts, she'll set on those eggs (fertile or not) for three weeks, come hell or high water. A broody hen is easy to recognize by her plumped-out plumage, self-important air and aggressive defense of the nest. Commercial hatcheries have deliberately bred broodiness out of some breeds and crosses, while other breeds, particularly among the bantams, seem naturally inclined toward motherhood. Hatchery catalogues often specify which breeds will or won't set.

Many flock owners consider a reliable broody hen as an asset. Since she'll hatch someone else's eggs as readily as her own, she can serve as the flock's official incubator. If you want to let a hen set but you don't think her nest is in a safe place, you can gently relocate her at night. Other than that, all you have to do is keep feed and water close at hand and disturb her as little as possible. When the chicks arrive, you can leave them in the hen's care or move them to a brooder. Their survival rate will probably be better if you take charge at that point.

Sometimes when a hen turns broody, you will want her to snap out of it. There are a number of old-fashioned techniques for "breaking up" a broody bird, most of them apparently invented by the Inquisition. They include pouring water on her, passing a feather through her nostrils, and hanging her up in a burlap bag for a day. I haven't tried any of these procedures. A more reasonable prescription is to move the hen to a small pen in a separate shed, give her plenty of feed and

The Classic Coop

COMFORTABLE QUARTERS FOR THE FAMILY FLOCK

A good chicken house is safe and comfortable for the chickens, easy to take care of, and attractive enough to be an improvement – or at least not a disgrace – to your yard. It should be snug enough to keep the chickens warm in a winter gale, but well ventilated and well lighted. And it should be strong enough to withstand a determined assault by a large dog.

For convenience, the building should include space for storing feed and fresh litter. I designed my chicken house with a high peaked roof to provide space for a partial loft, where I keep bales of wood shavings or straw. It's also a good idea to partition the space inside so you have an entrance area that is not accessible to the tenants. Otherwise, they'll all rush out to seek their fortunes in the wide world as soon as you open the door. There should be a board at the bottom of the partition to keep the litter from spilling out. For the same reason, the door into the chickens' quarters should have a sill about 6 inches high.

Laying hens need nest boxes, and they prefer them to be relatively dark and elevated about 2 feet off the floor. Each box should be about 14 inches square and open in the front, except for a 1x3 sill. Provide one box for every four birds.

Roosts should be located along the most sheltered wall of the building, out of drafts and about 2 feet off the floor. Never let the birds roost near a window that is covered only

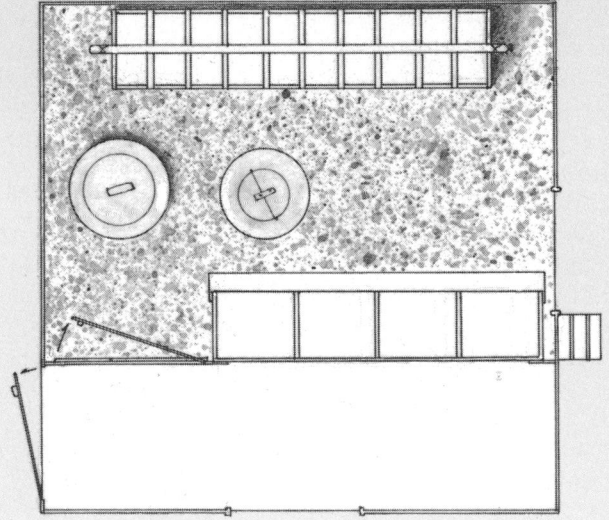

An uncluttered floor plan makes it easy to maintain the chicken coop.

by chicken wire; raccoons are quite capable of reaching in through the wire and grabbing a sleeping hen. A hardwood sapling about 2 inches in diameter makes a perfect roost. Allow about 10 inches of roost space for each chicken, and if more than one roost, at least 18 inches between them.

Manure tends to pile up under the roosts, so you may want to install a manure box with 2x6 sides and a hardware-cloth top. This prevents the chickens from walking in their droppings and scattering them around the rest of the coop. The manure box should be removable for easy cleaning.

Feeders may be of either the tube or trough type. I've used both, and I prefer a hanging tube feeder because the chickens spill less feed. Water should be provided in a container that can't be spilled, stepped in or roosted on, like the cone-top waterers you can buy at feed stores. Freezing is a problem in the winter. I keep a backup waterer on hand so I can replace the one in the chicken house whenever it starts to freeze. The waterer should sit on top of a small platform just high enough to keep litter out of the bowl.

The outside run should be just as large as you can reasonably make it, surrounded by a 6-foot chicken-wire fence that is tight enough to keep the chickens in and strong enough to keep predators out. It should have a little door into the coop for the chickens and a full-sized gate into the yard for you. Make sure that the door into the coop is closed at night; the fence around the run is no obstacle to weasels, and it won't deter raccoons or foxes if they have all night to think of a way to get inside.

–J.C.

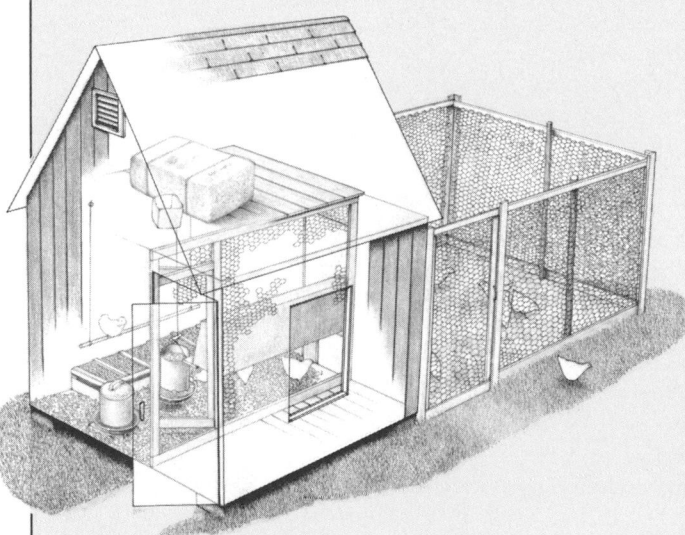

This illustration shows the layout of a well-designed chicken house; it is not intended to provide construction details. Basic plans for a variety of chicken houses and other outbuildings can be obtained from any Cooperative Extension Service office.

ILLUSTRATIONS BY RAY MAHER

water but no materials to use for a nest and hope for the best. Usually the hen will have a change of heart within a few days.

Since the productive life of a chicken — either a rooster or a hen — is about three years, you should plan to introduce some young birds into the flock every year or so, either by buying more chicks or by letting the hens hatch their own replacements. Colored leg bands, available from poultry supply companies, can be used to distinguish different generations at a glance.

By the time a hen is past her prime as a layer, she is too old and tough for roasting, but she can still contribute to a soup or stew. The best time to identify and cull nonlayers is during the peak laying season in the spring; that way, you won't accidentally condemn an unfortunate hen who is just going into or out of a molt. When a hen is in good laying condition, her comb and wattles are large and red, her vent (where the eggs come out) is dilated and moist, and her pubic bones are flexible and at least three or four inches apart. Of course, one way to be sure whether a hen is laying is to put her in a separate pen for a week or so.

Once you have established a backyard flock, it will become an entertaining part of your daily life. You'll soon understand why chickens became leading characters in so many old folktales and fables. They have a flair for the dramatic, and the minor triumphs, intrigues, feuds and tragedies that unfold in the chicken yard every day could provide inspiration for a dozen different soap operas. They were never meant to spend their lives standing shoulder to shoulder in little cages. They deserve a larger stage, an expanse the size of your backyard. ❧

SOURCES

Mail-Order Chicks

Cackle Hatchery
P.O. Box 529
Lebanon, Missouri 65536

Grain Belt Hatchery
P.O. Box 125
Windsor, Missouri 65360

Ideal Poultry Breeding Farms, Inc.
P.O. Box 591
Cameron, Texas 76520

All of the hatcheries listed above have good selections of traditional chicken varieties. All provide free catalogues or price lists.

Murray McMurray Hatchery, Inc.
Webster City, Iowa 50595
This 72-year-old hatchery publishes one of the nicest poultry catalogues, with color pictures of each available breed. It includes a number of rare and unusual breeds, as well as poultry books, equipment and supplies. Catalogue free.

Stromberg's
Box 400
Pine River, Minnesota 56474
In addition to chicks, Stromberg's sells adult chickens for exhibition at $50 a pair and up. This is a good source of equipment. Catalogue free.

Information About Traditional Breeds

American Minor Breeds Conservancy
Box 477
Pittsboro, North Carolina 27312
The AMBC recently conducted a survey of hatcheries to locate sources for 17 minor breeds of poultry. The results of the survey have been published in a booklet which can be purchased for $4. If you are looking for a breed or variety that was not included in the census, the AMBC may still be able to help you locate a source.

Equipment & Supplies

Sidney Shoemaker
P.O. Box 331
Mount Gilead, Ohio 43338

Nasco
901 Janesville Avenue
Fort Atkinson, Wisconsin 53538

Animal Pharmacy

THE BASIC MEDICINE CHEST FOR LIVESTOCK AND PETS

BY MICHAEL WEBSTER

It is the sleepy Sunday morning of a long weekend and chore time is comfortably late when you notice something wrong — a cow has the first blinking, watery symptoms of pinkeye, or the ear of a young pig looks scabby with ear mites, or the dog appears listless and has no appetite. What to do? Neither the feed store nor the pet-supply outlets will be open until Tuesday morning, and the thought of asking the veterinarian to make a house call on his day off makes your wallet cringe.

The well-prepared livestock raiser, be he or she a full-time farmer, a homesteader or, like nearly half of all Americans, a pet owner, draws on the knowledge gained from years of experience. She can select a course of treatment from a battery of ready-to-hand tools and medicines, preferably after telephoning the vet for a quick confirmation of diagnosis and remedy. The years of experience can only be obtained after, well, years of experience, but a supply of veterinary implements and pharmaceuticals can be laid up by the greenest novice. These are best gathered in the calm and reasoning light of day, thus avoiding a mad 20-mile dash to town or an embarrassing hat-in-hand trip to a better-prepared neighbor — "Mind if I borrow a cup of penicillin?" Such a collection of husbandry necessities will never replace the advice and services of a good veterinarian, but it can largely restrict one's need of them to office hours. And a proper inventory of livestock medicines will prevent a good deal of suffering and, in some cases, the premature death of the creatures in one's care.

In addition to the items noted here, your barn's medicine chest will include a variety of vaccines, parasite treatments and, perhaps, vitamin and mineral supplements to offset local diseases, worms and soil or dietary deficiencies. Consult a vet for specifics of the dosages and timing that are the foundation of good health maintenance. Although these regular preventive treatments are essential to the health of one's herd, flock or pets, the medicines seldom store well and are best purchased as needed; nevertheless, a number of articles should be stockpiled by the owner of any animal, whether it be an Arabian stallion, a Persian kitten, a Charolais cow or a black Labrador.

Foremost among these is a thermometer. A body-temperature reading is as useful an indicator of illness for animals as it is for humans and can also be a valuable diagnostic tool, so be sure to report a fever — or its absence — to the vet. Animals' temperatures are more variable than humans', so only a reading two degrees or more above normal should be considered significant. Specially sized thermometers are available for large animals, but a standard 4½-inch model will do for all pets and farm animals. The best buy is an ordinary human rectal thermometer, for sale at any pharmacy.

Normal Body Temperatures

Animal	Temperature (degrees F)
Cow	101-102
Pig	101.5-102.5
Sheep	101-102.5
Horse	100-100.5
Dog	101-102
Cat	101-102

Many courses of treatment call for an injection, and although farm-supply stores display ornate stainless-steel hypodermics with glass vials, most farmers — and a good many veterinarians — reach for the plastic disposables on the bottom shelf. Packaged in a sterile plastic bag and intended for one-time use, they are sturdy enough to last through several courses of treatment if properly disinfected after each use. Keep a couple of each of three sizes on hand: 3 cc for small animals or small dosages to large animals; 12 cc for general, all-round duty; and 35 cc for drenching (force-feeding liquids). As for needles, once again the disposables are a good value at about 10 cents apiece, but though many farmers treat several animals on the same needle, disinfecting them is difficult and the practice is not recommended. Use an 18-gauge needle for barnyard animals (1½-inch for cows, 1-inch for calves or sows) and a 20-gauge needle for pets and other small creatures.

Anyone with the nerve to poke holes in an animal while it is still breathing can give an injection, though picking the right spot on a horse can be critical, and intravenous injections on any animal should be left to those who know what they are doing. Intramuscular injections are as easy as jabbing the needle into a muscular part of the hip or neck—with cows, a few slaps with the back of the hand on the target area just before inserting the needle will usually prevent the injectee from kicking the injector in the kneecap. Subcutaneous injections are best given under a fold of skin on the back or side of the neck. Most important, though: holding the syringe up to the light and squirting a little antibiotic into the air immediately puts one in a class with famous surgeons like Hawkeye Pierce and is sure to instill confidence in the most sickly of beasts.

Though an antiseptic mouthwash can be used in an emergency, syringes are normally disinfected with rubbing alcohol, and it should be used liberally. Alcohol can also be used to disinfect minor cuts and scrapes, to soothe insect stings and bites and to cool down hot spots caused by staphylococci skin infections. As a bonus, it will temporarily paralyze fleas, a useful trick for de-infesting puppies too young to be treated by other means. Touching the flea with an alcohol-soaked Q-tip will render it immobile long enough for it to be plucked off and killed.

For the treatment of bacterial infections, antibiotics are truly the wonder drugs they are supposed to be, but they are of no value for other conditions and are widely overused. Most antibiotics are systemic, thus leaving residues in milk and meat, and the withdrawal period stated on the label must be treated as the absolute minimum. Antibiotics should never be administered as a knee-jerk reaction to the first signs of distress, but although overuse is their worst abuse, underuse is the second worst—treatment should always continue for three or four days after the symptoms have disappeared.

With all that in mind, though, antibiotics are still an important farm curative when used

A collection of medical paraphernalia does not make a successful husbandry practice or a mutually enjoyable pet-owner relationship. Other requirements include a respect and liking for animals, a willingness to spend time learning their habits and just hanging around with them.

MATTHEW NEAL MCVAY

wisely — never administer an antibiotic without consulting a veterinarian. Indeed, many veterinarians would prefer amateurs not to keep any antibiotics on hand, but for those who insist, penicillin G is a good all-purpose drug that has only a 5-day withdrawal period. Like any penicillin, though, it can cause a fatal anaphylactic ("allergic") reaction if accidentally administered in a vein or artery. To ensure that an intramuscular injection is not accidentally intravenous, after sticking in the needle, draw the syringe plunger back slightly before pushing it home. If the syringe begins to fill with blood, the needle has struck a vein and must be withdrawn, then placed in a new site.

Mineral oil is a multipurpose medication, useful in treating constipation in cows, colic in horses and ear mites in pigs and rabbits. As a final sales point, orphaned piglets will be accepted by a foster sow if the smell of all the pigs is masked by an application of mineral oil.

For a deep cut, the best initial treatment is to wash it thoroughly with warm water, but an emergency is no time to go looking for a clean container, so try to resist that almost overwhelming temptation to steal the veterinary bucket to mop the kitchen floor or soak a batch of pickles. After washing, use hydrogen peroxide, which is an effective antiseptic. Veterinarians are divided about the virtues of sprays and ointments — one school of thought approves because they keep flies away from the cut; the other worries that they attract dirt.

Of course, wounds are not restricted to livestock — barbed wire, thorns, farm machinery and the normal collection of scythes, axes and workshop tools can cause human injuries ranging from minor cuts and scrapes to broken limbs and life-threatening mishaps. Every farm — indeed, every household — should have a portable first-aid kit stocked with Band-Aids, gauze bandages and pads, adhesive tape, pressure bandages and a triangle bandage with safety pins for making a sling. Painkillers and other medications are not part of first aid, and they should be stored in a separate place, safely out of the reach of children.

Paper towels, hand disinfectant (a bar of unperfumed, nondeodorant soap will do in a pinch) and plastic gloves for internal examinations are all useful accessories, but none will be as well-used as a good reference book. Standard works are *The Merck Veterinary Manual* and *Black's Veterinary Dictionary*, although there are a variety of less expensive — and less thorough — handbooks on the market. Regardless of price, though, buy a new one — that 1948 edition (revised 1953) found at a garage sale is no bargain. In addition to these general items, which comprise a basic veterinary kit that should be standard equipment on every farmstead, each class of animal has its own needs, related to its size and physiology.

Cow Correctives

After about two weeks of age, a frisky young calf is all but impossible to catch in an open field, and an adult cow, weighing 1000 pounds or more, is not going to put up with being poked, prodded, needled or felt up by anybody she can knock flat. Ideally, every cow owner should have a squeeze chute, headgate or stanchion to hold an animal for treatment, though many part-time farmers get by with a sturdy pen and a rope halter or pair of nose tongs to restrain the animal's head.

Anyone who has adult cows should have a set of calf-pulling chains, although as with forceps for human births, in a perfect world they would never be used. Unless the cow is obviously having trouble, the best course of action is to sit back and enjoy the show. If she needs help, calving chains, which are smooth-surfaced and can be easily disinfected, are the correct tool: the nylon ropes and pieces of baler twine often used in their place leave the cow open to infection. Never attempt to pull a calf without ensuring that it is correctly placed in the birth canal — protect the cow's delicate membranes by squirting liquid dish soap on your disinfected arm to keep it slippery — and only pull when the cow pushes. Above all, and this is true not just of birthing difficulties but of every animal health-care problem, do not let a misguided sense of thrift or self-sufficiency cause you to wait too long before calling a vet.

One nemesis of calf raisers is scours, a debilitating diarrhea that leads to dehydration and death. Effective remedies are fairly new and are available as a pill, which must be force-fed — pop it in the back of the calf's throat, then hold its mouth shut and stroke its throat until it swallows — or as a liquid, which can be added to the calf's milk. In advanced cases in which dehydration is a factor, oral electrolytes should be given. Drenching, or force-feeding through a tube into the calf's stomach, is not a difficult technique once learned from a veterinarian, but a mistake — inserting the tube down the windpipe instead of the esophagus — is fatal. An esophageal feeder, form-fitted to help prevent such errors, is recommended.

Farmers who pasture their cows in fields containing alfalfa or clover should be prepared to deal with bloat, a potentially fatal condition caused by the tendency of legumes to bubble in the rumen, or first stomach. The resulting foam blocks the normal eructation of gas (that is, belching) and causes the poor beast to swell up like a balloon. Since a cow normally belches about 200 gallons of gas a day, mostly carbon dioxide and methane, clearly the situation can get serious in a hurry. In bloat's later stages, the only treatment is to puncture the rumen (on the left side, just under the short ribs) allowing the accumulated gas to escape, and although this is best done by a professional, one veterinarian says, "If she's all blown up and down on her side, you'd better stab her." The correct tool for the job is a trocar (a pointed surgical instrument), but a 14-gauge needle or even a pocketknife will serve in an emergency.

Sharp objects such as nails, fence staples and pieces of wire can cause "hardware disease." The metal objects are readily swallowed by grazing animals, which, of course, do not chew their food the first time round. Further down the digestive tract, these prickly hors d'oeuvres are subjected to severe contractions and often perforate a stomach lining, causing peritonitis and sudden death. An inexpensive preventive treatment for a cow likely to pick up some metal is to drop a special magnet down her throat—it is heavy enough to lodge in the reticulum and will collect any hardware there, where it is less likely to do any harm. One magnet retrieved at the abattoir was safely clutching 25 nails to its metallic bosom.

Pinkeye (infectious keratoconjunctivitis), commonly transmitted by face flies, is a highly contagious inflammation of the eye that can cause blindness if untreated. Symptoms—a swollen, weeping eye, often held shut because

Pigs are not only stubborn and greedy; they are also known for their intelligence, adaptability, and vigorous good health.

of an acute sensitivity to light—appear with little warning, usually in late summer. When caught early, pinkeye responds well to an antibacterial powder applied to the eye and is easily treated—but only if the medication is already on hand at the first sign of trouble.

The only surgical procedure most small farmers will attempt with their cattle is the castration of young bulls. Two implements that allow bloodless castration, or nonintrusive surgery (at least in the medical sense of the phrase) are elastrators and pinchers. The former stretches a rubber ring over the scrotum—be sure it contains both testicles. When the ring contracts, it cuts off the blood supply, causing the entire sac to fall off in about three weeks. Pinchers crush the spermatic cords, leaving the testes to atrophy. Neither instrument is entirely painless, and since intact males grow faster than steers and produce leaner beef, the procedure can be safely eliminated with animals that will be slaughtered before reaching puberty at about one year of age.

Pig Prescriptions

The list of implements in a swineherd's veterinary kit is a short one. Once called mortgage-busters because they provided such a reliable income, pigs are known not just for their stubbornness, greed and bad manners, but also for their intelligence, adaptability and vigorous good health. Indeed, the only procedures that should be attempted without the advice of a veterinarian deal with preparing newborn pigs for the six months of eating and sleeping that will fill their short lives.

The first tool required is a pair of sharp, clean, side-cutting pliers to clip off the eight appropriately named needle teeth. Buy a new pair and don't use them for anything else. Performed within a day or two of birth, this dental surgery is quick and painless and protects the sow's udder from cuts that could easily become infected. Sow's milk is poor in iron, and pigs that are raised indoors where they are not able to stick their noses in some fresh dirt are susceptible to iron-deficiency anemia. Oral supplements (a sort of swine Geritol) are available but must be given weekly; one shot of injectable iron—use a 20-gauge needle—at two days of age will see the piglets through until they are eating enough solid food to get their iron the old-fashioned way.

The final treatment for pigs is to castrate the males sometime between the ages of three and six weeks. The correct tool is a scalpel, though an X-Acto knife or even a straight-backed

L.L.T. Rhodes/ Animals Animals

razor blade will do, and ideally, the blade should be changed for each animal. In practice, of course, most farmers cut a whole litter with the same blade, and if this is the case, disinfect the blade between patients. Iodine is better than rubbing alcohol for this use because it disinfects instantly—alcohol must evaporate before it is done working.

Sheep Balms

Much more delicate than pigs, sheep are rather like miniature cows regarding the sorts of conditions to which they can fall prey, and the good shepherd will have, in addition to the basic kit, many of the cattleman's tools: pinkeye powder, scours treatment (use smaller doses of the calf medicine), a stomach-feeding tube and a castrator (the rubber rings can also be used for docking tails), although the Basque sheepherders of the West are legendary for their ability to "fix" lambs with their teeth. In addition, the shepherd should have hoof trimmers, bottle nipples for hand-feeding orphan lambs and, according to Randi Kennedy, partner in a 400-ewe commercial market-lamb operation, a stethoscope for early detection of pneumonia. Those with a seamster's bent and the confidence to stuff a prolapsed uterus back in place may keep it there by stitching across the vulva with a mattress needle (a large darning needle may suffice) and some flat-seam binding.

Horse Tonics

Horse medicine is a specialty practice, and vets such as James Herriot, whose tales of the Yorkshire Dales are so popular, are unashamed to admit they have little talent for it. Amateur practitioners are seldom as able as even an untalented vet, and only a few medical items beyond those in the basic kit should be kept in a tack room. Among them is a good lead shank with a chain and a twitch to restrain the horse for treatment. Interestingly, although a twitch is commonly believed to work by inflicting pain, recent research indicates that it causes the animal to release endorphins, naturally occurring painkillers, into the bloodstream, thus calming itself with a "natural high."

Horses, like sheep, are prone to intestinal parasites and must be wormed regularly. They are also susceptible to tetanus; this can be prevented with an annual vaccination, which enables you to doctor small cuts without worrying that the animal will be afflicted.

Aside from the usual collection of grooming aids, ointments or sprays for cuts and possibly an injectable muscle relaxer for severe cases of colic, most horse medications are related to their long, delicate legs and feet. Hoof care is best left in the calloused hands of a capable farrier, and although experienced riders may wish to keep leg bandages and cottons, their incorrect use can do more harm than good,

Cows that graze in alfalfa or clover fields may suffer from bloat— the potentially fatal blockage of gas caused by the bubbling of legumes in the stomach or rumen. A cow normally belches 200 gallons of gas per day.

causing bowed tendons and other problems. A wealth of advice about horse care, much of it conflicting, is available for the asking – and sometimes more cheaply than that – but perhaps the best recommendation is to avoid any treatment you have not seen performed by a professional and that you don't feel confident in tackling alone.

Canine Cures and Feline Physics

Farm animals are herbivorous creatures that are happy with a steady diet of greens or grains, but dogs and cats are from predatory stock, and even the most pampered house cat is still a creature of fang and claw best suited to a diet of meat. This striking difference in metabolism means pets are more independent and, in many ways, more forgiving of changing diets and inconsistent care, but it also means there are fewer treatments that can be performed by the pet owner. And more care must be taken with them, both for your own protection from the teeth and claws of ungrateful patients and for the welfare of the animal, which is generally smaller than a farm animal and correspondingly more affected by, say, a small change in drug dosage. "I don't want to appear self-serving," says small-animal veterinarian Darcy Reade, "but unlike horses and cows, the majority of things that go wrong with dogs and cats have to be treated by a vet."

The most common complaint, especially for dogs that run loose or that are given a lot of table scraps, is an upset stomach, a malady for which Reade often prescribes a little Pepto-Bismol until he can see them during office hours. Other discomforts, such as cuts, bruises and sore paws, can often be alleviated with ordinary human painkillers. In rare cases, cats will have a fatal allergic reaction to aspirin, but in any case, never administer any medication, human or otherwise, without the approval and dosage recommendation of a veterinarian.

Next to stomachs, ears are the greatest source of trouble, and a nystatin-based antibiotic ear ointment is useful for treating both yeast infections and mite infestations, as well as serving as a first-aid cream. Like most medications, it is probably good for about a month after its expiration date, but watch the label and be sure to have a current batch on hand.

The primary concern of most pet owners is external parasite control, but since only about one in ten of the fleas that plague an animal are on it at any given time, bathing is an ineffective solution. Also, many flea shampoos are harsh, and Reade has had to treat dogs whose well-meaning owners bathed them every two or three days. "By the time I see them," he says, "their skin is so dried out that the fleas are a secondary problem." Flea collars only work on cats and small dogs – like geese, fleas on a large dog migrate south when conditions become uncomfortable – and, like systemic medications given orally, flea collars contain powerful insecticides. Children who hug or play with an animal wearing a flea collar are likely to be exposed to harsh chemicals, most of which function like nerve gas. It seems odd that many consumers who garden organically and are concerned about chemical residues in food, air and water do not extend those concerns to their pets' care.

For severe infestations, Reade recommends an insecticidal flea spray – a pump sprayer is not as frightening for an animal as an aerosol – or powder, though either must be applied with strict adherence to the cautions listed on the label. Organically derived garden insecticides like rotenone and pyrethrum are naturally occurring and quickly break down into harmless components, but they are not completely safe. Those compounds, which are designed for garden and large-animal use, can, under some circumstances, be absorbed through the skin and may poison your dog or cat as well as its fleas.

Regularly applied, diatomaceous earth, a powder of cellular skeletons that scratch an insect's shell, causing it to dehydrate, is reputed to be effective but, as always, a program of prevention is preferable to a course of treatment. Adding brewer's yeast (½ teaspoon daily for cats, 2 teaspoons for a large dog) or garlic (½ to 2 finely chopped cloves daily) or both to the diet of dogs and cats will make them unpalatable to fleas, which will pass them over for tastier morsels. Be careful, though – that new and more appetizing entrée may be you.

As with larger stock, worms can be a problem with pets. Most supermarket worm medicines are based on piperazine, which is effective against roundworms but not much else. Instead of a blanket treatment every six months or so, have the animal tested, then treated for what it has, if anything. Worming should be viewed as the serious medical treatment it is. The only reliable way to rid an intestinal system of an existing worm problem is to kill the worms and their unhatched eggs with deadly chemicals; home remedies like a few drops of turpentine are not safe or natural just because they use a familiar household product. A suggested diet to prevent recurrence of worms includes garlic at the same rate as for fleas, ½ to 2 teaspoons of bran for roughage, and grated carrots, turnips or beets.

Dog owners will, of course, want to have pliers handy to extract porcupine quills, and a large can of tomato juice should be kept by the door. If the dog arrives home reeking of skunk, you can then quickly head outside with what it takes to cut the smell. Douse the sprayed area with the juice and wait at least a half hour before washing the treatment off. (Better yet, let the juice dry overnight and brush it out in the morning.) The animal will not come out of this smelling like a rose, but pet owners will be thankful for the improvement.

Finally, dogs and cats are every bit as curious and orally fixated as children, so keep household poisons out of the reach of both. Should a pet get into the wrong container, it is a fairly safe rule to induce vomiting for non-corrosive poisons but definitely not for corrosive substances – check the label. (To induce vomiting, place 1 or 2 teaspoons of hydrogen peroxide, salt or powdered mustard in the back of the throat; repeat in 10 minutes if necessary.) Tell a veterinarian immediately about the substance consumed, but if no vet is available, call the local poison-control center or follow the instructions on the container label. If the poison is unknown, administer a dose of universal antidote and rush the animal to a veterinarian without delay. A concoction suited to treating a wide range of poisons, universal antidote consists of 2 parts charcoal (burnt toast will do), 1 part magnesium oxide (milk of magnesia) and 1 part tannic acid (strong tea). Keep some on hand in a sealed container and administer 2 teaspoons to a cat or up to 8 ounces to a large dog.

One common poison against which the universal antidote is ineffective is automobile antifreeze (ethylene glycol), the sweet taste of which is fatally attractive to both dogs and cats. Little more than a teaspoon of it will kill a cat, and a small radiator leak on the garage floor or a spill while topping up the car's coolant reservoir could provide a pet with a deadly dose. If you catch an animal in the act of winterizing itself, induce vomiting and rush it to a vet; if found later, just rush it to a vet.

Making a Case

A homestead veterinary kit is useless if one cannot find it when it is needed, and dividing its components between a shelf above the laundry tub, the bathroom medicine chest and a handy beam in the barn reveals a careless approach to animal health that is unfair to the creatures for whom one has accepted responsibility. Ideally, at least for effect, the well-stocked kit would be kept in a doctor's black

bag, but more practical equivalents include a fishing-tackle box – the fold-out divided tray is just right for needles and other small items – and a mechanic's toolbox. At the very least, keep all parts of the kit in one place, whether it be a shelf in the mudroom or a small cabinet in the barn.

Of course, a collection of medical paraphernalia does not make a successful husbandry practice or a mutually enjoyable pet-owner relationship. Other requirements include a respect and liking for animals, a willingness to spend time learning their habits and just hanging around with them and, at least for the farmer, a careful and complete record-keeping system. Unfortunately, despite all possible vigilance, accident and illness are as much a part of farm life in the barn as in the farmhouse. A well-stocked veterinary kit will go far in easing the creatures' discomfort, but for complete animal care, there is one article that is inarguably the single most important accessory in the kit. As such, it should get more use than any other item and should therefore be kept where it is most easily accessible. It is the veterinarian's telephone number. ❧

Because pets are more independent than livestock, fewer treatments can be performed by the pet owner.

Creature Comforts

DESIGNING A USER-FRIENDLY BARN

BY MICHAEL WEBSTER

"If I were to give you a definition of animal well-being," says Frank Hurnik, "it would be something like this." He pauses. A Czechoslovakian immigrant, Hurnik often takes a moment to collect his thoughts before expressing an important point in English. "Animal well-being is the condition of harmony – physical and psychological harmony – between the organism and its surroundings.

"Now that's a nice definition, and the beauty of it is that everyone from farmers to animal rights activists will agree with it." As a farmer, a professor in the department of animal science at the University of Guelph and one of Canada's leading authorities on farm-animal behavior, Hurnik should know. "The only problem," he continues, "is with the definition of harmony.

"You see, a farmer will say, 'I have reasonable production, and I am making a profit, so there must be harmony.' An animal scientist will look at individual performance. If you put a laying hen in a battery cage, you may get 350 eggs from her in a year. If you put two hens in the same cage, they may give you 300 eggs each, and if you put in three hens, 250 eggs each. You have doubled production, but at the cost of individual performance. A veterinarian will say, 'I couldn't care less about production. I want to know if they are all healthy.' An animal welfarist wants to know that there is no suffering, and an animal rights person will say, 'Don't talk to me about harmony – you still kill the creature in the end.' "

So much for a human consensus on the surroundings that are harmonious with animal well-being. But what about the animals? Has anybody asked them for their definition of harmony? To put it another way, what would barns look like if they were designed by the animals that live in them? It is a question that would not have been asked a few generations ago, but the recent trend toward intensive animal husbandry – "factory farming" – has made it worth examining. The all-day-every-day confinement of livestock, most commonly practiced with pigs and poultry but now also being extended to cows and sheep, has made it easier to meet their physical needs, but it has demonstrated that animals also have social and psychological needs.

A genuine interest in farm-animal housing has recently sprung up among farmers and agricultural researchers (who want to keep animals healthy, strong and well adjusted enough to produce profitable quantities of food), animal welfarists (who want to protect animals against the cruelties of excessively intensive agricultural practices) and animal rightists (an umbrella term describing those whose opinions range from an extremely broad view of animal welfare to those who believe humans have no right to use animals for their own ends). The debate among these groups has led both producers and consumers to think about the architectural possibilities of a barn designed, like an owner-built house, by the creatures that have to live in it.

Good barn design is, of course, a question of animal welfare, not animal rights. It assumes that the domestication of food-producing animals is moral. It assumes that people are not going to stop eating eggs and that they are not going to release all dairy cows and let them fend for themselves. And because, of all the commonly raised farm animals, only turkeys were once native to this country, it assumes that all species of farm livestock require a building to protect them from the elements.

And one more thing. "If I were a pig, for example, designing a pig barn," says Agriculture Canada researcher Brian Thompson, "I don't think I would include a loading dock." A barn

THE PERFECT BARN

PLAN

ELEVATION

tshoffner

A dramatic departure from the farrowing crate used by most pig farmers, the Edinburgh pigpen, shown here as a model, houses four sows for their entire breeding lives plus their progeny from birth to market.

may be designed by a pig, but it will be paid for by a farmer, and the pigs will still have to go to market. Sustainable agriculture — and that includes ethical animal farming, assuming there is such a thing — must sustain profitability as well as soil fertility. The farm animals that design their own barn are going to have to work under the constraints of maintaining a level of production that will persuade Old McDonald not to pave over the farm and take a job in the city.

Lastly, since farm livestock lack pencils, T-squares, opposable thumbs and other drafting necessities, they will have to tell us what they want in their living quarters. Or rather, they will have to tell us what they *need*. "It's an important distinction," says Hurnik. "Many animal welfarists who speak about animal needs mean animal desires. I would define a need as something that is essential to developing good health, physically and psychologically. Desire is a more motivational term, and not every desire is also a need. In fact, some desires may even be harmful to the animal's health. A racehorse may wish to drink too much cold water when it is overheated, for example, or a sheep may want to eat something that is poisonous." Like parents who refuse to accommodate their children's requests to serve pizza and ice cream at every meal or to let them play too long in the hot sun, farmers, too, have a responsibility to take a long-range view of their livestock's desires.

The study of farm-animal desires and behavior is known as applied ethology, a rela-

tively new field whose practitioners, says David Fraser, a research scientist at the Animal Research Center in Ottawa, "could be counted on the fingers of a guillotine repairman." Fraser is one of only four ethologists working for Agriculture Canada. With Thompson, a statistician, and engineer Peter Phillips, he is part of a team that specializes in housing for pigs. The three men agree on a list of animal priorities that must be juggled when designing a barn. In no particular order, they are: basic needs (proper access to food and water); good health; freedom from fear (of predators, people and aggressive peers); comfort (based on animal behavior and physiology); and the freedom to perform those types of behavior that are important for the animal to perform (largely unknown, but chickens, for example, may need to roost or to dust-bathe).

As such lists go — and it seems that everyone involved with animal welfare has his or her own list — it is fairly complete, but some people include access to fresh air and sunshine on their lists. "What's so great about outside?" snorts Phillips. "I mean, you see a steer or some animal out in a field, and you say, 'Isn't that nice,' but then you go inside and spend the night in a house that has locks on the doors and screens on the windows. The steer stays outside and endures insects all night, plus the fear of dogs or other predators and goodness knows what else. People underestimate those kinds of stress. Farmers don't want to spend a lot of money building an expensive barn, but for the sake of the animal, they feel they need to. For example, confinement housing allows us to achieve a high degree of disease prevention. Here at the experimental farm, we have eliminated mastitis in our sow herd, and we have been able to stop feeding antibiotics to our poultry."

"Sometimes people miss the obvious signs of animal welfare," adds Fraser. "In our pampered society, we tend to take the necessities for granted and concentrate on the nonessentials that make up what we call our quality of life. But you can't do that with animals."

Hurnik agrees. "How you feel — whether you are happy or unhappy — depends on how your other needs are satisfied. You may be lonely or depressed, but those feelings disappear if you are hungry. As long as you are hungry, you don't think about anything but food. Once you get something to eat, though, the unhappiness reappears." On Hurnik's list of necessary creature comforts are: adequate fresh air, feed and water; enough exercise to promote normal growth and prevent atrophy; a sufficiently complex environment to avoid boredom; and enough interaction with other

JIM PANOU

animals to allow the development of social skills. "In general," he says, "we should provide an environment for which the animal's genetic makeup is predisposed."

The trick, of course, is in defining that make-up and what it requires. Animal scientists use their observations of animal behavior along with the results of preference tests to try to reach conclusions. "I don't *know* that other humans feel pain," explains Hurnik, "but if they react in a certain way to a certain stimulus, then I can judge that against my own experience and assume that they're feeling physical or psychological pain. And we can extend that to animals. I know their physiology is similar to mine, and when they show the same type of behavior, I assume they are sharing the same type of experience. There is a very real danger of anthropomorphism here, but on the other hand, just to reject behavioral observations because there is a danger of being anthropomorphic would be equally inappropriate."

Ethologists and other researchers spend a good deal of their time designing experiments that allow animals to make choices about their environments, and according to Fraser, they are often surprised by the results. After the 1965 Brambell Commission in England condemned chicken-wire floors in laying-hen cages because of the damage they caused to the birds' feet, tests showed that the hens preferred the wire to any other surface tested. Other research concluded that broiler chicks raised on wire floors preferred them to "natural" straw litter. When animal welfare groups in Europe objected to a huge new broiler-gathering machine that uses vibrating rubber fingers to crowd the birds onto conveyor belts, tests showed that the birds were far less disturbed by the machine than by the hand-collection method it replaced. Presumably, the chicks recognized the people as predators and panicked, but they were simply baffled by the machine.

One of Fraser's own experiments, in which he offered young pigs a choice between concrete and straw floors, produced what he calls "surprisingly noisy results" — the pigs showed no clear preference. "Then the penny dropped," he says. "We know pigs are very keen on a comfortable thermal environment, so we repeated the tests at 20 and 25 degrees C. At 20 degrees, the pigs preferred the straw, and at the warmer temperature, they preferred the bare concrete."

"We have done a tremendous number of preference tests," says Hurnik, "and the results are always interesting, but they change according to age, sex, experience, maturity, and so

Studies show that chickens have an instinct to spend the night off the ground, but unless they have been reared in an environment that offers access to a variety of levels, they will not roost as adults.

on. Every test is so specific that we still don't have enough material to make generalizations." Furthermore, even a strong preference is not necessarily indicative of a strong desire, much less a need. "If you offer me a choice between banana cream pie and apple pie," says Thompson, "I'll choose the banana cream every time. That's a strong preference on my part, but it doesn't mean I wouldn't be perfectly happy with apple pie if I didn't have a choice."

One lesson can be learned from preference testing, however, and it is that few elements in barn design operate independently. "Every time you resolve one problem," says Hurnik, "you create another one. For example, if you give hens more room so they can exercise, you are giving them more opportunity for aggression. And if you put a sow in a farrowing crate, that is a system that gives higher priority to the survival of the piglets than to the comfort of the dam."

Farrowing crates, which are used by virtually every commercial pig farmer in Canada, are narrow stalls made out of steel pipes that house sows for farrowing (birthing) and suckling. The sow has food and water in front of her, but her range of motion in any direction is limited to a few inches — she cannot turn around — and she never leaves the crate for the three to five weeks between farrowing and weaning. The piglets can run under and around their mother, and they have free access to heated compartments on either side of her, which allows them to get out from under her when she lies down but still get a drink of milk

Battery cages, which effectively provide birds with food, water and protection from predators but offer no opportunity for exercise or social interaction, have been banned in both Switzerland and Sweden.

no matter which way she faces.

"The Europeans emphasize the welfare of the sow," says Fraser, "and certainly, if you asked the sow, she would want the freedom of movement. But this is where it gets interesting. The welfare of the sow and the welfare of the piglet are in conflict. The most common causes of piglet mortality are starvation and crushing by the sow — both unappealing causes of death from an animal welfare point of view. If the sow is free to turn but at the cost of one piglet, then my sympathies lie with the piglet, who would undoubtedly want the farrowing crate. Having said that, though, we are trying to design a farrowing crate that allows the sow to turn around and still keeps piglet mortality at 5 percent."

"If you make a comparison with humans," says Hurnik, "the farrowing crate may be

reasonable. Often, a mother will compromise her own comfort for the comfort of her child. Perhaps that is a natural behavior. Still, I don't think the farrowing crate has reached its final stage of development. We can design one that has a high degree of safety for the piglets and also more comfort for the sow."

Despite the difficulties of interpreting the results of preference tests, juggling priorities and sorting out animals' needs from their desires, scientists have arrived at some conclusions that are useful to those farmers — particularly small farmers — who want to provide living quarters that will be to their charges' liking.

Cows

For beef cattle, pasture is both nutritionally adequate and inexpensive. During the growing season, all they require is good fences and access to shade and clean drinking water at all times and to salt and other mineral supplements as required. In winter, beef animals should have a dry and completely draft-free shelter in which they can escape wind, mud and freezing rain. Beyond that, they need a water source that does not freeze over and feeding equipment that allows all the animals to eat at the same time. Cows appreciate birthing facilities that offer privacy and reduced light. Agriculture Canada recommends providing 35 square feet of shelter space per adult cow, plus 325 square feet of exercise yard, figures that producers should consider rock-bottom minimums.

The dairy industry is generally given a low priority by animal welfare activists. "I don't know why," says Fraser. "I mean, where do they think veal calves come from?" Still, as far as housing is concerned, cow comfort is directly tied to health and milk production, and commercial dairy farmers have moved ahead of many small producers to "free-stall" systems in which cows are restrained only while they are being milked. For the rest of the day, when they are not on pasture, the cows have access to a feed bunker, a waterer and a private stall. Agriculture Canada recommends that a free stall for a 1,100-pound cow should be 44 inches wide and 90 inches long, dimensions that have been exposed to the rough-and-tumble of commercial farming but have not been tested in controlled experiments. Dairy cows are typically not as hardy as beef cows, and they prefer quarters that are above freezing.

Chickens

If there is one image that symbolizes the approach of agribusiness to animal husbandry,

J.C. ALLEN & SON

it is the battery-cage housing system for laying hens. For their entire 12-month laying period, hens are housed in tiers of wire cages in a windowless barn. Automatic feeders and waterers provide their dietary needs, and conveyors remove their eggs and manure. *Canadian Farm Buildings Handbook*, published by Agriculture Canada, suggests placing three birds in a 12-by-18-inch cage or four birds in a 15-by-20-inch cage and notes that this is one bird fewer per cage than the manufacturers recommend. Even the more generous options provide only half a square foot of floor space per bird, however, and animal welfare groups have been vocal in their opposition to the system. In a French experiment that allowed laying hens to establish the size of their own cages at anything from 70 to 160 square inches per bird, the hens settled for a little less than 120 square inches each, about 0.8 square feet.

Recent legislation in Sweden outlaws battery cages and requires farmers to provide daily outdoor exercise, straw floors and barns with windows for all their animals. In Switzerland, where a 10-year phase-out period for battery cages will expire in 1991, farmers have almost completely switched to an aviary system. Ruth Newberry, an ethologist and poultry specialist at the Agriculture Canada Research Station in Agassiz, British Columbia, describes it. "There are about 2,000 hens in each aviary, and they are free to move around the whole building," she says. "There is a litter floor provided for dust-bathing, and the birds have access to two or three different levels, with automatic feeders and waterers on each level. The levels are far enough apart for the birds to walk around and flap their wings, and under each one is a conveyor belt to take away the manure. The hens can enter individual nest boxes, where there is some loose material, perhaps buckwheat hulls, that is nice for them to lay their eggs in. Most of them lay their eggs in the morning, and in the afternoon, the doors open and they go outside. They come back in of their own accord when it gets dark."

In short, it stands in stark contrast with the battery system. "For the aviaries to work well," says Newberry, "you don't want them highly populated. It makes it hard to see all the birds, it makes disease transmission easier, and it increases the number of eggs laid on the floor." Depending on the size of the birds, aviaries provide 0.75 to 1 square foot of floor space per bird, not counting the extra space provided by the different levels. Agriculture Canada recommends a total of 2 square feet per Leghorn or other egg layer and 2.4 square feet for larger breeds such as Barred Rocks.

Preference testing on chickens has produced results of interest to the manager of a backyard flock as well as to commercial poultry operators. "Birds have an instinct to roost for the night at a higher level," Newberry says. "But it's very important to realize that if they are expected to fly up to a roost as adults, they have to be reared in an environment that provides an opportunity to move up to different levels. If they don't do it from a very young age, they won't do it as adults." Almost anything will do: a wall of concrete blocks on their sides, a tier of perches, a few chunks of firewood, an overturned wooden box, a discarded kitchen chair. As for flock size, Newberry says that one chicken is capable of recognizing about 100 other birds. "Some studies say to limit the population so they can all recognize each other, but new studies suggest that the birds adapt just as well, if not better, to larger populations.

"Chickens should never be isolated from the rest of the flock, and they prefer not to be mixed up a lot, especially the males. Some farms in Switzerland keep a few cockerels in with the laying flock, and the farmers say it relieves aggression and social tension. As to the birds' behavioral needs, we don't have a very good handle on that," she continues, "but we know that they desire a sandbox or some other place to dust-bathe. They want to peck and scratch in litter, they want to roost at night, and they want to move away from the crowd to lay their eggs. Even hens in a cage will pace before laying. They appear to want to move a distance and inspect various nesting sites. And they want to have some moldable nest material."

According to Hurnik, "You have to supply enough nest boxes. If you have 20 or 25 hens and you only have four nest boxes, then you are assuming that four birds will lay at a time and then get out. Actually, though, 80 percent of birds lay their eggs between 10:30 and 11:30 in the morning. Then in the afternoon between 1 and 3, they all want to dust-bathe, so again, you have to have space for more than a few at a time. You just can't program the birds to be like machines. Biology requires a different approach." To Newberry's list of behavioral desires, he adds only two. "If they have a choice, they will go outside, and they like to mate, starting in the early afternoon and increasing in the late afternoon. Actually," he says, reconsidering, "we don't know if they all like to mate or if it's just the males."

As for young meat birds, Newberry says the most important requirement is that they be kept in a warm, draft-free environment. "From the birds' point of view," she says, "it's best to provide sources of heat in localized areas rather than heating the whole barn. Their ability to regulate their own temperature is poorly developed, but this way, they can move closer to or farther away from the heat." Unlike layers, which she describes as "more agile and flighty," broilers do not make much use of different levels, either to satisfy a need to perch or to avoid aggressive penmates. "In the wild, hens brood on the ground, not in trees, so the chicks have no natural tendency to go into trees until they can flap their wings sufficiently, at about 7 weeks of age. Different levels might be useful to give them more exercise, but broilers are bred to be pretty docile – either they are eating or they are just sitting around. They grow so quickly, they spend a large portion of their time resting to metabolize their food."

Newberry's final word of advice is to allow the birds to become familiar with their environment. Although major changes in the birds' surroundings are at times unavoidable, flock managers should keep them to a minimum.

Pigs

As with chickens, there are few hard-and-fast rules of barn design based on the established behavioral patterns of pigs. But enough is known about their basic physical and psychological needs to offer some guidelines. Pigs prefer living quarters with at least three clearly defined areas: dining room, bedroom and bathroom. And because pigs also seem to want to do the same thing at the same time,

At the Animal Research Centre in Ottawa, David Fraser is experimenting with a farrowing crate that allows a sow freedom to turn around and gives the piglets access to her without danger of being crushed.

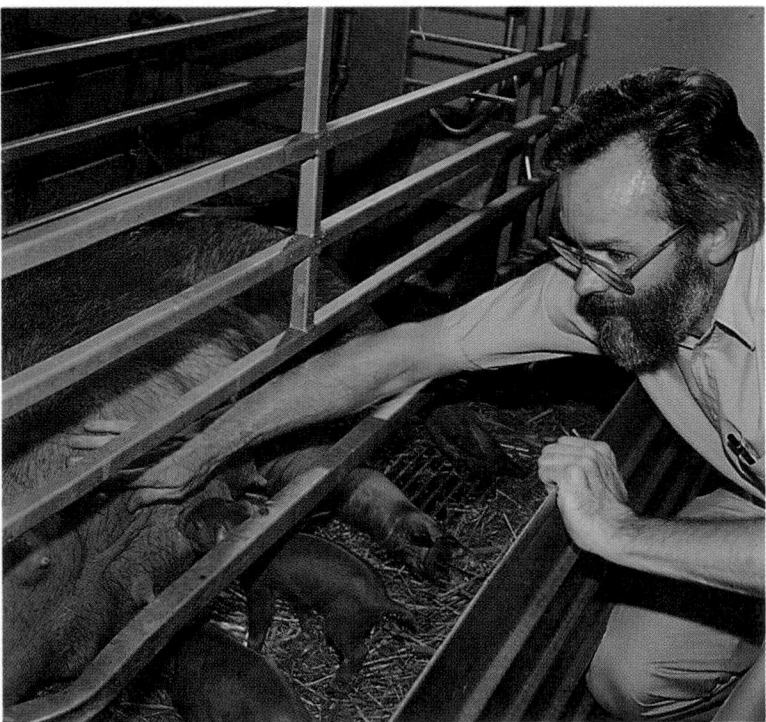

Hurnik recommends that each area be large enough to accommodate all the pigs at once; that is, enough feeder space to allow them to eat together, enough resting area that they can all lie down and enough dunging area to prevent the sort of early-morning lineups experienced in some human households.

Pigs prefer to be neat in their toilet habits and are encouraged in this by a pen that is 2.5 to 4 times longer than it is wide. Typically, the feeder is at one end, and the floor slopes to a dunging area at the other, with the waterer placed below the resting area to keep it dry. Hurnik says that pigs do not defecate near solid pen partitions as much as they do around open barriers made of wire or bars. Pigs that persist in dunging all over the pen are under some kind of stress, most often because they are too hot.

Feeder pigs are very social animals and should therefore be kept in groups, but in order to minimize aggression and other social vices, the size of the group should be kept small – 10 to 20 animals at most. Hurnik says that new research verifies what common sense suggests: Pigs from the same litter get along with each other better than with a random group of strangers. "Siblings are more mutually tolerant," he says, then smiles. "On average, of course. There are exceptions, very similar to humans."

Also like human siblings, some pigs are more aggressive than others, and weaker pigs need to be able to avoid or at least escape abuse from their peers. Although aggression is triggered by facial signals, pen designs that offer partitions or recessed corners where submissive animals can hide their faces have had only limited success. Fraser, however, has introduced a two-tiered pen in which the upper level is used for eating and resting and the lower level for drinking, dunging and resting in hot weather. In addition to offering the pigs clearly defined areas and a choice of microenvironment, the two levels provide more opportunity to avoid aggression. Finally, moving between floors gets the pigs accustomed to ramps, which reduces stress during loading and shipping.

Another innovative arrangement is the Edinburgh pen developed in 1984 by Scottish researchers A. Stolba and D.G.M. Wood-Gush. Designed to offer an approximation of natural social conditions, the large, complex pen houses four sows for their entire breeding lives plus all of their litters from birth to market. It includes a dunging area, socializing area and farrowing crates that allow each sow to get away from her piglets. The pen breaks all the accepted rules concerning hygiene, disease prevention and the special needs of newborn piglets, and many ethologists agree with Fraser, who says, "Whether it represents a net improvement in animal welfare remains to be seen." Even the pen's proponents are cautious. "It's gaining credibility," says Tom I. Hughes, former president of the Ontario Humane Society and an active participant in the farm-animal welfare debate, "but it's not necessarily the ideal." Nevertheless, commercial pig barns in the future may well look more like the Edinburgh pen than current models, the most intensive of which confine sows in farrowing crates for birthing and three weeks of mothering, then confine them in individual stalls the rest of the time.

Harmony Meter

What the world of animal husbandry needs is a device or symptom that would reliably measure Hurnik's elusive state of harmony. Unfortunately, it doesn't exist. The best we, as animal caretakers, can do is to try to eliminate the most obvious signs of disharmony. Production, even based on individual performance, is not a reliable indicator of animal satisfaction. "In fact," says Fraser, "I suspect that the most productive animal is a slightly unhappy one." A lack of good performance, on the other hand, definitely points to a problem. Lack of disease does not equate with good health or happiness, but persistent health problems are unquestionably symptomatic of an inappropriate environment. And although suffering is evidence of mistreatment, its absence is no guarantee of happiness.

Another signal that animals are out of sync with their surroundings is what scientists call nonfunctional behavior. "That's an unfortunate term," says Hurnik, "because it obviously does have a function." Perhaps a better description would be inappropriate behavior, because it usually consists of doing the right thing at the wrong time. The most common example of this is stereotyped movement, the almost autistic repetition of an inappropriate behavior, like the patterned pacing of wolves and other hunters kept in zoo enclosures. There is some evidence that this has a calming effect on animals, perhaps by stimulating the production of endorphin, a morphinelike analgesic. The stereotyped movements of farm animals include tongue rolling by cows (a repetition of the tongue movement they normally use when gathering a mouthful of grass). Others, not as harmless, are directed at the animals' penmates and are often lumped under the heading of social vices: feather pecking by chickens, tail biting by pigs, and

wool pulling by sheep.

It takes no great flash of genius to recognize that these movements are related not just to the animals' mouths but also to their food-gathering activities: chickens peck for their food, cows and sheep graze, and pigs root and chew. The problem is that we are feeding our livestock so much better than we used to that they can get their daily dietary requirements very quickly. Chickens, for example, would put in a full eight-hour shift of food gathering in the wild, but presented with a trough full of carefully formulated, concentrated and pelletized feed, they meet their dietary needs in about 2½ hours. Like workaholics forced to take some leisure time, livestock find the extra hours full of boredom and frustration, which they relieve by turning to social vices related to their food-gathering behavior.

Introducing anything that adds diversity to an animal's environment gives it something to do and is helpful in reducing inappropriate behavior, but according to Fraser, "What a pig really wants to do to dispel boredom is chew. If you put a TV in every pen, the pigs would be delighted, but only because they would be able to chew on the cord." Cows and sheep want to tear off mouthfuls of grass, and chickens want to peck and scratch. Fortunately, farmers can provide a universal chewing, pecking and scratching material for pigs and chickens: straw. "The thing about straw," says Fraser, "at least from a pig's point of view, is that every mouthful is new." Aside from giving their livestock the run of a large pasture — an option that is impractical for much of the

Frank Hurnik, an authority on farm-animal behavior who raises his own beef cattle, says that, in addition to food, water and fresh air, livestock need exercise, companions and a stimulating environment.

year in colder climates – the easiest and best thing farmers can do to relieve boredom and its associated stresses is to provide a generous supply of clean straw so the animals can satisfy their food-gathering urges.

Even so, we are left without a positive measure of animal welfare. All we can do is assure the absence of such negative symptoms as disease, poor production and inappropriate behavior and hope for the best. As Phillips pointedly asks, "How do you demonstrate that something is better for the animal if it doesn't improve performance?"

"That's a very difficult question," says Hurnik, "and I wish I knew the answer. But I believe there is an approximate way to assess an animal's well-being. The better its needs are satisfied, both in quantity and quality, the longer an organism will live. Longevity is not completely reliable – there is always the extreme example of something kept alive artificially – but I believe it is the best tool we have to measure animal welfare. For me, it always comes back to longevity."

Given the realities of meat production for steers, weaners and broilers, farmers will have to restrict themselves to examining the longevity of their breeding stock and leave the rest to Hurnik and other researchers. Whether they operate a commercial farm or raise a few pigs and chickens in their backyard, however, producers should provide an environment for their charges that meets their needs and promotes the potential for a long life. In this regard, it is important not to assume that farm animals of previous generations were happy simply because they were outside. In many cases, they suffered from poor nutrition, parasites, predators, temperature extremes, diseases and high mortality.

"Remember, it's not just housing that's important," says Newberry. "There are many factors, including the caretaker." The best-designed henhouse in the world offers little comfort to chickens whose owner is careless about filling the waterers, removing the manure or closing the door at night.

"Management is so important," says Newberry, who is reluctant to categorically endorse aviary or free-range systems even though she is convinced that birds need the exercise they are denied in battery cages. "A well-run operation of either type is better than a poorly run operation of the other. We don't know enough about how the birds perceive the situation, but we're trying to find out." ❧

Pantry

Memorable Muffins

SAVORY OR SWEET, A SPECIAL START TO A MORNING OR A MEAL

BY JOANNE CATS-BARIL WITH PHOTOGRAPHY BY GLENN MOODY

For six years, Mozart's town was my town, a place where the Alps and Renaissance architecture wrap themselves around a river valley. Salzburg is a town flooded with music, where cafés flourish, each with its own distinct reputation for pastry, coffee or clientele.

My favorite was the Café Tomaselli, where the morning ritual included a semmel, the national bread, with butter and jam, and a mélange—a wickedly strong cup of coffee with whipped cream. Newspapers from simply everywhere were mounted on wooden dowels worn smooth through years of wear, and I, like the 50 or so Salzburgers around me, sat quietly reading, eating semmel, listening to Mozart and feeling like a privileged guest in the private drawing room of a country estate.

My return home to a land where genteel breakfast places are rare or nonexistent in most towns was tempered by a dream of opening a coffeehouse of my own, a café modeled after the Tomaselli but with a spirit of its own. There was no doubt in my mind that the idea would cross the Atlantic successfully, that a nonboisterous atmosphere would be welcome, that Dylan could replace Mozart, that rich coffee and the newspapers of the world would attract those for whom Dunkin' Donuts had little appeal. But what about the bread? Ours is a country without a true national bread.

I briefly considered imitations: a semmel, croissant or brioche. But what I wanted was neither an Austrian coffeehouse nor a chic Gallic café; it had to be homegrown or nothing at all.

After much deliberation and some very tasty experimentation, I made the choice: muffins. Not exactly a national bread, but certainly part of our heritage, I reasoned, a fresh, hot muffin is a heartening start to any day. Plans went ahead and Sunprint, as the café

was called, opened on a September morning amidst high hopes (which were not to be disappointed) and the wonderfully pervasive aroma of bran muffins baking.

The muffin, lodged somewhere between cake and bread, is an aromatic package that is easily made and just as easily varied to suit the baker's whim or the ingredients at hand. Originally, the word muffin referred to small, round English griddle breads leavened with yeast. With the invention of baking powder in the mid-1800s, however, yeast was supplanted as North American cooks quickly adopted new, fast-rising recipes. Technically, the muffin is a batter bread made with two parts flour to one part liquid, plus leavening and shortening. Given a hot oven and a well-greased, heavy-gauge muffin tin filled right to the top with batter, the result will be a generous muffin with a slightly crisp exterior and a moist, properly crumbly interior. Start to finish, a batch of muffins can be mixed, baked and served in 30 minutes.

The mixing itself requires a light touch—no more than 15 to 20 seconds of gentle stirring or, preferably, folding. Although some lumpiness in the batter is to be expected, insufficiently mixed batter can yield a soapy, bitter-tasting muffin. A general rule is that there shouldn't be any hidden dry spots, but the dough should still be rather coarse in texture and never mixed so much that it can be poured. Overworking the batter allows gluten in the flour to develop, and the final result will be tough muffins full of tunnels and air pockets.

The secrets of leavening must also be mastered. "Just because your cat has kittens in the oven," goes the old folk saying, "you don't call them muffins." The alchemy that produces light and tender muffins is relatively simple; double-acting baking powder makes carbon

Sweet muffins, left: the transcendent combination of orange and chocolate.

dioxide bubbles in two stages: first when liquid is added, and then when exposed to the heat of the oven. Trapped within the batter, the bubbles cause the muffins to rise.

However, the leavening power of double-acting baking powder begins to decrease 15 to 30 minutes after the batter has been mixed. If baking doesn't take place promptly, the gas bubbles will escape, leaving a batter that cannot hope to rise properly. The solution: get the muffins into a hot oven without delay.

Disturbing the acid-alkaline balance of an existing recipe should be attempted only when one can afford to experiment. Recipe improvisers may also have their creative efforts foiled if they arbitrarily add, subtract or substitute acidic ingredients (such as citrus fruits or juices, sour cream, yogurt, buttermilk, molasses, apples or bananas) without altering the corresponding alkaline (baking soda) content. Most muffin recipes call for either baking soda or baking powder, or both, depending on the acidity of the batter, in order to produce sufficient carbon dioxide. Uninformed tampering with these ingredients is not advised.

For me, that lesson was a public one. After baking myriad muffins in the café and attracting a clientele who had integrated a Sunprint Bran Muffin into their morning ritual, I saw my business growing and hired bakers to keep up with production. On a very cold November morning, I arrived at work only to find a basketful of heavy-as-lead muffins with an uncanny resemblance to a collection of hockey pucks. I headed straight for the kitchen. In his most apologetic voice, the baker explained that he had read somewhere that baking soda was bad for you (it is not), and he had decided to make the recipe with baking powder instead.

Though ignorance can sometimes be blissful, where muffins are concerned, a good collection of time-tested recipes is usually preferable. The recipes that follow are recommended as a nicely balanced repertoire — muffins sweet or savory, for breakfast, teatime or formal dinners. Knowing the few basic procedures, one needs only a half hour and a loving hand to start any morning or evening with a basketful of piping hot, homemade muffins.

Note: The precise yield of muffins in any recipe depends on the volume of the individual muffin cups — they can vary from 5 to 8 ounces. Add about 3 tablespoons of water to any empty muffin cups to protect the pan during baking.

Honey-Mustard & Cheddar Muffins

These savory muffins are among our favorites — tangy with mustard, sweet with honey and rich with Cheddar. They can accompany almost any soup and are also excellent with eggs at brunch.

2 cups all-purpose flour
1 Tbsp. baking powder
¼ tsp. salt
freshly ground pepper, to taste
1 cup sharp Cheddar cheese, grated
1 egg
3 Tbsp. honey mustard
2 Tbsp. honey
1¼ cups milk
¼ cup butter, melted

Combine flour, baking powder, salt, pepper and cheese in a large mixing bowl. Whisk together the rest of the ingredients and gently but thoroughly fold them into the dry ingredients. Fill greased muffin tin and bake in a preheated 400 degree F oven for 20 minutes or until done.

Yields 12 muffins.

Ginger, Lemon & Walnut Muffins

These unusual muffins are especially good with fish or Chinese food; they are also suitable for afternoon tea. For a better blend and balance of flavors, let them cool to room temperature before serving.

grated peel of 2 lemons
2 Tbsp. fresh ginger
1 cup sugar
½ cup sweet butter
2 eggs
1 cup sour cream or yogurt
½ cup walnuts, chopped
½ tsp. powdered ginger
1 tsp. baking soda
2 cups all-purpose flour

Place lemon peel, fresh ginger and sugar in the bowl of a food processor fitted with a metal blade. Process until all large pieces are broken down. Add this to the butter and beat until fluffy. While beating, add the eggs and sour cream. In a separate bowl, combine the nuts, ginger, baking soda and flour, then fold gently into the wet batter. Fill greased muffin tin and bake in a preheated 400 degree F oven for 20 minutes or until done.

Yields 12 muffins.

Orange & Chocolate Muffins

This classic combination of orange and chocolate translates well into a muffin. Bits of chocolate melt and merge with the orange flavor, making these muffins, developed in our test kitchen, fast favorites. Great with hot coffee, tea or cocoa.

½ cup sweet butter
1 cup sugar
grated peel of 2 oranges
2 large eggs
½ cup sour cream
½ cup orange juice, freshly squeezed
1 tsp. baking powder
½ tsp. baking soda
2 cups all-purpose flour
3 oz. bittersweet chocolate, preferably a fine eating chocolate, chopped into small pieces

Beat butter and sugar together until fluffy. Continue beating while you add the orange peel and one egg at a time, then the sour cream and orange juice. Combine the dry ingredients and the chocolate, and fold lightly into the wet batter. Fold only until well blended, then fill greased muffin tin. Bake in a preheated 400 degree F oven for 20 minutes or until done.
Yields 10-12 muffins.

Pumpkin Pecan Muffins

These muffins have a melt-away quality; they are moist and cakelike. Excellent with soup and salad dinners, they also make a fine addition to a breakfast/brunch menu.

½ cup sweet butter
¾ cup dark brown sugar
4 Tbsp. maple syrup
1¼ cups mashed, cooked pumpkin
2 eggs
1 cup heavy cream
1½ Tbsp. baking powder
1 tsp. nutmeg, freshly grated
1 tsp. cinnamon
½ tsp. salt
1 tsp. vanilla
2½ cups all-purpose flour
½ cup pecans, toasted and chopped

Beat butter and sugar. Add the maple syrup, pumpkin, eggs and cream and continue beating. Mix the remaining ingredients and gently fold them into the wet batter. Fill greased muffin tin and bake at 400 degrees F for 20 minutes or until done.
Yields 10-12 muffins.

Sunprint Bran Muffins

These muffins have several great qualities: they are delicious, high in fiber, and the batter keeps for up to six weeks in the refrigerator.

3 cups bran flakes or bran bud cereal
1 cup boiling water
1 cup vegetable oil
2 eggs
1½ cups light brown sugar
2 cups buttermilk
2½ tsp. baking soda
1 tsp. salt
2½ cups flour

Soak 1½ cups bran in boiling water. Meanwhile, combine all other ingredients. Add the soaked bran and mix; spoon batter into greased muffin tin. Bake in a preheated 400 degree F oven for 20 minutes.
Yields 24 muffins.

Pumpkin Pecan Muffin

Oatmeal-Apple Muffins

The nutty flavor of oats and the perfume of vanilla come through nicely in these subtle breakfast muffins.

¼ cup sweet butter, melted
¾ cup dark brown sugar
¾ cup milk
2 tsp. vanilla
2 eggs
1 cup old-fashioned oats
1½ cups all-purpose flour
2½ tsp. baking powder
½ tsp. salt
1 apple, grated

Beat together the butter, brown sugar, milk, vanilla and eggs. In separate bowl, combine the oats, flour, baking powder, salt and grated apple, then fold gently into the wet batter. Fill greased muffin tin and bake in a preheated 400 degree F oven for 20 minutes or until done.
Yields 12 muffins.

Blueberry Muffins

These have a surprise cluster of berries in the center, which makes them more intense than other blueberry muffins. Delightful for breakfast.

Blueberry Muffin

1½ cups blueberries
2 Tbsp. white sugar
grated peel of 1 lemon
½ cup sweet butter
¾ cup light brown sugar
2 eggs
1 cup milk
4 tsp. baking powder
½ tsp. salt
2 cups all-purpose flour

Mix 1 cup of the blueberries, the white sugar and lemon peel in a small bowl and set aside. Meanwhile, cream butter and brown sugar until fluffy, then add the eggs, one at a time, then the milk. Combine the baking powder, salt and flour, then add the remaining ½ cup blueberries, tossing lightly to mix. Gently fold into the wet batter. Fill greased muffin tin halfway with batter, add 1 tablespoon of the blueberry-lemon mixture to each muffin and top with more batter. Bake in a preheated 400 degree F oven for 20 minutes, or until done.
Yields 12 muffins.

Note: If blueberries stick to the pan, the muffins can be difficult to remove; try to distribute the batter accordingly.

Corn Muffins

These are my favorite corn muffins. They are especially good with chili or spicy soups and stews.

1¼ cups all-purpose flour
¾ cup yellow cornmeal, preferably stone-ground
3 tsp. baking powder
½ tsp. salt
¼ cup white sugar

½ tsp. baking soda
1 cup sour cream
1 egg, beaten
buttermilk (optional; add up to ½ cup if muffin batter appears too dry)

Put all dry ingredients, except the baking soda, in a large mixing bowl. Mix the baking soda with the sour cream until it bubbles a bit, then gently but thoroughly fold this and the egg into the dry ingredients. Fill greased muffin tin and bake in a preheated 350 degree F oven for 20 to 25 minutes or until done.
Yields 12 muffins.

Maple Walnut Muffins

These marvelous muffins have a subtle flavor and crisp outer edges — the qualities of a great waffle.

1¾ cups all-purpose flour
2½ tsp. baking powder
¼ tsp. salt
1 cup pure maple syrup
¼ cup sweet butter, melted
1 egg
¼ cup milk
½ cup walnuts, chopped

Combine the flour, baking powder and salt in a large mixing bowl. Beat together the maple syrup, butter, egg and milk and add, along with the walnuts, to the dry ingredients. Fold the mixture gently but thoroughly. Fill greased muffin tin and bake in a preheated 400 degree F oven for 15 to 20 minutes or until done.
Yields 10 muffins.

Herbed Cottage Cheese Muffins

Try these with your favorite tomato soup or as a special treat with smoked ham, sandwich style. They have a smooth, crisp surface and a moist interior.

2 cups all-purpose flour
1 Tbsp. sugar
2½ tsp. baking powder
2 Tbsp. dried dill
½ tsp. salt
freshly ground pepper, to taste
1 egg
1 cup cottage cheese
¾ cup milk
4 Tbsp. butter, melted
1 Tbsp. shallots, chopped fine

Combine the flour, sugar, baking powder, dill, salt and pepper in a large mixing bowl. Whisk egg, cottage cheese, milk, butter and shallots together. Add the liquid mixture to the dry ingredients and fold gently but thoroughly. Fill greased muffin tin and bake in a preheated 400 degree F oven for 20 minutes or until done.

Yields 12 muffins.

Carrot-Coconut Muffins

Chock-full of fruit, nuts and fiber, these muffins are coarse-textured but not dense, and especially nutritious.

2 cups all-purpose flour
1 cup sugar
2 tsp. baking soda
2 tsp. cinnamon
¼ tsp. salt
2 cups carrots, grated
½ cup currants
½ cup walnuts or pecans
½ cup shredded coconut
1 apple, peeled, cored and grated
3 eggs
1 cup vegetable oil
1 tsp. vanilla

Combine first 10 ingredients in a large mixing bowl. Beat eggs, oil and vanilla together and combine with the dry ingredients. Fold thoroughly. Fill greased muffin tin and bake in a preheated 400 degree F oven for 20 minutes or until done.

Yields 12 muffins.

Summertime Soups

Brisk Blends from the Vegetable Garden

By JoAnne Cats-Baril

When my husband's work took us to Portugal recently, we used the occasion to make a journey through the Moorish countryside of Spain to the ancient towns of Cordoba, Grenada and Seville. In Lisbon, we eagerly packed our rented car with the sustenance necessary to keep the appetites of a 2-year-old and a pregnant woman under control. Rural roads in Spain have had a long-standing reputation for being difficult, and they lived up to their notoriety. Nevertheless, the beauty of the landscape — dotted with gnarled olive trees, fragrant groves of orange and almond trees and expansive haciendas where, for centuries, fighting bulls have been bred — was more than generous compensation for the bumps and curves in the road. The raw countryside, unblemished by the commercialism of roadside junk-food stands and billboards, foretold of the honest, Andalusian food that awaited us each midday and evening.

We ate tapas and drank delicious local wines, but again and again we found ourselves ordering the superb gazpacho. Back home, our garden lay under several feet of snow, but here was the essence of summer captured in a bowl. Spain claims gazpacho as part of its patrimony, and almost every restaurant, be it grand or quaint, proudly features gazpacho on its menu. In most cases, we were served bowls of the opaque red soup accompanied by finely diced bits of cucumber, green pepper, onion and tomato and toasted croutons. These crudités were spooned onto the soup, providing a fresh, crunchy version of the blended ingredients that made up the soup itself. This soup bore no resemblance in either taste or appearance to the flashy V-8-red version of gazpacho so often served outside of Spain. One would be hard-pressed to think of a more refreshing and healthy lunch dish or starter for a warm-

weather meal, and we vowed to take better advantage of our own garden's potential to provide a delightful season of authentic home-made gazpacho.

Of soup itself, there is much to be said. "Soup is cuisine's kindest course," De Gouy wrote in *The Soup Book* in 1949. "It breathes reassurance; it steams consolation; after a weary day it promotes sociability. . . ." Soup can be basic nourishment in the form of an entire meal or can be the overture to a festive dinner. The foundation for good soup depends entirely on the simplest of things: utterly fresh ingredients and pure, cold water. As Auguste Escoffier said of soup, "A comfortable and thoroughly bourgeois dish that nothing may unseat."

Unfortunately, for most of us hot weather manages to unseat the appetite for steaming soup. During the dog days, even the most enthusiastic cook enjoys freedom from a hot stove. Cold soup, which is sadly missing from the repertoires of most North American home kitchens, is a worthy answer.

Simple to make, cold soups tap the nutritious harvest of the summer garden and require either no cooking at all or a brisk session in the cool morning hours of the day. Certain fresh vegetables, like tomatoes and avocados, invite a preparation without the use of heat — just confident spicing, pureeing and thinning with yogurt, buttermilk, cream or sour cream. Other soups best for chilling include consommés and vegetable purees, which require some modifications if you intend to serve them chilled.

A consommé is a broth made by cooking a beef or chicken broth a second time with fresh meat and vegetables and clarifying it with egg whites if necessary. The charm of consommé rests entirely on the flavor and gelatinous quality of meat and/or poultry and the subtlety of fresh vegetables and herbs. The idea of a consommé may take some getting used to — the

Cool, fresh Andalusian Gazpacho, right.

broth sets up as it cools – but the melt-away, light, gelatinous broth is purity itself, and the shimmering beauty of a well-made consommé can be irresistible.

A vegetable puree, on the other hand, depends on cream and broth for richness and proper consistency. Though almost any vegetable can be used successfully in soup, some vegetables have particularly high starch contents and therefore need almost no added thickeners. Among these starch-rich vegetables are potatoes, carrots, peas, lima beans and celeriac. All of these vegetables make lovely soups with the flavor added by some members of the onion family – leeks, onions, chives, garlic – and herbs; they achieve the proper texture by balancing broth and cream.

The broth you use will be higher in natural gelatin if you make your own (recipe follows), but canned broth can be used if necessary. When using potatoes as a thickener, choose the mealy baking types; they are superior to boiling potatoes because they disperse more easily in soup.

Potatoes, of course, form the base of classic vichyssoise, whose origin can be traced back to a hot potato-leek breakfast soup served in Burgundy. More specifically, it is Louis Diat, the French chef-de-cuisine of the famous Ritz-Carlton in New York City, who is credited with the invention of cold potato soup. The chilled version of a boyhood favorite is said to have been born out of an attempt to create an elegant soup course to be served on swelteringly hot summer days. Diat's experimentation began with the memory of his mother's soup in his hometown of Montmarault; it ended with a deliciously cool white soup that he named after the nearby spa village of Vichy. Voilà: vichyssoise.

Celery, watercress and sorrel, to name just a few, are other prime ingredients for cold soups. These are lacking in natural starch, but they do not profit from the addition of vegetable thickeners: Their delicacy is canceled by the texture and flavor of other, heavier vegetables. In these instances, a velouté-based soup is just the answer for fine texture and virtually no competitive taste. (A velouté is a concoction that depends on flour as a thickener and egg yolks and cream for enrichment.)

Yet another thickening agent appropriate for cold soups is rice, and its most famous application is in Greek avgolemono. Lemon, the dominant flavor in this soup, has a refreshing tonic-like quality, just perfect for a hot summer's day when our appetites have become listless.

Lightness is the key to warm-weather cooking, and neither consommés nor vegetable purees should contain much butter or animal fat, which only coagulates in an unfortunate and unappetizing way when chilled. All soups both thicken and lose flavor when chilled; the taste, especially that of salt, is muted by this process. The soups, therefore, should receive their final seasoning after being chilled, just before serving. To assure intense flavor, serve these soups just cool, not icy cold.

The word soup itself comes from the Germanic "sop," which originally referred to the bread over which a hot broth was poured. Today, in some regions of France, "la soupe" still refers to the type of bread over which soup is ladled. Bread and soup have a history of being inseparable, and that habit is still happily alive today. There are countless examples of the companionship of hot soup and bread – like the raft of bread in French onion soup – but even cold soups have their traditions. Bread is used as a thickener in gazpacho, and a gorgeous hot-pink borscht is more handsome and delicious with wedges of buttered black bread on the side.

Cold soups are dramatically enhanced in appearance when sprigs of fresh herbs (dill, tarragon and chives are personal favorites) or julienned vegetables are carelessly set afloat just prior to serving. Bold pinks and reds, as in borscht and gazpacho, become artfully striking with a dollop of sour cream or tiny geometric squares of dark green pepper splashed in the center of the bowl. For special occasions, chipped ice surrounding any bowl of chilled soup promises refreshment before the tasting begins. Both the eye and palate are sure to be satisfied by these healthy, invigorating soups of summer.

Andalusian Gazpacho

An authentic and simply made version of the zesty Spanish classic. Most North American vegetable gardens will be able to supply all the fresh ingredients.

2½ cups chicken broth, homemade or canned (see recipe below)
1½ cups cubed white bread, crust removed
4 cups concentrated crushed tomatoes, strained to remove seeds
1 small white onion
1 green pepper
½ large cucumber, peeled and seeded
1 clove garlic
¼ cup red wine vinegar
2 Tbsp. mayonnaise
1 cup half-and-half, or mix milk with heavy cream in a 1:1 ratio
salt and pepper, to taste

Garnish:
1 cup each toasted croutons, finely diced white
  onion, green pepper, and cucumber

Pour ½ cup of the chicken stock over the bread cubes and let soak while you put all other ingredients, except mayonnaise, half-and-half, and salt and pepper, in a food processor or blender and puree until smooth. Add soaked bread cubes and puree. Run the mixture through a food mill to remove remaining tomato seeds and green pepper skins. Chill for at least 3 hours so the flavors blend. Whisk in the mayonnaise and half-and-half. Season to taste with salt and pepper. Serve with the garnish.
Serves 6 to 8.

Chicken Broth

This is a simple and flavorful broth that serves as a great foundation for any soup calling for chicken broth.

7-8 lb. stewing hen
4 quarts cold water
1 large onion, studded with 3 whole cloves
2 carrots
1 garlic bulb (not clove), unpeeled
bouquet garni: bay leaf, parsley, lovage
  and thyme
1 tsp. coarse salt

Put everything but salt in a large stock pot and bring to a boil. Skim off all scum that rises to the surface. Lower to a gentle simmer, add salt and simmer, partially covered, for 2 to 3 hours. Strain and cool. The fat will rise to the surface during chilling. When broth is completely cold, skim fat from the surface.
Yields approximately 3 quarts.

Consommé Madrilene

The tomato gives this clear, shimmering soup a slightly rosy tinge. It is lightly gelatinous, elegant and refreshing.

3 quarts chicken broth
1½ lbs. lean beef chuck, cut into small chunks
2 carrots, finely diced
1 leek, white part only, finely diced
6 tomatoes, seeded and chopped
1 tsp. coarse salt
chives for garnish

Put everything into a stock pot and bring to a gentle boil. Skim the scum off the surface and lower the flame to keep the soup at a gentle simmer, uncovered, for 1½ hours. You should have about 3 cups of liquid when finished. Strain through a double thickness of dampened cheesecloth, then chill consommé until lightly set, about 2 hours. Serve garnished with chives.
Serves 2.

Avocado-Coriander Soup

No vegetable is as creamy as an avocado, and it is shown off at its best in this delicate, pale green soup.

2 ripe avocados
2 scallions
2 cups half-and-half
juice of ½ lime
½ cup chicken broth
¼ tsp. salt
¼ tsp. cayenne
¼ cup fresh coriander leaves,
  or 1 Tbsp. dried

Put all ingredients in a food processor or blender and process until smooth. Refrigerate for 3 hours, until completely chilled. Thin with more chicken broth if necessary and season to taste with salt and pepper. Garnish with fresh coriander leaves.
Serves 4.

Green Vichyssoise

A green-flecked cool soup with a hearty texture, this is ideal for a light meal in itself. Serve with a green salad and fresh bread.

5 small leeks, white part only (about 2 cups)
2 Tbsp. butter
6 cups chicken broth
2 medium baking potatoes, peeled and diced
  (about 1½ cups)
4 bunches watercress, leaves and tender stems
  (about 4 cups), or 4 cups fresh spinach leaves
1 cup heavy cream
salt and pepper, to taste
sprigs of watercress or parsley

Sweat leeks in butter for 10 minutes, then add the chicken broth and potatoes and simmer until the potatoes are tender, about 20 minutes. Add the watercress or spinach and simmer 5 minutes longer. Puree the soup, leaving flecks of green, and chill for at least 3 hours. Add the heavy cream and season to taste with salt and pepper. Garnish with sprigs of watercress or parsley, and serve.
Serves 6.

Garden Pizza

FAST FOOD WITHOUT GUILT

BY JOANNE CATS-BARIL

It was midnight in Venice; my husband and I had just left La Fenice, a venerable opera house with the roisterous atmosphere of a baseball stadium and a reputation as the launching point for the singing careers of many operatic greats. The Venetians take their opera seriously, but not necessarily with hushed solemnity: they sing along, with libretto in hand, comment loudly on the stage design, squeeze and kiss their dates, laugh and cry. Some visitors from opera's stuffier outlands are visibly annoyed, while others watch with bemusement and wish they were Italian.

We had just seen *Don Quixote* and left La Fenice humming, caught up in a lighthearted spirit that led us onto the patio of the Café del Teatro, an open-air restaurant with an extensive pizza menu that seemed to suit our mood.

North Americans visiting Italy commonly don't know what to expect when ordering "real" Italian pizza—indeed, there is a rather widespread belief that real Italians may not even eat pizza as we have come to know it. Greeted by one of Café del Teatro's veteran waiters, we let him order for us and found ourselves served a platter of a dozen or so small, crunchy-crusted pizzas. Each was just four bites big, and each had a different topping: artichoke hearts in a creamy white sauce, tomatoes with not-quite-melted chunks of flavorful aged cheese, and sautéed eggplant with oregano are ones I remember.

It is not surprising that Italians are credited as the orginators of the pizza: the Italians who sing along at the opera are the same breed who throw just about anything onto a piece of raised dough and produce a superb meal. Whereas the mass market pizzerias of North America have standardized a tomato/mozzarella/pepperoni/sausage version of pizza, the Italians have always shown a greater willingness to be versatile—a trait now spreading among a new generation of American pizza makers.

Perhaps because of the heavy-handed use of fatty sausage and thick mantles of oily cheese, pizza in this country is high on the list of junk foods perceived as carrying a megadose of calories and less than healthy ingredients. In the trendier urban centers, all this is changing, as avant-garde young chefs have turned pizza into a light appetizer or pre-appetizer with toppings of wild mushrooms, mussels, clams, homemade lean sausages, smoked salmon, avocado and all manner of nontraditional cheeses, from Monterey Jack to blue.

For those whose local pizza parlor has yet to see the nutritional light and for those of us who live well beyond the delivery zones of the pizza couriers, there remains an option all too few cooks consider: make your own.

Gardeners, especially, should consider learning the simple skills needed to make pizza, for this is a dish ideally suited to making memorable use of fresh vegetables and herbs as they come into season. The very nature of pizza makes this a fast food—but not necessarily an unhealthy food. "Pizza pulls its weight nutritionally," says a recent report of the American Council on Science and Health, which notes the "substantial" amounts of protein, calcium, vitamin A, thiamine, riboflavin, niacin and iron. The crust supplies carbohydrates; the cheese, meat or fish provides protein; the vegetables and herbs lend vitamins, minerals and fiber.

Indeed, pizza is a perfect trencher, an edible plate to hold other foods. From the provender of the home garden, one can select almost any combination of tomato, asparagus, zucchini, pepper, spinach, eggplant, broccoli, cauliflower, onion, garlic and leeks. The use of low-salt and low-fat cheeses can yield a pizza

Pizza is ideally suited to making memorable use of fresh vegetables and herbs as they come into season, left.

befitting the regimen of the strictest spa – the same savory tastes and textures that all pizza lovers crave, but without the guilt.

Two Secrets

Although the popularity of pizza in North America dates back only to the homecoming years after World War II, its origins can be traced directly back to the Greek settlement of the Magna Graecia region of southern Italy in 750 B.C. Accomplished bakers, the Greeks taught the Romans the skills of leavening, flavoring and baking, and breads evolved that made use of local olives and olive oils, cheeses from the herds and herbs from the hillsides.

Virgil, after visiting Naples, immortalized in poetry a bread known as *moretum* – a flat round of dough baked with a sauce of olive oil herbed with garlic, parsley, rue, coriander and sprinkled with dry cheese. Only in the late 1800s did pizza as we commonly know it begin to achieve widespread popularity outside Naples. Legend has it that Queen Margherita, visiting Capodimonte Palace, had the most noted local pizzeria cater a baking session so that she could sample this much-talked-about regional specialty. Her favorite, it is recorded, was topped with tomatoes, mozzarella and fresh basil – appropriately displaying the red, white and green of the Italian flag.

The good taste of royalty notwithstanding, the truth of the matter is that pizza is a simple peasant food, made with simple tools and methods little changed down through the millennia. Whether rustic or refined, homemade pizzas depend primarily on your ability to follow a simple dough recipe and to assemble a well-balanced topping. Beyond this, the difference between mediocrity and excellence comes in knowing two basic secrets: bake on a pizza stone and use a very hot oven.

An unadorned piece of unglazed natural stoneware that has been fired at over 2000 degrees F, the pizza stone imitates the lining of a professional pizza oven; it produces a desirable crust texture because stoneware characteristically absorbs moisture and distributes heat evenly. Gourmet equipment shops and mail-order suppliers offer pizza stones from about $15 to $30, depending on size and the presence or absence of a very handy wire carrying rack. A stone with a diameter of at least 15 inches is recommended.

Equally good results can be obtained using unglazed quarry tiles from a building supply outlet or tile store. Be sure to specify high-fired (1500 degrees) quarry tile, as those fired at lower temperatures will crack in the oven. Such tiles cost about $3 per square foot, and

their only drawback is in being less convenient to handle than a one-piece pizza stone; however, they can be left in the oven. In any case, the stone or tiles are necessary to render a crisp, nicely browned crust.

The second tip – using a very hot oven – is especially important. Italian pizza ovens achieve temperatures of 800 degrees F, which creates a great crust and smoky flavor. Domestic ovens, therefore, should be used at their highest setting.

Foolproof Dough

Crust being the downfall of so many commercial pizzerias, one might assume that pizza dough is difficult to prepare. In reality, there is nothing mysterious about pizza dough, the making of which is straightforward and less time-consuming than making bread. It will need 1½ to 2½ hours to rise, but large batches can be made and the excess refrigerated or frozen for convenient later use.

In the following recipes, we are not aiming for heavy, deep-dish Sicilian-style pizza, but rather a more classically Neapolitan crust – thinner, with a crisp outer texture and light, fresh, savory toppings. We will leave room for much interpretation, but the end product should never be gummy, sweet or quiche-like.

Crust choices include whole wheat, semolina and white; the decision depends both on personal preference and on the intended aesthetics and ingredients of the final product.

In Italy, semolina is ground to a silky cream-colored flour and used in most of their bread, pizza and pasta doughs. It is milled from the heart of the durum wheat berry, producing a high-gluten wheat flour. Although often grainier than its Italian counterpart, American semolina can be improved by grinding it with all-purpose flour in a blender. Health food and Italian specialty shops are likely sources.

Whichever flour you choose, the goal is to achieve a light, crisp and chewy crust, substantial enough to hold up to a variety of toppings. The lightness of the crust is related to the type of dough you mix: a soft and sticky dough will increase the likelihood of a light crust. The addition of a fruity olive oil to the dough lends elasticity and eventual flavor and crispness. Spreading olive oil on the surface of the shaped crust creates a seal between dough and topping and keeps the crust from getting soggy. Pizza dough has almost twice as much yeast as a bread dough, but since pizza is baked at high temperatures for such a short time, it needs the extra yeast for the dough to rise.

Finally, whether you choose whole wheat,

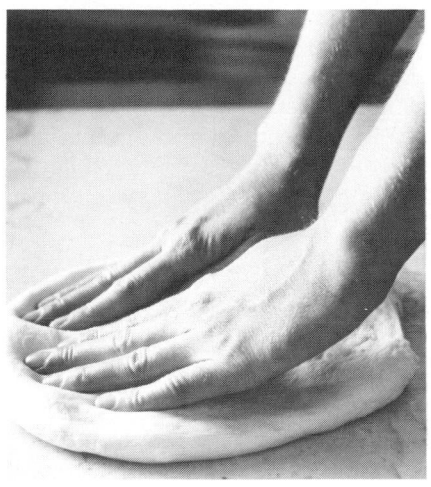
1.

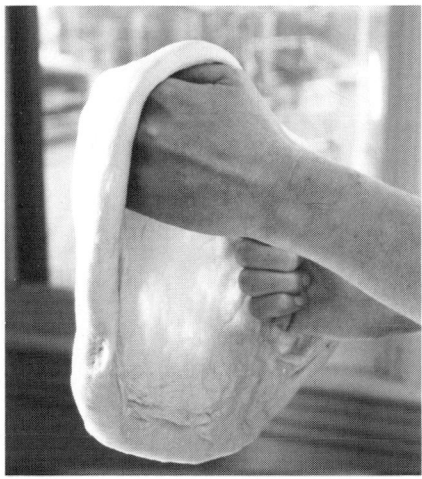
2.

3.

semolina or white flour for your crust depends on the topping you have in mind. The addition of whole wheat or semolina flour gives a grainy texture and a nutty flavor; these crusts are more substantial and are therefore ideal for pizzas with a good helping of cheese. If you opt for whole wheat or semolina flour, it should still only constitute a portion of the recipe or the crust will be too heavy. If your intentions run to the extravagant – pizza with smoked salmon and golden caviar, for example – then a white crust is the only appropriate choice.

There are many ways to shape pizza dough. You can press, roll, stretch or toss it. Rolling and pressing the dough compresses it and can create a dense and heavy crust unless done gently. Stretching and tossing the dough into shape is the better method and quite easy after a little practice: simply make two fists and drape the dough over them, then rotate and stretch the dough by moving your fists apart. We find that using a combination of rolling and stretching works best. In any case, you should rest the dough afterwards to relax the gluten and insure a tender crust. Preheat the oven and stone for at least 30 minutes and bake the pizza as briefly and as intensely hot as possible. Whatever your intentions are, remember that pizza is a deliciously flavored bread, so make your crusts with passion.

Embellishments

In deciding which topping to use, a good rule of thumb is to exercise restraint in the heavy, wet items like cheese and meat and to be lavish with seasoning agents and vegetables. Sauces are the first order of business since they are spread right on top of the olive oil-glazed dough. The sauce can be either an herbed ricotta, a simple white béchamel, a pesto or a tomato type but, in any case, it should be suitably thick, the consistency of sour cream, to avoid a watery or soggy pizza.

When using vegetables, it is important to tenderize them and rid them of excess water. You can do this by sautéing, as in the case of mushrooms; steaming, for cauliflower, broccoli and asparagus – no more than *al dente*; breading and frying, for zucchini and eggplant or slicing and air-drying for tomatoes. Among the tomatoes, the Roma or plum tomato is best for pizza because it is meatier and has less water content than other varieties. Herbs should be bruised and snipped, then sprinkled over the vegetables but under the cheese.

And finally, cheeses are grated and dappled over the top. There are wet cheeses like mozzarella, Cheddar and Gouda, and there are dry cheeses like Parmesan, Romano and provolone; keep this distinction in mind when choosing your cheese so that it complements the rest of the topping. Also, Parmesan cheese burns quite easily so it is best to put it under another cheese or add it a bit later, after the pizza has baked for five minutes or so. Though we haven't discussed the addition of sausage, pepperoni, or other meats, they should be added before the cheese, if desired.

In putting together these garden pizzas, be sure to keep moisture, its absence and presence, in mind. Using olive oil, sauces, vegetables like eggplant, zucchini, asparagus and tomatoes, and whole milk moist cheeses will increase the moisture level of your pizza: guard against watery, sticky results. Slimming down to no sauce, drier vegetables like broccoli and cauliflower and low-moisture cheeses like Parmesan and Romano will increase the risk of a dry pizza. Mix, prepare and combine your ingredients judiciously to create a well-balanced pizza.

In the *Italian Baker,* Carol Field reminds us

1. Flatten the dough into a circular shape.
2. Rotate and stretch dough with fists.
3. Push dough outward for final stretch.

that "the Neapolitans start with the sun and the fish of the gulf and add strong local tastes without intricate mystery or shadings – let that be your guide."

Tips

Making and raising the dough requires but a few minutes of attendance; shaping the dough and preparing the toppings are also quick steps that tend to attract volunteer helpers. Truly the only tricky moment in the whole pizza-making process comes in getting the prepared and dressed dough transferred to the hot stone.

This is accomplished nicely with a professional pizza paddle, known as a peel, available from restaurant suppliers. The peel comes in very handy for checking under the crust during baking and in withdrawing the piping hot pizza from the oven, but one can make do easily enough without this tool by using the following sleight-of-hand tips:

1. Keep dough well oiled and covered during the rising stages to prevent it from drying out.

2. Use a fruity olive oil which will give a subtle taste to the crust.

3. Use generous amounts of cornmeal on the surface where you do the final shaping – the back of a cookie sheet or pizza peel – to aid in moving the crust to the preheated stone. Be careful not to make a pizza that is larger than the stone (because the stone is in the oven heating, this is easier to do than you might think).

4. Place your stone or tiles directly on the floor of your oven and preheat at 500 degrees F (or as high as your oven will go) for at least 30 minutes to maximize the available heat.

5. Shake the cookie sheet or pizza peel occasionally while the dough is rising for that last 30 minutes to prevent it from sticking. Put the toppings on and transfer the dough immediately to the preheated stone; give it one energetic shake to slide it onto the stone.

6. Bake the pizza quickly and serve immediately.

Crusts

White Pizza Crust

This crust is heavenly and foolproof. It is easy to work with, quick to rise and produces a beautiful, puffy edge. If you stretch it really thin, you will get a 15-inch pizza and some extra dough. You can also divide it into two or four pieces for individual pizzas.

1¾ tsp. active dry yeast
1⅓ cups warm water (105 degrees F)
pinch of sugar or 1 tsp. honey
¼ cup olive oil, preferably extra virgin
3¾ cups all-purpose, unbleached white flour
1½ tsp. sea salt

Semolina Pizza Crust

This crust is more crackerlike and, some insist, authentically Italian. It requires a longer rising time, is very easy to roll and has a delicious flavor. The edge is narrow and crunchy rather than puffy.

2 packages active dry yeast
1 cup plus 4 Tbsp. warm water
  (105 degrees F)
pinch of sugar or 2 tsp. honey
6 Tbsp. olive oil, preferably extra virgin
2 cups semolina flour (available at health food
  or Italian specialty stores)
1½ cups all-purpose, unbleached white flour
2 tsp. sea salt

Whole Wheat Pizza Crust

This recipe produces a relatively light whole wheat crust. It has a lovely texture, a nutty flavor and works especially well with slightly heavy toppings.

1¾ tsp. active dry yeast
1 cup plus 2 Tbsp. warm water (105 degrees F)
4½ Tbsp. olive oil, preferably extra virgin
¾ cup whole wheat flour
2½ cups all-purpose, unbleached white flour
1 tsp. sea salt

Method: Stir yeast, water and sugar together, let sit for 5 minutes or until foamy. Stir in the oil and add the flour, 1 cup at a time, and the salt, and mix until all the lumps are gone. You can do this by hand, in a heavy-duty mixer with a dough hook, or in a food processor. If using a mixer or food processor, put the flour and salt in the work bowl and add the wet ingredients while the motor is running. Knead for 8-10 minutes until the dough is satiny and elastic; this can be done in the work bowl but I knead by hand for the sheer pleasure of it. Place the dough in an oiled bowl, turn to coat, cover tightly with plastic wrap. For the *white crust,* let rise 45 minutes to 1 hour; for the *whole wheat* and *semolina crusts,* let rise for 2 hours or until double in bulk – this will help lighten these crusts a little bit.

Roll or press the dough lightly into a flattened ball. Pick the dough up and stretch it with your fists, from underneath, until you achieve the desired size and thinness. Place it on a cookie sheet or pizza peel that has been sprinkled generously with cornmeal.

At this point, push the edge of the crust outward with your fingertips to give it a final stretch and pinch the edge lightly (don't build up the edge, or it will rise too high in proportion to the rest of the pizza). Cover with a kitchen towel for the second rise of 30 minutes. Shake it occasionally to keep it from sticking to the work surface.

When ready to bake: top the dough, leaving about one inch of edge uncovered; transfer the pizza to the preheated pizza stone or tiles, and bake in a 500 degree F oven for 10 minutes or until done. Watch the pizza while baking because at these temperatures it could burn quickly. These recipes will make at least one 15-to-16-inch pizza, two 10-inch pizzas, or five to six 4-inch, single-serving pizzas.

The dough can be frozen at any stage in the process; simply wrap it in aluminum foil and label it as to whether it has risen once or twice. Defrost it in the refrigerator for at least 8 hours and pick up where you left off.

Toppings

(all recipes suitable for 1 large, 15-inch pizza)

Ratatouille with Red Peppers, Parmesan and Mozzarella

This pizza is reminiscent of classical, Neapolitan pizza. The added flavor comes from using a version of ratatouille instead of tomato sauce.

2 large eggplant, diced
2 Tbsp. salt
¼ cup olive oil, preferably extra virgin
2 medium-sized yellow onions
2 cloves garlic, pressed
3 medium-sized zucchini, diced
2 red peppers, roasted and peeled
8 ripe plum tomatoes, blanched, peeled and diced, or 28-oz. can Italian tomatoes, diced
2 tsp. fresh thyme or 1 tsp. dried thyme, crumbled
1 Tbsp. red wine vinegar
1 cup grated Parmesan
1½ cups grated mozzarella

Method: Sprinkle eggplant with the salt, toss and let sit in a colander for 1 hour; this helps remove any bitterness. Meanwhile, put the olive oil in a pot and add the onions and garlic, rinsed eggplant, zucchini and roasted red pep-

pers sequentially. Sauté each for 5-10 minutes before adding the next one. Finally, add the tomatoes, thyme and vinegar and simmer everything until the vegetables are soft, the water is mostly cooked off and the flavor is mellow – about 30 minutes. Taste for seasoning and add whatever is necessary. Put the mixture, in batches, into the work bowl of a food processor and pulse until the mixture has a medium-fine texture, like a chunky sauce. Brush the prepared dough with olive oil, spread with ratatouille, top with Parmesan then mozzarella, and bake in a preheated 500 degree F oven for 10 minutes or until done.

Smoked Ham, Asparagus Tips and White Cheddar

If you mound the asparagus generously, this pizza is as beautiful as it is light and delicious. The smoked ham underneath adds the perfect depth to the fresh taste of asparagus.

olive oil
¼ lb. smoked ham, sliced paper-thin
6 cups asparagus tips and stalks, washed and cut into 1-inch pieces and steamed for 5 minutes or until *al dente*
2 cups grated white Cheddar

Method: Brush the prepared dough with olive oil. Lay down a single, thin layer of the smoked ham, top with mounds of asparagus and sprinkle the Cheddar on top. Bake in a preheated, 500 degree F oven for 10 minutes or until done.

Ricotta, Zucchini and Tomato

This is a meal in itself. Full-bodied, rich and satisfying. It takes some extra time to prepare but is well worth the effort. It is excellent with the semolina crust.

1½ cups ricotta cheese
2 small eggs, beaten
¼ cup chopped parsley
½ tsp. salt
3 plum tomatoes
1 cup bread crumbs
1 cup finely grated Parmesan
1 clove garlic
2 tsp. dried basil
1 tsp. dried oregano
2 medium-sized zucchini
3 eggs, beaten, for coating the zucchini
olive oil
1½ cups grated mozzarella

Method: Mix the ricotta, 2 eggs, parsley and salt; set aside. Slice, salt and air-dry the tomatoes. Put the bread crumbs, Parmesan, garlic, basil and oregano in a plastic bag and shake to mix well. Slice the zucchini into ¼-inch wheels, dip in the beaten egg wash, place in the bag of crumbs and shake to cover. Fry in a hot skillet with olive oil and drain on paper towels. Brush prepared dough with olive oil. Spread the ricotta mixture on the bottom, and arrange the zucchini and tomatoes, alternating them in a circular pattern, over the ricotta mixture. Scatter the mozzarella evenly over the top. Bake in a preheated 500 degree F oven for 10 minutes or until done.

Fresh Spinach, Caramelized Onion and Gorgonzola

This pizza is a favorite. The spinach adds a fresh, earthy flavor and the caramelized onions and Gorgonzola bring rich and contrasting tastes.

4 medium-sized yellow onions, sliced
4-6 Tbsp. olive oil, preferably extra virgin
2 Tbsp. sweet butter
2 lbs. fresh spinach
1 tsp. salt, or to taste
6 oz. Gorgonzola or blue cheese, crumbled

Method: Caramelize the onions slowly, over moderate heat, in 4 Tbsp. of the olive oil and in the butter; this will take nearly an hour. Meanwhile, sort and wash the spinach. When the onions are a deep caramel color, add the damp spinach and cover to wilt it, about 5 minutes. Since you have such large quantities to work with, it is easiest to add the spinach in batches. Toss the mixture gently and taste for salt and oil; add as needed, but be sure the spinach is well oiled because this pizza has no sauce. Spread the mixture on the prepared dough, sprinkle the cheese over the top and bake in a preheated 500 degree F oven for 10 minutes or until done.

Plum Tomato, Scallion and Parmesan

Almost tartlike in its simplicity, this pizza is easy to prepare whether for dinner or as elegant finger food with cocktails.

olive oil
10-12 plum tomatoes, sliced very thin, salted and dried for at least 1 hour
3 scallions, sliced into thin ringlets
1½ cups grated Parmesan

Method: Brush prepared dough with olive oil. Arrange the tomato slices in a circular, slightly overlapping pattern and sprinkle with the scallions and lastly, the Parmesan. Bake in a preheated 500 degree F oven for 10 minutes or until done.

Cauliflower, Béchamel and Gouda

This unusual pizza is delicate and especially lovely as an appetizer. The soft texture and mild flavor are highlighted by the tang of aged Gouda.

1 large head cauliflower
4 Tbsp. sweet butter
4 Tbsp. flour
2 Tbsp. minced shallots
2 cups milk
½ tsp. salt, or to taste
olive oil
2½ cups grated aged Gouda

Method: Trim cauliflower into flowerets and steam for 5-8 minutes or until *al dente*; set aside. Make a béchamel sauce with the sweet butter, flour, shallots, milk and salt. Brush the prepared dough with olive oil, spread with béchamel, lay the cauliflower on top of the béchamel in a circular pattern and top with the grated Gouda. Bake in a preheated 500 degree F oven for 10 minutes, or until done.

Broccoli, Cherry Tomato, Parsley Pesto and White Cheddar

A lovely pizza—the Cheddar melts to the bottom leaving the pattern of broccoli and cherry tomatoes visible. The parsley pesto with tarragon is delightful, adding sparkle to the broccoli.

Pesto:
2 cloves garlic
2 cups chopped parsley
¼ cup fresh tarragon, or 2 Tbsp. dried
⅓ cup olive oil, preferably extra virgin
⅓ cup grated Parmesan
¼ cup walnuts, lightly toasted
½ tsp. salt, or to taste

4 heads broccoli, steamed *al dente*
4 cherry tomatoes
1 cup grated white Cheddar

Method: Put all of the pesto ingredients into a blender jar or the work bowl of a food processor and blend until smooth. Spread the pesto on the prepared dough and lay the broccoli in a circular pattern on top; leave a space in the center and put the halved cherry tomatoes there. Sprinkle the Cheddar on top and bake in a preheated 500 degree F oven for 10 minutes or until done.

Porcini and Cultivated Mushroom with Mozzarella

Italian woodland mushrooms bring exotic aroma to this pizza. For mushroom lovers only.

3 oz. dried porcini mushrooms
10 oz. cultivated mushrooms
4 Tbsp. sweet butter
1 Tbsp. minced shallots
1 Tbsp. cornstarch
3 Tbsp. tamari
½ tsp. salt, or to taste
2 cups grated mozzarella

Method: Soak the dried porcini in 1 cup warm water for 30 minutes. Meanwhile, clean and slice the cultivated mushrooms. In a skillet, melt the sweet butter and sauté the shallots until tender. Add the cultivated mushrooms and sauté over a moderately high heat until nicely browned. Drain the porcini, straining the water through a double thickness of cheesecloth to eliminate sandy residue. Chop the porcini and add to the skillet along with the water. Reduce for just a few minutes – don't let the mushrooms get too soggy. Mix the cornstarch with the tamari and salt, and stir in 2 Tbsp. of the hot mushroom broth; then add the mixture slowly to the skillet and allow to thicken for a few minutes. Spread this mushroom ragout onto the prepared dough, top with the mozzarella, and bake in a preheated 500 degree F oven for 10 minutes or until done. ❧

Sources

Dean & Deluca
560 Broadway
New York, New York 10012
(800) 221-7714 / (212) 431-1691
Baking stone: 14-inch x 16-inch rectangle, $28, plus $7 shipping and handling charges.

Sassafras Enterprises
P.O. Box 1366
Evanston, Illinois 60204
(800) 537-4941 / (312) 226-2000
Pizza stones: 13-inch round, $16; 15¼-inch round, $22. Prices include shipping and handling. Illinois residents add 8% sales tax.

Williams-Sonoma
Mail Order Department
P.O. Box 7456
San Francisco, California 94120-7456
(415) 421-4242
Pizza stone: 12-inch x 15-inch rectangle, $25, plus $4.25 shipping and handling charges.

Sausage Savvy

HOLD THE SALT. HOLD THE NITRITES. KISS THE HOG LIPS GOODBYE.

BY RUX MARTIN AND JOANNE CATS-BARIL

"Could the sausage speak," observes an old German proverb, "many a butcher would be embarrassed." Indeed, a sausage may be the ultimate anachronism in an age of consumer awareness and health consciousness. A hank of hog or sheep intestine stuffed with an unknown amalgam of abattoir by-products and stodge laced with hypertensive amounts of salt and possibly carcinogenic additives, the typical commercial sausage is increasingly being shunned by those who care what manner of food passes their lips. Masquerading in spices and slathered with mustard, such a sausage may have its gustatory charms, but what, exactly, are you eating?

The ingredients on a typical label seem innocent enough: "Beef and pork, water, salt, corn syrup, spices, sodium erythrobate, sodium nitrate." What the labels so often do not specify is that the "meat" consists of "meat by-products" or "variety meats," government-sanctioned euphemisms defined in a USDA handbook as: pork stomachs or pork snouts; tripe; hearts; tongues; fat; lips; spleens; weasands (gullets) and "partially defatted fatty tissue."

Commercial sausages are typically bloated with fat, which can legally comprise up to half their total weight. Even those marked "lean" and "lite" can carry fully 80 percent of their calories as fat. Salt, a cheap flavoring, is added in whopping amounts, with a single sausage serving delivering 50 to 100 percent of an individual's total recommended daily sodium intake. Finally, there are the nitrates and nitrites, linked to the occurrence of cancer in laboratory animals.

Ralph Nader called the ubiquitous hot dog "America's most deadly missile" in 1972 after he found that the frank was just 60 percent as nutritious as it had been in the Depression and contained nearly twice as much fat as meat. Instead of protein, which had decreased by half in 40 years, it was inflated with water, salt, cereal fillers, nitrites and nitrates. Although the preservative content has since been lowered, the average commercial sausage is a modern nutritionist's nightmare.

Enter a new generation of American cooks and a radically new style of sausage made with quality cuts of duck, veal, chicken and even seafood, seasoned with fresh herbs and greens, grilled or poached and served with fresh chutneys, pepper relishes, reductions or other garden-inspired condiments. Even the casing can be dispensed with to create a sausage made at home in minutes and guaranteed to provide a memorable appetizer or main course for family members and guests alike.

The following recipes, all developed in HARROWSMITH's test kitchens, vary from subtle and light to bold and spicy, but all share a fresh and distinctive taste achieved with a bare minimum of fat and salt. None contains preservatives; the sausages can easily be frozen or stored for a few days in the refrigerator if not eaten immediately.

Surprisingly, we found that the most quick and convenient sausage-making approach produced results superior to the traditional, somewhat time-consuming stuffing session. Every sausage mixture tested tended to be consistently juicier when broiled or fried as patties rather than stuffed into natural casings. Conventional recipes, even for duck or veal sausages, almost invariably call for added pork fat, perhaps to compensate for the drying effect of the longer cooking time required for stuffing sausage. Properly garnished, the sausage cakes can make very attractive fare, but those who prefer the traditional sausage shape can form the mixture in kitchen plastic wrap and poach before grilling. The use of actual casings is really only a matter of appearance and choice, ex-

A trio of light sausages, right: seafood with watercress, duck flavored with oranges, and French-style chicken and veal links.

cept when the goal is a sausage that requires a skin to remain intact when simmered in soups, sauces or stews.

The Techniques

All methods of sausage-making require that the meat or fish be ground or minced. A food processor fitted with a steel blade will grind the meat quickly in small batches, and an old-fashioned meat grinder or a sharp knife, although slower, will also do an excellent job. In any case, the blade must be extremely sharp. A dull blade will tear and mash the meat and purée the fat. The results will be rubbery and dense sausage. When using a food processor, chill the meat in the freezer for a short time until it begins to firm up; it will cut much more cleanly in this state.

If you haven't the equipment or inclination to do it yourself, most service-oriented butchers will be happy to grind the ingredients to your specifications. Remember that the taste and texture of sausage is determined not only by the ingredients but by the grind itself. In general, the larger the grind, the meatier the flavor.

Patties: To make skinless sausage patties, simply mix the ingredients together, handling the meat gently, and form the patties loosely. Do not pack firmly or the texture will become dense and tough. Broil or fry in a small amount of butter or oil, in a hot skillet, only until browned. Do not overcook.

Shaped in Plastic: Place approximately ¼ cup of the sausage mixture on the center of a large piece of plastic wrap and roll firmly into a log shape. Twist the ends of the plastic wrap to eliminate air pockets and tighten the sausage; tie with a string. Cut off the excess plastic and repeat the procedure with the remaining sausage mixture. Refrigerate for at least 30 minutes or up to two days before cooking. Poach in simmering water for 10 to 12 minutes. Unwrap plastic and serve immediately, or refrigerate in plastic and serve cold.

Stuffed into Casings: Although some texts advise the use of a wide-mouthed funnel or pastry bag to stuff sausage, this is extremely difficult to do well, and is nearly impossible without a two-person team. If you are at all serious about making this type of sausage, consider investing in a hand-powered meat grinder with a stuffing attachment, or a small sausage stuffer. The latter resembles a small meat grinder with a plastic funnel that neatly stuffs the casings as the handle is turned.

The casings themselves can be obtained from a local butcher or meat packer (a few calls may be necessary), or by mail order (see Sources). Hog casings are used for sausages that are the diameter of Italian sausage, sheep casings for the smaller breakfast-type link. They are usually sold by the hank, a looped bundle that is enough for 115 pounds of meat. They come in a compact box and will last indefinitely in the refrigerator. (Avoid artificial casings made of collagen, which are less tender and can't be twisted into links.)

Before working with the casings, first cover them with cold water acidulated with one tablespoon of white vinegar and soak for 30 minutes. Then attach the casing to your kitchen sink faucet and run the water through the casing for two minutes. Casings should be odorless, soft and slippery before being stuffed.

Prepare your sausage mixture and set up the stuffer. Ease the entire length of casing (two feet for each pound of meat if using sheep casings; one foot per pound if using hog casings) onto the nozzle, leaving four inches free at the end. Feed the sausage mixture through the hopper, and as soon as the mixture appears in the casing, tie off the end carefully to avoid trapping air.

Now, crank out the entire quantity of meat and set your long length of sausage on the work surface. Twist the sausage into links, any length you desire, alternating the direction of the twist at each sausage end. Tie off with butcher's twine if you wish.

Refrigerate finished sausage for at least 30 minutes to firm, then prick each link several times with a needle, especially where air bubbles have formed. Sausages can be broiled, fried in a little butter or oil or baked in a buttered pan at 400 degrees F for 8 to 10 minutes. Do not overcook.

General Guidelines

1. Keep the mixture as cold as possible at all times to prevent spoilage and insure good texture.

2. In recipes calling for fat, grind lean meat and trimmed fat separately to control the fat content. (Most butchers will do this upon request.)

3. The texture of sausage is controlled by handling. Use a very sharp blade for cutting and handle quickly and gently.

Whatever method you choose to employ, sausage-making can be an addictive skill, with the temptation to experiment almost overwhelming once one has followed an established recipe or two. When in an inventive mood, you may want to emulate the Spanish tradition of testing the sausage-in-progress. After the mixture is prepared, family and friends gather in the kitchen for *la prueba*: the tasting. The spiced meat is grilled and each critic tastes it and delivers an opinion: "Much more of that!" "Less of that!" "Delicious!" "Ruined entirely!"

Then again, perhaps the best policy is just to follow the advice of the German folktale: "Cook your soup alone, little sausage, and do not tell anyone why it tastes so good."

(Except where noted, each of the following recipes can be made into patties, shaped in plastic wrap or stuffed in casings.)

Chorizo (Mexican Sausage)

Fiery hot, this stuffed sausage adds zip to paella, chili or bean dishes. Sliced, it makes an excellent hors d'oeuvre—but not for the meek of palate. Cook first in a small amount of water, then grill or fry. Do not overcook, or it will become dry.

1¼ lbs. pork butt, cubed and chilled
1¼ lbs. beef chuck, cubed and chilled
1 tsp. paprika
1 tsp. cumin
1 Tbsp. oregano
3 tsp. salt
2 tsp. freshly ground black pepper
4 tsp. ground cayenne pepper
¼ cup finely diced onion
¼ cup finely diced bell pepper
4 cloves garlic, crushed
¼ cup Burgundy
2 Tbsp. brandy
3 feet medium hog casings (32-35 mm.)

Grind meats together in batches in a food processor or meat grinder and place in a large bowl. Add remaining ingredients and mix well with your hands. Refrigerate for at least 30 minutes. Fill casings and twist into 8-inch links. To cook, boil in a skillet in a small amount of water, then fry until brown, adding a little oil if necessary.
Makes 2½ lbs. or about 12 to 14 sausages.
Serves 8.

Boudin Blanc

This is a version of the mild and delicate French classic and is best made with the traditional casing method. Grill and serve with hot potato salad and cornichons, or sauté with apples, cider and cream.

1¼ lbs. veal, cubed and chilled
1¼ lbs. skinless, boneless chicken breast, cubed and chilled
3 onions, minced

4 Tbsp. butter
1 cup water
1 cup milk
1 cup bread crumbs
1½ tsp. salt
1 tsp. white pepper
¼ tsp. allspice
¼ tsp. ground nutmeg
¼ tsp. ground cloves
¼ tsp. ground cayenne pepper
1 Tbsp. chopped parsley
1 Tbsp. chopped chives
½ cup heavy cream
2 eggs
3 feet medium hog casings (32-35 mm.), optional

Grind meats in batches in a food processor or meat grinder and place in a large bowl. Place onions, butter and water in a skillet and boil until the liquid evaporates.

Cook a few more minutes, stirring, until the onions are soft. Add them to the meat mixture. Place milk and bread crumbs in a saucepan and cook, stirring, until mixture forms a paste. Add to meat mixture. Add remaining ingredients and mix thoroughly with your hands. Make skinless sausages or fill casings and twist into 6-inch links.
Makes 3 lbs.
Serves 8.

Veal Sausage

This is a subtle sausage with traditional origins. The addition of spinach provides a twist—both visually and in the delightful flavor.

1 lb. ground lean veal
¼ lb. ground veal fat
¼ cup finely minced parsley
¾ tsp. salt
½ cup finely chopped spinach
1 tsp. thyme
1 shallot, minced
1 egg
freshly ground pepper

Mix all ingredients together. Refrigerate for at least 30 minutes. Gently form into patties and fry in a little butter or oil until nicely browned. Do not overcook.
Serves 4.

Lamb Sausage with Avgolemono

The Greeks would approve of this succulent combination of tastes: the lemon sauce adds zest to the sweetness of the lamb.

Sausage:
½ cup fresh bread crumbs
1 Tbsp. red wine or water
2 Tbsp. tamari or soy sauce
1 lb. ground lean lamb
1 shallot, minced
1 Tbsp. dried mint or 2 Tbsp. fresh mint
2 Tbsp. minced parsley
grated peel of ½ lemon
1 egg, beaten
freshly grated pepper

Avgolemono (egg and lemon sauce):
1 Tbsp. cornstarch
⅓ cup fresh lemon juice
2 egg yolks, beaten
1½ cups hot chicken stock

To make the sausage, soak the bread crumbs briefly in red wine and tamari. Mix with remaining ingredients and refrigerate for 30 minutes. Gently form into patties (or stuff into casings and prick). If patties, fry until browned. If links, bake at 400 degrees F for 10 minutes, turning once.

To make the avgolemono, dissolve cornstarch in lemon juice and add to beaten egg yolks. Whisk in the hot chicken stock slowly. Heat over medium flame until slightly thickened.

Spoon sauce onto serving plates and arrange patties on top.

Serves 4.

Glazed Duck Sausage

Oranges and green peppercorns bring a fragrance all their own to the richness of the duck meat.

2 4-lb. ducks (about 1 lb. meat)
3 Tbsp. duck fat
2 Tbsp. butter
1 clove garlic
3 carrots
3 mushrooms
1 large onion
10-12 dry black peppercorns
1 bay leaf
4 cups cold water
2 oranges
1½ Tbsp. green peppercorns (in brine)
1 tsp. salt
freshly grated pepper

Remove breast and thigh meat from ducks and set in the freezer for 30 minutes to chill.

Meanwhile, put duck skin and fat (from breast area and cavity) into saucepan and render. Put in freezer to firm up.

Melt butter in stockpot, then add duck, bones and carcass, garlic, carrots, mushrooms and onion and brown well. Add peppercorns, bay leaf and cold water, bring to a simmer and cook, stirring occasionally, for 1½ hours. Strain and continue to simmer until reduced by half.

Zest the orange peel into shoestring pieces; blanch for 1 minute in boiling water, rinse with cold water and set aside.

In a food processor fitted with metal blade, place the duck meat, zest from 1 orange, 1 Tbsp. of the green peppercorns (rinsed), salt, pepper and duck fat. Process until fine-textured.

Refrigerate mixture for at least 30 minutes. Then form into patties and fry in butter or oil in a hot skillet for only 1 to 2 minutes on each side or until nicely browned. Add remaining orange zest, 1 Tbsp. fresh orange juice and remaining ½ Tbsp. green peppercorns to reduced stock. Serve sausage with the sauce.

Serves 4.

Chicken Sausage with Velouté

The simple elegance of this chicken sausage is made unusual with a hint of carrot and dill. It is also excellent as a cold lunch with mayonnaise.

Sausage:
1 lb. chicken breast meat
2 egg whites
¼ cup heavy cream
2 Tbsp. dry vermouth
⅔ cup finely diced carrots
3 Tbsp. diced scallions, green part
2 Tbsp. diced fresh dill
½ tsp. salt
freshly grated pepper, to taste

Sauce:
4 Tbsp. sweet butter
3 Tbsp. flour
2 cups chicken stock, heated to boiling
1 Tbsp. finely chopped parsley
2 Tbsp. finely chopped fresh dill

Put ¾ of the breast meat in a food processor fitted with metal blade. Process for 2 minutes and add, through the feed tube, the egg whites, cream and vermouth. Process 1 minute more, scraping down the sides, or until smooth. Meanwhile, chop the remaining breast meat. Blanch the carrots for 2 minutes in boiling water, then drain, reserving ⅓ cup carrots for garnish. Fold carrots, scallions, dill, chopped breast meat, salt and pepper into processed mixture. Refrigerate for at least 30 minutes. Using about 3 Tbsp. of the mixture per sausage, form into sausage shapes in plastic wrap and poach in simmering water for 10 to 12 minutes. Do not overcook.

While the sausages are cooking, make the velouté: Melt butter in a saucepan, whisk in flour and cook 1 minute. Whisk the boiling stock in all at once, add herbs, then spoon over the sausage. Garnish with diced carrots.

Serves 4.

Seafood Sausage with Watercress Cream Sauce

Colorful flecks of pink and green, combined with the delicate flavors of the sea, create an elegant main course for company.

Sausage:
½ lb. sea scallops
¼ lb. Pacific salmon
¼ lb. haddock
2 large egg whites
¾ cup heavy cream
¼ cup dry vermouth
1 Tbsp. plain yogurt
¾ tsp. salt
½ tsp. white pepper
½ tsp. grated lemon rind
½ cup spinach
1 cup watercress
1 Tbsp. butter
1 tsp. chopped fresh chives
freshly grated nutmeg

Watercress Cream Sauce:
1 cup fish stock or clam juice
1 cup heavy cream
½ cup dry vermouth
salt and pepper to taste
¾ cup finely chopped watercress

Cut 4 scallops and Pacific salmon into small dice; reserve.

Put in food processor fitted with metal blade the remaining scallops and the haddock and process for 2 minutes. With motor running, add egg whites, ¼ cup heavy cream, vermouth, yogurt, salt, pepper and lemon rind; process for another 2 minutes. Refrigerate mixture.

Clean and chop, then wilt spinach and watercress in a small amount of water with butter. Squeeze out excess liquid and fold greens into the processed mixture. Add chives and nutmeg. Whip the remaining ½ cup cream and fold into the mixture. Refrigerate up to 2 days or until ready to use.

Lay plastic wrap on work surface and put ¼ cup of the mixture in the center. Roll into a log shape and twist the ends to firm the sausage. Tie with twine. Poach in simmering water for 10 minutes.

To make the watercress cream sauce, mix all ingredients except watercress and reduce by half over medium flame. Stir in watercress and serve immediately.

Serves 4.

SOURCES

The Sausage Maker
177 Military Road
Buffalo, New York 14207
(716) 876-5521
Carries a complete line of sausage-making equipment, including natural casings ($19.95 per hank); grinders (beginning at $47.00) and stuffers ($79.00 and up).

Great Sausage Recipes and Meat Curing by Rytek Kutas. The Sausage Maker (address above), 1984. Hardcover, $22.95 plus handling.
Probably the most complete book on conventional sausage-making available, offering a comprehensive explanation of the history of the sausage, sausage-making equipment and recipes for almost every sausage in the world. Kutas's recipes contain nitrites and additions like powdered dextrose, but the book is a valuable reference.

Home Sausage Making, by Charles Reavis. Storey Communications, Pownal, Vermont, 1989. Paperback, $10.95.
Clear explanations of all aspects of sausage-making and includes a wide variety of sausage recipes.

Rising Again

SOURDOUGH MAKES A WELL-DESERVED COMEBACK

BY RUX MARTIN

Picture, for a moment, an isolated farmhouse in the early 1970s, inhabited by eight communards, furnished with Salvation Army furniture and, thanks to someone's Zen flash, decorated with chintzy '50s prom dresses displayed on the walls. A newfound friend of mine, who was part of this collective, recalls the rigidly ordered sharing of work (marching orders taped to the refrigerator with especially strict rules to correct a tendency among the men to shirk their bathroom-cleaning chores) and the ritualistic evening meal of lentil loaves, brown rice and sourdough bread. The bread was the exclusive responsibility of one female member, who wore heavy work boots as she baked and who guarded her sourdough starter with something bordering on ferocity.

Kept in a crock near the kitchen sink, the starter was a mysterious, gooey mixture that bubbled with seeming malevolence and was strictly off-limits to all but its master. She had affixed various dark warnings to the pottery vessel: "Do not throw out!" "Do not touch!!" "Hands off!!!" My friend gave the crock wide berth and has nothing particularly good to say about the bread it produced.

Skipping forward several years, we find my friend enrolled in a famous French cooking school, where one day she is astonished to discover that the deeply flavorful, sturdy country breads she has come to love in France are also made with sourdough. That the hair-shirt hippie cookery of her commune days could have anything to do with the secrets of France's best bakers is a revelation. Today, with Cordon Bleu credentials and a successful stint as a gourmet caterer to her credit, my friend lives in a renovated farmhouse in our community and is locally famous for her magnificent crusty loaves of bread – tantalizing in flavor and light but perfectly chewy in texture. Sourdough is her secret.

This ancient form of baking, which uses little or no yeast, has had its ups and downs in North America, but its most noteworthy heyday was certainly the gold-rush era when packaged yeast was even more rare than precious metals. Ranging across California and up into the Yukon, sour-smelling prospectors carried sourdough starter in glass battery jars discarded by telegraph workers, turning out batches of tangy pancakes and swigging the alcoholic "hooch" that collected on the surface of the precious cultures. A number of today's fashionable bakeries in San Francisco (the scene of what one social critic has dubbed the Yuppie Bread Lines) claim their sourdough cultures to be directly descended from frontier stock.

Sourdough's potency was recognized at least as early as 4000 B.C., when the Egyptians discovered that mixtures of flour and water left in the sun produced lighter, more palatable bread. The unseen miracle agents, we know now, were invisible, ubiquitous wild yeasts in the air, which settled on the dough and fed on the flour's natural sugars, releasing ethanol alcohol and bubbles of carbon dioxide to lift the dough.

Throughout medieval Europe, bread was made almost exclusively by this natural leavening system. Flour and water were left in a wooden trough to ferment for a day, after which the remaining flour and the salt were added to make the dough. Before baking, a portion of dough was set aside to leaven and flavor the next day's batch. In France, the indispensable reserve was called, appropriately, *le chef,* while in the north of Italy, it was *la madre* (the mother) and in the south, *il babbo* (the father).

Intrigued by the pungent lore of sourdough baking, I nonetheless approached it with trepidation, worried that my house would not be hospitable to the proper aerial fungi. Within

Breads with character, left: sturdy loaves of sourdough range in flavor from tantalizingly sour to gently mellow.

JIM SCHERER

a few days, however, several starter cultures were fervently percolating in a warm corner of the kitchen, and the house began to smell like a large, yeasty bread box. Five days after beginning my first sourdough culture, I took my first sourdough baguette from the oven and cut open its crackling crust to smell the creamily tart interior. Success!

Unlike the predictable packets of commercial yeast, my young, still-wild sourdough culture rarely produced the same style of loaves twice, ranging from mouth-puckeringly sour to gently mellow. Although sourdough breads take longer to make than ordinary yeast recipes, requiring an overnight fermentation of starter, flour and water, as well as two risings, they actually involve no extra work. For the days I don't have time to bake bread, the starter brings forth biscuits, English muffins, coffee cakes and the best pancakes I've ever made.

Every sourdough baker has a favorite starter. Many bakers start with a bit of culture from a friend, but starting one's own can be fascinating. I experimented with several recipes, from combinations of potato, flour and water, and raisin, flour and water, to simple mixtures of yogurt and flour. My favorite, it turned out, was the simplest of all. Made solely with milk and flour, it was lively, reliable and tart. Powdered sourdough cultures from California are also available in health-food stores, but I'm not convinced they are any better than homemade.

"Bread With Eyes..."

Although many starter recipes do call for bakers' yeast in the starter, or later in the bread, presumably as a kind of insurance policy, too much will retard the tang of the wild spore. Bakers' yeast, *Saccharomyces cerevisiae*, is a botanically different creature from wild yeast, *Saccharomyces exiguus,* which lives companionably with a bacterium, *Lactobacillus sanfrancisco.* The bacterium eats maltose and discharges acidic by-products that give the dough its distinctive flavor. Unlike the wild yeast, which does not metabolize maltose, bakers' yeast gobbles it up, thus annihilating the bacterium's food, and in the process, the sourdough taste.

Like all yeasts, starters are alive – and they are not exactly shrinking violets. In fact, like some tough houseplants, they can thrive on minimal attention. Their needs are simple. After each use, they must be replenished with flour and either water or milk. When not in use, they should be refrigerated, as cold slows their metabolic activity without killing them.

High temperatures, on the other hand, are deadly.

The traditional French method of making sourdough bread takes a bit longer, but it does not require maintaining a liquid starter and, many believe, results in a better-textured loaf. A fresh starter mixture, containing a small amount of yeast, is made one day, and on the next, more water and flour are added to make a "sponge" (in French, *levain*), which is allowed to ferment for another day. After that, the remaining flour and salt are added to make a dough, which must rise twice. (Maturing the dough at room temperatures – 65 to 70 degrees F – seems to produce a better flavor.) The longer it ferments, the stronger the flavor of the bread and the better developed its cellular structure.

"God grant me bread with eyes and cheese without them," is a saying favored by French bakers. I have had good luck achieving the "Swiss cheese look" by leaving the dough slightly more moist than usual for the final shaping and letting it rise in a floured wicker basket to give it form. The loaf is placed on the baking sheet just before baking.

The effects of a wood-fired stove, which produces a superb crust, can be approximated in an ordinary oven by placing two firebricks on the floor of the oven to retain heat and preheating the stove to 450 degrees F for at least 20 minutes. A steamy atmosphere in the oven will soften the crust of the dough and allow it to rise even further. I spray water on the bricks and directly on the bread before putting it in the oven, and several times again during the first 15 minutes of baking. For the same effect, the bread may be baked under the top of a clay cooker that has been first soaked in water. The emerging bread will have a crackling, glossy crust and the flavor of a venerable French *pain de campagne* or a Nob Hill loaf with breeding that goes back to the Gold Rush of '49.

The Care and Feeding of Sourdough Starters

Never store starter in a metal container or use a metal spoon to stir it, as metal will interfere with the yeast reactions and spoil the flavor. Store in a glass jar, ceramic crock or a plastic refrigerator container, with the lid ajar – the gasses can blow off a tight lid. After the starter has fermented, it should be kept in the refrigerator. Before using, stir in the alcoholic liquid that has collected on top. After each use, the starter should be replenished with a cup each of flour and milk or water.

If you do not use the starter for 10 days, if it fails to raise the dough properly, or if the bread has an "off" taste, pour out half and replenish with a cup each of water and flour. (You may also wish to sterilize the starter container with boiling water.) Let the starter sit at room temperature, lightly covered, for 4 to 5 hours, or overnight, before refrigerating it again.

Traditional Sourdough Starter

Of all the starters I've tested, this is my favorite. It has a smooth, but distinctly sour, flavor and performs reliably, improving with age.

2 cups milk
2 cups unbleached white flour

12 to 15 hours ahead: Mix milk and flour together with a wooden spoon in 2-quart non-metallic container sterilized with boiling water. Cover with lid slightly ajar, and let stand overnight in a warm place (75 to 80 degrees F) until the starter bubbles and has a sour smell. **Note:** If the starter turns any color, or if mold appears on it, throw it out and try again.

If, for some reason, this recipe fails to spark a viable culture, start again. For better assurance of success, substitute buttermilk for whole milk and add 1 Tbsp. active dry yeast and 1 Tbsp. sugar.

Whole Wheat Sourdough Biscuits

Quicker to make than sourdough breads, these biscuits are ready in less than two hours. Fluffy and moist, they have a delicate nutty flavor and are best served hot from the oven.

1⅔ cups unbleached white flour
1 cup whole wheat flour
1¼ tsp. salt
1¼ tsp. baking powder
½ tsp. baking soda
½ cup butter
1 cup sourdough starter
¾ cup buttermilk

Sift together flours, salt, baking powder and soda. Cut ½-inch lumps of butter into the dry ingredients and work them in with fingers until they are pea-sized. In a separate bowl, combine starter and buttermilk. Stir gently into dry ingredients, just until blended. Do not overmix or biscuits will be tough; dough will be very moist. Turn out dough onto a well-floured board; lightly flour and roll out to a thickness of 1 inch. Cut with biscuit cutter. Place on ungreased baking sheet so that sides of biscuits touch lightly. Let rise in warm place (80 to 90 degrees F) for 45 minutes, or until doubled in height. Bake in a preheated 400 degree F oven for 15 to 20 minutes or until light brown.

Makes 1 dozen 2-inch biscuits.

Light Wheat Country Sourdough Bread

Chewy and resilient, with a porous interior, this French-style bread owes its excellent texture to a three-day fermentation; the starter is made the first day.

1 tsp. dry yeast
1 cup warm water
1 Tbsp. nonfat dry milk
1 cup whole wheat flour
2 cups warm water
3 cups unbleached white flour
1 Tbsp. salt
1 cup wheat germ **or** 1 cup cracked wheat
    soaked in boiling water, cooled and drained
    or ¼ cup raw sunflower seeds
2½ to 6 cups unbleached white flour
oil to grease pan
cornmeal

Day 1: Mix together yeast, 1 cup warm water, nonfat dry milk and 1 cup whole wheat flour in a large, nonmetallic bowl. Cover with plastic wrap and let sit overnight.
Day 2: Stir and add 2 cups warm water and 3 cups flour. Cover with plastic wrap; allow to rest overnight again.
Day 3: Stir in 1 Tbsp. salt and wheat germ (or cracked wheat or sunflower seeds) and at least 2 cups of flour. (Cracked wheat requires more flour than wheat germ or sunflower seeds do.) Turn onto a board and knead for 10 minutes, adding flour so that dough is pliable but not sticky.

Place in greased bowl and cover with plastic wrap. Allow to rise at room temperature (65 to 70 degrees F) until doubled in size, about 1½ to 2 hours. Push dough down and cut off about 6 ounces to use in future bakings, if you wish. Shape into two rounded loaves. Place on greased baking sheet sprinkled with cornmeal. Cover with a cloth and allow to rise until tripled, about 2 hours.

Preheat oven to 425 degrees F. Slash bread in tic-tac-toe pattern with sharp blade, spray with water and place in oven. Bake 35 to 40 minutes until bread sounds hollow when tapped. For a thicker crust, spray bread twice during the first 10 minutes of baking.

Note: The reserved dough (*levain*) should be

allowed to stand at room temperature overnight, covered with water. In this fashion, it will keep for up to 10 days in the refrigerator, or it can be frozen. It can then be added to the next batch in place of the starter.

Makes 2 loaves.

Upland Bakers'
Sourdough French Baguette

This California-style baguette has an almost creamy interior with a tart character and a crackling crust. The recipe was graciously contributed by Jules and Helen Rabin, owners of Upland Bakers in Plainfield, Vermont.

1 cup sourdough starter
2 cups warm water
10-13 cups unbleached white flour
1½ cups warm water (110 degrees F)
1 Tbsp. salt
olive oil for greasing bowl
cornmeal

Make the sponge 12 to 15 hours ahead: In a nonmetallic bowl, combine starter and water and gradually stir in 2½ cups flour, with a wooden spoon, beating in air. Cover with plastic wrap, and set in warm place overnight until light and bubbly.

For the dough: Stir down sponge, add 1½ cups warm water, salt and enough of the remaining flour to make a fairly stiff dough; add flour ½ cup at a time, about 8 cups in all. Knead for 10 to 15 minutes, working in up to 2 more cups of flour so dough is not sticky. Place in a lightly oiled bowl and set in a warm place to rise until doubled, about 2 to 3 hours.

To shape: Divide dough into 4 to 6 parts and shape each into a long baguette. Place seam-side down on a lightly greased baking sheet sprinkled with cornmeal and allow to rise, lightly covered with a cloth or plastic wrap, until doubled, approximately 30 to 45 minutes. Slash loaves diagonally with a sharp blade, sprinkle them liberally with water and bake in a preheated 450 degree F oven for 15 minutes. Reduce heat to 350 degrees F, and bake 20 minutes more, or until loaves sound hollow when tapped.

Makes 4 to 6 baguettes.

Sourdough Oatmeal Bread

My favorite part of this slightly tart bread is its chewy crust, which tastes of lightly toasted oats.

1 cup sourdough starter
1 cup warm water (110 degrees F)
4½ cups unbleached white flour
2 tsp. salt
3 cups rolled oats (not quick-cooking)
⅔ to 1 cup water
additional flour for kneading
oil for greasing pans and bowl
yellow cornmeal
1 egg white, beaten with 1 tsp. water
additional oats for topping

Make the sponge 12 to 15 hours ahead: In a large, nonmetallic bowl, stir together starter, water and 1½ cups flour. Cover with plastic wrap and let stand in a warm place overnight, until bubbly.

For the dough: Stir in remaining 3 cups flour, salt, oats and enough water to make a soft, pliable dough. Turn out onto floured board and knead until dough is smooth and elastic, working in additional flour as needed. Place in lightly oiled bowl and turn to coat sides and top. Cover with plastic wrap and let rise at room temperature until at least doubled, about 2 hours.

To shape: Punch down, divide in half, roll each half into an oval by pushing it with the heels of your hands. Fold in half down the middle; flatten again, and fold down the middle once more. Pinch seam to seal. Place loaves seam-side down on greased baking sheet sprinkled with cornmeal, cover with a cloth, and let rise until doubled, about 1 hour. Brush loaves with beaten egg white, sprinkle top with oats, and slash diagonally. Bake in a preheated 425 degree F oven for 35 to 40 minutes, or until loaves sound hollow when tapped.

Makes 2 loaves.

Sourdough Dijon Rye

A delicious rye sourdough: perfectly balanced, tinged with the aromatic flavor of caraway seeds, mellow and sour. The high-gluten flour called for is available in health-food stores.

1 cup sourdough starter
1 cup warm milk
1 cup rye flour
½ cup unbleached white flour
1 Tbsp. salt
¾ cup warm water
2 Tbsp. molasses
2 tsp. Dijon mustard

¼ tsp. allspice
2 Tbsp. caraway seeds
2 cups rye flour
½ cup high-gluten flour
1½ to 3 cups unbleached white flour
oil to grease bowl and baking sheet
cornmeal
1 egg white, beaten with 1 tsp. water

Make sponge 12 to 15 hours ahead: In a large, nonmetallic bowl, combine starter, milk, 1 cup rye flour and ½ cup unbleached white flour. Stir until smooth, cover with plastic wrap, and set in a warm place overnight.

For the dough: Stir into the sponge: salt, warm water, molasses, mustard, allspice, caraway seeds, rye and high-gluten flours. Gradually stir in enough remaining white flour to make a soft, pliable dough. Knead until smooth and satiny, about 10 minutes. Place dough in an oiled bowl and turn to coat. Let rise, covered with plastic wrap, until doubled, approximately 2 hours.

To shape: Gently cut dough in half and pat halves into oval shape, placing seam-side down on greased baking sheet sprinkled with cornmeal. Cover with cloth and let rise in a warm place until doubled. Slash loaves diagonally with a sharp blade and brush with beaten egg white. Bake in a preheated 400 degree F oven for 40 minutes, or until loaf sounds hollow when tapped.

Makes 2 loaves.

Bubble, Bubble, No Toil or Trouble

BACK TO THE STEWPOT AND PRESSURE COOKER FOR WONDERFULLY SIMPLE MEALS

BY RUX MARTIN

My mother hated to cook. A rigorous budgeter with an Irish-born husband, she shopped with great pragmatism in our small town grocery and indifferently turned out a predictable succession of boiled vegetables, boiled cabbage, boiled corned beef, meat loaves, stews, shepherd's pies and mutton roasts. For us, spaghetti was an exotic rarity. Her own mother, ironically, loved food, and in her rural kitchen introduced me to salmon roe and clams on the half shell even as chicken smothered in cream and mushrooms bubbled in a double cooker on her stove.

If the passionate interest in cooking somehow skipped a generation in my family, it reemerged with new vigor when I went off to college, moved into an apartment and suddenly discovered the glorious freedom of having my own kitchen. I celebrated my liberation in urban supermarkets and delicatessens, eagerly searching out shrimp, artichokes, fresh pineapples, tiny imported cans of snails and other hitherto untasted extravagant delicacies.

Reality finally interrupted this gleeful gourmet binge on a bone-chilling winter day when the daily mail brought a notice of insufficient funds from my bank. I found myself seized by a longing for home and the smell of my mother's beef stew. Innocent of wine, cognac or *fines herbes,* it was a savory Irish-Italian-New World hybrid, filled with fork-tender hunks of beef, carrots hacked into serviceable rounds, canned tomatoes, sweetly disintegrating onions and potatoes – all pervaded by the piney tang of rosemary. It was not the kind of recipe I could ever reproduce from a cookbook. I called my mother, and

several hours later a close approximation of the dish was simmering on my stove, filling the apartment with the unmistakable scent of home.

Stew is one of those happy dishes consistently full of rich, complex flavors – even when prepared with frugality and a minimum of effort in the kitchen. Simmering in what food writer M.F.K. Fisher once called "natural rather than fabricated sauces," and often served in the same rustic casserole dishes in which they are cooked, one-pot dinners are appealingly simple for everyday eating, and when company is planned, they can be wonderful alternatives to the fussy four-course productions that keep the cook shuttling from table to kitchen.

The rise of the redoubtable stew would undoubtedly have pleased Escoffier. *"Faites simple"* – "Make it simple" – counseled the chef who created over 7,000 new recipes for an age when "a thousand worries of industry and business occupy the mind of man, and he can devote only a limited place to eating well." Earlier in his career, Escoffier had proved himself a master of limited circumstances: when supplies ran low during the Franco-Prussian War, he found a rabbit, browned it in hot lard, added some finely chopped onions and a soupçon of cognac and white wine, simmered it over the fire and *voilà!* – presented his men with a fine stew.

The birthplace of the modern stew, however, was not the nineteenth-century battlefield but the Mediterranean melting pot, where the availability of Eastern spices made possible international combinations that rival today's. The earliest surviving cookbook, writ-

Simmering stews reward patience with simple sustenance and complex flavors, left.

ten by the Roman gourmet, Apicius, in the first century A.D., contains recipes for "minutals," innovative ragouts of meatball and leeks, ham and apricots or seafood and dumplings. Since Roman times, stews have become nearly universal, appearing in the form of goulashes, pepper pots, pot-au-feu, daubes, English hotchpotches, jambalayas and assorted other moist-heat dishes in which patience and creativity play equal roles.

Although the idea of serving stew to guests would have horrified me in my sophomoric years, Creole jambalayas, Mediterranean bouillabaisses, Moroccan tajines with their spicy blends of cinnamon, cumin and ginger, and even old-fashioned chicken fricassees with dumplings, are now among my favorite choices for special occasions. For special effect, they may be embellished with capers, chopped fresh herbs, grated lemon rind or dollops of homemade garlic-and-red-pepper mayonnaise. Not the least of their appeal is that they can – indeed should – be made well in advance, as their flavor appreciates greatly with a day or two of aging.

While precision is not necessary and can even hamper the making of a good stew, a sense of proportion, timing and a knowledge of technique are crucial. "Stews, above all, were responsible for the brilliance of old French cookery, yet it is stews which bring disgrace on contemporary cuisine, especially that of England," complained novelist Alexandre Dumas in the nineteenth century. Unfortunately, we, too, have tasted our share of bad stews, in which the meat acquired a mealy texture, the vegetables disintegrated to mush, or the seasonings came through as insipid or harsh.

Although it may sound elementary, the most important rule in making a stew is to choose the ingredients carefully. While some cookbook authors suggest that the best cuts of meat yield the best stews, in our experience frugality at the butcher counter can make for superior stews. To prove the point, we cooked two beef dishes, identical but for the fact that one was made with tenderloin and one with shin. A panel of more than a dozen tasters unanimously favored the shin stew for flavor, texture and finish. Likewise, shank is a most economical cut of meat and one ideally suited to stewing. On the other hand, cheap supermarket chickens can be ill-suited to long stewing because their meat tends to fall off the bone and become mushy. Old hens or free-range birds with more developed muscles are ideal, but when these are not available, we have found that chicken breasts, skinned and boned, remain fairly firm during cooking.

Despite variations in individual recipes, the process of stew-making is essentially the same. The meat (and often the vegetables) is first browned to intensify its flavor. After browning, wine, stock, water or a combination of these is added. While a fine wine is unnecessary, a vinegary vintage will ruin the stew: if it isn't fit to drink, it isn't fit for the stewpot. Sometimes brandy, cognac, Pernod or other liqueurs are added for flavor as well.

Early in the cooking, vegetables like leeks, onions and carrots are added to flavor the broth, along with dried herbs, while "garnish vegetables" – additional onions, carrots, potatoes and so on – are added later so they retain their shape. When garlic is added near the beginning of cooking, it ripens to mellow softness; added near the end, it can be aggressively pungent. Quick-cooking vegetables and seafood are always held out until the final moments of cooking.

Thickening can be accomplished by one of several methods. The meat can be rolled in flour, or for more exact measurement, added to the oil and cooked gently into a roux, or mixed with a bit of cold liquid and added during the last half hour of cooking. Arrowroot, a white Caribbean starch that Escoffier considered the purest and silkiest of thickeners, may be added at the last moment without producing a raw, starchy taste and is excellent for making last-minute corrections. Cornstarch, which produces a glossier sauce, is particularly recommended for vegetable stews. Alternatively, the stew liquid may be reduced through boiling, resulting in intense flavor and velvety texture.

The best vessels for making stews are enamel-covered Dutch ovens or heat-proof casserole dishes, in which ingredients can be both browned and simmered. An electric crockpot, left to cook slowly all day, also produces admirable results. That old-fashioned timesaver, the pressure cooker, streamlined and made fail-safe by recent technology, can greatly speed the production of a stew, reducing preparation time to less than one hour.

The process is fundamentally the same as in the traditional method: the meat is first sautéed in the cooker with the lid removed, and after the flavoring vegetables, herbs and liquids have been added, the cooker is brought up to pressure. After about 20 minutes of cooking, the pressure is released, and the garnish vegetables and thickening agent are added. Again the pot is brought up to pressure, and the stew is cooked for a short time longer. We found the flavor of pressure-cooked stews perfectly acceptable, but in side-by-side tastings, they were noticeably less rich than the long-simmered versions. Better results can be obtained by refrigerating the stew overnight and slowly reheating it with the pressure-cooker lid removed.

Regardless of how long they have been simmered, all stews benefit substantially from chilling. Before reheating, their fat can then be removed, making them among the healthiest of meat dishes. If time does not permit thorough chilling, ice cubes may be skimmed through the liquid to degrease it. With the exception of the oyster stew, all of the following stews taste rounder and riper when made in advance and served the next day.

In the end, when I think of the generational flip-flops in my family of on-again-off-again cooks, I suspect that my mother and grandmother, whose tastes and kitchen habits were so very different, would nonetheless share an appreciation for the enduring qualities of stew.

Chicken Fricassee with Cheese-Herb Dumplings

The creamy richness of this traditional chicken stew comes from the roux, which is cooked slowly to a golden brown.

4½-5 lb. chicken, split and jointed
ground nutmeg
white pepper
paprika
2½ Tbsp. vegetable oil
3 Tbsp. flour
1 cup dry white wine
2 large shallots, cut into slivers
1 medium onion, finely chopped
3 leeks, cut into ½-inch pieces
4 carrots, cut into ½-inch pieces
1 cup celery, cut into ½-inch pieces
2 Tbsp. butter
½ tsp. thyme
1 Tbsp. chervil
1 tsp. salt
½ tsp. paprika
Cheese-Herb Dumplings (recipe follows)

Sprinkle chicken on both sides with spices. Heat oil in heavy stewpot and brown chicken in batches. Set aside. Reduce heat, and add flour, scraping up browned bits with spoon. Cook the roux until it colors to a light brown, mashing lumps. Be careful not to burn. Whisk in 3 cups water and the wine and return chicken to pot. Simmer 45 minutes to 1 hour, covered.

In Dutch oven, sauté vegetables in butter until softened. Strain stock through a col-

ander, add to vegetables, and continue simmering. Skim fat. Stir in seasonings. Meanwhile, cool chicken in colander over a bowl and prepare the dumplings. Remove meat from chicken and add to Dutch oven, along with any drippings. Spoon in dumplings, cover and cook for 15 minutes, keeping stew at a slow boil. Uncover and cook for 5 minutes longer.

Serves 6.

Cheese-Herb Dumplings

These fluffy dumplings with crusty tops may be adapted for beef stew by substituting rosemary and thyme for chervil and omitting the cheese.

2 cups flour, sifted
1 tsp. salt
4 tsp. baking powder
1 tsp. chervil
⅓ cup grated Cheddar cheese
1 egg, beaten
3 Tbsp. melted butter
⅔ cup milk

Sift together flour, salt and baking powder. Stir in chervil and cheese. Mix egg, butter and milk together, and stir into flour mixture to make a moist, stiff batter. Using 2 teaspoons, drop dumplings over bubbling stew.

Makes about 2 dozen.

Spinach-Oyster Stew

This "stew" takes just minutes to prepare. The secret is to cook the oysters just until their edges curl; they should be hot but still have a limpid appearance.

2 Tbsp. unsalted butter
2 large shallots, minced
¼ cup finely chopped celery
1½ tsp. lemon juice
1 lb. oysters, with liquid
2 Tbsp. bottled chili sauce
3 cups chopped spinach, tough stems removed
2 large potatoes, peeled and diced into ¾-inch cubes
5 cups milk
1 cup heavy cream
1 tsp. paprika
¼-½ tsp. cayenne pepper
salt and pepper

Melt butter in skillet and sauté shallots and celery until softened. Whisk in lemon juice, oyster liquid and chili sauce. Add spinach and cook until slightly wilted. Set aside. In separate pot, cook potatoes, drain, and place in stewpot along with contents of skillet. Add remaining ingredients. Heat on low flame just until liquid is hot and edges of oysters begin to curl. Do not overcook.

Serves 6.

Veal Stew with Winter Vegetables

"Red" veal, which has been fed a diet of grain and allowed to roam, is a fine choice for this delicately seasoned, aromatic stew. For best results, use fresh dill, but 1 teaspoon dried may be substituted.

4 Tbsp. butter
3 Tbsp. olive oil
3 lbs. boneless veal chuck roast, trimmed and cut into 1½-inch cubes
freshly ground pepper
¼ cup brandy or cognac
2 leeks, cut into 1-inch rounds
4 carrots, cut into 1-inch rounds
2 medium onions, quartered
1 tsp. dried thyme
1 cup dry white wine
4 cups chicken stock
4-inch strip orange peel
1 butternut squash, peeled and cut into 1-inch cubes
4 potatoes, peeled and quartered
1½ tsp. Dijon mustard
1 cup light cream
1 Tbsp. plus 1 tsp. chopped fresh dill
½ cup chopped fresh parsley
salt to taste

Preheat oven to 350 degrees F. In a large Dutch oven, melt 2 Tbsp. of the butter and 1 Tbsp. of the oil over moderately high heat. Lightly brown veal in batches, on both sides, seasoning with pepper; don't crowd the pan. Set aside.

Add brandy to Dutch oven and, averting face, ignite with a match. When the flames subside, add remaining butter and oil. Add leeks, carrots, onions and thyme. Simmer, stirring, until vegetables are softened, about 15 minutes. Add wine, stock and orange peel and scrape up any browned bits. Return veal to pot, and add squash and potatoes. Heat just to boiling, and bake in the oven for 1 hour, or until meat and vegetables are tender.

Skim fat. Using a slotted spoon, remove vegetables and meat from broth and place on serving dish; discard orange peel. Boil broth and reduce by half. Whisk in mustard, cream and herbs, heat briefly and adjust seasonings. Pour over vegetables and meat, and serve.

Serves 6.

Greek Artichoke Stew with Garlic Mayonnaise

The flavors of the Mediterranean permeate this light but sturdy vegetable stew, a favorite in Greece during Lent. A pressure cooker can speed the cooking of the vegetables.

4 large cloves garlic, crushed
⅓ cup olive oil
8 medium artichokes
2½ tsp. salt
juice of 1 lemon
1 cup dry white wine
8 medium russet potatoes, cut into 2-inch wedges
12 carrots, peeled and cut into 2-inch lengths
1 bay leaf
1 Tbsp. dried oregano
2½ Tbsp. cornstarch, mixed with 1 cup cooled artichoke water
½ cup chopped fresh parsley
pepper
6 slices good French bread
olive oil
Garlic Mayonnaise (recipe follows)

In a stockpot, sauté garlic in oil until golden. Let stand. Parboil artichokes in 12 cups water and 1½ tsp. of the salt for 20 minutes, or until softened. Reserve water.

Remove leaves from artichokes and set aside for another use. Remove stems and spiny "chokes." Quarter hearts and place in a little water mixed with 2 tsp. lemon juice; set aside. Discard garlic from stewpot, add wine and heat until vapors have evaporated. Add 4 cups artichoke water, potatoes, carrots, bay leaf, oregano, remaining 1 tsp. salt and remaining lemon juice. Simmer 20 to 30 minutes, or until vegetables are tender. Add artichoke hearts, and simmer a few minutes longer. Thicken with cornstarch mixture, stir in parsley and adjust seasonings.

Fry bread lightly in olive oil and place a slice in the bottom of each soup bowl. Ladle stew over bread and top with a dollop of Garlic Mayonnaise.

Serves 6.

Garlic Mayonnaise

1 egg
½ tsp. salt
½ cup olive oil
¼ cup vegetable oil
4 cloves garlic, crushed
2 Tbsp. lemon juice

Beat egg with salt, using a whisk or a food processor. Beat in ¼ cup of the olive oil drop by drop, until mixture is thickened. Add remaining oil in a thin stream, beating continuously. Beat in garlic and lemon juice.

Serves 6.

North American Bouillabaisse

Monkfish, a firm, white fish readily available in the winter, takes on the flavor of shellfish in this fennel-scented stew. Top it with a slice of crisply fried French bread, a spoonful of Garlic Mayonnaise generously seasoned with red pepper, and a sprinkling of Parmesan cheese.

4 large cloves garlic, crushed
1 medium onion, chopped
1 green pepper, cut into 1-inch chunks
1 red pepper, cut into 1-inch chunks
2 Tbsp. olive oil
¼ cup chopped parsley
¼ tsp. red pepper
½ tsp. dried thyme
½ tsp. salt
¼ tsp. black pepper
2 qts. fish stock (recipe follows)
3 canned plum tomatoes, drained and chopped
2 lbs. monkfish fillets, cut into 1½-inch pieces
1½ lbs. mussels, washed and debearded
1½ lbs. shrimp, shelled and deveined
6 slices French bread fried in olive oil
Garlic Mayonnaise (previous recipe) seasoned with Tabasco
Parmesan cheese, grated

Sauté garlic, onion and peppers in oil in a heavy stockpot until softened. Stir in parsley, red pepper, thyme, salt and pepper, and sauté briefly. Add fish stock, tomatoes and monkfish, and simmer until monkfish pieces are opaque. Steam mussels in 1 cup water, add water to stockpot, and shell mussels. When monkfish is done, add shrimp and simmer just until they turn pink. Stir in mussels and serve. Top with bread, Garlic Mayonnaise and grated cheese.

Serves 6.

Fish Stock

2 medium onions, chopped
2 stalks celery, chopped
4 cloves garlic, crushed
1 tsp. fennel seeds
½ cup chopped fresh parsley
¼ cup olive oil
1 canned plum tomato
shrimp shells
2 fish heads from nonoily fish
1 bay leaf
½ tsp. dried thyme
1 strip orange peel
2 cups dry white wine
salt and pepper

Sauté onions, celery, garlic, fennel and parsley in oil in a stockpot. Stir in remaining ingredients and 6 cups water. Simmer 30 minutes and strain.

Makes 2 quarts.

These recipes are from Simmering Suppers, *edited by Rux Martin and JoAnne B. Cats-Baril. Camden House Publishing, Inc., 1988.*

Small-Batch Canning

QUICK PICKLING AND PRESERVING WITH NEW, PINT-SIZED RECIPES

BY ANDREA CHESMAN

I share a cellar with my husband. He has his workshop at one end, I have my canning shelves at the other. One day recently, I caught him studying the rows of dust- and cobweb-covered jars.

"When are you going to throw that stuff out?" he asked.

"What do you mean?" I said. "That's perfectly good food."

"Then why don't you ever serve it? Some of those jars are labeled '1983.' That's before we moved into this house."

He had me there. All that canning was done at a time when I spent marathon sessions in the kitchen, following recipes that weren't exactly to my taste, using overripe and past-their-prime vegetables. Some of the pickles are too salty; some are too bland; others taste great but have grown soggy with age. They are all what I call "too good to throw out but not good enough to eat."

It used to drive me wild to follow a pickle recipe slavishly only to find that it didn't make enough brine to cover the vegetables. I used to struggle to adapt a recipe for seven pounds of cucumbers to five pounds – until I discovered how to make pickles in small batches. Now I know how many cucumbers fill one pint jar (about 2½ cups of thin slices measured before salting) and how much brine is required to cover them (about ¾ cup). This simple formula enables me to make as many or as few jars as I have cucumbers, without complicated mathematical calculations.

Once I got into the habit of working out canning recipes by the jar, I found that I can pickle my cucumbers as fast as they ripen, sometimes at the rate of just a few a day. Because they don't pile up in the refrigerator getting limp, the resulting pickles are crisper.

With a small batch, I can also experiment with new flavors. This year, I have been trying liqueurs in my canned fruit. Sometimes the recipe works; sometimes the flavor of the liqueur disappears. I've found, for example, that Grand Marnier and grated orange peel add wonderful depth to the flavor of Blueberry Apple Compote, while the flavor of Chambord is lost in Peaches in Raspberry Sauce. When the experiments are less than successful, I'm not saddled with rows of jars languishing and breeding guilt in the cellar.

The main advantage of small batches, of course, is that they save time. I can start a recipe as I prepare dinner, crisping cucumber slices in a salt brine and preheating the water in the canner. Then, when dinner is over, I finish up. If I'm lucky, my husband does the dishes and keeps me company while I fill and process the jars.

With recipes worked out by the jar, I can make all the classic pickles – dills, bread-and-butters and pickled beans, flavored with dill, caraway or basil, depending on my mood and what's plentiful in the garden. My mixed vegetable pickles make great antipasto, eaten with fingers, straight from the jar. Using recipes that make enough pints to fill one canner load, I also "put up" salsa, which I use to rev up a quick layered casserole of tortillas, refried beans and cheese. Canned fruits, made in small batches, become instant elegant desserts for winter, served plain in glass bowls or with ice cream in layered parfaits.

The high-acid vegetables and fruits in the following recipes provide a relatively inhospitable medium for dangerous bacteria and therefore don't require the high-heat treatment of a pressure canner. They are easily preserved: immerse them in a boiling-water bath and follow simple canning procedures. (See "Canning Basics," next page.)

For especially busy times, I rely on methods that require even less effort than water-bath canning. Because tomatoes ripen in large quantities and take hours to can, I prefer to set aside

DIDIER DELMAS

a large part of them for drying and preserving in oil, a technique that dates back at least to the ancient Romans (see "Preserving Dried Tomatoes in Oil," page 304). After drying them in my oven on low heat, I pack them in olive oil with a garlic clove or fresh herbs. Like the sun-dried Italian tomatoes in specialty stores, they add intense bursts of flavor to cream sauces for pasta and can be used in lieu of tomato sauce on pizza. One of my favorite ways to use the oil, which is infused with a rich tomato flavor, is to drizzle it over sliced fresh tomatoes.

Nonacid vegetables, such as cucumbers and peppers, can also be packed in oil, if they are first soaked in pure, undiluted vinegar for two to ten days, depending on the density of the vegetable. These marinated vegetables make spirited additions to salads. Use a little oil from the jar, add a splash of wine vinegar and you have a completely dressed salad. Chili peppers preserved in this fashion can be chopped and

added to Mexican dishes, and the peppery oil can be used for extra flavor in sautéing meat, poultry or vegetables.

As the harvest season progresses, I try to remind myself that no one will starve if we run out of dilly beans. So what if there are only five jars of barbecue sauce? Those brief summer canning sessions in the kitchen have become my pleasure, not my doom.

Canning Basics

If you are new to canning, you may want to arm yourself with a reliable reference guide like *Putting Food By*, by Janet Greene, Ruth Hertzberg and Beatrice Vaughan (The Stephen Greene Press, 1988; paperback, $9.95). Then borrow or buy a boiling-water bath canning kettle. If you don't own one, you can use any large stockpot. The only requirement is that it be deep enough for the jars to sit on a metal

Putting up fresh produce a few jars at a time takes the drudgery out of canning.

rack and be covered by two inches of water with at least an inch of boiling space to spare. Buy glass canning jars and metal lids at a supermarket or hardware store, and you are ready to begin.

1. Preheat the canner filled with water. Wash jars with hot, soapy water and rinse them well. Prepare the lids according to the manufacturer's recommendations, usually by washing them in warm soapy water, rinsing, and immersing them in boiling water. Leave the lids in the water until you are ready to use them.

If the jars will be processed for fewer than 10 minutes, they must be sterilized first by immersion, upright, in boiling water. Boil for 10 minutes.

2. Pack the jars tightly, trying not to squash the vegetables or fruit. Pour in the hot brine or syrup to cover, allowing the specified amount of headroom (the space between the rim of the jar and the top of the jar's contents). Remove any air bubbles inside the jar by running a chopstick or plastic blade around the inside. Add more brine or syrup to cover the vegetables or fruit, if necessary.

3. Wipe the rim of the jar clean with a paper towel. Place a lid on the jar. Secure with a metal screw-band hand-tightened into place.

4. Set the jars on a rack in the preheated canner. If you don't own a rack, place each jar on a metal screw-band set on the bottom of the pot. The water should be hot, not boiling, or the jars may break. Add more hot water, if necessary, to cover the tops of the jars with about two inches of water. Cover the pot. Turn the heat on high and allow the water to return to a full boil, and then begin counting processing time. The water should remain at a moderate boil throughout the processing.

5. When the processing time is up, remove the jars from the canner and set them where they can cool undisturbed, away from drafts, for at least 12 hours. Never tighten the screwbands after the jars have been processed.

6. As the jars cool, you may hear a distinctive popping sound, which tells you the jar has sealed. The center of a sealed lid will be slightly depressed. Gently remove the screw-bands and test any questionable seals by lifting the jar by its lid, holding a towel underneath to catch the jar in the event it has not sealed. Unsealed jars should be stored in the refrigerator and used quickly.

7. Store sealed jars in a cool, dry place. Pickles should sit for at least six weeks to allow their full flavor to develop.

Note: Some of these recipes call for "pickling salt." Available in bags in the supermarket, it does not contain the additives used in table salt that can make pickling liquid cloudy.

Preserving Dried Tomatoes in Oil

Although virtually all tomato varieties can be preserved in oil, I prefer the meatier Italian or plum types. Select ripe, unblemished fruit. Wash and dry them carefully and slice them in half lengthwise. Sprinkle them with a little salt. Tomatoes can be dried in a dehydrator starting on high for 2 hours and reducing the heat to 130 degrees F for 8 hours more, or in the oven for 7 to 8 hours at 150 degrees F, with the oven door propped open. They should be dried until they are still flexible but no longer sticky to the touch.

Experts at the U.S. Department of Agriculture caution against drying tomatoes outdoors, since weather conditions are too variable to ensure that enough moisture will be removed before tomatoes are invaded by pests or by bacteria, yeast and mold growth.

According to Dr. George York of the Department of Food Science and Technology at the University of California, Davis, there are two safe methods for preserving dried tomatoes in oil. Pack the tomatoes in hot, sterilized pint jars with either a sprig of fresh basil, oregano or rosemary, or a peeled garlic clove that has been soaked overnight in a mixture of half water and half vinegar. Heat olive oil to 190 degrees F (use a thermometer) and fill the jars with the oil, leaving ¾ inch headroom. Wipe the rims carefully to remove any oil. If the oil and jars are hot enough, the jars should seal themselves.

The second method is to pack the tomatoes in clean jars, add garlic or herbs and fill with unheated olive oil, leaving ¾ inch headroom. Simmer them in a bath for 25 minutes to seal.

According to York, if tomatoes are dried to about 20 percent moisture levels and are kept submerged in the oil, there is no danger of spoilage, but washing the tomatoes carefully and using clean utensils is a necessary precaution.

Gardener's Salsa

This salsa is rather mild. For a hotter version, use more chili peppers and proportionately fewer sweet green peppers. For nachos, cover corn chips with grated cheese and salsa and broil for about 10 minutes. Or make a Mexican torte by layering salsa, tortillas, refried beans (or ground beef) and cheese in a pie plate. Bake for about 25 minutes and serve.

24 cups, or approximately 12 lbs., quartered
    ripe tomatoes
2 cups white vinegar
1 cup finely diced hot chili pepper
1 cup finely diced sweet green pepper

3 onions, finely diced
1 Tbsp. salt or more to taste

In an enameled or stainless-steel saucepan, combine tomatoes with vinegar. Cover and cook until tomatoes are very soft, about 45 minutes, stirring occasionally. Puree briefly in batches in a blender or food processor; tomatoes should be slightly chunky.

Return pureed tomatoes to the saucepan and add chili peppers, green peppers and onions. Simmer until salsa thickens, about 1 hour. Add salt to taste.

Ladle hot salsa into clean, hot pint jars, leaving ½ inch headroom. Seal. Process in a boiling-water canner for 15 minutes. Let cool undisturbed for 12 hours. Check seals. Store in a cool, dry place.

Makes approximately 8 pints.

Blueberry-Apple Compote

This compote makes an instant dessert, served in glass dessert bowls or spooned over ice cream or pound cake. An attractive parfait can be made by alternating layers of compote and whipped cream, yogurt or ice cream.

6 cups peeled, sliced apples
3 cups apple juice
1 Tbsp. lemon juice
2 cups sugar
6 cups fresh or frozen blueberries
1 Tbsp. grated orange peel
1 Tbsp. cinnamon or 6 Tbsp. Grand Marnier

Combine apples, apple juice, lemon juice and sugar in a saucepan. Cook over low heat for about 10 minutes, until apples soften and sugar is completely dissolved. Remove from heat and fold in blueberries and orange peel. Add cinnamon or Grand Marnier.

Ladle hot fruit into clean, hot pint jars, leaving ½ inch headroom. Seal. Process in boiling-water canner for 10 minutes. Let cool undisturbed for 12 hours. Check seals. Store in a cool, dry place.

Makes approximately 6 pints.

Herbed Pickled Beans By the Jar

Pickled beans are complemented by various herbs. Caraway beans have a buttery flavor; oregano beans are a nice addition to antipasto. Basil beans are my favorite.

1 cup white vinegar
2 cups green beans, trimmed to 4 inches
   in length
1 clove garlic
2 sprigs fresh dill, basil, oregano or cilantro,
   or 1 tsp. caraway seeds
1 tsp. pickling salt

In an enameled or stainless-steel saucepan, combine vinegar and ½ cup water and bring to a boil. Meanwhile, pack each hot, sterilized jar with beans, garlic, herbs and pickling salt. Pour hot vinegar over the beans, leaving ½ inch headroom. Seal. Process in a boiling-water canner for 5 minutes. Let cool undisturbed for 12 hours. Check seals. Store in a cool, dry place.

Makes 1 pint.

Giardiniara By the Quart

These mixed pickled vegetables couldn't be easier — and you can use whatever vegetables are on hand. For the tastiest and most attractive mix, use as many different vegetables as you can, and keep their relative size the same.

1 quart mixed sliced or chopped vegetables
   (cucumbers, zucchini, cauliflower, green
   beans, green tomatoes, sweet red or green
   peppers, carrots, okra, small pickling onions)
pickling salt
1¾ cups white vinegar
3 sprigs fresh basil, tarragon, oregano
   or cilantro
1 clove garlic

If you are using cucumbers and zucchini, slice them thinly and toss them with salt, using 1 tsp. per cup of vegetables. Let sit for 3 hours. (This process draws off excess moisture and ensures a crisper pickle.) Rinse and drain again before packing into jars.

In an enameled or stainless-steel saucepan, heat vinegar to boiling. Into each clean, hot quart jar, pack herbs, 1 tsp. salt, garlic and vegetables. Pour hot vinegar over vegetables. To cover the vegetables completely, finish filling the jar with boiling water, leaving ½ inch headroom. Seal. Process in boiling-water canner for 10 minutes. Let cool undisturbed for 12 hours. Check seals. Store in a cool, dry place.

Makes 1 quart.

Classic Barbecue Sauce

Slightly sweet and subtly spiced, this barbecue sauce tastes like the best commercial variety, but without the preservatives and artificial flavors. If you like a spicier sauce, add a dash of cayenne and more cumin. One pint is sufficient for 3 to 4 pounds of barbecued chicken.

25 cups, or approximately 12 lbs., quartered ripe tomatoes
1¼ cups cider vinegar
2 onions, finely diced
4 cloves garlic, minced
1 cup brown sugar
2 Tbsp. chili powder
1 Tbsp. cumin
1 Tbsp. molasses
1 Tbsp. soy sauce
salt to taste

In an enameled or stainless-steel saucepan, combine tomatoes with vinegar. Cover and cook until tomatoes are very soft, about 45 minutes, stirring occasionally. Puree in batches in a blender, food mill or food processor.

Return tomatoes to the saucepan and add remaining ingredients, except salt. Bring to a boil and simmer until the sauce is quite thick, about 1 hour. Stir occasionally to prevent scorching. Add salt to taste.

Ladle hot sauce into clean, hot pint jars, leaving ½ inch headroom. Seal. Process in a boiling-water canner for 15 minutes. Let cool undisturbed for 12 hours. Check seals. Store in a cool, dry place.

Makes approximately 6 pints.

Dill Chips By the Jar

These classic dill chips are perfect in sandwiches. One secret for making crisp pickles is to slice the pickles thinly and uniformly, so as to get as great a proportion of crisp skin to soft center as possible. I use a food processor to slice them.

2½ cups thinly sliced cucumbers
1½ tsp. pickling salt
½ cup white vinegar
1 tsp. dill seed
1 clove garlic
1 tsp. mixed pickling spices
½ tsp. black peppercorns

Combine sliced cucumbers and salt. If you are making more than 1 pint, increase the salt up to a total of 2 Tbsp. only. Toss to mix well. Add cold water to cover. Let stand for 3 hours. Drain. If the cucumbers taste salty, rinse and drain again.

For each jar, combine vinegar and ¼ cup water in an enameled or stainless-steel pot and bring to a boil. Into each hot, sterilized pint jar, put dill seed, garlic, pickling spices and peppercorns. Pack the jars with cucumbers. Pour hot vinegar over cucumbers, leaving ½ inch headroom. Seal. Process in boiling-water canner for 5 minutes. Let cool undisturbed for 12 hours. Check seals. Store in a cool, dry place.

Makes 1 pint.

Salad Pickles By the Jar

These pickled cucumbers taste more like marinated vegetables than sour pickles. They can be served as a condiment, but they also make wonderful additions to salads, and their oil can be used for dressing. For best flavor, use extra-virgin or virgin olive oil.

Important note: *Oil will destroy the seal on the canning jars, so take special care to wipe clean the rims of the jars before setting the lids in place.*

2 cups sliced cucumbers
½ cup thinly sliced red pepper
1 Tbsp. plus ½ tsp. pickling salt
approximately 1 cup white vinegar
1 cup extra-virgin olive oil
1 tsp. sugar
½ tsp. crushed red pepper
1 clove garlic
1 Tbsp. fresh oregano, or 1 tsp. dried

Combine sliced cucumbers, red pepper and 1 Tbsp. salt. If you are making more than 1 pint of pickles, increase the salt up to a total of 2 Tbsp. only. Toss to mix well. Add cold water to cover. Let stand for 3 hours, then drain. Rinse if the cucumbers taste salty and drain again.

Pack cucumbers and peppers into a clean pint jar. Add vinegar to cover. Place a lid on the jar and set aside for 2 to 3 days. (The exact timing isn't critical, but after 5 days or so the cucumbers will become mushy.) Drain off vinegar.

Combine olive oil, the remaining ½ tsp. salt, sugar and red pepper in saucepan and heat to 190 degrees F, stirring to dissolve sugar.

Into a fresh, hot, sterile pint jar, pack garlic, oregano and pickled cucumbers and peppers. Pour the hot oil over the vegetables, leaving ¾ inch headroom. Cover with a lid and screwband. If the jar does not seal on its own, store in the refrigerator.

Makes 1 pint.

Zucchini-Tomato Relish

Zucchini relishes often seem poor excuses for using up extra squash. But this version, with its slightly crunchy texture and barbecue sauce flavor, is perfect with hamburgers.

12 cups grated zucchini, packed
6 cups finely chopped tomatoes
1 onion, finely chopped
2 sweet red peppers, finely chopped (green peppers can be substituted)
3 Tbsp. salt
1¾ cups malt or cider vinegar
1 cup brown sugar
1½ Tbsp. celery seeds
1½ Tbsp. chili powder
6 Tbsp. prepared mustard
salt to taste

In a large bowl, toss zucchini, tomatoes, onion and red pepper with salt. Add cold water to cover and leave for at least 3 hours. Rinse vegetables with fresh water and drain well in a colander. Weight with a heavy plate and drain overnight.

In a large enameled or stainless-steel saucepan, combine vinegar, sugar, celery seeds, chili powder and mustard. Bring to a boil, stirring well to dissolve sugar and mustard. Add drained vegetables. Return to a boil. Salt to taste.

Pack hot relish into hot, sterilized pint or half-pint jars, leaving ½ inch headroom. Seal. Process in a boiling-water canner for 5 minutes. Let cool undisturbed for 12 hours. Check seals. Store in a cool, dry place. Let jars sit for about 6 weeks before opening to allow the full flavor of the relish to develop.

Makes approximately 6 pints.

Peaches in Raspberry Syrup

These peaches, which take on a lovely purple hue, make wonderful gifts for people who appreciate homemade presents — if you can bear to give them away. Serve in clear glass dessert bowls.

5 cups fresh or frozen raspberries
2½ cups apple juice
½ cup sugar or more to taste
5 Tbsp. lemon juice
21-24 ripe peaches

Combine berries with approximately 1 cup of the apple juice in a food processor or blender, and puree. Press through a fine sieve to remove seeds. Combine puree with remaining apple juice, sugar and 2 Tbsp. lemon juice in an enameled or stainless-steel saucepan. Bring to a boil, stirring to dissolve sugar. Boil gently for about 30 minutes, stirring frequently. Remove any foam that forms on the top.

Blanch peaches for about 30 seconds in boiling water to loosen the skins. Peel, cut into halves, discard pits. Place peaches in cold water to cover. Add the remaining 3 Tbsp. lemon juice to prevent discoloring.

Pack peaches into clean, hot pint jars. Fill with hot raspberry sauce, leaving ½ inch headroom. Remove any air bubbles. Seal. Process in a boiling-water canner for 25 minutes. Let cool undisturbed for 12 hours. Check seals. Store in a cool, dry place.

Makes approximately 7 pints.

Bread-and-Butters By the Jar

A classic bread-and-butter pickle, not too sweet, not too spicy. Resist the temptation to skip the first step of soaking the cucumbers in salted water. The salt draws out their excess moisture and results in snappier pickles.

2½ cups thinly sliced cucumbers
½ cup thinly sliced onion
1½ tsp. pickling salt
½ cup white vinegar
3 Tbsp. sugar
¼ tsp. turmeric
1 tsp. mustard seeds
½ tsp. mixed pickling spices

In a large bowl, combine cucumbers, onion and salt. Toss to mix well. If you are multiplying this recipe, do not use more than 2 Tbsp. salt. Be sure to rinse the cucumbers before packing them into jars. Add water to cover and let stand for 3 hours. Drain. If the cucumbers taste salty, rinse and drain again.

In an enameled or stainless-steel saucepan, combine vinegar, sugar and turmeric for each jar. Heat to boiling.

Into each hot, sterilized pint jar, place mustard seeds and pickling spices. Pack with the cucumbers and onions. Pour hot vinegar over cucumbers, leaving ½ inch headroom. Seal. Process in boiling-water canner for 5 minutes. Let cool undisturbed for 12 hours. Check seals. Store in a cool, dry place.

Makes 1 pint.

Some of these recipes first appeared in Summer in a Jar: Making Pickles, Jams & More, *by Andrea Chesman. Williamson Publishing Co., 1985.*

Cultured Cooking

THE HEALTHY VERSATILITY OF YOGURT

BY RUX MARTIN

Believing that evolution had dealt mankind several unkind anatomical blows, Russian scientist Ilya Metchnikoff in 1904 touched off one of the more bizarre phases of twentieth-century medicine. A distinguished embryologist and pathologist, Metchnikoff contended that, of all Earth's species, *only* humans were in dire disharmony with nature: suffering the pain of childbirth because of reproductive misdesign; being poisoned by our own systems because of our colon, the final section of the large intestine. Metchnikoff said the colon was teeming with bacteria that upset digestion and produced toxins that slowly poisoned the body, leading to premature death.

Medical practitioners began prescribing antiseptics to kill these insidious bacteria, while eager surgeons developed procedures to bypass or remove the offending colon. Metchnikoff, however, recognized that these approaches could kill not only the bacteria, but also the patient. Convinced that a dietary cure might be the answer, Metchnikoff embarked on a study of the eating habits of populations with extraordinary longevity.

In Bulgaria, he found his answer: a culture where the elders commonly reached ages well past 100 and — *Aha!* — where yogurt was eaten in great quantities. Metchnikoff isolated a bacterium in their yogurt and dubbed it *Bulgarian bacillus*, which later became *Lactobacillus bulgaricus*. The researcher believed this to be a beneficial bacterium that secreted lactic acid and created an inhospitable environment for the life-shortening bacteria commonly found in the large intestine.

Metchnikoff began an enthusiastic yogurt regimen of his own, and an enterprising Spaniard named Isaac Carasso used Metchnikoff's bacterial cultures to found a commercial yogurt dairy in Barcelona. He called the business Danone, after his son Daniel, and when the company moved to New York at the end of World War II, the name was Americanized into Dannon, and the rest, as they say in the yogurt business, is history.

As for Metchnikoff, he disappointed his followers by dying at the unremarkable age of 71. And although his theory was eagerly seized upon 70 years later in advertisements in which ancient peasants extolled yogurt as the elixir of life, it was repudiated by scientists, who maintained that the large intestine is indispensable after all, that Metchnikoff's bacterium could not survive in the human digestive tract and, finally, that the Bulgarians were not nearly as old as previously believed.

Subsequent research, however, has shown that Metchnikoff may not have been entirely wrong. Another bacterium found in some yogurts, *Lactobacillus acidophilus*, can replace beneficial bacteria depleted by antibiotics or illness; for that reason, many doctors prescribe yogurt for diarrhea. Though the results are far from conclusive, other studies suggest that *acidophilus* may lower cholesterol in children and may even prevent or delay the formation of cancerous tumors.

Regardless of the effects of its bacterial cultures, yogurt has a proved and indisputable health benefit that Metchnikoff overlooked: it is both rich-tasting and low in fat, making it an admirable substitute for other dairy products. Low-fat yogurt contains only 144 calories per cup; sour cream, cream cheese and mayonnaise have 320, 868 and 1,580 calories respectively, and derive 80 to 100 percent of their calories from fat, compared to yogurt's meager 22 percent.

Yogurt begins as milk, which is pasteurized and injected with live bacteria. The bacteria feed on the milk sugar, producing lactic acid, which coagulates the milk, imparting the dis-

Yogurt, which is low in fat, makes a fine substitute for cream cheese in this lemony, rich-tasting cheesecake, right.

ERNIE SPARKS

tinctive tangy taste. After the inoculation stage, the yogurt is sometimes pasteurized again, killing the bacteria; check the label to make sure that the ingredients include "live, active cultures." Most yogurt companies use *Lactobacillus bulgaricus* and *Lactobacillus thermophilus*; the label will specify if the beneficial *acidophilus* is present.

Yogurt that has been inoculated with bacteria in the container in which it will be sold—a process used by most smaller companies, as well as Dannon—is considered superior to yogurt that has been inoculated in a vat and transferred to cups. Transferring breaks the "set," and thickeners in the form of modified food starch, vegetable gum or gelatin must then be added later.

Most people find low-fat yogurt, made from skim milk, virtually indistinguishable in taste from whole-milk yogurt, but it contains half the fat. Nonfat yogurt, which gets less than 10 percent of its calories from fat, has a relatively bland flavor, but is a boon to those watching their fat and cholesterol intake. The "boutique yogurts" that are made from the milk of Jersey, Brown Swiss or Guernsey cows are slightly higher in butterfat than yogurt made from Holstein milk, and are creamier and more like sour cream in flavor and consistency.

Next to its low fat content, yogurt's chief merit is its versatility. Two years ago, a recipe contest sponsored by Stonyfield, a small yogurt company in Massachusetts, brought forth more than 400 recipes for soup, entrées, salads, sauces, whipped toppings, baked goods and desserts—all made with yogurt.

At our table, plain yogurt often appears as the basis of quiche, in a cold savory salad of cucumber and yogurt, or in luxuriously rich-tasting cheesecake. The lactic acid in yogurt acts as an excellent tenderizing marinade for meat, which then becomes part of a flavorful sauce. Yogurt also appears on our menu in small ways: with maple syrup on French toast or pancakes, as a substitute for whipped cream on fruit compotes, over warm fruit crisps or pies, or in place of sour cream on baked potatoes, bean tacos, chili, soups, curries or blintzes. We routinely substitute yogurt for all or part of the mayonnaise in creamy salads, including tuna, as well as in salad dressings. Instead of adding milk to mashed potatoes, we enjoy yogurt's piquant taste.

Yogurt can also replace milk or heavy cream in soups like vichyssoise and can substitute for sour cream in stroganoffs. A cup of yogurt becomes a delicious ice-cream-like dessert when folded into three beaten egg whites, mixed with 8 tablespoons of fruit preserves and chilled briefly in the freezer.

There is no mystery to cooking with yogurt, provided a few simple rules are followed. It responds best to a gentle hand, and whenever possible, it should be stirred rather than beaten, or it will become thin. When adding yogurt to salad dressing, it is best to stir the sauce or dressing into the yogurt to keep the texture smooth. In substituting yogurt for other dairy products, acid ingredients like wine, lemon juice or vinegar should be reduced to compensate for yogurt's natural tartness.

Yogurt also adds tenderness and moistness to baked goods, in which it can replace sour cream, sour milk or buttermilk. When replacing milk with yogurt, it is necessary to counteract the acidity by adding ½ teaspoon baking soda for each cup.

Heating yogurt too rapidly or at too high a temperature can cause it to separate into unattractive curds and whey. Several precautions will help prevent curdling. Try to have yogurt at room temperature before heating it. For foolproof results, it can be "tempered" by stirring in a tablespoon of cornstarch or flour and a beaten egg white before heating. Whenever possible, it is best to add yogurt near the end of cooking and to keep the heat low.

Finally, yogurt can be made into a delicious low-fat "cheese" that can be used in place of Boursin or cream cheese simply by placing it in a double thickness of cheesecloth over a bowl and leaving it overnight to drain. (A yogurt-cheese funnel is a handy tool for this job.) The resulting fresh cheese, which is halfway between sour cream and cream cheese in consistency, can be covered with herbs and olive oil or seasoned with pesto or tomato paste and spread over crackers. Whipped with sugar and vanilla, it makes an excellent dessert topping, and it can virtually replace cream cheese in desserts.

The following dishes, adapted from winning recipes submitted to Stonyfield Yogurt's contest, should bring considerable pleasure, if not the longevity sought by the Russian doctor.

Lemon-Yogurt Cheesecake

Lemony and properly dense, this cheesecake invites guiltless indulgence.

Crust:
1 cup graham-cracker crumbs
½ cup gingersnap crumbs
⅓ cup crushed walnuts
⅓ cup vegetable oil or melted butter
½ tsp. cinnamon
½ tsp. ginger
1 Tbsp. honey

Butter and chill an 8-inch springform pan. Mix all ingredients together. Press into the bottom and sides of the pan. Chill at least 15 minutes.

Cheesecake:
8 oz. low-fat cream cheese
8 oz. yogurt
2 cups yogurt cheese made from 48 oz. yogurt (recipe follows)
1 cup sugar
2 Tbsp. lemon juice
1 Tbsp. grated lemon peel
4 eggs, room temperature, beaten until thick

Topping:
1 pint fresh strawberries, hulled and sliced in half
½ cup sugar

Beat together cream cheese, yogurt, yogurt cheese, sugar, lemon juice and peel with an electric mixer. Stir in eggs. Spoon mixture carefully into the crust-lined pan.

Bake at 300 degrees F for 1 hour and 10 minutes, or until the center sets. Cool in the oven with the door ajar for 1 hour. Refrigerate 3 hours or more and unmold. Mix strawberries and sugar, let stand for 1 to 2 hours, and spoon over cheesecake.

Yogurt Cheese

Line a colander with a large cotton towel or double thickness of cheesecloth and place the colander in the sink. Pour in yogurt. After 15 minutes, transfer colander to a bowl. Cover with plastic wrap and refrigerate overnight. Gathering the edges of the towel together, gently squeeze out any remaining liquid. Transfer cheese to a separate container. Refrigerate until ready to use. Keeps 1 week.

Marinated Yogurt Cheese

This delicate, fresh cheese is a sensational appetizer.

32 oz. yogurt
¼ cup olive oil, preferably extra-virgin
2 cloves garlic, finely minced
½ tsp. dried thyme
½ tsp. dried rosemary
½ tsp. dried basil
1 Tbsp. chopped fresh dill

Make yogurt cheese according to directions above. Divide into 4 rounds, shaping patties

with your hands. Place in a wide, shallow bowl. Pour oil-herb mixture over cheese. Let stand at room temperature for ½ hour; cover and refrigerate overnight. Remove from refrigerator ½ hour before serving. Serve with crusty French bread or crackers.

Makes 4 small cheeses.

Chicken Curry with Yogurt

The addition of apricot preserves makes this curry taste faintly of chutney. A tablespoon of curry powder from a health food store may be substituted for the coriander, cumin, cardamom and cayenne combination, but don't use supermarket curry, which is too flat and sweet.

2 cloves garlic, minced
1 onion, chopped
1 Tbsp. olive oil
4 boneless chicken breasts, skinned and cubed
1½ tsp. ground coriander
¾ tsp. ground cumin
½ tsp. ground cardamom
⅛ tsp. ground cayenne or more to taste
1 tsp. ground ginger
¼ cup apricot preserves
½ cup golden raisins
2 cups yogurt
salt and pepper

In a large skillet, sauté garlic and onion in oil. Add chicken and sauté until browned. Add ¼ cup water, seasonings, apricot preserves and raisins. Simmer uncovered for ½ hour, stirring occasionally. The liquid will be mostly absorbed. Fold in yogurt and heat briefly, but do not boil. Season with salt and pepper.

Serves 4.

Yogurt-Dill Salad Dressing

Light, creamy and not too tart.

½ large cucumber, peeled and seeded
1 Tbsp. olive oil
1 Tbsp. minced fresh dill, tightly packed
½ tsp. dried oregano
¼ tsp. garlic, finely minced
¼ tsp. salt
⅛ tsp. black pepper
2 tsp. lemon juice
1½ tsp. honey
¾ cup yogurt

Combine all ingredients except yogurt in blender or food processor and stir into yogurt.

Makes approximately 1 cup.

A Twist of Tradition

BRINGING BACK THE ART OF COOKING WITH ORANGES

BY RUX MARTIN & PAMELA CROSS

I f Christmas today means Transformers and transistorized Teddy Bears for many children, a friend of ours still associates the Yule season with the exotic simplicity of a Mandarin orange. Growing up with seven brothers and sisters, she remembers Christmas as a time of minor intrigue and furtive trips to their father's cool basement workshop to see if family tradition was going to be upheld. Unfailingly, just days before the holiday, two curious pine-slatted crates would mysteriously appear, each roughly 14 inches long and 8 inches deep, their lids uncompromisingly nailed shut. A mood of excited impatience mounted day by day.

Finally, on Christmas Eve, one of the slats was gently pried open, revealing perfect rows of little oranges, individually wrapped in pale green tissues. Each child was allowed to pluck one and, sitting in the semi-dark of the living room with a log fire crackling and the tree lights sparkling, savor the tiny seedless sections welling with bittersweet juice. Indelible in her memory are the brilliant orange color and the loose-fitting skins that could be zipped, Velcro-like, from the fruit by even the youngest of fingers. The next morning, the toes of their Christmas stockings would be bulging with familiar round shapes, and within days, all the little oranges would have been eaten. She imagined them to have come directly from China, and marveled that they could arrive with such perfect timing each Christmas. It was years before she realized that mandarins could be bought from the grocer, and not just at Christmas time.

As she had imagined, however, the orange did originate in China, and for centuries it was among the most prized of fruits, a luxury for royalty and the very rich outside its homeland. Following the trade routes, oranges made their way to India, on to the Middle East, and thence into Europe, arriving in Italy in the first century A.D. French and German royalty spared no expense to build huge greenhouses to protect their indoor groves, importing trees from the south and bathing their roots in milk or honey before planting. At Versailles, Louis XIV, whose passion for oranges was legendary, commissioned a combination ballroom-*orangerie* in the shape of a C, with a circumference of 1,200 feet, where guests danced under clouds of fragrant blossoms. Royal gardeners systematically deprived these trees of moisture, forcing them into full bloom by adding water just as they were about to expire, thus assuring the king a display of orange blossoms in all seasons.

From Europe, the orange traveled to the Caribbean in the pockets of the Spanish explorers, whose sailors were each required by law to carry 100 seeds for planting in the Americas. The resulting groves were intended to be strictly for medicinal purposes, stopping off points for future seafarers sick with scurvy.

It was not until the early 1800s – 300 years after Ponce de Leon is believed to have dropped the first seeds in Florida – that commercial orange production began in the United States. California's citrus industry started somewhat later, in 1841, when an ambitious Kentucky trapper named William Wolfskill planted 70 acres of oranges. He was called a fool by his neighbors. Today, the United States grows more than 11 million tons of oranges a year, making it the second leading producer in the world, surpassed only by Brazil.

To sun-starved northerners, the sight of a bowl or bin piled high with fresh oranges still seems nothing short of a midwinter miracle. Fortunately, the orange crop peaks at the time when other fresh fruit is scarce, giving us an inexpensive, potent source of vitamin C. Winter oranges, in fact, contain more vitamin C than summer oranges, according to the

Orange flavors bring an exotic taste of the tropics to the Yuletide table, left: Almond Tart, Spicy Tea, Refrigerator Cookies.

ERNIE SPARKS

USDA. One orange provides 60 milligrams of vitamin C, the full recommended daily allowance for an adult and almost three times as much as limes, nine times more than apples and five times more than bananas. Oranges and orange juice are also high in potassium, which recent research suggests may play an important role in lowering blood pressure and lessening the risk of strokes.

Alas, with all that oranges offer and considering their cheap, year-round availability, many of us have forgotten just how useful they can be in cooking. Oranges can be a true winter pleasure for the cook, instantly enlivening the taste of simple chicken, fish and meat dishes and providing inspiration for tarts, scones and other baked goods, as well as condiments and beverages.

Because commonly available sweet oranges have just a tenth the acidity of lemons, the two are not interchangeable in recipes. For this reason, orange-based sauces must often be bolstered by the addition of wine, vinegar, lemon juice, capers or tomatoes. Cut in halves and placed inside the cavity of a roast chicken with a little rosemary, however, the orange imparts a delicate, fruity flavor.

The most versatile and concentrated part of the orange is the aptly named zest, or peel. Rich in citric oils that, undiluted, are flammable and can redden the lips, it can be used as a spice in pound and tea cakes. Added during the last stages of cooking, zest imparts a sunny depth to tomato sauce, rice dishes and couscous.

When buying oranges, look for fruit that is heavy in proportion to its size. The peel should have no discolored places or water-soaked spots. Avoid spongy or puffy oranges, which will be dry. Green fruit, though not as aesthetically pleasing, is still fully ripe.

Orange Almond Tart

Orange and almond flavors blend beautifully in this simply made tart. It offers a striking finale to a festive dinner.

½ cup plus 2 Tbsp. unsalted butter, softened
½ cup plus 2 Tbsp. sugar
1 egg yolk
1 tsp. vanilla extract
1 tsp. almond extract
1½ cups flour
1 cup sliced almonds
8 oz. cream cheese, softened
1 tsp. Grand Marnier or other orange liqueur
zest (grated rind) of 1 orange
3 large oranges, peeled, deveined and seeded

⅓ cup orange marmalade
2 Tbsp. fresh orange juice or Grand Marnier or combination

Cream together butter and ½ cup sugar. Beat in yolk, vanilla and almond extract. Mix in flour and almonds to form dough. Press into 11-inch tart pan. Prick shell. Bake at 375 degrees F until golden, about 10 minutes. Cool and set aside. Beat cream cheese and remaining 1 to 2 Tbsp. sugar until smooth. Beat in Grand Marnier and zest. Peel and remove pith from oranges and separate into segments. To remove the transparent membrane from each segment: slit the concave side with a sharp knife, peel back membrane and pinch it off. Work carefully to keep segments intact. Place fruit on top of filling in concentric circles. Whisk marmalade and liquid together over medium heat until melted; boil 30 seconds and strain. Cool slightly; brush fruit with glaze. Serves 8 to 10.

Orange Napa Salad

Napa, or Chinese cabbage, is generally available in large supermarkets or Oriental food stores. The quantity of ginger root can be varied to suit individual taste.

1 small head Napa cabbage
6 oranges
1 cup orange juice
½ cup oil
⅓ cup malt or cider vinegar
3 Tbsp. soy sauce
2 tsp. black bean sauce
2 Tbsp. grated ginger root
salt and pepper

Slice Napa in half lengthwise. Remove core and chop cabbage into strips. Remove skin and pith from oranges and slice into rounds. Toss with cabbage. Whisk remaining ingredients together, pour over salad and toss. Serves 6 to 8.

Orange Walnut Chicken Salad

Serve this as a luncheon main course on a bed of lettuce accompanied by freshly baked muffins.

8 oranges
3 cups diced, cooked chicken
1 red onion, thinly sliced
1 cup chopped walnuts
2 Tbsp. chopped parsley
2 Tbsp. mayonnaise

Peel and pith oranges, then slice in rounds, removing seeds. Add remaining ingredients and toss. Serves 4 to 6.

Orange Currant Scones

Offer these as a special breakfast treat, and the lazybones will get out of bed in no time. Preparation time is about 30 minutes.

2 cups flour
1 Tbsp. sugar
1 Tbsp. baking powder
½ tsp. salt
¼ cup cold butter
¼ cup orange juice
¼ cup heavy cream
2 eggs, lightly beaten
grated rind of 1 orange
½ cup dried currants
sugar

Sift together flour, sugar, baking powder and salt. Cut in butter until mixture resembles coarse meal. Make a well in the center and add orange juice, cream, 1 egg and orange rind. Stir until dry ingredients are moistened. Add currants and stir to distribute—mixture will be crumbly. Press into a ball, then turn onto floured board and knead until dough holds together. Roll into a rectangle and cut into 10 triangles by cutting dough into squares then cutting squares in half diagonally. Place ½ inch apart on ungreased cookie sheet. Brush with remaining egg and sprinkle with sugar. Bake at 400 degrees F for 15 minutes or until golden brown. Makes 10 scones.

Spicy Orange Tea

This is a quick and simple way to dress up a pot of tea. It is best made with regular tea; if herbal teas are used, the flavors tend to overwhelm one another.

10 whole cloves
2-inch cinnamon stick
⅓ cup honey
1 cup orange juice
4 tea bags (black tea)
Angostura bitters

Combine 1 cup water, cloves and cinnamon stick and simmer, covered, for 10 minutes. Add honey, 1 more cup of water and orange juice and bring to a boil. Remove from heat, add tea bags and let steep, covered, for 5 minutes. Remove tea bags and spices. Add bitters to taste. Serves 4.

Scallops in Orange Caper Vinaigrette

These scallops are delicately flavored with orange and slightly piquant. Serve them at room temperature as an appetizer, or warm over linguine.

2 lbs. sea scallops
1 cup fresh orange juice
1 cup dry white wine
4 large scallions, including green tops
2 medium tomatoes, seeded and diced
1 1-inch green chili pepper, minced
2 Tbsp. capers, drained
¼ tsp. orange zest
1 cup olive oil
salt and freshly ground black pepper

Place scallops in skillet, cover with orange juice and wine, and heat to boiling or just until scallops are barely cooked through and have begun to lose their translucent look. Do not overcook. Using a slotted spoon, transfer scallops to a bowl; cover and set aside. Bring liquid to a boil and reduce to ⅔ cup. Add scallions, tomatoes, chili pepper, capers, and cook briefly until vegetables have softened slightly. Add zest, whisk in olive oil and season with salt and pepper. Combine with scallops and serve. Serves 4.

Orange Refrigerator Cookies

The dough for these light cookies can be prepared a day ahead and baked at your convenience. They are delicate and delicious.

zest of 1 orange
2 cups sugar
½ cup butter
1 egg
3 oz. cream cheese
2 Tbsp. orange juice
1 tsp. vanilla
2 cups flour
⅛ tsp. baking soda
⅛ tsp. baking powder
½ tsp. salt

Chop orange zest with sugar in food processor for 10 seconds. Set aside 1 cup of this sugar, then add butter and egg to remaining sugar in processor and process for 1 minute. Add cream cheese, orange juice and vanilla, and pulse to mix.
Sift together flour, baking soda, baking powder and salt; spoon into food processor and pulse to mix. Do not overmix.
Line a small bowl with plastic wrap, place

dough in bowl, cover and refrigerate until firm – approximately 4 hours.

Divide dough in half and shape into 2 rolls, each 1½ inches in diameter. Place in freezer for 1 hour.

Line 2 baking sheets with parchment paper, then brush paper lightly with melted butter. Slice rolls into ¼-inch slices and place on cookie sheets, leaving 1½ inches around each cookie. Sprinkle each cookie with a little of the remaining orange-sugar mixture.

Bake at 375 degrees F for 8 minutes. Cool on paper, then remove. Makes 40 cookies.

Orange-Glazed Roast Chicken

Orange-zested butter inserted under the skin permeates this chicken with aromatic flavor. The glaze is light and citrusy, not cloyingly sweet, and pan drippings make rich brown sauce.

1 roasting chicken, about 7 pounds
5 sprigs parsley
1 tsp. marjoram
¼ tsp. pepper
1 onion, peeled and quartered
3 oranges
2 Tbsp. minced orange rind
4 Tbsp. unsalted butter
1 tsp. minced shallots
1 Tbsp. lemon juice
½ tsp. pepper

Sauce:
½ cup orange juice
¼ cup honey
3 Tbsp. unsalted butter
2 Tbsp. lemon juice
2 Tbsp. Worcestershire sauce
1 tsp. ground ginger
⅛ tsp. cayenne pepper
3 Tbsp. butter or more, if needed

Preheat oven to 425 degrees F. Sprinkle cavity of the bird with parsley, marjoram and pepper. Fill with onion and one quartered, unpeeled orange. Remove rind from 2 remaining oranges using a vegetable peeler. Blanch rind for 5 minutes in boiling water, drain and pat dry, and mince. Combine rind with butter, shallots, lemon juice and pepper. Loosen skin from the chicken breast with your fingers, starting from the neck and working back. Push butter mixture between skin and flesh, working down as far as possible to the legs, being careful not to break skin. Rub outside with more orange butter. Roast for 10 minutes. Combine sauce ingredients, except last 3 Tbsp. butter, and boil until thickened. Reduce heat to 350 degrees and roast for 20 minutes per pound, basting with orange sauce, or until juices run clear when thigh is pricked. Remove bird from pan, and pour off juices into a saucepan, scraping to remove browned bits of meat. Heat to boiling, and whisk in 3 Tbsp. butter until sauce is thick. Serve with chicken. Serves 6.

Index